X-RAY OF THE PAMPA

The Texas Pan American Series

X-Ray

OF THE PAMPA

by *EZEQUIEL MARTÍNEZ ESTRADA*

TRANSLATED BY ALAIN SWIETLICKI

Introduction by Thomas F. McGann

UNIVERSITY OF TEXAS PRESS, AUSTIN AND LONDON

The Texas Pan American Series is published with the assistance of a revolving publication fund established by the Pan American Sulphur Company and other friends of Latin America in Texas. Publication of this book was also assisted by a grant from the Rockefeller Foundation through the Latin American translation program of the Association of American University Presses.

International Standard Book Number 0-292-70140-3
Library of Congress Catalog Card Number 70-165913
© 1971 by Agustina M. de Martínez Estrada
All Rights Reserved
Type set by G&S Typesetters, Austin
Printed by The University of Texas Printing Division, Austin
Bound by Universal Bookbindery, Inc., San Antonio

CONTENTS

VI. *Pseudostructures*

INTRODUCTION

As an X-ray strikes through all human substance, so this great book, *X-Ray of the Pampa*, penetrates the experience of the people of Argentina and, through its piercing analysis of their history, also reveals much about man's condition in the Western world during the twentieth century.

Ezequiel Martínez Estrada's book resembles Argentina's vast plains, the pampa: extended, repetitious, and, therefore, at times monotonous, but unforgettable.

First published in 1933, when its author was approaching forty years of age, *X-Ray of the Pampa* is multidimensional: part history, part essay in social psychology, part prophecy. Seen from the 1970's, this work by the Argentine essayist, poet, novelist, and playwright is the self-fulfilled testimony to a first-class analytical talent dissecting national and universal problems. From the author's deep perspectives on national and Western culture, Martínez Estrada's criticism of Argentina as a dysfunctional and anomic society has been largely proven true by the events of the last forty years. Neither the civilians nor the generals of that rich but disturbed land know how to rule.

Colonial Argentina lacked minerals; it had wild, nomadic Indians rather than densely settled native populations; it lay far from the principal colonial capitals and routes of trade. The earth was its wealth, but there were no markets for the products of the land, until Europe's industrial revolution created the demand after the middle of the last century. The conquistadorial spirit trapped men into searching beyond the far horizon, while the gold they sought actually lay in the agricultural potential of the deep, humus-laden soil under their feet. This was no North America of yoemen farmers, but a society of a few great landowners and the rest: defeated tenants, and peons, and swarming immigrants who clung together to build the massive city of Buenos Aires. There too they found defeat—the defeat of the urban proletarians who can neither escape nor revolt nor prosper; or so it has been down until today. Such failures and frustrations, which Martínez Estrada relentlessly exposes, have created in Argentina anomic attitudes compounded of disillusionment, distrust of others, and self-doubt.

Some of these attitudes are observable in Martínez Estrada himself, despite his courageous, life-long intellectual struggle to tell the truth about Argentina. He had a hard life. He worked for thirty years (1916–1946) as a subordinate postal employee to earn his bread and butter, although during part of that time, and in the last decades of his life, his income came from teaching, writing, and lecturing. The fact that this cadaverous-appearing man was an autodidact in a land that lusts after professional degrees, that he was a disheartened collaborator in a stifling bureaucracy, and that for five years in the 1950's he was bedridden by a repulsive and undiagnosable skin disease—these experiences may help to account for his personal pessimism and pervasive sense of social isolation. Late in life he left Argentina: in 1959 he went to live in Mexico, and in 1961 and 1962 he lived in Fidel Castro's Cuba. He praised the Cuban revolution passionately and wrote much about it and about Cuban history. But after a time, not having made any great impact on his new compatriots, he returned to Argentina. There he died of cancer in 1964.

He was a man of profound humanitarianism and radicalism, a poet and social critic and teacher who loved his nation, and all the people of earth, but sadly. He framed his message in this book within Argentine history and geography, and he traces the growth of this backwater of the Spanish empire in America through its independence from Spain after 1810, and its modernization in the nineteenth and twentieth centuries, until it became, by material standards, a leading nation of the Atlantic world. But to Martínez Estrada civilization and modernization as exemplified in the megalopolis of Buenos Aires with its seven million inhabitants were misnomers for the barbarism that he saw inherent in the condition of Argentine men and women, and modern men and women everywhere.

He speaks for disinherited Western man: for the individual, against the machine. He drew upon his acute observations, and upon his deep knowledge of Western thought, in which he was widely read, from Socrates through Nietszche and Thoreau to Sartre and Weil. He will read beautifully, especially, perhaps, to younger people who do not yet know him.

A pessimist, a spiritual anarchist in the sense that he rejected the state as an alien body, a man possessed by deepest moral indignation, Martínez Estrada could yet validly claim at the end of his life that he was, in ultimate analysis, an optimist. Only an optimist who believed in the perfectability of man could struggle so hard against evil.

Vitriolic, antibourgeosie but also antitotalitarian, whether of the right or the left, this poet-prophet fights with fierce anguish for the underdog trapped in a closed society.

As Martin Stabb has pointed out, Martínez Estrada viewed man as estranged from reality by self-imposed falsehoods, such as gross materialism and false erudition. He himself displays that "glandular rancor" which he attributes to the morally and socially imprisoned settlers of Argentina, and he sums up his grim dialectic of his nation's history in such phrases as "The land conquers the conquerer, defeats him, and forces him to become the servant of all that which he loathes."

What Martínez Estrada is talking about is the great lie of the establishment: more than that—the lie of life. Do we not today, young and old, hear and understand his words about the rootless Argentines who have no ancient, indigenous cultural remnants to

cling to, nor anything other than the synthetic, imported European
and United States models to guide them: "There was nobody who
could claim possession of nothing except a nobody."

Estranged people: the dispossessed gaucho, the *porteño* (the resident of Buenos Aires) isolated by the mighty city, the immigrant
betrayed by his dreams and his leaders—these are the characters in
the politics of immorality, the castaways of the society of the lost.

Events in Argentine history since Martínez Estrada wrote *X-Ray
of the Pampa* nearly four decades ago have remarkably borne out
his grim prophecy of the hollow condition of the nation. Argentina
has been beset by political instability, by the corrupt Perón dictatorship, by economic stagnation, and by social unrest. No solutions are in sight to these problems, because of fundamental flaws
in social consensus, which Martínez Estrada correctly identified
long ago. As Peter G. Earle puts it in his book about the Argentine
author, entitled *Prophet in the Wilderness*, these flaws are "the
civic scorn and distrust of human motivation which [Martínez
Estrada] believes to be typical of the Argentine mentality."

Here then we have this existentialistic, puritan skeptic, who is at
the same time a true believer because he believes in what is impossible to believe: the secular redemption of the human condition.
Dogmatic, bitterly biased, Martínez Estrada is nonetheless one of
the three or four important authors of twentieth-century Argentina; more, he is a leader in Western social criticism. Few paid heed
to him in 1933; many do today, in Argentina and elsewhere in
Latin America. Now, the English-speaking world has a chance to
judge him, in this excellent translation by Alain Swietlicki.

Martínez Estrada's early perception of vital issues that have only
in recent years become central concerns in the West may be
demonstrated by his exposure in *X-Ray* of the sordid sexuality that
he portrays as woven darkly through the history of Argentina.
"Male chauvinism" and "women's lib" are merely new, catchy
terms for the powerful messages on these subjects conveyed decades
ago by the Argentine essayist.

The reader who is unfamiliar with Argentine history will of
course find in these pages many references to persons and places

unknown to him. Perhaps this fact, which will not impair appreciation of Martínez Estrada's themes, may lead the reader to search into the history of Argentina, to find out about Sarmiento and Mansilla and Pellegrini and the other Argentine people and places to whom the author refers. Thus the history of Argentina, a nation even yet curiously remote from much of the rest of the world, in time and space, may come closer to us—at least be as close and meaningful as places in Africa and Asia.

Poets who write history and social criticism are dangerous. They see more deeply, especially if they are both powerfully rational and powerfully emotional about the fate of mankind. Admittedly, Martínez Estrada's style is difficult. It is dense, epigrammatic, laden with inverted constructions and overly complex syntax and neologisms—a difficult, irritating, powerful style. But it conveys a most modern message, out of an alien, isolated environment. His is a deeply ecological message, concerned with the conservation of men and women on a corroded planet.

The people, Martínez Estrada wrote in 1957, "are hungry, but not for bread. They are hungry for honor, for love, for cordial treatment, for human consideration."

Liberation is the message and goal of this book.

Thomas F. McGann
The University of Texas at Austin

I·TRAPALANDA

1 COMPASS BEARINGS

The Adventurers

The new world, just discovered, was not yet fixed on the planet, nor did it have any form. It was a chance expanse of land peopled by images. Born of a mistake, the routes that led to it were those of the water and the wind. Those who embarked for the new world came dreaming; those who bade them farewell remained to dream. Both carried America in their imaginations, and by necessity this world, which had suddenly appeared before a people just stirring to freedom, was bound to take the shapes of ambition and pride of a victorious awakening. It is difficult now to reproduce the vision of world, carried in the narrow minds of those brutal men, who at that moment were freeing themselves from the Arabs and from things Arabic. What feats of imagination were performed by the impoverished hidalgo, the breadless artisan, the unemployed soldier, the beggar, the parish priest of a land without miracles upon hearing the fabulous news about America? Without wishing it to be so, even those who listened lied. A poor vocabulary and slow wit exaggerated the adventure upon its narration. The old maps cannot even give us an approximation of those other absurd maps of marches, dangers, and treasures, all drawn by word of mouth. Few were able to return, because hunger and disease took their toll; but those who survived affected success to save themselves from derision and were thus able to gain converts. To embark was, first of all, to flee reality; to cast at sea was already to work for the kingdom of God. In the second place, the ocean crossing freed the one who dared to turn his back on the Peninsula and cast his eyes on chance. It freed the voyager from the nemesis of his isolated, adulterated race and a penniless family lacking influence. To him the new world was the antithesis of the old one. There was nothing tranquil about this business, nothing that might require a period of gestation, no long-range project that would demand moderation, respect, thought, hope. Navigating through so many days and so many nights, following a wind-set course, they arrived unprepared for the very simple and poor reality of America. They imagined it populated by monsters, difficulties, riches. America was, on their disembarking, a swift disillusionment; a contrast that kindled their frustrated purpose and tempted them to recuperate their wasted illusions by sublimating the goods they had obtained. In the roadless plains they once again faced the sea. America was not America; it had to be forged and superimposed with the reality of a crude dream. On an immense land, which itself was the unalterable reality, would rise the precarious works of men. Between one expedition and the next these would turn into ruins, and the harsh reality of the land would cover the utopian dream. Nothing that had been built, planted, or made could compete with the certain existence of the earth itself. Ownership of things, authority over men, relationships among inhabitants, trade in goods, family: all were subject to unforseen changes, in a manner of plants freshly transplanted that might take root but might also die.

A path had to be opened in the solitude; and the plains, destroyers of illusions, had to be filled with something. That which coincided with the preexisting structure of this world prospered; that which rose by the will of man fell when he died. What but the possession of land could be yearned for by the new arrival to these lonely parts where force would yield the only dividends? The ideal of the newcomer was not to colonize or to settle. To have thought about such matters then would have been equivalent to conceiving complex machinery by the inspiration of a distaff. The environment lacked the incentives that stimulate the need to settle and colonize. There was no type of human activity to which the newcomer could aspire or of which he was competent that would allow him to play a decent role. He put into action all his primitive energy, but life would go on with the events alternating between his inept hands and a formless reality. The native had learned to live in relation to this world by submitting to its demands. But what the native might accomplish was also taboo to the newcomer. What was within anyone's reach—sowing, building, becoming resigned to one's lot and waiting—turned out to be depressing and beyond the scale of values for conquest and dominion. To work, to yield a little to the demands of nature, was to be defeated, barbarized. Thus a false scale of values was born, and men and things moved by different routes. By the classification of tasks into servile and free, the old system of the hierarchies of haves and have-nots was reinitiated. The pinnacle was represented by landownership, which meant submission to that which was easier to acquire and demanded less intelligence to retain.

On this basic plan were future courses drawn, and since then the units of measure would be the hectare and the bushel. Those who no longer had to "sell behind the counter" looked upon the retail merchants as salaried clerks. A distinction was made between the merchant who personally conducted his business and was excluded from elective posts and functions and the one who, directing his establishment from afar, was fit for those posts and functions. Here again, distance became a desirable value. To captain a band of smugglers and to traffic in slaves was more honorable than to build a wall; to sell fabrics was much more honorable than to retail articles from overseas; to steal was better than to work. The quantity of what was possessed was not a basis for judgment as it would later be. Two categories were established: the entrepreneur and the wage earner. The prestige posts were reserved for those with sufficient money to buy them, and so it was in the infinitely graded scale of authority. Spain was the government, and within its jurisdiction the citizen was respected, but the road was forbidden to the common run of men. Judicial and teaching posts fell to vociferous lawyers and priests, who formed the intellectual class, while intelligence was denied free avenues to manifest itself. The hollow forms of discredited institutions were brought over from Spain, and into them were poured the minds and the manners of the young. Everything that grew in its own climate, according to its laws of development, was persecuted and scorned to the point that the outlines of these fictions of culture and wealth scarcely resembled the authentic shape of the American reality.

It was an extremely simple world as to things and acts but ruled by a very complicated bureaucratic protocol. The nakedness of this forgotten part of the planet had to be concealed in a dress of legality sometimes difficult to comprehend. The complexity was in the mechanisms and the procedure, in the decorousness that would be used to cover disenchantment, that is to say, in an antitruth. Over an uncomplicated world was drawn a world full of complexities. The newcomer weighed the potential of the only thing that remained fixed in this whirlwind of dialectical forms, the one thing that only the government could take away from him, since the government arrogated to itself the right of engaging in banditry and despoilment on a grand scale. To gain the government's favor he could count on another extremely complicated work of interests and influences. Consequently, the immovable security of this one solid and static type of property also contained its own kind of adventurousness. The land was measured according to the lawyer's deed, authority was affirmed by royal decrees, and worth was acquired through the Church's recognition.

The Lords of Nothingness

The vastness of the horizon, which always looks the same as we advance, as if the whole plain moved along with us, gives one the impression of something illusory in this rude reality of the open country. Here prairie is expanse, and expanse seems to be nothing more than the unfolding of the infinite within, a colloquy of the traveler with God. Only the knowledge that one is traveling, fatigue, and the longing to arrive give scale to this expanse seemingly without measure. It is the pampa, the land where man is alone, like an abstract being that will begin anew the story of the species—or conclude it.

Landscape is lacking, and man is lacking; bottomless chasms open toward the past and the future; one's mind improvises arias on well-known themes, creating its own free, unleashed destiny. One's body is a miracle; through its senses penetrates the breath of a novelty that quickly and nervously subsides into a cosmic weariness that falls with all the weight of the sky.

The landscape of the plains, if such there is, assumes the form of our own dreams, the shape of a chimera; it becomes sterile when the dream is unworthy.

We advance and our plans for the future grow unrestrained: projects of dominion without obstacles but without definite goal. Man puts up no resistance against nature; he has given up the struggle and surrendered. The pampa is an illusion: it is the land of disordered adventures in the fantasy of a shallow man. Everything glides ceaselessly by, animated by an illusory motion in which nothing changes except the center of this mighty circumference. Here the coarse man discovers new beginnings; the cultivated man finds his end. This was the chimerical realm of Trapalanda, of which Father Guevara said, "Its discovery was never made; it was a wasting force that consumed rich resources without bearing fruit." This was the imaginary city of solid gold that almost destroyed the expeditions of Francisco de Aguirre and Diego Abreu, and that led to the founding of La Rioja and Jujuy, in order to lay siege to Trapalanda and to seize it from the natives. The Quixote also was a victim of the plains: the barrenness of La Mancha nourished in his mind the deeds born of his solitary readings. It was natural for the conquistador, limited by the bounds of his own personality, not to conceive ideals of permanence, stability, or restraint. A son as a perpetuation of the family line, a house as a home, a family, and seasonal tasks were impossible. The dominant, universal, historical fact was the prowess of the individual; biography was history and what had been buried or hidden did not exist. To these limited mentalities the limitless, level land or the endless monotony of the arid mountains gave promise, as in the desert of the ascetics, of the appearance of saints or of marvelous cities full of opulence and bliss. One expected to come suddenly upon accumulated treasures in some unsuspected place, ready to be carried off. Nor was the kingdom of God seen to exist, but exist it certainly did. Absurdity was the most logical fact of all. When objects take form and move of their own accord and man follows after them, then we can expect none of the fruits that the earth produces when man populates it and settles down upon it. The dragon is still the animal native to the plains where the mylodont grazed. Nowhere did the newcomer find signs that would help him to conceive of the world as a continuing, rational system. The whole continent appeared to him a magic world drawn out of a dicebox, despite the fact that it was a rational continuum.

Disillusionment as Stimulus

In the forbidding emptiness it was useless to think of towns sharing a productive life, of domesticated animals, of orchards and market places. What was natural was Trapalanda with its city where the native Caesars hoarded precious stones and metals, elixirs of eternal youth, beautiful women, and any other hidden thing that might appear at the swearing of a cabalistic oath: not what displayed itself to the eyes of the searcher for unreality. It was for this that he had come, and because he hoped to use the treasures he found to carry on the war in the Holy Land, he persisted in his belief that somewhere he would discover that for which he longed. In this way he closed his eyes to reality.

The conquistador had taken possession of all that he surveyed; he was the conquering hero over a vanquished land in which his every whim was a command. He had not come to colonize, to remain, or to hope: he came to demand, to despoil, to be obeyed. Thus he lost the very concept of moderation, of order, of time. Vastness, the immeasurable eternity in the present filled his imagination:[1] thousands of leagues, hundreds of thousands of cattle. The Crown divided the continent into various sections: to Pizarro, two hundred leagues to the south of the Río Santiago; to Almagro, two hundred leagues of the country beyond; to Mendoza, two hundred leagues from Almagro's concession; to Alcazaba, two hundred leagues closest to the borders of the area given Mendoza to govern. Azara calculated that there were about forty million head of cattle in those lands. Animals did not need so many months for gestation and so many for weaning: they multiplied like the numbers in one's head. Minerals did not require extraction by laborious methods: they were already piled up, smelted into bars, minted, made into crucifixes and swords. Illusion replaced truth. Reality—the limitless and empty land, the solitude—went unnoticed, since it formed the very flesh and bones of the traveler: an unheeded bulk in which stirred a dream that spilled out beyond the limits of the real, stretching beyond the horizon.

Nor did the dream diminish as these parts began to be peopled: it remained to fill in the interstices of reality, like all frustrated dreams born of the ambition and the longing of uncultivated men. The dream gave way to reality in a concrete, material sense; but insofar as reality was ambiguous it was deformed into a symbol of that ambiguity.

This land had no precious metals to be picked up on the surface or ancient civilizations to destroy; it possessed no fabulous cities, only handfuls of naked savages; yet it continued to be a metaphysical asset in the minds of the sons of the conquistador. It came to represent power, domination, rank. To possess land was to possess cities that would be built in the future, to rule over people who would populate them in the future, to own haciendas that would multiply fantastically in the future. Nothing else had value. Land

---

[1] "They revile you, my people, because they say you went to impose your faith by fire and steel, but the sad part is that it was not entirely so; you went mainly to snatch gold others had amassed: you went to rob" (Miguel de Unamuno, *Vida de Don Quijote y Sancho* ["The Life of Don Quixote and Sancho"]).

was security put up for hope; the latter, its collateral. No one sought from the land what it could produce immediately, only what it might produce someday—including the cities and treasures that had been sought by expeditions. No riches were found, a sure indication of a dormant potential. The cities and the treasures that gradually assumed more sensible forms were better possibilities for wealth than bars of gold. This future, preconceived in a present full of resentment and rancor, was the cause of the delirious dreams of grandeur that caused the idealist Alberdi so much indignation. We still live with the mines of Trapalanda in our souls. The old conquistador yet rises in his tomb: he is dead, but within us he looks across his frustrated dreams at this immense and still-promised land, and our eyes moisten with emotion. We are at the same time his tomb and the stone of his sling. In Europe, to establish a bond of ownership with the land was to marry into history, to weld a genealogical link, to enter the dominion of the past. But in America—in South America—which has no past and consequently, it is thought, must have a future, owning land is one part vengeance and another part greed. By means of land one gains dominion over the future, and a mortgage is the financial method of carrying the past into the present. At the outset, land was seized as booty; the lands left behind by the fleeing savage were the only plunder that later could be displayed as a trophy of war. Those spoils came to be the prize of combat; the expanses of land taken affirmed the power of the victor.

Upon the fact of ownership were built new scales of values based upon prices. It was a map of a nonexistent kingdom: a cyanide process by means of which a poor couple might have their own house, yet unadorned with children or even parents. Thus did this land acquire a supervalue, a psychological overvaluation brought about through an effort of the imagination: the fictitious value of what might come to pass through a compact with ambition. This land of wild cattle was a "seedbed and a gold mine," according to Valdivia, another diviner of the future. This gold would become more pure and more valuable with the passing years. It was also power but of a secondary order. The conquistador who conquered nothing lost sight of the veins of ore as he advanced southward from the northern plateaus; the one who came by sea, drawn on by the fable, who met only wretched Indians, in his sexual abstinence and mental torpor saw in the pampa the final adventure that would prevent him from declaring that he had been defeated. He was conquering space and space was power; he was dominating thousands of leagues crisscrossed by fugitive savages, and he reckoned the quantity of empty land as though it were ounces of gold. There were so many thousands of square miles in the viceroyalty of the Río de la Plata from the ocean to the highest peaks of the Andes—and no gold. He did not count gold coins though, only his own fingers. The rule that he had was the rule of his pride over his ignorance. He was vanquished. There was no need for him to conquer, only to colonize; not to reap, but to sow; he was not about to enter into governorship of his island, but to labor and suffer. He took possession of this empty land in the name of God and the king, but in the depth of his conscience he was disillusioned. He had to lie about the real value of his dreams, as he did by giving laughable names to the regions where he failed to find what he was seeking. Thus he set up the cross and boundary stones, mocking the voice of his own conscience when he armed himself and brandished his sword in defiance of absent rivals. For there was nobody who could claim possession of nothing except a nobody. And that nobody, who existed only within the conqueror, was the voice of his own failure.

Dominion as Reprisal

But the earth is not a lie, though man may traverse it in delirium, demanding of it what it cannot give and christening it with paradoxical names. It is the surest thing man knows underfoot and under his back when the day's journey is done. The dumb brute stands and feeds upon it and by this intimate contact is aware of a sense of life. The earth is the definitive truth, the first and the last: it is death.

Instead of building, fencing, or laboring, man made laws to give a theological and judicial value to his possession. He treated the Indian as he would have treated the dragon, had it existed. The Indian would cast an evil eye over the enchanted treasure and cause it to disappear. To destroy the Indian was to assume reaping in peace the benefits of the land and at the same time doing away with the evidence of failure. The Spaniard treated his fellow man as the witness of his defeat, and he exploited the *encomiendas* and *mitas* according to the prudent counsel of the Jesuits. It was the way to conquer nature, to make it produce by means of the man come forth from her womb, the aborigine, what it had refused to yield of its own accord so as to have it ready for the conqueror's arrival. In this manner the Spaniard took reprisal against both nature and man for the legends that had tricked him: against the former for Christ, against the latter for the Crown. The possession of land gave him additional claims in society. The earth was an immense fief, a domain implying nobility. That is why even today our land-owner is the nobleman in the hierarchy of our barbarous capitalism.

Vastness is not greatness: it is merely the idea of greatness. It is not wealth: it is the possibility of mortgage credit. It is nothing. Space was given value because it became an ideal and for that reason attained the imaginary price per hectare of land in Trapalanda. To wish to acquire land, to desire for power through its possession, is a residual product of the invader's fury and a residue of medieval times. A property title represents a document of one's capacity to command. He who possesses it is lord and master, not because of the money it represents, but because it is a barony, a county in the form that ambition and rancor take. Since ancient times it has been the military man who possessed the land, and the land served to reward acts of heroism and feats of arms. It is something like dominating a part of the globe to take revenge for one's personal wretchedness: it is plunging up to the waist in the Pacific Ocean to take possession of it in the name of the king.

Those were the captains; the troops followed with their more humble dreams. There is a difference only of degree between the ownership of a vast estate and a small plot of land. The contemporary dream of owning a house without a corresponding desire for a home is a degenerate, bourgeois form of the old dreams of grandeur. These are the daydreams of the man who deep within himself feels incapable of aspiring to a more courageous and more active fortune, that of making himself master of other riches. But just as there breathes nothing more than the spirit of an insecure man (with all the poetry of a bird) in the humble desire to have a house, in the ownership of thousands of leagues there is a lordly drive (that of a digitigrade). Each craving corresponds to a common type, different in the élan of their aspirations but identical in their esteem for counterfeit values. The third angle of the triangle is the tomb into which man enters whole, dreams and flesh, in a condition of inanimate matter, of earth, of place. These are the three positions of the same unconscious renunciation of life and of whatever gives life its human texture: the bitterness of having destroyed all other values, and of wanting to sink oneself within the only value that is equivalent of one's corpse.

The Advance to the Rear

The immigrant who drifted to these shores was fundamentally, as he is today, a dreamer of personal dreams. On the other hand, he who came and resolved to stay was a more dangerously desperate man than the one who arrived to rob and leave. Ships loaded with jailbirds or with men crazed with ambition and faith made the crossing of an ocean of forgetfulness. Those few who renounced the return voyage home and resignedly fixed their lives so far from the beaten path of reality became declassed beings without a definite goal in life, as is the case today with the immigrant who lands and accepts the first job offered him.

With his help, however, the adventurer in a hurry to return could leave something behind him. The man without hope was the right hand to this other's daring plans. A sterile brute with a one-track dream, he owned a hundred leagues of land and he wanted a thousand or ten thousand; he owned twenty thousand head of cattle and wanted two hundred thousand or two million; he owned a house and he wanted ten or a hundred. His desire was always for greater quantities of what he already owned, and these were always things intimately linked to the land. He desired in a primitive way, with his sense of touch. The idea of geometric progression was embedded in his brain. There were other desires that mattered besides these, but only as functions of them, adjuncts, coordinated with them, measured and weighed by hectares and fanegas. His ambition lay in multiplying units by tens, in adding zeros, as later on he would build floor upon floor, publish book after book, accumulate appointments, professorships, and titles. In the imagination of this anachronistic primitive, land and livestock were the only dynamic forces. All other vital social and economic energies became polarized or they revolved around this central hub. Thus an insensible degeneration took place in the life of this two-dimensional being who knew no ideals, no spiritual struggles, and no mystic disquietude, but who did know fear. Fondly attached to a wealth so easily acquired, he was remote from everything else. To strike roots in this no-man's prairie land, he had had to tear himself away from an ancient land, watered with sweat and tears. He was the center of the universe, but he was alone. In front, to the sides, behind, he had the earth—but it was roadless. Little by little he filled the hollows left by his rending separation with matter alien to his own human self until even his most instinctive movements were filled with the substance of the place. In the past he had prayed often; now he raised his eyes to heaven seeking rain in the clouds that moved over the land cracked open by the sun. He gazed far into the distance as if he were aboard ship, but now so as to see if Indians were appearing on the horizon, or the tax collector who despoiled him, or the militiaman who conscripted him by force. Beneath the roof of his hut, he felt that he was crumbling away faster than the mud and straw that supported his sagging shoulders. His wife and children by his side merely confirmed his feeling that he was alone. He avoided looking within himself, for there it was more desolate than the pampa; neither did he look back in remembrance of his life in other places. The world was what was around and in front of him. He had been deceived, and now only two roads were left for him to take, since it was no longer possible to return home. He could think of himself as chosen by God for some lofty end in Church or State, or he could come to terms as courageously as possible with that formlessness which faced and surrounded him. He struggled against reality and thus became reality's instrument. At the same time, the tenacity with which he hung on to it, trying to change its face, drove and defeated him. He moved backward and thought he was going forward by pushing against the future with his back. The history of our colonization is one continuous march backward.

In his letter to Viceroy Del Pino, Viceroy Avilés stated that the families brought to settle the Río Negro province had fallen into an abject state. Some lived buried alive in caves they themselves had dug. Others lived in huts, that is to say, in caves built outward, open-air caves. They submerged themselves in their caves and in the past. Darwin witnessed the saturnalias of the Argentine Huns: the enjoyable slaughter of cattle, the orgy amidst smoking blood.[2] It was the victory of the earth, the triumph of the prehistoric, the defeat of an irrational dream tossed on the lap of a nature in which the Pleistocene still held full sway. Under imperceptible influences the population regressed into an inferior state; and such regressive states, relapses into barbarism, are cruder than the natural state. They involve the surrender of civilization and the return along many paths, such as one may stumble upon in the prairie land, to the lowest level of animality. The families that came to colonize had cheated themselves, but they had also been defrauded by the companies of slave traders who recruited them in Spain only to cast them away upon our limitless spaces. Dead cattle were shipped abroad and live human beings were brought back in exchange. To submerge oneself in a cave and to slaughter cattle and sheep was to strike back at oneself and at the entrepreneur. Disillusionment leads to destruction and mockery of everything that reminds us of

---

[2] Dogs fled from homes and became ferocious enemies of herds and of men. They were turned wild by the abundance of meat abandoned in the fields; these were the remains of cattle after their hides, horns, and fat had been removed. The dogs formed immense packs to attack the herds; they were more like jackals than dogs. It was necessary to organize military expeditions to contain them. In just a few years they had regressed countless centuries.

the superior state we abdicated, not only in objects around us but in ourselves. The love for what we have is hate for what we cannot have, and vice versa. Much of what has been taken for barbarism is simply the disillusionment of an ordinary dreamer. Those who in their homeland had worked to improve their stone villages and their plots of ground surely must have aspired to better homes and better properties.

The Sting

The settlers kept coming from less productive lands, from more molded and exacting social systems to these promissory lands. They abandoned a known environment in which they were misfits and flung themselves into the unknown, hoping to mold it into their own image, never dreaming that this amorphous and retarding reality would become incarnate in them. They arrived unarmed in dauntless legions along the same paths trod by the conquistador: more sordid than he, expecting less, content with little, but without the epic daring of the conquistador or the hyperbole with which he crowned his works. They were the conquistador reincarnated from the descendants he had left on the Spanish peninsula, from the populace made up of the timid who remained there on the piers awaiting the gold-laden ships that arrived stinking of rotting meat. This rabble, fragments broken off from a robust body, also came to dream and to pursue their dreams. There was the same hope, the same ambition, the same anxiety to evade a fate of irredeemable want; complementing the concavity of the digitigrade ancestor was the corvidae. They came looking for money as others had come looking for kingdoms, title, and fame; to work, as others had come to fight; to collect and leave. These bastard children of the conquistador did not settle down any more than he. They wandered from one place to the next because in the beginning they were drawn hither and yonder by the wild cattle and by the possession of a ground as movable as the cattle's hooves. What one of them attained he held fast to; it was his booty. He became cruel in his treatment of the mestizo whenever he gained advantage over him, as he was to all objects and beings that submitted to him. He possessed without loving. He gloated on his possessions without enjoying them, with that glandular rancor with which we engender a child in the woman we despise. Through material fortune he attained high position; but no one took him seriously as to his character, his rank, or his family background. He inspired a kind of contemptuous respect. If the rich man paid him court, it was only because of the tacit connivance that existed between them. Instead of letting his wealth be known in a frank and open way, he misrepresented what he owned, hiding behind a false smile. With his fortune he bought the right to human status, achieving his dream at the cost of his failure. Ignorant and miserly, he sought to wash the dung off his hands at the holy-water basin; and he transferred a part of his own brutishness to the Church. He did no works of philanthropy, having no interest in the greatness of a country he scarcely knew, a country he despised, which he had never loved, which he resented because its success had defeated him. He was the family fragmented, embodiment of untold paternal and conjugal guilts. But about him there was no one with a more legitimate right to claim precedence and rank. He measured himself against the rest, man for man, hectare for hectare, bushel for bushel. The privileges accorded to noble birth or intelligence did not exist, because everyone led the same wretched life. He mistrusted the intellectual as the cow does the automobile: he planted himself in the middle of the road and refused to let the other go by. He piled up his fortune in solitude, deep in his fields or behind the counter that was a barricade against society, watching the corruption of his daughters who married the servants who seduced them or married no one, losing the power of descriptive language and abstract thought so that his fortune became hate and resentment, a backward leap. All his interest was in what was inferior, in subverting the ethical scale of values, in emptying the cruelty and . ignorance of the country upon the city to give an appearance of honesty to the game he played. Like the North American pioneer he blazed new trails along the tangled meaning of life, along which his children would later travel. And these defeated ones were the successful dreamers; many—most—made no fortunes at all. They grew old, they died, and their children inherited disillusionment. The myth of wealth disheartened the majority, especially the boldless and the ignorant, those least fit to succeed in such a severe test. And there was no other road to take. Abundant crops and their high prices had deceived them as Trapalanda had deceived the conquistador. Reality was the countryside, solitude, brutishness, fallen mud walls instead of magic cities of gold. The moral state of the disillusioned settler was the same as that of the ragged conquistador, starving among his harem of filthy Indian women. Crops were hypothetical: they depended on chance. The price of his labor was hypothetical: it depended on the demand for grain and meat in unknown markets. He worked, but after paying rent to the landowners and bearing the cost of transporting his crop he had nothing left. He had sheep, cattle, and his hut, while to the landowner and the financier he was himself but so much livestock.

The Land: Standard of Value

The ideal of the land—a land without history —as a religion and a design for conduct either is a cloak over a great disillusionment or is a representative of the renouncement of many unattainable aspirations. At the opposite pole is the ideal that goes no farther than an untroubled house, a faithful wife, and hardworking children. The latter is the desire of a sick soul, the former a brave denial of the past, the challenge of a celibate alienated from human society. The bird seeks the nest, but the wild beast aspires to the dominion of nature. It attacks the surrounding world because it wants to flee from the loneliness inside it, enraged because it has no allies or companions.

In the absence of consolidated social order, of rules based on experience, of stimulus arising from custom, an attempt was made to identify all good with the earth, with what lay there with no form other than the vague one that goes beyond the eye and the ear. The earth was a metaphysical value: it was space. It could yield fruit for the newcomer whether he knew how to farm or not: its fecundity would be a substitute for assiduous dedication, making both labor and intelligence unnecessary. Land was all that could be found, so it had to be worth risking one's life. The adventure was in the finding. Furthermore, land gave to the younger sons a certain kind of primogeniture that the sons of the conquistador lacked. The conqueror's domain raised him to the level of an absolute monarch, the founder of a dynasty. In the beginning all that was necessary was to let loose in the prairies a few dozen horses and cattle, or to even abandon them because it was difficult to take them back as Irala did; and they would multiply. Garay would discover when he came with a few more that they had turned into numberless herds. All that was necessary to grow wheat and corn was to throw the seed on the ground; for other tasks one enslaved the Indian and took away his woman.

These lands were the poorest of all the conquests made in America and for that reason should have contained hidden wealth, future profit. Disappointed, Irala went away to Paraguay; and out of the abandoned remains of his inadequacy, from the loose livestock, would sprout forth that inexistent gold. Livestock was our precious metal, as the excrement of the birds would in the long run be the real gold of Peru. For here there were no metals; the earth gave no fruit and it had no cities. Soldiers often returned naked from their expeditions, their bodies barely covered with untanned hides, famished. They would eat even the leather trim of their saddles, and their desperation drove them to sexual excesses. In Venezuela, which produced institutions and types of men analogous to ours, they descended to cannibalism. They chose their victims from among the Indians who guided them through the mountainous terrain by holding daily lotteries as told in pirate tales. The same thing took place during the first founding of Buenos Aires. But none of these deprivations was real; reality was the conquest of a world. In Nicaragua they kept seeing gold and silver boiling in the crater of Masaya; the lands with the treasure were over there in Catamarca, in Neuquén, in Tierra del Fuego. One had to persist and keep on looking.

Those who came with Garay found riches in the form of livestock; and although not as prestigious as precious metals, these were riches nevertheless. They were in the hands of the savage with whom the newcomers had made common life, joining their destinies in common solitude. Savages and animals formed a curious entity for resistance and mutual defense, sharing the patterns of existence imposed upon them by the wilderness and their enemies. Thus were laid down in categorical terms the standards of conduct to be followed: nature and its creatures against the invader. The struggle would be remorseless, rejecting any kind of transaction or pact. It was the conquistador who laid down this norm of hate. Here he coveted what he had disdained in his own land and proclaimed himself lord of the earth, of men, and of things; but he never really possessed them, nor did he value them except as a form of portable wealth because the eagerness to expand was precisely the opposite from the desire to settle down. The capture of wild cattle and the harvesting of the land required other methods than those used in extracting gold from the mines. The herds were treasures, since they were the Indian's, and taking them away from the Indian was a higher enterprise than raising and tending them.

In the open country, rounding up cattle and fighting the Indians, man established an involuntary relationship and identification with his cattle. In this land the feudal lord was aborted in the cattleman; henceforth there would be no great lords, only rich men, and the value of land would be that of the cattle upon it. Thus the physical environment triumphed over ambition and forced it to be content with what nature offered: grain and cattle. More than that, the ambitious man was forced to accept a set of terrible conditions: a vagabond spirit, the zeal for accumulating things, the worship of quantity and size, the haste to leave, the disgrace of poverty, the breaking up of the home, the impossibility of a culture based on respect alone, and the emptiness of love.

It was at the same time a victory of land over its conquerors, avenging its native sons by incarnating in the victors the reality they had ignored. This was the first battle won by America, the triumph of the wilderness, and the first step toward decadence by the conqueror, a humiliation that took the appearance of triumph. There were meat, corn, and wheat aplenty: food, that is to say the most basic but the least significant element of a civilized life. In return, the child of Europe and the sixteenth century and centuries following had to acquiesce to a most primitive life. He was forced to regress to the cave in order to buy fortune with his own degradation. Those who were most ductile to the process of deformation were the ones who prevailed, and those who best accepted their condition did the right thing. In the end they became machines, tools for the production of cattle and grain, herders and butchers dedicated to the feeding of the Europeans from whom they were separated by thousands of centuries.

The conquest of the territory for the Crown was followed by another absurdity, the conquest of the means to feed the foreigner, and finally by still another absurdity, which is but the third and present aspect of the same lack of logic: the conquest of wealth for the benefit of foreign capital in the railroads, the refrigeration, and the grain trust. These were the conditions under which was begun the struggle that would decide the fate of these lands for many years. It was a stupendous struggle, like no other in history perhaps: the land conquers the conqueror, defeats him and forces him to become the servant of all that which he loathes.

Life and Movement of the Earth

The first battle was joined with man as the temporary victor to the detriment of his status as a civilized being, but in the end he succumbed to the slower and infinitely greater forces of nature. He must resign himself and settle down, submit to the inert laws of the earth, obey it, and become as the sediment that covered its subsoil. His soul rebelled from the intimate depths of its ethnic existence against the renouncing of his personality, his passive submission to a nature that absorbed and mastered him as it would a fallen edifice in ruins. He did not want to lower himself to the status of the Indian, a product of the conjunction of forces that surrounded him. He fought against this force burrowing deep into his flesh, but in the end he adopted the customs of the native he despised: he learned the Indian's way of fighting and living; he used the Indian's weapon, the knife; he mated with the squaw; he built his casual hovel; and he left offspring behind him. But one supreme recourse was left him: he did his best to convert that harsh domain, no more valuable than a scrap of legal paper, into riches, into something movable, portable, salable. This had been his way in Spain (in Andalusia, in Castile, in Vizcaya); and when he found himself face to face with a featureless world, a world that imposed its hollow and fleshless reality upon him, he looked for some way to keep his pride intact in the midst of disaster.

He did not wish to see his adventure crystallized; for the form it could take would be that of want. His instinct for possession turned out to be after all an abortive form of another that was even more absurd; and as he put out roots and vegetated, it left him abruptly. He attempted to make this dead domain, this endless land, into something living. Agricultural work was repugnant to him; and, as his grandfather in Spain, he considered it degrading; submission to the sod was not part of his history. In his own country he had never been tied down to the land: the traditions of his race had disdained any kind of attachment to a place. From the days of the Cid he had loved mobile riches and the conveyance of power. He required a kind of wealth that would rise up to the surface and walk, and all the prairie land began to move in the form of endless wild herds. These animals which had multiplied in the mystery of the plain were, by adoption, the Indian's. But he brought the Indian's cattle under his control as he also brought the Indian who submitted to being his ally.[3] His estate, his assets were those which came to be called hacienda as in old Castile. But he would dissolve his ties with the earth in order to link himself to this spontaneous and miraculous product of the earth and to fight a war of spoliation against the Indian who controlled the land where the cattle roamed. He became a floating being, parasitically dependent on the cow and the horse, with nothing to restrain him in his ambitions or his career, since nothing knew bounds here— neither the law nor property nor life. He became a traveling pseudopod, a twig torn from the seignorial tree and forked upon a horse.

---

[3] When war was waged for territory, the Indian was sought as an ally; but when it was conducted for political domination and to make a fortune, the Indian was sought out and exterminated.

On the other hand, ownership of cattle included ownership of the land, which was the same thing. It even came to have the value of coin when no silver arrived from Potosí and there was a scarcity of metallic money in circulation. Cattle came to be money in transactions that were countenanced by the smuggling trade, which became common because of necessity and restrictions imposed, and, what is more important to another aspect of our history, it also became the legal form of commerce. The hunting of cattle gave its name to a whole colonial era, "The Age of Rawhide," and it also perhaps gave Argentine life a definitive character. It was one of the forms of the tradition of the great estate, which had bifurcated in different directions: one, following the old traditions, cultivated the landed estate and sought to create a new Spain in these lands; the other followed the estate on the hoof, seeking to trade, to live, and to promote America.

2 THE AGE OF RAWHIDE

The First Sowing

Did Bishop Lué really believe—as Castelli accused him in open assembly on the eve of the revolutionary movement—that the Spanish conquistadors and settlers had begot sheep instead of men in America? Bishop Lué was of a reactionary habit of mind and could not see the truth as it was seen by Castelli, one of the few men of the time who could tell the men from the sheep. America had not been populated by sheep; but the children of the conquistador and the settler grew and multiplied in the country, in the towns, in the fortresses, and in the Indian camps without transforming their nutriment into human substance.

An inconceivable blindness to the future and to his own responsibilities drove the white to beget on Indian women, as though he were making some abstruse reprisal against America. His furious lust crowned the humiliation of the native, whose naked poverty inflamed his goatlike instincts as well as his contempt. But from that unhappy seeding there sprang forth enemies as did the Spartans from the dragon's teeth. He affronted both nature and the native, and both would later call him to account for his transgressions in what he had done and engendered.

The conquistador did not love this land. He saw its future only through his avarice and lust. He populated a vacant land given up to its own norms according to the physical and physiological laws of nature. He brought from his ancestral home none of the virtues that had made it possible for him to resist the invasions of warlike peoples for seventeen hundred years, virtues that seemed to belong to the place and not to him. He brought with him a heroism based on race, caste, and religion, very soon overwhelmed by the vastness of a prodigious landscape that impelled him to embark on a purposeless journey.

Almost never was he accompanied by women of his own race with whom he might have contemplated the adventure with less haste and more indulgence. In his plans there never entered anything that might demand permanence, reverence, or waiting. He brought with him a strange avidity for time and rapine that made no valid sense to the native peoples who were used to living according to the slow rhythm of the land. But his son, begotten into a bitter truth, came here to stay and to understand what the father had ignored as he confronted his helot's fate. He came to oppose the delusion of grandeur with the humble truth of his tattered form.

The Indian had not been extirpated or even defeated. His pursuer preferred to employ against him only inferior forces; and the native would triumph in the end, for even dead he lived on in the tactics he had imposed on his enemy as the prize of his death. The Indian became stronger than ever when he was attacked because he finally understood his situation. He was ready enough to fight beings he now knew were flesh and blood like himself and not gods or demons or immortal souls. For if the white man gave the Indian an imperishable soul by means of papal bulls and councils, the Indian returned the compliment by endowing the white man with perishable flesh. The Indian redoubled his will not to submit, and he did not die.

At best he was held in check; he would threaten from the frontier, disturbing his enemy's peaceful enjoyment of the spoils. He was always out there in the distance, like a loaded gun; the knowledge of his presence beat on the gates of the city's stable life. Then he was back in a sudden raid to recapture his stolen women, his enslaved children, his livestock, and his lands that had been unjustly confiscated.

But between the city and the frontier began to rise the creole and the mestizo who took sides with the tribe against the trading post, with the trading post against the city, and with America against Spain. The mestizo had been begotten in infamy with the repugnance one feels in satisfying sexual appetites on vile flesh. If he was recognized in his status as an illegitimate son, he owed it to the requirements of the Church. He was more Indian than Spanish, survivor and fiduciary of his maternal race.

His father was one of the invaders and he would leave. His mother belonged to the vanquished and she would die. But he was the people who would remain. Nothing could incline him toward respect for the past, for the family, or for legal and ecclesiastical customs and forms, he who carried a name that meant nothing to his blood. Abandoned to wretchedness and contempt whether he was recognized or not, he was closer to nature than to civilization. He would always abominate the past and throw himself at the future, destroying everything in his path to avenge the stigma of his origin.

Seeds on Fertile Soil

Since the naked Indian had nothing but himself to serve as inducement to ambition, the conquest was postponed for several centuries. Without the conquistador's awareness there was developing a population born of irregular unions between white and Indian that in the course of time would comprehend all the shame of the past. In the Indian's eyes, the Spaniard must have taken the aspect of an insatiable animal, plagued by barracks diseases and the perversities of a lord.

The casual unions between the invader and the women he enslaved left their irredeemable consequences in the mestizo, who would turn against society and the past when his hour came. Out of them would burst forth the civil wars and the political convulsions that followed them with mestizo chieftains almost always at their head. But they also left a shamed but immortal substance that would perpetuate the humiliation of the female in every act of copulation. Against the eruption of the masses certain more or less efficacious means could be found, principally money with which peace could be bought. But against this flowing out of repressed outrage neither money nor the law could do anything.

At the same time the pastoral letters and edicts consummated the ruin of love. An abysm yawned between marriage and concubinage; the law of God was not the law of America. Cortés, Alvarado, and Núñez de Balboa brought mistresses with them and set the example for their troops. Spanish law prohibited a viceroy from establishing a legitimate family, but he was allowed to court loose women. We see in the *Comentarios* of Alvar Núñez that "the friends, acquaintances, and servants (of Irala) were given license to go through the villages and settlements of the Indians and to take from them their wives and daughters and hammocks and other things they had." At once dishonor and despoliation: hate was implanted very deeply indeed. And this hate was given the name of love. But love is a form of attachment and fixed habit; it is born of repose because it is the transmission of imperishable life and the seal of eternity. It requires a fixed place—the nest, the lair, or the house. The random union of the sexes engenders a sense of insecurity in the spirit and passes it on to future generations. The sexual act incompletely realized produces one of the forms of neurotic affliction: haste, disgust, the very murder of one's life.

The Indian woman served the white-skinned invader as a night's enjoyment after an idle day, giving her blood to feed the germs of boredom and disillusionment; and out of pleasure was born heartache. Love was not expected of her, or even fidelity, since male and female came together only anatomically. When he got up she began her long physiological task. Many men later legitimized these unions, more as an act of contrition and compassion than of love; and up until recently groups of priests would go into the outlying districts to bring together in heaven what was not united here on earth either in body or in soul. The truth is that more of the Indian women were turned into courtesans than became wives, and the wives were not any more highly regarded than the concubines with whom they lived under the same roof, under the eye of the master as beasts of burden and pleasure to the point that the chroniclers had to confess that contact with the white had depraved the purity of the Indian's savage life.

Even today, concubinage and prostitution are above all a dreadful moral problem. Woman was lowered by making her do heavy tasks, suckle children, and satisfy concupiscence; therefore, she became an inferior being without control over her own conduct, the loss of which destroys both dignity and conscience. She suffered the fate of all idols in whom faith has been lost: ritually respected, she did not inspire the values of enthusiasm and hope.

South America resembled a vast market of pleasure, a brothel managed by authorities and directed by speculators. In 1844 Valparaíso was "a horrible market of women" to which came girls from all countries to contract clandestine unions because marriage of persons of different faiths was forbidden abroad. "Concubinage took the place of matrimony, and thousands of prostitutes roamed the city, hundreds to the block, crowded in rooms."[1] Cunninghame Graham describes the brothels at their height where an important personage, adored by his fellow citizens and "elected by thousands of noses," could go after lunch to smoke his cigar and drink his coffee. In 1880 regular troops were camping on the treeless plazas, accompanied by their camp followers. During these times, undoubtedly the high point in the flowering of Argentina, ladies used to visit the Riachuelo waterfront in Buenos Aires when boats arrived from the south to choose from the children of the Indian women who had to part with them, as if they were picking out ponies from a herd. In his *Memorias* Paz refers to the license and laxity of Lavalle's armies in 1840. He contrasts these troops, which

---

[1] D. F. Sarmiento, *Conflicto y armonía de las razas en América* ["Conflict and Harmony among the Races in America"].

made open-air bordellos of their encampments, to the armies of 1828–1829 and to those of Belgrano and Urquiza, which were disciplined and manly. And in the provinces today the dregs of these depressive bawdyhouses live on as crudely as they did one or two centuries ago.

The contempt for the feminine soon converted the female into an animal. The habit of humiliating the woman turned the feminine sex into a separate fauna born for insult and contempt. Mares may be used as beasts of burden but not as mounts. Only the foreigner will ride a mare. The mare is given tasks analogous to those of a woman; it is not for show. Neither mare nor woman is taken to town; both embody a sexual taboo, a contemptuous one. The gaucho's poetry from *Martín Fierro* on is plagued by this dual disdain: the gaucho thought it humiliating to fall in love and marry, as much as riding a mare.

Under the tent made of hides or in the store or straw hut, the Indian woman had her place as mother, wife, sister, or daughter. She was a woman in a social, an emotional, and a physical sense. She was not a sex, even when naked. Marriage, usually monogamous, was subject to a native morality free of anomalies, and adultery was punishable by severe penalties. But when the white came to the tribes he destroyed these innocent customs and did not replace them with anything else. He tore women from their homes and took them with him to satisfy his lust or to entertain his superiors. If he thought them beautiful he kept them as his concubines. Those few who brought wives with them kept them under the same roof with their mestizo mistresses. The children of one and the other female—those born under the laws of God and those born under the laws of America—grew up regarding each other with rancor. Indian women were considered as booty; loaded down with children they could still be repudiated and sent back to the tribe to be killed or jeered at. They were predestined to be pregnant with the weight of the world. The mestizo and the gaucho knew no compassion or clemency. They did know contempt. Darwin tells of a slaughter of Indian women over twenty years of age and of the natives, forming the greater and more dynamic part of López's troops, who worked themselves into a frenzy over the massacre. Their misfortunes are sung in old epigrams while even today they are chastised in the words of the tango, that lock of horsehair on the adolescent body of art. They were burdened with the tasks the men considered humiliating: farming, tending domestic animals, weaving, drawing water and gathering wood, cooking, cleaning. Even a nobody could herd them into his hut in whatever number he could support, while he devoted his time to rounding up maverick cattle, to brigandage, and to playing the role of the dominant male.

The woman took charge of domestic tasks and of the field; furthermore she bore children. The man was the one who lived outside. He belonged to the home only at night when he came to beget more children upon her. Man and wife lived in a state of divorce, living a life that shamed them. To be affectionate, to work for his children, and to be concerned about the honor of one's family were negative qualities. On the other hand, to be intractable, insensitive, and nocturnal signified prestige, manliness, and paternity. Positive values were debased, and by compensation negative ones were held in esteem. Men and women were born in those homes, in the country and in the city, differing only in their external features; they grew up, and the same characteristics were multiplied in their children and their children's children. Legitimate marriages thus acquired the exterior aspects of concubinage, the husband imitated the bad habits of the lover so as not to appear inferior while the wife resigned herself to a kind of legalized prostitution as the fate of her sex. The man accentuated his status as lord, master, and male by referring to his wife and child in a somewhat disparaging tone. He had lost his mastery over real estate, but he could still exercise it on his movable property—his family and his horse. The woman became resigned to his disdain, accepting it as a natural thing. She left the hut and rode on the horse's croup; she accompanied the soldier, dressing his wounds, giving him the warmth of her body in the nights at camp, satisfying his appetites, inciting him to battle. She marched with the armies, bearing their provisions; she was part of the army. But in her condition as a passive and vegetative being she served as a brake upon the soldier's impulse to conquest on a grand scale, being content with the booty of victory or the theft of a few chickens. She turned the soldier into a bird of prey, the conquistador into a miser. She made of great marches a series of advances and halts, raids out of full-scale invasions. That knapsack on her back was heavy after all.

Between the native and the outsider there could be neither pacts nor alliances. The Christian was always a felon and a liar; without father or sister to watch him, he lacked dignity and morality. He promised peace and rewards, the respect for life and friendship; but he made a mockery of all. There are no lasting pacts between the powerful and the oppressed. One side has the privilege of meeting or disregarding its obligations and the other is enslaved by its own inferiority. Between Christian and Indian no friendship was ever possible; they had differing interests and were widely at variance in their cosmic conception of things. Their relationships were based on deceit, and the Indian always got the worst part of the bargain. He ended up by making mistrust his most salient psychological trait. Almost all the Indian's spiritual tasks are scars upon his body. Such simple souls are deeply impressed by any deep emotion and in this they never change even though one can convert them into anything at once. Life leaves deep organic prints on their unmodeled matter. Deceive them once and they become living rancor. They are plastic enough to incorporate into their character any fraud that disturbs their mental structure, to the point of passing it on to their descendants. They are feminine souls. The germ inoculated in their blood incubates slowly, and it progressively develops at the expense of the whole organism. The Indian turned suspicious, withdrawn, and disaffected; the mestizo inherited from his mother these same traits in both body and soul. The Spaniard had taught the Indian to be cautious, not to believe in words, to rake up with infinite care the most insignificant details that might help him understand the white man's demoniacal psychology, moved by passions and purposes with mysterious ends. There exists today, perhaps, no better diviner of intentions. He became an expert in following the trail of an intention beneath the words that concealed it, so he could be ready to strike first. His good faith, his trust in mankind, the simple goodwill that had made him yield without malice —all these had failed him. He was hurt in his most sacred customs and ideas; he was led astray and his mind was corrupted. He learned to answer in vague phrases, to withdraw both physically and spiritually. He talked from a distance and slept on his horse, adopting the wiles of a bird that leads the hunter away from the nest and then becomes an undistinguishable clump of grass. Bitter experience in his dealings with the white man made him wear a knife at his belt night and day, and his daughter learned to think of herself as an object that could be used and cast aside. In remote areas the local governments lacked any formula that would meet even the outward exigencies of modesty, and they made the inevitable child into a silent witness of dishonor. Someday he would have his revenge, but meanwhile he perpetuated the same customs on the sisters of his friends. Promiscuity and insolence were common while feelings of kinship and paternity curdled into arrogant impulses. The man valued the quality of the male animal, the *macho*, in all things: human character, words, attitudes. Women and objects were goods over which the male exercised phallic mastery. The sons born of concubinage followed the customs of their fathers, but deep in their consciences they were not content. They had no home; they were pariahs of the plains, more like ownerless animals than men. Even the creoles of the cities, when they had reached a comfortable state, preferred to make prostitutes of their daughters rather than to marry them to the mestizo, brutalized as he was by the vices of the pampa—by alcohol, license, and thievery. The known father was worse than the unknown. Meanwhile this population grew and multiplied, becoming multitudes, although its precise number was not known. It was impossible that the masses would forever remain in their abject condition. The only way left for them to free themselves from the hell they lived in was to rebel against their oppressors. But they were not united, they lacked leaders to bring them together and tell them which way to go.

Executors for the Indian

A mixture of native and European blood, the mestizo produced an ethnic type inferior to both the mother and the father. He was considered a Spaniard and paid no tribute as did the offspring of an Indian male and a European woman. This latter was fierce and rebellious. When the occasion arose to distribute prebends or offices, he was excluded. He grew up without rules of conduct, without education or law; and on becoming of age he demanded an accounting for his brutishness. The Indian, his closest relative, accompanied him all the way to the city or to the white commander's tent. They were mysteriously affiliated in a barbaric order of chivalry. The Indian never was an obstinate enemy even when he was given cause for being so; there was no reason to break all relations with him or to pursue him relentlessly. He was simply a free force susceptible to being controlled and led, a psychic force. The missionaries had known how to make use of the Indians and so did our generals who found them tractable enough. López used to say to Paz, "The Indian is very useful when he is led and given orders." Zeballos and Mansilla describe their customs as morally superior to the invader's. They drank and made war, but they kept their word once given. They did not rape other men's wives, and their raids took the form of rescues rather than of robbery. They had no civilization of any kind except for some vestiges of the Inca, the rudiments of which faded out gradually as one moved southward. Those Indians and their hybrid descendants were roaming tribes, enemies among themselves; but they were susceptible to taming influences, to obedience, and to work. They defended nothing, having nothing to defend; and whatever was given to them as a gift they considered good. But they were stupidly used, made allies when the need arose, and persecuted afterward. The chieftain Catriel fought as Mitre's ally in the luckless revolution of 1874, wearing the insignia of a colonel in the nation's forces. Later he was defeated, his tribe annihilated. When a Brazilian invasion threatened along the Río Negro, Rosas based his defense on the Indians. Rosas hurled them into the abyss, but they respected him because to them he was an idea to which they might anchor their errant strength. With Güemes in the north; with Ramírez, Hereñú, and Artigas on the coast; with Facundo, Peñaloza, Aldao in the west; with Bustos, Ibarra, López in the interior; with Rosas in the south—everywhere they were a valuable element in the national armies. With the mestizo the Indian swelled the ranks dressed in red with an ostrich feather in his hat. They were the knights of truth mounting an assault on the knights of a gross illusion. They both came to restore to the Conquest its true sense, to awaken the dreamer from his dream. There they were, mounted, sounding their horns, beating their war drums, saying they must be reckoned with, for they were reality oppressed, the unspoken taboo. They served all sorts of purposes in the hands of the military leader, but they were ideal in the fight against the *godo*. López and Quiroga manipulated them, now to augment their forces, now to weaken those of the rebels raised against them. They were conscious of nothing but a burning resentment, of a secret desire for vengeance against everything that smacked of centralism in politics because it was presumed to be the embodiment of civilization and the ideal of grandeur. Tattered and starved, with matted hair, barefoot and armed with bamboo lances or fragments of unserviceable weapons, they were the embodiment of mass humiliation. But a sinister contract was being made with them, one that would be impossible to annul by still another dream. The structure taken by the towns was Indian as was everything else. They who were but matter would give form to the colony, which was ignorance. Generals and statesmen stained themselves with bribery and fraud when they sought them or persecuted them. The Indian and the mestizo were the armed force, and the commander who could count on them had to be bought, for which end the legislatures were always quick to vote appropriations in secret sessions. The armies of these chieftains adopted their own ways of fighting and their own tactics of war. The women accompanied the troops, camping with them. Out of this sooner-or-later-necessary awakening came a great evil. In the armistices the Indians were the faithful, the whites the perfidious ones, and if perfidy triumphed the victory was theirs also. For it was during the struggle that this land was peopled. That network of towns born as a result of the persecution of the Indian gave the Republic a military rather than a political or an economic aspect. The map of populated places is a map of trenches converted into stores and saloons. It was the Indian who forced us to give this arbitrary pattern to our settlements and consequently to the railroads that fixed them forever. Exterminated, the Indian still left these cadavers which could never be buried. Universities might be founded to explicate theology and teach canon law, but such an approach was part of the lie. The truth operated obscurely and relentlessly, and its inferiority was emphasized in the spaces that were being populated haphazardly with animals and men. It was necessary to fill in the hollows left by the Indian, who had been molded to his environment. The expeditionary forces had none who could take their places; as always they were composed of sensual celibates, clerics who had abandoned the cassock for the sword, *colonists*. The harvest of lost children went on.

A clearer vision of reality was possible after this irruption of the subject hordes. No longer was it possible to count on a lucky fortune. One had to look along harder roads: work the land, sow, and reap. And this reaction was a result of those hordes.

The psychology of the gaucho will never be fully understood, nor will the soul of the anarchic Argentine multitudes unless one thinks about the psychology of the humiliated son and dwells upon the results that may come about through an inferiority complex irritated by ignorance in an environment favorable to violence and whim.

The so-called Conspiracy of the Mestizos in 1580 already is a revolt based on ancestry: seven creoles attempted to seize control of the city of Santa Fe. They were executed. In 1711 in Venezuela a mulatto was proclaimed king during a mestizo revolt. The armies that Belgrano, San Martín, and Alvear found impossible to discipline—hybrid mobs of Indians, mestizos, and foreigners—were a human counterpart of the wild herds of horses and cattle. The in-

surrectionist armies, originally made up of mestizos, attracted the
Indian thirsting for vengeance. Whole tribes swelled the groups of
revolutionary horsemen of a century ago: Minuanes, Charrúas
(who were cannibals only in fits of sacrilegious rage), Taros, Gue-
noas, Guaycurúes, Ranqueles, Puelches, Tapes, and many more,
mixed with wild, mestizo gauchos. They were the sons in rebellion
against their fathers, men of solitude born of the desert, debauch-
ery, and rape. Like nightmare fragments in a drunkard's imagination they took form in the far reaches of the plains and descended
in a gallop upon the towns. They were the successors of those jailbirds and rogues who had poured into the New World to populate
it since the times of Ferdinand the Catholic to those of Charles III.
They fought for liberty, equality, destruction of the past, and possession of those goods belonging to all, to which the landholder
could not lay claim with equal authenticity. They had suffered all
sorts of insults because of the fathers who had repudiated them,
considering them children of error and sin even when legitimized.
Numberless storms and wants had belabored their bodies and souls.
Their mothers had never found words that could dissipate the ac-
cusations of society; in the confessional Christ reproached them
behind the lattice, while the tribes looked upon them with disgust.
This kind of life, which held both mother and child in contempt,
seemed to them to be rootless and to be chained down by an artificial moral code. They at least had a sure impetus, an ideal: the
mastery of all the land that their power could reach. They knew
but one law: courage. The provinces, the fief of corregidors, attained in the eyes of the native son the attributes belonging to clan
and fatherland, more powerful than the vague totality of conquest,
nationality, and abstract religion inculcated upon him as an adolescent and catechumen in obvious contrast to the world before his
eyes—barbarous, free, and sure. The province would rise up
against the city—against Buenos Aires, which for the mestizo was
no longer Argentina but Europe, a piece of Spain with its customs
house, its centralized authority, its lawyers, and its laws. In this
diffuse and inflamed effervescence America began to be aware of
itself, and the awakening was as violent as the dream.

Independence

Independence was both an act and a thesis. Out in the country it was an act slowly gestated in the state of inferiority, abandonment, and ignorance in which the people had been sunk. In the cities it was a thesis inspired in democratic and liberal doctrines still in a period of trial. As an idea it was born in churches and town halls, encouraged by citizens of means. But it soon became flesh in the poor peoples of the hinterland; otherwise it would not have progressed much farther than a Pan American ideal. Until then the back country had not thought of independence, because no movement was part of its plans that would demand unity and leadership, which was in sum a juridical and diplomatic matter. It lived in discontent, subject to extremely hard conditions, lacking cohesion, scattered about in villages, hamlets, and huts. It was not a people, nor did it have any of the ideas conceived by an organized people. The city, on the other hand, had been secretly incubating its plans like a decapitated but living head. And yet, the true revolutionary state was that of the back country —disorganized, chaotic, violent. What the cities—principally Buenos Aires—wanted was to resolve a legal, administrative, and mercantile problem. The independence movement split into two as soon as it was proclaimed: into revolutionary medium and revolutionary idea. What was important was not the revolution of principles or emancipation adopted as a new system of thought but the inevitable conflict that came about as a world held together by a fictitious unity burst asunder.

For the promoters in the city it was enough to change a few of the details of government and administration to judge that the revolutionary ideal had been achieved. It was not even deemed necessary to change the flag, which was chaste and noble and worthy of hyperdulia. They thought that only a change of insignias and nomenclature was necessary, and that the problem would be resolved by means of arbitration or according to the texts of Helvétius, Filangieri, or Mably. They had no clear concept of the magnitude and transcendence of the step they had taken, because they were a fragment of the mother country, detached from the vital ethnic and economic problems of the rest of the country. As late as 1840 the feeling of nationalism and a total view of the enterprise could scarcely be detected. Not until 1853 did the idea of unity and the revolutionary idea finally triumph. The city revolutionaries did not suspect that by the cancellation of one state of things another was being inaugurated. Had they foreseen it, deducing its final and inevitable consequences, their leaders might have hesitated. Those who abandoned themselves to the natural results of a declaration of independence brought about the anarchy that was implicit, according to Paz, in the declaration itself. And they were right. The others aspired to maintain a strong and legal state, and they had recourse to a monarchy tempered by sophistry to lend stability to government and regularity to commerce. More than an expedient to consolidate a state of things, it was an extreme attempt to preserve a state of affairs that had been overthrown. Civil war is not only implicit in a revolution: it saves the revolution. The very heads of the movement for independence suddenly assumed the roles of counterrevolutionaries. The revolutionary thesis failed as a movement but it gave birth to irrevocable consequences. The execution of Liniers and Álzaga was the death of a system, that of Dorrego the death of an idea.[2] Neither of these happenings would seem to have an explanation; yet they obeyed a pragmatic logic with involved repercussions. The popular forces moving the back country had their origin in facts rather than rights; their source was America itself. These chaotic forces dragged into the struggle everything that had been left out of the calculations of the patricians. A full-scale war was being fought inland and on the coasts in the name of ownership of cattle, division of land, and freedom of commerce. Later a democratic, republican, and liberal ideal was revealed in what was only the consequence of an old resentment that took refuge behind two masks: politics and free trade. For this reason we call social conflicts civil wars.

[2] The two transcendent acts of our authentic history are two executions: those of Liniers and Dorrego. The two transcendent episodes—Paso de los Andes and Tucumán—are two dishonorable acts.

The separation of Uruguay and Paraguay from Argentina under the pretext of incompatibility came about through the determination to maintain a free commerce in beef and its by-products, which were carried on through Montevideo without regulation, and to take away some of its importance from the port of Buenos Aires, which was weakening Asunción, threatening to put the wealth of the viceroyalty at the service of Europe, as unfortunately did occur. For the back country the problem went deeper, as can be seen: it aspired for independence from Buenos Aires as well, and from Córdoba and all the other cities all the way to Salta, because they had to be made independent of the independence movement.

The revolution put into motion a paralytic, prostrate, and stagnant world, agitated it and put it into circulation; it also produced a simultaneous awakening of a feeling of inferiority at all levels. When country and city came into contact with each other, solely through the contact of one army with another, the boundaries of these two antagonistic fields were clearly marked. The countryside awoke, but upon its awakening the centralized revolutionary movement became a hindrance. The role of protagonist passed from the junta, the directory, and the generals to the masses—from the decapitated head to the headless body. The disarming of Belgrano's troops at Arequito is a symbolic prototype of error personified. The concept of liberty that awoke with the passing of the armies brought with it the concept and the consciousness of an infamous past. It was necessary to free oneself from it also. A new perspective opened before the murky soul of the bastard, the child of the village, with the possibility of establishing himself in spheres monopolized by the centers of power in the cities. His first goal was the control of local government, separating it from the center: disunion. Independence historically was a decisive but premature step in the prophetic march toward its own eventual fulfillment. With the loosening of restrained forces a floodgate was opened for the congealed torrent of a people maintained in barbarism by the laws and regulations of the Crown. The peasant—the mestizo most of all—experienced an intuitive vision of a better life immediately to be realized, and it gave him a clear idea of the distance between the present and the past, between today's truth that opened without limits before him and that humiliating yesterday adorned with coarse and metaphorical embellishments. The proclamations of the leaders who carried the movement to the frontiers of the viceroyalty awoke in the common man a desire for individual freedom, and this was perhaps—in spite of all the disorders that followed—their most salutary effect. The clandestine traders and the land pirates raised their banner under the pretext of nationalism. Their interest was in moral rehabilitation and freedom of trade, not in politics they did not understand; yet the curious fact is that their habit of pronouncing heroic phrases without restraint moved them toward politics and patriotism. Thus the diversity of banners proved the oneness of the ideal.

In the confusion every participant soon attributes to himself part of the revolution's ideals as if he had created the whole movement for himself. In such an amorphous and incongruous state of things the individual has to assume a cardinal role. But every revolution is the critical point in a process of decomposition and is the more legitimate the less it seems to serve anyone, and is the more profound the harder it is to understand.

The Legacy and Its Compound Interest

The colony had lived in hunger, in misery of all kinds, in fanaticism and ignorance. In 1810 it had reached a low point in economic values, one of its great periodic crises, while at the same time it felt stimulated by the knowledge of its strength in the recent repulse of the English invasions. It is true there were many who owned the land they farmed, but their land had no real value. Surrounding their paltry plots, the great estates stretched out in fiefs that covered hundreds of leagues. Wealth was concentrated in a few hands just as power was diluted among the many.

Independence meant nothing for the poor man and the peasant; notwithstanding, they were the ones who supported it and who lighted the purifying blaze of anarchy. Independence did have meaning for the export trader and the beef salter, for the smuggler and the cattle thief, all of whom were interested in preventing the return by whatever road to the age of privilege, monopoly, trade restrictions, duties, and other taxes. When generals like San Martín, Paz, or La Madrid attempted to enunciate an ideal of patriotism and liberty, they were not understood. The generals did not understand it themselves beyond the limits of their duty; and the angelic Belgrano—an economist and a polyglot—would go into mystic raptures before the enormity of the contrast between the ideal and the reality. It was a social war, not a war for independence; its second part, foreseen by few and soon opposed, would be the really important one. The revolution seemed to alleviate hunger and ignorance, but soon hunger and ignorance turned against it, and then the revolution was left behind and became conservative and monarchical. The negotiation with foreign countries, which was necessary as a kind of countermarch, and the congresses that sanctioned hybrid constitutions that would never go into effect showed that success was assured, for theory was now defenseless before the act. The situation of the soldier and of the militant patriot who found themselves in the service of an act and a theory clearly in opposition was unfortunately the comic scene in the drama.

Never in his military career was our soldier able to go into battle in a decided spirit, disposed to sacrifice in the name of an ideal or a cause that imposed itself on his consciousness as superior to himself and his own instinct for self-preservation. Each battle was merely one more occasion in which he risked his life for trifles, and for trifles he neither understood nor cherished; that is to say, for a new cause that did not as yet have its own martyrs but instead demanded them with excessive urgency. These soldiers would end by turning the hero who brought them safely through the adventure into a chieftain who would make himself, and them as well, both the banner and the cause for which they fought, since their lives were what was at stake and thus worth defending.

Those military men, like the politicians who were their contemporaries, did not fight to defend a cause or to sustain an order of things. They struggled to create a motive for fighting that would convince and arouse them; they argued in the congresses, seeking a doctrine that would allow them to choose sides. The ideal was being born formlessly from these same skirmishes and debates, so that it was quite possible for the hero to appear too late or to make his entrance prematurely. And in either case, he could appear as a rebel and against the system. The means employed in searching out both action and ideal were converted into veritable ends, and when the moment arrived to have a cause and an order to defend, the search itself had been passionately embraced as the final aim. Above all, men had died or suffered exile in the search; and that was enough to consecrate the cause as a patriotic and legitimate one.

The First Fruits of Liberty

The victories of the armies excited the spirit of plunder in the soldiers. An ambition to possess, to dominate, led them to form parties that would assail in the name of liberty the very men who had first supported it. Every town council became the center of a zone of political action, furthering its own interests; and there even was a Bernabé Aráoz who proclaimed the autonomous republic of Tucumán. Every chieftain aspired to the hegemony of his province, and he alone was its embodiment. Only the province of Uruguay was successful in a try for autonomy, aided by its marginal location and its status as a producer of half the cattle raised for export and a mistress as well of the clandestine port through which the products of the Río de La Plata region were shipped abroad. The chieftain was the being about whom the province's consciousness of self took form. With rhetorical injustice the hoarder Artigas has been called a bandit and a smuggler, but he embodied a universal ideal. Banditry and smuggling were at the time the regular forms of government and trade. The commerce controlled by the Casa de Contratación and the policies of the Spanish magistrate, the judge, and the soldier were in fact unrealistic systems, anomalies that would perforce fall into pieces.

Where no unity of any sort existed, only a vague idea led the people to consent to a federal union. Many of the soldiers were pressed into service by threats of violence, or they were talked into enlisting by others who had a greater vocation for military life.

They deserted or changed leaders according to the turns of fortune. The city taken was a city looted. Looting led to a greater understanding of the rights of property and the inviolability of the home. The people of Corrientes province, according to Paz, were all acquainted with looting techniques; and they hastened to loot each other—so they said—in order to leave nothing for the enemy should he be victorious. Lavalle became a chieftain at the head of an army of cosmopolitan gypsies, fugitives, and whores.

There was no people as such and no government. The armies measured their effectiveness according to numbers of soldiers, the boldness of their commanders, and the physical condition of their mounts. For example, at Gamonal the battle was lost by the horses. Only by an infectious, inorganic stirring could a conglomeration of men become a people; only through systematic error and violence could a government be formed. It was the gaucho who precipitated a state of consciousness of the totality, the unity, and the internal functions of the country. He had become accustomed to living without a head, and that dawning of consciousness was like the formation of gastrula. The new era arises from the total dissolution of its chrysalis: that is why Rosas embodies the idea of order and Artigas that of patriotism. Rosas had a system to offer; the others did not. Alvear, Lavalle, and even Paz compared to him seem to be capricious, disorganized, almost anarchic. For Rosas had systematized barbarism, while the others—without a plan of any sort much of the time, with nothing but an idea to offer in opposition to this frank system which took the form of existing reality—in the end came to appear as the barbarians. The professional general had already taken definite shape when all things else were barely beginning to take form; from this we can judge the stature of men like Quiroga and Güemes and the magnitude of their error as well. It was not easy to know the direction in which the course of events would move or which party would end up as the really patriotic one.

The role of the great hero cannot be maintained unimpaired for any length of time. A military leader who began by fighting for a worthy cause, if he fought long and resolutely enough, would appear to be fighting for a bad cause. The leaders divorced themselves from everything around them in order to follow one fixed idea, and in the course of time they found themselves in a retrograde and obstinate role in regard to the wishes of the majority. San Martín was right as long as the state of things in his country allowed him to be, but he came very close to seeing his disinterested and noble ideas become something base and treacherous because he followed a definite program. Belgrano was lucky enough to die just as he had begun to assume this role, and the same happened to Rivadavia. Misfortunes suffered by men like these and the lack of understanding shown them by other leaders, who went so far as to call them insurrectionists and corrupters of public morals, show that they no longer were understood.

The generals and the statesmen did not espouse barbarism, but they were its most genuine products, and they worked unknowingly in its favor. They were barbarians because their ideals of independence and national unity, of discipline and order were nothing more than abstract aspirations with no basis in Argentine tradition or history. They were mere theses violently opposed to reality, and they could only excite imagination with their last word on foreign military and philosophical schools, Napoleonic tactics, Spanish uniforms, and republican ideas from the United States. Güemes was much more effective because he adapted his plans to his gauchos; had he insisted that they follow his plans, he would have been unsuccessful. The advantage that the chieftains had over the rule-book generals was that they did not meet reality head-on; they hit it on the flank instead. Even in the best cases, when they were inspired by clear thinking and generous impulses, these civilized ideals were exotic to the situation here and were consequently opposed to the natural order of things. We must remember that all this chaos was no accident. It was an organized, constituted state of things, while the attempt to destroy it was based on techniques that were out of tune with this birth of unbridled life. Our barbarism has been in certain aspects fomented by dreamers with delusions of grandeur. Many of our most serious ills are due to the fact that this barbarism was not reduced into civilized forms by means of slow persuasion;

it was instead supplanted suddenly and brutally by its diametrically opposed extreme. That is to say, it merely changed labels.

The New Values

The branding of cattle became a way of marking out the limits of the possession of land. For example, the brand on the steer's flank denoted the twenty thousand leagues of land Rosas had taken from the man of the pampa; and it served as a warning to others not to settle in the land where those cattle roamed. The steer carried the earth along with it, for to it were tied both boundaries and value of the land. Although the land had ceased to be a happy find to the discoverer, the cattle remained alluring with the additional incitement of a victorious struggle against its adventitious owner. It was at about this time that cattle began to establish a standard of value for the land, while man continued to be an artifact of a betrayed and misunderstood nature. The cattle roamed at will across the plains, man's dominion over them being hypothetical and, at all events, challengeable. Being ownerless goods, they belonged to the hunter, that is to say to the herder who dared to take them from the Indian, who by legitimate right had incorporated them into his way of life rather than establishing ownership over them (what belonged to the Indian was not property). Cattle were liberty; man found them an inexhaustible source of money. But soon he was forced to violate another legal structure: the laws that obstructed or made impossible the traffic in hides, hair, and meat. So he learned to break through another barrier, that of the law. With this new aspect of his adventure he developed a new concept of freedom and self-determination, a barbarous one to be sure, but one that would rule the life of these regions for many years to come. It stems from the same sources as the Declaration of Independence (preceded by three proclamations in favor of free commerce in hides and having as its background the Cattlemen's Committee), the civil wars (which had no clearer objective than the legal ownership of the cattle), political sovereignty (guaranteed by the cattle rancher turned provincial governor), and the Accord of San Nicolás (perhaps not an assembly of guerrilla chieftains, as Sarmiento called it, but certainly a pact in defense of the cow, as he also said). In sum, it was a barbarous sense of self-determination but one of obedience to the same mechanism of brutality and fantasy of the conquistador. This was the type of adventure that could interest the nomad emigrated from Spain, displaced by the Arab's departure. He thought he would find both wealth and freedom in America, as did those who followed him and profited by his experience.

The newly arrived foreigner grew more and more attached to the land, attempting to reconstruct, out of the fragments and residue that had remained with him, the civilization he had abandoned. The mestizo took up arms against him, resolutely espousing the interests of cattle against those of the land. The Spaniards would incline toward a central system of government with programs based on the fiscal ownership of the land and on its usufruct without responsibilities on the part of the tenant, including rights of emphyteusis as well. The mestizo—the patriot, the new American—held a bolder and more dynamic concept in his political program (federalism) and his armies (groups of mounted horsemen). In this way cattle and land interests confronted each other: motion and promise ranged against quietude and denial. The mustang stallion, too, was a being in rebellion against the law, since the law meant for it submission, work, and suffering. The gaucho, without any legal context to guide him understood the wild horse and made it his totem. There was between them the same mysterious relationship as between Edvige and the wild duck. He took the herds, not to subject them to civilization, not to hand them over to their common enemy, the man of the city, but to assure his own liberty by placing it upon the horse's back.

Toward a Conditional Acceptance of Reality

The land, when it is conceived of and held in enormous quantities, has nothing to do with the family. It belongs to the single man, not to his progeny, to geography rather than to private institutions. On the other hand, the outlying settler had to submit to exigencies of nature that tore him from his origins, his race, his religion, and his landscape. He could farm only extensive acreage because only quantity could compensate for distance and isolation. He would not be able to sink roots in the future or to do things in depth or to dedicate himself to family or cultural matters. He would have to extend himself, spread out, disperse, and become a number, a statistic, until he even derived his significance as a human being from the quantity of land or cattle that he owned. He became part of a nameless society based on subhuman values. He was forever forced to renounce love and to surrender himself to hate, overt or covert, the pattern of distance and solitude.

Ranged against him was the man in rebellion against the law— who prospered and grew strong. This man owned nothing but he symbolized a violent and discordant force with his incorporeal domain of epic proportions. For he was a lord without estates, a knight errant, a child of the plains, and an ominous brother to the horse. Yet his ideal stemmed from the feudal tradition. He owned neither lands nor cattle (that is to say he had no power), though before him he saw the earth covered with animals as nomadic as himself. The awareness of his poverty blended in hybrid mixture with an illusion as to his wealth. Riding on horseback through the prairies with no clothes on his back, homeless and wandering, he was lord of that measureless nothingness where legal title belonged to the king in Spain. He was a Don Quixote come home in defeat, the tatters of an absurd dream. He swelled up in his pride and preferred to rebel against a law that denied him the title of ownership but not the enjoyment of what could well be his according to the laws of nature, well known to the medicine man, the range rider, and the chieftain. Like a knight, he enlisted the rabble of the plains under his banner and was a prince in his hut. He raised an army from the cattle and confronted the landowner, the unknown man from the city. So the spirit of the countryside (federalist and barbarous) was dissociated from the spirit of the city (centralist and monarchist), each of them attracting into its magnet the iron shavings of many disparate interests. The first chose to live in the vastness of its untamed dominions, refusing to bow to the will of the intruder from the city. Its consciousness was molded by the landscape and it rejected all traditions. The result was the gaucho, the covetous lord, the man of the ignorant multitude following close on the footsteps of a thwarted dream. In his solitude he came to think of himself as one who had been despoiled, victim of the injustices of distant tribunals and legal codes. He made common cause with the Indian, whom he continued to look upon with the rancor and contempt of the bastard he was. He was himself a product of a prolonged dream of grandeur, victim of a desert mirage, the desert's living phantom. If he could not legally defend what he possessed he would defend it with the knife, the instrument of his daily work. If the port city would not permit him to ship his products and to barter for merchandise, he would achieve his ends behind the back of the customs official by means of tips and bribes. Such vague aspirations coalesced into a political program, and this was the focal point for the era of organization culminating in 1880, the year the gaucho died.

The cult of courage is just that, a cult. It had its poets and panegyrists, its devotees who now dissemble by exalting its literary image. But it never was a poetic theme, only the ethnographic example. Some gauchos ended as outlaws; others began as foremen or cowhands on the great ranches and rose to commanders and generals; still others took the path from horsebreakers to presidents of the Republic, from bosses of beef-salting gangs to tyrants or liberators. "At Pavón," Sarmiento used to say, "the fate of the country was decided by the best horsemen."

But that same craving for power, buoyed by the prestige of some notorious crime, could lead in the direction of politics, of personal influence, of finance and pedagogy, and even of medical quackery or simply of a wandering through the countryside.

The borders of the provinces marked the limits of the birthright, though in a new and spiritual sense. The chieftain symbolized an unconscious yearning for legitimacy in conduct and security of material profit. Among all the hazardous forms taken by institutions in their beginnings, he was the least aleatory. He also embodied a spirit of rebellion against civilization, which was about to organize and become systematized. The caudillo represented the triumph of power, the leadership of the mob, but at the same time was the personification of something superior and harmonious.[3] Out of the old, tattered ideal there appeared this new and extravagant personage with the friar as his agent and clerk. In a confused ferment he embodied the ideas of stability, direction, sense, form. Later he became the standard-bearer for a political doctrine; and he cloaked under the name of federalism his efforts to bring symmetry to chaos, to give an aspect of legality to power attained precisely by illegitimate means. But at least it was an ideal, the concrete form assumed by a barbarism that sought to perpetuate itself under a decorous name. It was not a matter of changing working methods or giving up one set of tools for another, since the hands that wielded arms exercised no other trade (and perhaps not even that of arms). This was true even of the common soldier who attempted to change his calling but did not know how because it was a matter of inventing new kinds of jobs, since there was no experience available to apply to the conditions of the new land. And above all it was necessary to remove from the mob all the charac-

[3] There have been attempts to see the caudillo as a replica of the feudal baron, but he rather resembles another character who played the role of deuterogamist in medieval epic drama: the robber. The robber was not necessarily an antisocial being. He formed an apocryphal society in opposition to another society; he had his principles, his code, his ritual. In *The Robbers*, Schiller has described this chivalry with its romantic archetype, Karl Moor, who believes himself divinely ordained to punish with fire and sword a society bereft of its standards of justice. The caudillo was not a feudal baron, but a bandit gifted by nature with an inborn social consciousness and lacking, in the same strong and solid measure, a society and a true sense of justice that would allow him freedom of choice. It was quite logical for him to invoke Divine Providence in his proclamations while ordering mass executions; thus, it was natural that the priest should have a certain tendency to follow and to succeed him. He passed through cities like an avenging angel, and the tenacity of his barbarism could convince anyone that he was in the right. In the worst of cases, he greatly resembled the epic horses, who also were bandits, that is to say, antisocial types only when viewed in isolation from their environment. In appropriate surroundings, the bandit is equivalent to the demigod. In America, which lacked a society, he was the embryo of one. He could say: I am the State—because there was no State. He was Power and Law in the dominions of chaos, a Messiah whose tragic destiny was to bear the burden of his people's sins, to be sacrificed, and in the course of time to be disbelieved.

teristics it possessed—as work—which tended to lower the individual in his expectations and self-esteem. Because to resign oneself
to the obtaining of wealth through the opprobrious use of one's
hands in the frankly plebeian tasks of sowing, reaping, herding, and
selling was already to admit defeat. An attempt was made to give
work at least an appearance of something else: an exercise similar
to military drill, while the tools used were made to resemble weapons as much as possible. In early days all heavy work was in the
charge of women and Indians; later the owner stooped to such
labor but in the role of speculator or middleman for his own interests. Since then the owner of any kind of capital has been the
worst of speculators with his own profits and the destroyer of his
own satisfactions.

Agriculture and the raising of livestock were classed with the extraction of metals as essentially mining industries. Hides were the
raw materials for an industry that replaced mining; and, without
stretching the point, rawhide supplanted iron, wood, and willow
even in the construction of dwellings. Knives were the tools of this
industry but were used more like swords than picks and trowels. In
Facundo we learn the value acquired by the knife in the hands of
the impoverished conquistador and his son, the gaucho, and its
importance in civil wars. The knife was the implement used to
establish a "sphere of culture," to fix the character of the epoch
from the mustering out of the first soldier turned loose to shift for
himself to the wars of independence in the north along the coast.
Along the banks of the Paraná and the Uruguay and on the shores
of the Atlantic it created a roving population, which, from the days
of Artigas to those of López Jordán, was quick to rally around the
flag of the first chieftain who offered economic advantages with the
promise of markets for a product that they owned without being
its owners. The troops, rustics defending their own interests, were
used to the handling of the short blade, and they would break their
sabers to convert them into the gaucho knife, the *facón*.

Rhea hunting had the aspect of a game, but it was not a game;
it was a means of livelihood. There was something of a bullfight in

the struggle with animals in the open fields, and the slaughter of cattle had much in common with the cutting of throats that often followed a victory. It was all a process of transference: from war to play to work. The killer of cows became most cruel when, to use Homeric language, he ceased to be a killer of men. But did he cease to be a man-killer while he slaughtered cattle?

Aside from its utilitarian motives, cattle herding as a form of big-game hunting was a means of preserving a sense of mastery and pride. Agriculture came much later, brought by men of another speech, and it signified man's final surrender to his children: the true settlers. The general store was also the occupation of the non-Spanish immigrant.

The task of cattle slaughtering eventually perfected the killing techniques. The skillful hand will not be denied; the terrorists of the Mazorca Society attained true virtuosity in the cutting of throats, expert surgeons that they were in the work of the abbatoir. That knight errantry of the pampa rode with the knife at its belt; that symbolic tool was wholly a disguise for a shamed poverty. "The Unitarians castrated their prisoners; the Federalists cut their throats," according to Mansilla; and all this was due more to technical virtuosity with the knife than to barbarism. The man who conquered, knife in hand, was also the defeated knight whose hand wreaked his vengeance upon the flocks. He became cruel because the knife is a ferocious tool and a weapon that knows no clemency.

He turned from the pleasures of a tranquil life and became a roaming creature; he did not love the home, for it was the seam that joined him to his father. He begot children and disowned them; he became rich but did not love his wealth and gambled it away in one night at cards, or he carried it with him on his belt close to his knife wherever he went. He was alone. The knife speaks of solitude, like a wild beast's jaws. He lived like an outlaw; he made use of religion to proclaim it in his standards as an alternative to death, and in camp just before a battle he would read the Bible, which is the book of a solitary people. Such was the end of this creator of fraudulent structures, this counterfeiter of the soul's values, once the land had subdued him. Out of this new enslavement he could raise as a symbol the sword he used for a livelihood, the tool with which he had saved his life.

The Knife

The knife is carried out of sight because it is not part of the costume but part of the body itself. It pertains more to the man than to his apparel, more to his character than to his social status. Its study is related to the culture of the people who use it rather than to heraldry or to the history of costume. It is the most valuable object with which to define the limits of a whole technique.

It is an intimate accessory carried between the skin and the underclothes and is related to the most private and secret personal rights. It is brought forth only at a supreme moment as that of an insult, for it also is a way of tearing out a hidden part of oneself and casting it aside. The knife requires the modesty of the phallus, which it resembles because of similarities that a hundred obscene talks have broadcast. He who shows his knife when there is no need for it commits an indecent act.

The saber presupposes a duel; the knife is for dueling afoot. As Lugones said: "The patriotic saber/Shortened into a mere knife."

Because of its size, it does not allow for third parties in the struggle; it is understood that the quarrel is an intimate one, excluding both witness and mediator. As a weapon the knife is as fearsome as any object can be that is used but occasionally for these ends. It fails only when the arm behind it fails, so that self-confidence alone can assure the efficient use of this point of steel, focal point of violent impulse. No weapon gives greater faith in oneself after victory than does the knife; the victor feels that his success was due more to the hilt than to the blade. The entire hilt fits into the closed hand that clasps it to the very point where the edge begins. For the knife has just the right shape to be held in the hand and, though this is true of all hand weapons, no other is made so truly for the hand alone. The hand is like a pair of jaws closed tightly over the haft so that the knife becomes an extension of the body, accentuating its concentrated force. The hand is aware of the knife as the sharpened point of the body's will, and there is no thought of technique or fencing skill as knife and body act as one.

A well-given stroke may exalt the whole life of the man who strikes it; Necochea, for example, loved to remember the time when he rode bareback through a body of enemy troops and sliced the throat of a Spaniard who barred his way, down to the spinal column as required by best form in the art of cutting throats. Rosas considered the knife a proselytizing instrument and made a ritual of its use; he forbade its being worn on Sundays. Darwin relates how Rosas had himself punished once when through forgetfulness he violated his own orders. Rivadavia absolutely forbade its use and in so doing attacked one of the aspects of the religion. He was decreeing the suppression of an Order.

The sheath takes the knife away from the world: the sheathed knife has been withdrawn into the world of death. It is a utensil in repose though it is never completely at rest; it partakes of the feline's enigmatic sleep. Under one's pillow it is a faithful watchdog, and worn on the belt it is a watchful eye at the back of the head, guarding over that half of us which is behind us. It is worth more than money in our pocket or a woman in the house: it makes possible food whenever needed, shelter from sun and rain, tranquility during sleep, faithfulness in love, assurance along dangerous roads, and confidence in oneself. It is what stays with us when everything else is against us, all that is necessary to test the merit of our reputation and the lawfulness of all we own.

It carries the weight of authority because in the hands of a laborer it may symbolize a livelihood without ceasing to be the instrument of liberty and justice. With a knife a man may, in Alberdi's words, "carry the government with him." It is not without reason that its name also signifies the right to govern and to judge.

Through it we perceive the slashed body at arm's length and the death throes of the victim, and through the hot agony of the blood that bathes our hand we are aware of the spilling of life and the affirmation of our own personal existence. The knife is the short weapon that makes help difficult; it is the ego, objectified and inorganic, left to its own fate, to its unimpeded destiny. It is an arm for single combat, the weapon of the man who goes alone.

It is also useful to underline an argument, to speak sincerely; and in the hands of a woman or a child it can be a docile instrument for domestic tasks. It can slice bread and peel fruit, but it is dangerous to learn the whole secret of its employment and to become a master of its techniques. The full knowledge of its incisive art can be fatal, like the art of making good verses. A man could go along that road much farther than he may wish. For the knife may be used to kill, especially to kill other men in a way that demands the proximity of body against body, thus eliminating any special advantage or the safety of distance. It is the synthesis of all the tools man has employed from his very beginning. Ameghino discovered five kinds of tiny knives made of stone in our pampa.

It is the only weapon that is used for earning one's bread with humility and that betrays crime by the trace of blood adhered to its blade. On occasion it is quicker than the insult, and it is very difficult to measure or gauge the degree of aggression because the hand carries out unconsciously the first impulse even before the spirit can recant; therefore, we would say that it is swifter than thought and closer to will than thought itself. It enters to the hilt; the forefinger and thumb touch the body and this contact indicates the hopeless consummation.

The faithful part of the dueling weapon is that which remains firm and sure: the knife—which is the size of the blade that remains fixed to the pommel when the sword snaps. On breaking, it loses the part that belonged to chance, to the factory, to the worker who made it; the excess—the part broken, snapped off—is but useless metal. The knife is of a size well thought out with nothing of chance or the exotic; it is of a size without excess.

The saber and the fencing foil, even in dexterous hands are unwieldy by their length. The wrist must subdue the inert force of the trajectory and speed of the tip, while in the handling of the knife the force travels from the hand to the tip, and the blade is the slave of the master. The sword has its schools and its styles; the knife is intuition, self-taught. The maestro can teach the pupil nothing; if one possesses the indispensable inborn gifts and the courage, all can be learned with practice. It is as much an art of hand as of eye. The knife fight as an exhibition is senseless (it is an intimacy, not a spectacle), while in the test of the sword and the fencing foil the exhibition is the true end. The knife never lends itself to sham battles, and very rarely is it made a game of simple demonstration. The only sort of knife exhibition, target competition, is repugnant to the nature of this weapon in so far as one must cast it from one's hand, hurling and directing it with precision—all of which is foreign to its purpose and nature. Even marksmanship, which demands a set target point, cold-bloodedness, and reason, is repugnant, since in a fight aggression is directed toward whatever point of the body the adversary may make vulnerable. And it is not a matter of steady pulse and cold intent, but rather of the quick glance and the spontaneity and intuitiveness from which it surges forth with the unpremeditated instantaneousness of that indescribable quiver of reaction of a hunted animal—also present as a defense in the man under attack.

In a sword, that which was inherent in its master—that which formed a loyal unit with his arm—extended down to the very tip of the present knife. To shorten the sword to that point gave a man freedom, art, destiny. Further, that part is serious, merciless; the feint was all that was lost in longitude. There is no appeal remaining to the unforeseen or to theory.

Being tiny, the knife may be carried among one's clothes and so acquire the merit of an amulet borne next to the flesh. As an "interior" utensil it has a share of the magic. Its faithfulness is felt step by step while walking; it is the companion of the leg. One may carry it at the belt, which is the level of the body at which the arms naturally rest. At one's side goes the broad, short knife for skinning. He who wears it behind his back on the forbidden day, hiding in a crouch, is the dangerous one, the Sunday knife wearer.

From the butt one may hang the whip, for the butt is still the hand.

Suicide with the knife is rare; from the grip to the point, it is man's weapon for the outer world; like one's dog, which it most resembles, it does not turn on its master. It is supremely propitious, since it lacks a superstitious meaning in its character of an amulet. The naked blade is the warning of danger; it defines the width and depth of the wound; in the air it is the metallic measure of the hole in the flesh; in the cut there is a mysterious understanding between the steel and the flesh, and even on entering the sheath the knife warns that it can wound. Blood leaves the steel clean, but it accumulates and darkens the place where the blade joins the butt (where that which is of the world joins that which belongs to the hand), or it saturates the handle if it is of leather or the hoof of a stag.

There is a knife for everyday: a knife for work with a wooden or a leather handle, of worn blade and dull edge from much use. The silver knife for fiestas, initialed and engraved, of rectilinear cut almost without a trace of sharpening, is the ornamental weapon, with the *S* that is the stylized form of the hilt, which shields but does not deprive of contact during the blow. One may even have two lines of poetry inscribed on the blade, as did El Chacho. There is the *facón*: longer with two longitudinal grooves, with barely dulled double edges and an arborescent arabesque, in the middle of which is the mark of the maker—that of the weapons shop more than that of its owner. The knife has a sharp edge, delicately tuned by knife-sharpening steel with the voluptuousness of a personal shave. Its edge is tested on the fleshy tip of the thumb and the subtle sensation indicates its raw sharpness. With the fingernail one savors its temper, and striking with the flat of the blade is considered offensive. In a greeting it is customary to feign unsheathing it, and it suffices to carry one's hand to the handle in the manner of quieting a dog keeping too close a guard.

Well managed, it can merely scratch the skin, and there is a level of consummate skill that consists of tatooing the adversary like a slave, in putting a mark on him like a slave, which means subjection without possible emancipation.

The merit of the knife is in its point, just as in the fencing foil, but it does not end there; the knife is its apex, but it continues along the blade. A blow with the edge—an axelike blow—shows leniency or contempt, and it is thus that the peon wounds his master and the gaucho wounds the stranger. It is also the blow that the mounted gentleman gives to the poor man afoot.

3 ROUTES

The Path of the Draw-well

Legend attracted the ignorant conquistador; a mythology of grandeur, of liberty, and of easy success attracted the ignorant colonist. Trapalanda and Fortune were two products of torpid dreams and avarice. There was only one expeditious road, and one could not follow that way alone and poor. He had no faith; he was not a mystic whose conduct had a transcendent meaning; he was a fanatic for speculation who prayed to God for help in bad times—and later forgot Him. He had no character; he was not structured; he was as uncultivated as a swamp. He came to change his life, not merely to better it, so that he might fulfill his own destiny; he came to negate himself, to lose himself. He wanted to take a leap and test an adventure without breaking the ties to his homeland even though he had renounced it. He laid at rest that which he left behind, and he desired to obtain his advancement at full speed or drag down the world in his fall. His haste was out of step with the slowness of nature. The earth is slow. It can be forced to yield in a short time what it normally produces unhurried by itself, but in the long span the earth is right. It can be invaded, violated in its solemn parsimony; in the end, it invades and triumphs. The farmer, who urged it on, at best obtained the pleasures of ravishment. He made himself rich, but he did not enrich the country; not wishing to let go, he bequeathed nothing of his holdings. That fortune in his hands was not noble and useful, because it had not been developed slowly with the rhythm of normal wealth. He possessed forty leagues of land—yet four thousand men had no place to sleep. For one region to prosper another had to be impoverished; for a few to enrich themselves meant that thousands around them would be poor. Property did not circulate but stagnated in the hands of those who possessed it. All the wealth that for many years fascinated our governments kept the Republic in hypertension during more than half a century. These governments, born of an inclination to the absurd and the fruit of our illiterate dreamers, were eager to trust a fiction nourished on great domains made up of pound sterling. One lived anticipating the future—as people were fond of saying in times of Rivadavia—but the mortgage contracted on economic freedom to raise and adorn public buildings, to maintain six universities, and to have the full external apparatus of progress resulted in the sad truth of fourteen agonizing provinces and ten dead territories. The rich man who gave the State that unwise impetus involving it in his extravagant actions—but who at the same time received from the State the example of a mortgaged existence—did not dispose of his fortune, because it was not his. To him belonged the pleasure of a loaned wealth; he was but an administrator of another's property. Many enjoyed their own goods until the day when they would evaporate like an ephemeral dream. They did not possess any more nor did they ever; they held the titles to huge properties, but the wealth as an expression of national wealth was part of the vast illusion. Wealth was uncommon: it existed as a small barren island and the bad luck with which it might be lost was a composite of the insular, accidental, empirical state of the economy manipulated by stock-market players. Those proprietors and men of means might have been good administrators and businessmen, but their goods and their business affairs were constructed on a fallacy and planted on unsteady ground. It was the foreign gold, here where there was no gold, that produced the flowering of riches from the earth itself.

Their goods were mortgaged beforehand; they formed part of a general mortgage. Their fortune was an illusion; it formed part of a general illusion. The proof that it was badly gained or badly consolidated, that it obeyed no organic plan, is that it was lost. It was an individual gift to one's capacity or audacity. In the hands of the children the fortune dissipated in a puff of smoke, at best leaving them a diploma as a reminder of the fiction of another class. There were those who in order to deny the father, who had amassed his money by his sweat, went abroad without abandoning their possessions here. Their women wanted to become related to the nobility, and every time that a new public building was erected or that gold from the loans would spread, the glitter of an ancient name would be made to dazzle. They returned to the fatherland like desperate voices of their sire who wished to be reintegrated into the bosom of a life that was renounced but not forgotten. By spending and wasting far away they undermined the foundations of native wealth. Financially and morally the fruits of hard labor were wasted aboard the decks of transatlantic cruisers. Thus the gold returned to Europe. And when that property which still remained behind was finally able to function with a man reintegrated into a society that valued other goods, everything floated away like a dream at dawn.

The Routes of the Hands

Of all those itineraries, Buenos Aires was the point of arrival and departure. Lines of communication became established between Buenos Aires and Europe well before there were any with the interior. Port of embarkation and landing place of shiploads of people in search of well-being, Buenos Aires was from the start the magnifying glass through which the Republic was viewed. That port was united to Europe; it had to unite itself with the interior, and for that purpose routes of iron were traced.

These followed in part the direction of working hands, but much more importantly they followed the march of the wealth seekers. Upon establishing permanent lines of communication, the interior began to move and the different regions that make up the Republic began to fall into various categories according to their types of pasture ground, quality of tilling land, and other factors. Roads produced a displacement of lands and livestock; at the same time that some places were drawn into contact with the metropolis, others lapsed into regions of the past and of solitude. Wealth, population, and culture turned from their established channels, and we are still witnessing the move toward the center and the south. Insofar as livestock constituted a nucleus of aspirations and a fundamental topic of economic life, the population clustered on the edges of fertile pasture lands. The predominance of agriculture in the years of good prices for grain set the laboring people off in an ebb of vehement desire toward other preferable lands. The movement of this wandering, unstable interior was obeying demands for its products in unknown markets. Towns went on being organized and human beings scattered about according to the fluctuations of prices, at the service of interests whose central headquarters were on the other side of the ocean. Less and less will we be able to organize our independent existence or to produce other materials than those demanded by a world whose needs of consumption determine our necessities of production. The north has been displaced; it is becoming depopulated and impoverished; it has lost its hard-working character to such an extent that the pampa, that south which Lavalle said he could put in a bull's horn and seal with another, means much more than the formerly renowned "Upper Provinces." The port gave to the country a new physiognomy that almost had nothing to do with its geographic structure. Córdoba, Tucumán, Corrientes, San Luis, San Juan, Salta, and Catamarca suffered a loss in their industrial population from 1869 to 1914. Already in *Recuerdos de provincias* these words can be found: "The location of the majority of American cities reveals the dominant preoccupation of men's spirits. They are all way stations for easing the transit to the countries which have the gold; few are on the coast in a location favorable to commerce. Agriculture developed under the pressure of necessity and disillusionment, and produce found no outlet from the remote corners toward the ports where the cities were."

The wide coastal belt—which is the plains—is most fertile. Pasture grounds and farms that produce for the world attract gold and labor, gold and labor that produce for the world. The Republic lies behind and at the extreme limits of the fertile plains. Between these two areas, the foreign and the Argentine, the peripheral and the interior, there is a competition with unhappy results for the poorer and more isolated region. According to Alberdi, fertility was the cause of our own backwardness: the abundant land accustomed man to expect everything from earth and sky, which were converted into propitious divinities. Nevertheless, that fecundity, the essential cause of backwardness, was also the only incentive for the immigration of labor and capital. The prairie is to wealth as the jungle is to life: a breast to suckle and upon which to sleep. The history of the arid lands is that of civilization, and that of fertile lands is that of wealth. Only when the anthropoid had to obtain sustenance and shelter, defending himself from an inclement climate and harsh natural conditions, did his brain show signs of ingenuity. The progress that is to advance from the fertile lands to the arid ones, from the coast to the interior, will be very slow because it lacks the auxiliary forces of necessity and of faith. The confined towns do not interest the consumer, because they do not produce for him; our producer is interested in the consumer and the financier who allows him to produce more. In many cases he becomes a salaried worker: he collects as profit proceeds the salary that the buyer pays him, and the accumulation of goods is the savings from his wage. Even Rosas saw this problem with clarity— which is one of all Argentine life—when he persevered, blockaded, as a hero. After 1852, the date that opens the cycle of political and juridical violence, there begins a new tactic in relationship to that which is foreign. Buenos Aires has been invaded; the Republic falls prey to European commerce and banks. After the Nation was established all of it was a safe haven; immigration and capital poured in. The stability of the government attracted the colonist; the labor that came in the arms, the backs, and the bellies of the colonizing families attracted capital; and the government became stabilized by the gold and labor of Europe. The dream turned itself toward the world outside and now it was not only the newcomer who placed his faith and his ambition in that, but everyone who contemplated his future in what was arriving from outside, in the recently arrived. Governing was done by populating, but that population was arriving to pursue hopes that would remain unfulfilled, because with regard to the colonizing undertakings the State took the passive role of conceding undeveloped land but without the responsibility of distributing, encouraging, or educating the people.

The real problem and scandal was the land. The Congress of 1826, which needed to consolidate its external credit, ratified the law of emphyteusis. After 1822 it was seen that only the land could offer unequivocal guarantees for loans in pound sterling. The proclamation of the national constitution demanded that the nation be worthy of it. In 1853 the government contracted with Brougnes to transport forty thousand laborers within a period of six years, and in 1854 the first families recruited in Bordeaux disembarked. In combination with the firms of Vanderest and Company of Dunkirk, Textor of Frankfurt, and Beck and Herzog of Basel, Aaron Castellanos systematized the colonization of Corrientes. Hundreds of families arrived who found no kind of work, and Urquiza had to cede to them part of his great lands because there was no place to locate them. Corrientes was still that great, rich, and cultured province in which Echeverría and Paz had put their hope of the Republic's salvation. The methodical, intelligent colonization failed. It was thought desirable to channel tens of thousands of colonists upon tens of millions of hectares in Sante Fe, Entre Ríos, and Córdoba. Great companies were organized that speculated with the contracting of workers and whose only motive was to obtain enormous expanses of land and profit from the human cargo. This happened with identical characteristics until the end of the past century. Once the families had disembarked at the port and were brought to the countryside, they were abandoned. The promoters lacked funds to indemnify the grave losses suffered by the colonists, and the government lacked resources to shelter them. Thus, solitude was sown among desperate and indignant men. The colonist wanted freedom to settle, to reside or to depart, to apply himself most advantageously, to test fate as a man and not as a laborer. Long after Aaron Castellanos fulfilled his plan for colonizing Santa Fe with farmers, and Tandil with cattlemen, the Indians would raid up to Azul, killing and sacking the people of La Carlota and Río Cuarto. The government had nothing to offer to the settlers exposed to such horrifying dangers, but in a fifty-year period 100 million pesos were spent on defending the frontiers. Nothing had been prepared for the reception of the workers, who then ended up seizing weapons and dedicating themselves to cattle stealing. The fields were fenced in with wire and frequent communications were established. The first cattle were exported from Azul in 1871; the first grain left in the following year. An interchange of muscle and products was established; the worker had to improvise his labor as he sharpened his tools and raised his little house. The only thing that had form was the constitution that sheltered him. The countryside did not have form, nor did the government or the Nation; and life had that same consistency. We see the luck of these settlers in *Martín Fierro*: many of them ended up as grocers and salesmen of trinkets. That was the fate of the father of Guillermo Enrique Hudson. The Indian was still a stronger reality than the government across the rugged, uncultivated, and savage land, which could be populated only by those who had remained recalcitrant toward civilization in barbarous regions of the civilized world. The boldest, the most capable came—those who brought in their souls a bit of nature similar to our landscape. In accordance with the conditions, the fittest settled down and became rich. The arrival of those beings with their dreams gave the illusion of a very great economic potential, which the government was quick to exploit by raising loans for public works and sanitation. Urgent demands caused these loans to be diverted into smothering rebellions, buying off rebels, destroying the Indian, and containing Paraguay, which rebelled because it was being slowly absorbed by the pampa. That was the road followed by the hired hands recruited to populate the desert until from such dispersion towns were born and from these towns the present form of the Nation, which is also provisional.

The Outer Bounds of the Journey

The pioneer was a man who hurled himself into the conquest of nature and who in a given moment could say, "Far enough," or go on, since he was not alone. While he was advancing he was conscious of his march and of the human meaning of his journey. The settler of these regions was not the master of his will. He believed that he could advance or stop when he wished, but in reality it was the empty pampa that harassed him into moving on or holding back. He went where nature apparently carried him without hidden design; he went without plan, without limits fixed beforehand, without norms of conduct. Hence he did not push ahead conquering, but being conquered. He always advanced as long as he did not encounter difficulties that impeded him; when he could not continue, he turned or retreated. All this was taken for progress. The obstacles were immense, yet they were visible; they were never born from within him, from his conscience, from the notion of the distance already crossed or a feeling of remoteness from the departure point to which he would join himself by the normal communication routes. For him to return was merely to retrace; yet his journey had no end or destination. He needed neither compass nor map. The deeper into the country he went, the more ground he kept losing, since the adventurer's advance is but one-half of the conquest—the other half is knowing when to stay put. The persecution of the Indian, which served him rather as a pretext to dissimulate his instinctive vagrancy, was a flight; it was the very flight of the Indian. At the same time that he was pursuing the Indian, he was being dragged along by him; he marched at his heels like the rearguard of a fleeing horde. By such chance advances he went on sowing his routes with fixed points, and victory signified nothing because it was the complement of the flight of the savages. That itinerary could have been another one and then the pattern of roads and railways and telegraph lines would have been otherwise. Upon establishing a fort or making camp our settlers

did not reckon that that point would remain as a link in a chain,
serving as a knot in a net. They lacked the idea of a plan and a
vision of the whole. It was not a conquest but a dissemination in
the unknown. Once the conquest was made the settler took steps to
assure it. His haphazard approach left a shaky construction that
did not make allowances for soil and geography. It was the route of
defeat and nothing more. Later on, these places would form areas
of relative but isolated prosperity, according to whether or not they
were more or less suited to cattle ranching or to agriculture. They
would progress or be depopulated thanks to undeterminable circumstances. They were true oases of chance location that turned
out to be separated by even greater distances due to the interposi-
tion of arid zones, the cost of transportation, and the disillusionment of the worker.

The towns being thus situated, the railroad stretched these vast
distances because the costs of transportation across hundreds of uninhabited leagues would cast the products across an economic distance much greater even than the geographic distance. The animals
were better distributed. They occupied the best pasture lands and
moved about cautiously. We populated following the flight of the
aborigine from Salta to Córdoba, "following the tracks of Quechua
civilization and founding cities at whim" (Mitre). And the population also moved from the coast toward the interior in an overwhelming movement by which we expelled the native from four
great zones: from Cuyo under the rule of the Captaincy of Chile,
from the west and over the Andes, from Tucumán by sweeping
from Peru and Chile, and from Buenos Aires along the coast by
coming from Spain. The coastal regions, the richest ones, "are no
more than Europe established in America" (Alberdi). Catamarca,
Jujuy, and La Rioja maintained themselves only by suppressing
Indian uprisings, but without any foresight of an economic or a
demographic order. Cities were born from forts and towns from
outposts. The unit of measure between one outpost and another, as
between one Indian camp and another, was the capacity of a horse's
resistance during an unhurried day's journey from sunrise to sun-

set. Distance also was measured from outpost to outpost by the maximum range of vision on clear days and the ease of obtaining drinkable water. Along the Colorado River the measure was ten leagues; on the plains it was five leagues. That distance gives the measure of the savage in combat; it is the perimeter of military cavalry maneuvers; it does not measure the industry of manual labor. Even though today it may appear as a senseless modulation, there is a relationship of town to town like that of white to native and native to landscape. Progress was marked by intermissions of a purely horizontal, overflowing, universal force; the towns created in that march would remain isolated in a static and rigid situation beyond the possibility of union. Since the settlers had been scattered without method, three hundred years did not suffice for the occupation of even a tenth part of the territory. By the time a greater population density was achieved, the bad result was beyond remedy.

Even before the coming of population the rolling forms of nature predetermine the scheme of the future nation; they indicate the places where the great cities, the intermediate towns, the capitals, the key centers of communication, the industrial sites and those of livestock raising and agriculture will have to be established. But it is necessary that consciousness of the organic meaning of this landscape exist in the soul of the settler and that he understand what ends bring him to settle there. On the plains, nature does not preform the political structure, and even a government, motionlessly rooted there, is artificial. Man has nothing to do with the plains insofar as he ceases his wandering; the plains are on the march.

Men came, wandering, to people the plains: gentlemen, pilgrims, beggars. They came alone, passing through. Nowhere did they leave signs of their wish to settle down. The form they gave to institutions, to population, to the orientation of life is linear and superficial, ample and transitory. To alter the shape, it would be necessary to lift or destroy and anew create the forms. The eagerness to occupy the entire territory in a short time, to crisscross it, to gallop over it, spread just a few people over many leagues. From this galactic position of the communities stemmed an intrinsic necessity that would set the norm for Argentine life: distance, area, quantity, credit. The latifundium was the form of property suited to the soul of the navigator of the land and the sea, and the proper form for the cultivation and improvement of the soil. The latifundium was a prophetic geographic and ethnic message exaggerated by the distance and remoteness of the southern part of the continent from the densely peopled regions of Europe whose consumption exceeds production. Thus the density of the south and the consolidation of the north came to be fixed in harmony with the mechanical laws by which the water and the earth of the globe were distributed.

The necessity for a free-ranging agricultural pattern and for cattle breeding in quantities concordant with that planetary distribution obliged the settler and his children to take possession of enormous expanses and to fill them with cattle without thinking about men: Europe thought about the men. The pastoral and agricultural tone of these regions was becoming fixed and accentuated at the expense of economic subjection to the beef consumer, who in turn could dedicate himself to other activities and thus sealed his own industrial fate. Cattle do not require populations—they are the population. They are contrary to society and displace and dissolve it. Cattle are not sedentary although they may be slow moving; they change locations as they go on consuming grasslands, and since possession implies permanent custody the herdsman keeps pace with the cattle. The cow stays subject to the house, but the herd carries with it the house.

When in *Facundo* our country people are defined as having customs similar to those of the Tartars and of the Arabs, these characteristics are attributed to the plains; and the plains were responsible, but only as reflected through the quiet omnipresence of the horse and the cow. The horse is as much in the Hun and the gaucho as the plains are in the horse's hooves. Thus, man had to spread out and to remove himself far away. The Indian and the cattle were the forces that determined his position. That which ensued

simply ratified this truth. The railroad would come later to consecrate the disunity, to fix towns and roads, to provide an iron structure to the Indian's flight. The railroads to the north mark the
inverted itinerary of the treasure hunter; those to the south and
to the west show the path of the pursuer of savages and of the cattle
hunters—who were one and the same. It was not enough that our
Republic was badly formed and at the extremity of the planet:
it had to be badly settled in order that it might exist. Badly formed
and badly peopled, it serves foreign capital wonderfully and can
prosper by supplying remote markets. It would have been difficult
enough to rectify nature by the rational distribution of settlements,
but the demographic distribution, which did not even take into
account the dictates of topography, was doing violence to nature
by its inborn deformity, and the result was to turn nature into an
obstacle to progress. All the difficulties that arose in the development of the remote interior, in the education of its inhabitants,
and in the economic mobility of the provinces and of the immense
territories arose from that cause. And the coastal regions prosper
as a result of all that poverty and isolation. All that is not Europe
is Argentina; because of that the Congress of 1862 declared the
lands beyond the frontiers to be national lands. Those unknown
lands which were divided according to parallels and meridians and
which took on shape and area according to provincial boundaries
constituted that State within the State that is the national territory
—half barbarous and uninhabited.

The disproportionate value that the conquered land assumed
once it fell under the power of speculators was a form of isolating
it from the danger of a land without any value—where only recently the savage had roamed. The capricious value assigned to it
was yet another frontier beyond which the impoverished were cast
so that they might populate those economically vacant lands as
they wished. And of course the poor populated them in conformity
with the norms of vacant lands. They put up their huts and with
equal reason these later became towns or they became nothing. All
those points became united without being able to cause the disap-

pearance of distances—all kinds of distances—that stretched out between them. The roads indicated the routes where one ought not to advance.

The Steel Routes

Nor did capital come to serve the destiny of the native things of this land. It was attracted by the offer of all possible benefits, of all guarantees and prospects that might incite it to come. And under the same auspices that impelled the ships full of men, so liquid capital came sailing. In 1857 there were ten kilometers of iron road upon three million square kilometers without a track; the steam engine began its journey with the same urgent uncertainty with which man, three hundred years before, had thrown himself into the adventure. The potent and docile locomotive represents a future in which faith has already been placed during many decades, although just what that faith will come to consist in is still unknown. The machine is domineering and it makes its runs with regularity and intelligence. It seems to be serving the agricultural areas, although in truth it has succeeded in penetrating and dominating and casting a chain around them. In its march there are no obstacles; it goes across the plain, which since its arrival takes one only where it wishes to bring him: to Buenos Aires where the transatlantic liners anchor also at the service of Europe.

The railroad does not cross the most fertile fields or the least poorly populated regions, nor is it the circulatory system for the country's body. As a consequence its general utility is low; the value of the land is arbitrary; man's life is at risk. It irrigates a body that does not exist, but that for a long time was believed to exist. The very scantiness of its productivity and its superabundance proves that it is a fortuitous communications structure laid upon an ignored territory, to which was owed in conscience the duty of giving it form. Even the positive money calculations accepted the tragic deformity of the land and the illusory representation that was made of it at the outset, when it used to be little known and frequently violated. Capital was not greatly interested in whether or not the lines were of any service, and it even had a certain interest in their not being of use. The lender was just as attracted to investing in public works as in civil wars if the civil wars were going to assure him a better return than canals and docks. The lines that extended into regions of small production would work as brakes on the more fruitful regions nearer the port. The train is the vehicle of great quantities of cargo and passengers; it has to serve as the bridge uniting the geographic system and the economic system if it is to be anything but an object of pride. In its first significance it has value for commerce and in the last, for tourism. An absurd division of the population that does not coincide with the plan nature sketches with mountains, rivers, deserts, and forests makes an unrealistic fantasy of a rail route. Uninhabited lands and high cold regions are crossed without any other reason than that of arriving as soon as possible at other rich and distant regions. The straight line, in these cases, is the longest and slowest.

Going along the unpopulated latifundia one has the impression that the train is spinning its wheels over the same place and that the cars are traveling almost empty. An empty railroad car is a lie with wheels, and the passengers who travel inside with official passes are phantoms set in a fiction. The desert, which the train would show as nonexistent, weighs on the worker through the increase of transportation charges by which the enterprise must equalize the gross losses. Hope burdens the profits of what is being produced. The railroads form a financial, not an industrial, undertaking; they are not at the service of products and transportation —they serve the interests of capital invested in their exploitation. Rather than their serving commerce, commerce subsidizes them. They respond to statistics and not to impulse, and since their interests are very complex they are welded to other financial systems; the reason behind their decisions is almost always unknown. They have the key of this game which so excites us. Our railroads are investments in pound sterling, meant to provide a return, and not vehicles for the production of wealth. They are put in motion from London; thence these subsidiary branches originate and there they

die. One is dealing with static, inflexible capital that does not follow the curves of our national economy but of a vast international
economy. It goes along its own rails and not by our fields, responding to its own motives and without adjustment to a South
American industrial mechanism. The railroads have as their norm
a fixed dividend and a minimal list of recognized public services,
thus making up an orthopedic skeleton to which other activities
always dependent upon the railroads have to adapt themselves.

Since the pattern of the rail lines did not obey economic demands
or a study of the country's needs, capital had to back up its gains
not only with a guarantee from the State, but also, so as not to
arrive at that extreme, with branches more logically laid out in
terms of profit. The planning engineer for these routes was the
Indian chief, whose camp had caused the town to be located; the
construction engineer complied with the irrevocable verdict of the
chieftain and brought the iron rails to the town raised from the
clash. The network made in obedience to a transportation plan
justifies the network made without plan and with the simple idea
of linking scattered localities. Such a chance pattern is the equivalent of a sketch of the constellations in the zodiac.

The Atlantic Channels

The railroads brought loan money to the
country; with the guarantee of that iron money the government
entered into other loans that were not going to be invested in the
alleged objectives. As would naturally occur, the government came
to be lord and master of misspending. The money was spent in the
support of unnecessary troops and in the purchase of armaments,
as if all the weaponry were to guarantee the loan of the rails. The
lender reserved the right to administer the capital invested in
rolling stock and track and converted himself into an overseer of
the train. The useful quantity of work to be done was only of
secondary interest. By means of well-administered railroads, punc-
tual payments in cash of the installments of other loans were assured—loans which came from the same hand and were going to
end in the same place, financing development. Thus, the lender-

stockholder was permitted to hold the main key to national wealth, to open or to close it and at the same time to regulate new credit in conformity with the economic capacity of the country. The State infallibly bound itself to serve this capital, since it had contracted debts for other purposes, invoked and justified by a prosperity that was owed by chance to the railroads. Two-thirds of the relatively enormous amount of 18 billion pesos, figured at the current gold exchange rate for pound sterling, was invested to stimulate production so that it might become self-sufficient. This investment was for a utopian tomorrow because the present was continually exhausting the possibility of a future production. The transitory nature of tourism and the promotional character of those lines destroyed beforehand the possibility of a future return. To cast locomotives at chance is tantamount to making places already sterile yet more sterile, to pushing to the desert the boundary zone of the activity with nothingness. For the farmer who finds himself with a fat harvest that is not worth what it cost to produce it, the train that stops in front of his door is misery. Then the train is a death-dealing machine, and that which in the calculation of wealth figures as an element of progress is on the farm only a residue of arrogance.

The railroad arrived too soon for the normal development of most backward areas. The result was an intensification of poverty in distant or marginal regions and of those income-rich regions which were unfortunate to be single-product producers. Hence, activity and optimism crowded around the centers of consumption and exportation. The farm laborer and the peon from the country sought proximity to Buenos Aires and Rosario as a means of obtaining better recompense for their efforts, and it was the same train that carried them and hauled the cars full of riches. The railroad brought with it nominal, theoretical progress; but in fact it caused real backwardness. This development could be observed until relatively recently in Salta, where the arrival of the locomotive brutally uprooted the transportation companies and opened a channel for the consequent flight of the peasants. It depopulated and impoverished. Chascomús, Dolores, Mercedes, and a hundred other towns stagnated. Geographic, economic, and moral isolation increased after the migration of the working hands. Such distant regions cannot produce grain and cattle, because grain and cattle can be produced cheaper everywhere else; because of competition, not even their regional products can be marketed advantageously. Those trains which cannot carry their wheat, vegetable oils, or wines because they would cost too much in the markets bring them goods and objects made by foreign industries that displace those manufactured locally. Given the fact that the provinces are disconnected from each other, the population grows poorer and degenerates once the railroad has put the people in contact and competition with world markets.

The caudillo divided the Republic according to the *cabildos*, or municipalities; the railroad divided the nation according to freight rates. The absurd territorial configuration was ratified by the net of communications. The railroad lines represent on the map a diagram of anomalies very distinct from the anomalous configuration of the territory. Further, this defective structure within a defective structure caused agriculture to go on restricting itself before the advance of cattle ranching. Agriculture's civilizing struggle against the desert today depends on the tariff duties of the nations that buy meat and on the improvements in the refrigeration industry. The perfecting of the refrigerated lockers or the increase in the speed of the transatlantic cargo ships could benefit us in one sense, but in another sense they would destroy the main source of wealth. Faced with the fall of the price of wheat, a considerable area has been turned into pasture; the fall of livestock prices literally depopulates equally extensive areas. A regression of such proportions brings by force a change in the techniques of production, life, and business and induces a whole change of face on a sector of culture. The predominance of cattle ranching implies the victory of those ancient and inert forces which have blocked the way of the creative forces from the time of the Conquest: a defeat with long-range results. Freight charges favor the development of flocks of sheep, because Argentine meat is preferred over that of New Zealand and Australia.

Buenos Aires cannot regulate the economy of the whole interior, which is stranger to it than Europe. It is also necessary to renounce the fantasy of creating points of interchange in the north and west, the outermost ends of the world. The railroad, which is a closed system in motion, obstructs every effort at local liberation. An inevitable hemorrhage of men of talent and action is the result of the clash between the closed system in motion and the local static conditions. Those who resign themselves to vegetate tolerate the stay, and this anemia is the worst weevil of the grain and the most damaging epidemic influenza in cattle.

The Spider's Web

The railroad extended the national territory and then fractured it, leaving it reduced to a lineal sketch of its lines of track. The embankments of the railroad created a frontier: Europe was the railroad track—America was the rest. That which is not at the very foot of the embankment is at an unmeasurable distance, economically beyond the world of commerce. The railroad makes possible the exploitation of mines and forests; metals and lumber cannot reach the factories without substantially diminishing in value in transit. Whole forests and mines are not worth the transportation charges. The steam transportation cartel also makes impossible the existence of dirt or asphalt roads; it is interested that there be none and, if there must be some, that they be exclusively for tourism, for the simple reason that their trains are providing tourist services along two-thirds of the routes. The ruinous competition that trucks and buses are giving the railroads in North America, England, and France will never exist here, because the roads are ours but the rail lines belong to others. In order to have 38,000 kilometers of iron ways we have had to renounce hundreds of thousands of kilometers of paved roads. The extent of roads ought to be twelve times greater than that of the rail trackage, but it is scarcely more than half of it. Without highways an auto is a gas-driven dragon that sticks in the mud, like a diabolic artifact that the horse, pulling a sulky, contemplates without fear when he passes.

As a corollary to the dissolution of the interior into the economic distance, the railroad sharpened the umbilical destiny of Buenos Aires: progressively and irredeemably it made it into a head severed from the body. The iron ways were a dream of the metropolis, and they stretched out its predatory tentacles across the pampa. All political history from the time of the colony aimed at this and the train secured it, settling forever an old dispute because trains are centralizing.

To understand the destiny of South America it is enough to look at the map of railroads. In spite of its marginal location, Buenos Aires forms the center of a circle—a design that one finds in *Argirópolis*. That network best resembles a spider's web. The fundamental problem of our economic life is transportation because the fundamental problems of our existence are distances, quantities, sizes, and solitude. When the government, which is unexcelled as a deformed structure, participated in the construction of communications it was to show that its ideas were molded on old concepts. It is not accidental that the allotments of postal and telegraphic communications and those of the state-owned railroads were at the mercy of the whims of the government and were indices of its downfall. The government has laid out luxury lines for tourism under the pretext of development, and these have been extended into regions that are sterile not only geographically but also politically and economically. The epitome of astrological concepts in this regard is the branch line to Huaytiquina, the only straight nonstop route to Trapalanda. It can be considered the appendix to the conquistador's horoscope. Because Huaytiquina is a political, cultural, religious, and demagogical program it symbolizes an entire epoch of coarse arrogance of progress. A branch line to nowhere, on constantly shifting alluvial lands, it transports only families of passengers with free passes and paid traveling expenses. The closure of the tunnel and the return to transportation by muleback on this stretch has an air of the most nonsensical obfuscation. Thus the State pays in order that its functionaries may admire a lunar landscape without putting out any money. This myopia obeys the politico-military concept that determines for the Argentine leaders the overall view of Argentine problems. Huaytiquina is more logical than one hundred dirt roads, just as three submarines are more rational than one merchant ship. Dreadnoughts and submarines at anchor are ready to sail out upon the route of the caravels—and they never set sail. They are not war machines, thanks be to God; they are sentinels and escorts for the trains, placed where the trains link up with the transatlantic liners and America with Europe. Our rail ways are copies of the old strategic lines, but they are not mercantile or commercial, nor are they concerned with agriculture or cattle. We possess lines that are responses to panic, products of the eagerness for greatness and the fear of losing it.

Every day the trains follow the same routes as did Rondeau, Belgrano, and San Martín. It could be said that they follow their footsteps at a distance of one hundred years and that they are one hundred years slower than those men. Foreign capital—which came to serve that old politico-military need, not the true economic need—further demanded material guarantees of the interests on its loans and did so in clauses that were accepted in the face of the urgency to lay rails where there were no roads. The terms of the concessions condemned us to perpetuate our original condition as a colony. The railroads demanded the grant of a league to extend on both sides of the tracks along the entire route or a settlement to consist in a set number of leagues. What we call progress is what has been produced within a league on each side of the railroad lines. Land again fulfilled the role of a substitute for money, of an insurance policy good for redemption tomorrow, of a troglodytic money. On the other hand, it was a precaution analogous to the three years of prepaid interest that the firm of Baring and Company extracted when making us the first loan in 1824. With their leagues of land the railroads also established on their flanks a certain kind of natural frontier between the rich land of the company with its iron channel and the poor roadless land of the country. Since that league of width was the area of greatest value, the increase in value of the land that the railroad produced did not serve the country but the company. The area beyond the two leagues was fallowness, loneliness, and ignorance. From far away the lord of the land and the settler watched the· train pass; but they raised their rents, speculating on the distant benefit. From that moment the train was a hindrance, a system imprisoned within its net like the fish inside a basket: a captive train. It stimulated the greed of the landlord who raised his rental charge, and it stimulated the obfuscation of the settler who ventured too far. The company assumed the direction of cattle raising and agriculture and exercised it to the benefit of capital that was in London—not beside the rails. The company also gave value to the land according to a fantastic standard as if the locomotive were something fantastic; it hastened the lawyer's and the politician's eagerness to plunder as if the locomotive were something immoral. The government fell headlong before the mirage of this false valuation; it believed that to extend rail lines was to populate, without taking warning that the contrary could be the truth. And when the government had 36,000 kilometers of track, it said that the Republic was at peace and that culture had come to the depths of country life. In the depths of the countryside there was misery and ignorance, and that is the truth and not the lie.

Viewed from the train, all this truth appears to be a game of words, but it must be seen with the eyes of those who remain when the train goes. One should contemplate the railroad from the outside and realize that it is a living three-dimensional body and not a net of black lines on a white background as it appears on the maps. That white background is our countryside; full of truth and life, it is the guts and the source of the children of tomorrow. The progress of the Republic is opposed to the interest of those who made it prosper, and no progress can be achieved until this relationship is changed. It will happen when the entire body is in a state of health and not just the euphoria of a severed head.

II·SOLITUDE

4 ISOLATION

A World without Experiences

America had existed and lived its American
life in the diverse people who formed it. Some seeds fallen from
other cultures produced wild fruits that did not attain maturity
or flavor. Populated since the preglacial epoch, it remained isolated,
remote from man's other ascendant movements and without unity
in its customs. Before the Discovery this was the perfect world:
the American world, the most ancient, without an accumulation
of experiences, not molded by outside forces, without channeling
in a fixed direction the resultant of its energies. In general terms,
it was a botanic and geologic area held in check before the horizons of the Age of Iron were opened to it. That which had disappeared in other regions, that which in other places had been
transformed and put at the service of intelligence, here conserved
its telluric virginity and its mechanical character of an always
repeated experiment. When the caravels arrivel, the Pleistocene
men were intact with their industries of the Stone Age and their

languages of the Bronze Age. Beneath their cities and under fugitive feet lay the mutilated remains of an entire chapter of the history of vertebrates; in five or six insignificant groups spread out over the vastness of the land the shipwrecked people of archaic cultures of great style thrashed about in the agony of their splendor. But on coming into contact with destructive beings they were annihilated. Still the forces of the earth and the atmosphere continued their secret work against the invaders, forcing them to respect that which was not perishable.

The living of this continent had their reasons for being, more powerful than the upheavals that tended to destroy them. All America was the land of the Tertiary era and it formed a unit with its immense vertebrates, ambulatory mass bulks of bones and tissues. Linked by size and form to the planetary landscape, the gigantic animals were the autochthonous inhabitants. They no longer existed when the caravels arrived at the Antilles; the dramatic interlude of that deformed and titanic life had concluded many centuries earlier; nevertheless, the soil and the climate remained, like empty molds that had given consistency to the disappeared body. And so, together with some surviving examples of a most ancient flora and fauna, in a land among the richest in fossils, the human animal began the regressive trek toward total equilibrium with his medium. Living beings grew smaller or succumbed during the passage of long periods; nature continued immensely superior, destroying them just as it had created them. The most rigorous tasks of speaking, of living together peacefully, of bearing the human burden against the magnetic currents of the Tertiary beat down the last titans and reduced them to cities isolated in the midst of the solitude. A few peoples—Incas, Aztecs, Mayas—occupied zones beseiged by nature, and America was the whole continent extending around and far beyond these oases.

The land was divided into great natural zones and there was no regular communication between them as today there is none between the countries into which the land is divided. The countries came into contact by assault and by combat; after the pillage they made peace and the peoples again separated and forgot each other.

The forest was the absolute domain of vegetation; the mountains, of minerals; the plains and the hillsides, of viviparous animals. The clusters of civilization were produced in the mountainous lands in vague reminiscence of others—suffocated by the totally refractory medium. In general, the plains remained in a barbaric state. The forests were one world, the mountains another, the plains another.

Those inhabitants lived alone, floating or rooted, always alert to innumerable perils. Mayas, Incas, Pueblos, and Aztecs, all skillful builders, came to be architects and builders of fortifications from the necessity to erect a barrier against the world that surrounded them and to open a secret door to infinity where divinities no less cruel resided. Fear made them wall themselves up; the wall was a second isolation like a superstition in the enclosures of the temples. A people was an individual, and an individual was a monad. But individual and people made agreements with nature, and the terror and anxiety of saving themselves from the evil that everywhere menaced put them in the hands of the white man, who annihilated them. In Guatemala, in Colorado, Texas, and Arizona, in Peru and Mexico, those civilizations were at their highest point in the epoch when the Moors entered Spain; only the poetic Carib civilization, of which the Spaniards left no trace, was in bloom when the Spaniards landed. The onrush of the grandsons of the Vandals and of the Goths, who did not halt to judge the value of those societies and who could not conquer them except by the sword, exterminated them or corrupted them.

America had civilizations but it had no past. It was a world without a past and until then without a future; its life evolved in forms asynchronous and asymmetrical with the rhythm and structure of known and approved experiments. Its experience, ranging from architecture and art to law and religion, did not serve the great effort that man was trying systematically to accomplish in other places; for that reason it is absurd to wish to revive them in an archeological sense. However, they did serve a function in that great human effort: the rectification of very serious errors. They were the mirage that allowed correction of the telescopic vision, of the cosmic perspective of that experiment. Face to face the aborigine and the Spaniard did not understand each other, and from the first instant the conquest veered onto mistaken paths. Since he did not understand the native, the conqueror began by judging him as anarchic to all known laws. Upon seeing that the native remained indifferent before the cross and that he concealed metals and precious stones, the conqueror would explode in an aggressive rage.

Toward the Reversal of Time

Each day of navigation the caravels retraced one hundred years. The voyage was made across the ages, receding from the epoch of the compass and of the printing press to that of the chiseled stone. These lands standing at the threshold of the anthropologic ages were called New World; and this erroneous name, like that of America, endured. Henceforth the ancient vices of senility would be taken for defects of infancy. That which was populated and modified was converted into something new; the unpopulated still remains ancient and goes on depositing itself like sediment over the new by a certain impalpable and invisible osmosis. Atavistic tendencies that impel governments to systematized blunders cause people to err in their designs as though motivated by a free interior force and, in general, make them set improvisation above calculation, neglecting authentic human values to the benefit of a primitive scale of worth—these tendencies are taken to be defects of a recently formed society. Nevertheless they are very old defects now forgotten by other peoples; it is a new beginning after many centuries. As with children, all the novelties of the society are very old. Its occasional errors are but a systematized form of governing, of thinking, of living—far from the remote and unconquered nature. Barbarism is not an accidental state; it has its norms, its laws, its local morality, its powerful impulses of invention—all aged.

The point is that we are not a new people, a new landscape, or a final experiment. We were antiquity and we were peopled by an old nation that was already archaic in the Europe of 1500.

Spiritually we inherited a culture that remained stationary and lacked the internal power to evolve boldly within the general movement of the epoch toward complex civil forms. Let one consider how Spain was appraised at the end of the fifteenth century compared to the German, Gallic, Italian, or Saxon peoples; it was a sclerotic, stony, rupicolous people. It was an "American" people. While in other nations the unusual and promising forms of the Modern Age were advancing in knowledge, Spain was just appearing on the political scene by displacing a culture of vast capacity. Inflamed by victory, Spain conserved as the distinctive works of its race the sum of forces she had employed for her liberation. Spain made an emblem of the Pyrenees; she shut herself up in a stone world and in the year 1500 took up the existence of the year 700. Her glory was in being archaic, in being recalcitrant to progress; welded to fanaticism and valor, to moral, religious, and aristocratic prejudices, she stubbornly refused to look forward or allow herself to be invaded by other styles essayed beyond her frontiers. The untimely enterprise of the Discovery itself obeyed the desire to conquer a relic rather than the intrepid will to give life: the sepulchre of Christ, which was more material than his body, which had the structure of his life—the tomb. Recently awakened, centuries after the Crusades, she wished to undertake an anachronous adventure at a most untimely moment—determined in her will not to be Europe. The flight of her invader incited her to flee. In this sense it is certain that Providence was on her side, since it allowed her chimerical hosts to be cast out. The expeditions poisoned the soul with an itch for material dominance—impossible to satisfy with any booty. Here awaited them the "new" world petrified in its fossils, in savagery, in panoramas of an astral scale. Conquest was very natural for the Spaniards; for no other race was it so hopeless to try to be independent of America, because no other race was so identified with America, maintaining it in its barbarism. Our people of the South were most ancient; plainsmen without traces or residues of an enduring culture. Upon that people of Monte Hermoso was deposited the people of Tartessos, without strength to shape or create but with an aptness for amalgamating with the former. Theirs was blood of the same type and transfusion was painless. Nature yet conserved the unwithering fecundity of primordial eras. It was in full bloom: covered with growth whose fossil duplicates lay hundreds of feet below the strata of humus, both old and new intact. Ancient nature and ancient beings, to whose forms the invader adjusted himself by the plain phenomenon of symbiosis. He became acclimated; whatever he did that was illogical, censurable, the opposite of what is understood by colonizing, was called acclimation. His weighty sopor, routine, laziness, ignorance as a paradisiacal state of mind, are unequivocal proofs that the people of Tartessos had found their home. The Saxon, the Fleming, and the Frank fought and conquered despite the environment; none of America's prospects weakened them. On the other hand, the Spaniard and the Portuguese came to take repose and rest satisfied.

Where man skids jubilantly down the slopes of primitiveness, unsheltered and subject to telluric forces like the wild animals and vegetation, there reigns an archaic tone over what he thinks and what he does. The essential thing was what man had initially incorporated into his existence; that which would come later from other influences would take on the shading of the initial force. It will be in vain to assign the symptoms and the values of youth and health to an old world that bends old men to its standards. It is as though the difference between bold and restless adolescence and egotistic and astute old age were a mere play on words.

To Each His Region

In the conscience of the invader there was already a nonexistent region, a no man's land, isolated even in this isolated world that he was slowly beginning to settle. To that region the Indian and the Indian culture were confined, then and after. Once there, the Indian was considered dead—also nonexistent. The seriousness of the matter lay in the fact that the region of these expelled Indians was the tomb of the American man, a wasteland as dead as the Indian, not clearly demarcated but contaminating everything everywhere.

At one time it was necessary for the country's security to establish neutral zones along the frontiers, and to see to it that these were all the more neutral as it became more desirable to bury the danger and the shame. The frontier was the dike opposed to the indiscernible, unfixed danger: to contain not an organized force, but a blind, savage force, internally and externally a phantasmogorial living force of the inanimate—that which could not be reduced to concrete terms.

That belt of stone or furrowed earth, of water or of brush created a distance sufficient to give prominence to the isolation and the separation that were desired. In those days that which had been conquered was within; that which had no value was beyond. The necessity to defend the conquest caused embankments to be built, ditches dug, trenches constructed—to live enclosed. Thus, at the same time that dominion was assured, a complex was created made up of an uneasy conscience, of hate, and of deprecation. Civilization is the opposite of isolation, and the first settler brought loneliness to solitude. Backward peoples live in concentric circles of confinement: they are limited by language, custom, religion, money, artistic style, and industrial practice, until they cast themselves upon the world or are absorbed by it. Everything about them tends to stand out sharply and be encircled by a moat—from the totem to the law.

America had not evolved, because of its isolation—it stuck incrusted in its medium. Isolation is still the indigenous force that threatens to destroy the hermetically inclosed civilization created by the conqueror's fear and the ruler's ineptness and, in the end, by the proclamation of independence of all the republics reflecting the many aspects of Spain's taciturn soul. The vastness of the Empire seemed to form a unit—yet it was separated into insoluble parts; it imposed the isolation of its conscience upon the false unity of the land. Geographic unity remained fixed within the line of the frontiers that were sometimes traced according to the lines of longitude and latitude;[1] and thus at birth each was incommuni-

---

[1] The western boundary of Buenos Aires runs along the sixty-fourth meridian; the southern territories are divided by the forty-second, forty-sixth, and fifty-

cado. There were as many disconnected parts as there were disjoined portions—and there could have been many more or many less. Solitude was imposed upon them by the territory, by the ignorance in which the territory was kept, so that, even before the death of those dreamers who were called Miranda, Bolívar, Monteagudo, and San Martín, freedom forced each viceroyalty, intendancy, and captaincy to shut its frontiers to those who shared its boundaries. Therefore, people from one region could not affect those from another.

A people, spread out upon unmeasurable perimeters, who have not extended themselves progressively by exosmosis, and who are haphazardly expanding its area according to the increase in numbers and energy, cannot have strength or unity. The people fluctuate within their bounds in the event the territory has been originally much greater than the population. The territory belongs to the Nation in the same sense that the Pleiades are part of Taurus. It has no form because it has no internal unity; it will have grown to the point of almost overflowing the glass; and its development will be chaotic. To isolate oneself and contemplate oneself with misgiving is the great evil of solitude and of ignorance and the key for interpreting the enigmas of South America.

Frontiers and Dangers

The realization of the lack of danger along the frontier, of the emptiness of no man's land, psychologically broke the expectant tension of the people. To be alert to our environment is to be dynamically on guard: this is the true test of a nation's strength and organization. The lack of tension causes the aimlessness that turns aggression inward—into what we call revolutions, boundary wars, and a general state of belligerency in peace. This needed tension cannot be artificial nor can it merely

---

second parallels; and Tierra del Fuego is demarcated by a line parallel to the sixty-eighth meridian. La Pampa follows the direction of the sixty-eighth and sixty-fourth meridians and of the sixty-fourth parallel. The boundaries of the Chaco, of Santiago, and of Santa Fe have geometric forms in accordance with astronomic divisions.

assume its form. Once the logical causes for fear disappeared, it only remained by inertia to view the borderlands with mistrust; behind the map of the nation was a gloomy unknown land.

To amass armies on the frontiers, to litigate over boundaries, to break diplomatic relations, to hold congresses, or to sign such treaties as those of the ABC powers and international postal agreements has in substance no other purpose than the need to somehow establish contact with others. In turn, it is required that from within the territory there flow a consciousness of national integrity toward the frontiers, since the whole life of the organism keeps on guard to respond to the world beyond. By such means the spirit of the people is inflamed or pacified, but conscience is not imbued with a sense of right or of duty. All else is dream, indifference, forgetfulness.

An army can be no more than a false movement of guardianship when its preparedness has not slowly emerged from competition and dispute—from abrasive, imperceptible, but constant skirmish. The army that is in garrison simply for strategic reasons or because of the abundance of matériel and troops is a sleeping sentinel; the desert that marks the end of the world is a lonely sentry. In neither situation does a people gain vigor or acquire self-consciousness. States disappear for mechanical motives, foreign to men's wishes; thus they are formed; thus they are maintained. They cannot sustain themselves from their own substance, as hibernating beasts; they maintain themselves from that which they lose and gain in the exercise of their powers by opposing or by concerting with those outside themselves. If the score stays tied—they are dead.

The State needs living frontiers—not of stone, or water, or jungle—just as one's body requires its frontier of skin to maintain itself against the world on a level of workable relations. The frontiers in the case of newly inhabited areas are always distinct from those which are shown on the map. Every South American country has its political boundaries in addition to the true ones. Our real frontiers, for example, are the boundaries of the provinces of Buenos Aires, Santa Fe, Córdoba, Entre Ríos and their offshoots in the direction of the vast neutral zone. All the rest is at the threshold of the frontier from where the ancient world presses upon us. But it is certain that the tangential zone must be to some degree neutral—although not dead. Boundaries of poverty, of inaction, and of ignorance create the idea of a vague frontier beyond the national territory—and this in itself becomes a form of invasion. If the spiritual and dynamic forces do not confront an organized society, competitive in economy and culture and struggling for hegemony on any level on stimulation, they relax and, satisfied with their own share of misery, proceed by lazy dreaming to convert these dull facts into positive values. The greatest damage that can be done to a nation is to lack more powerful and advanced neighbors with whom to be in contact, and instead to possess neighbors who have descended to inferior levels or who live within themselves and have significance only as the names of states that are nonexistent in the reality of life or that are only pejorative points of reference. The reason for the insecurity with which the Argentine Republic advances is this peripheral paralysis, this vacuum beyond its borders from where the emanations of a deep soporific reach us, of a lethargic existence charged with menace. It is preferable that a nation be defeated and absorbed by a conqueror than for it to conserve the sovereignty of its backwardness.

While it is true that the fall of a state may bring on ethnic dissolution, it is also possible that ethnic dissolution may cause the loss of political sovereignty. In the first instance the phenomenon is quick; in the second it is slow, time consuming, and scarcely visible even to the farsighted. The state decays and dies while those in power judge it to be living and aggressive. The long-term process results in a cadaverous decomposition that is erroneously interpreted as the bubbling up of a vital existence. But these are larvae of putrefaction.

Lack of Communication

1. In the main, the South American countries do not have communication among themselves, because they do

not need it; each is also incommunicado with its own interior regions. If they were at opposite ends of the earth they could not be
more profoundly ignorant of each other's intellectual currents,
systems of government, means of increasing public wealth, or ways
of life. Independently they live darkened and opaque lives, although from within each seems enlightened and dynamic. A great
silence envelops this part of America, and the passage of time
covers it with yet deeper shadows. Today these countries are less
known to each other, less esteemed in each other's eyes, and they
help one another less than they did one hundred years ago. They
amount only to an amorphous mass of names and data, of ideas
taken from an atlas, from textbooks, from the succinct reports of
journalists—the latter abounding only in news of disasters. Essentially, we have only a vague notion of their shape and color from
the maps of Justus Perthes and of their sufferings from the inclinations of their dictators.

We are separated from Chile by a strip of stone and desert; nonetheless, the effort to rise above the destiny of geographic laws on
the other side of the Andes is similar to our own. Chile is perhaps
the worst constructed and worst located nation on this planet: it is
like a plant that sprouts between two stones. All along one side
runs the Pacific Ocean, which leads nowhere, since one must try to
avoid it while navigating to the Straits of Magellan or the Panama
Canal. The Andes enclose Chile at its back and the country lies like
the prisoner of nature, for it is no more than the juncture of sea
and mountain range.

Except for a few passes that the Araucanian Indians knew and
used, the height and compact width of the mountain range prohibited contact between the peoples of Chile and Argentina. Only contraband runners made light of this interdiction and these, principally in Patagonia, made the boundary zone a confused clamor of
nationalities, moneys, and products. The clandestine traffickers
have been pursued by authorities since the colonial era; yet, engaging in illegal traffic in the face of a barbaric customs system,
they have been basically right. The airplane, which is not a bird of
these lonely latitudes, daily crosses this strip of the planet. The

tunnel that was opened to exploit the capital invested in the railways, with their limited range of interests, has been closed. Chilean and Argentine interests could not be reconciled, and when ruin was heaped on that inexplicable republic it enclosed itself even more in self-defense; in the end communication was interrupted. There was a return to the mules and the roads that had been known for hundreds of years. Nor did the Trans-Andean Railroad serve the kind of relations we ought to have maintained, because it was not able to support by itself the burden of the totality of geographic and ethnic fate. The tunnel served as a focus of financial contact, but the road opened in the mountain served further to isolate us. Neither country has surplus resources, or curiosity, or sympathy; and consequently that tunnel could not even be what trenches are between two enemy lines: a cave where during a truce the soldiers exchange cigarettes and candy received from home in an act of human confraternity far above and beyond war's hate. By that tunnel we did not come to know each other but rather to watch each other with suspicion in an irrational war of mercantile interests. In its purpose, use, and historic significance the tunnel was the complete opposite of the Panama Canal. It interconnected two reservoirs of different economic levels, and the resultant flowage instead of leveling off produced an imbalanced condition. The identical reasons that proved the absurdity of adjudicating the provinces of Cuyo to the captaincy of Chile, today hinder a spiritual union. Cordillera and desert will continue to interpose themselves invincibly while men lack the tools necessary for their conquest. Those tools would cost as much as the possessions of both nations. The earth's aridity absorbs every effort, and even the cordillera interpolates difficulties along its slopes by means of the strangest geological and climatic phenomena. The sterile pampa embraces the length of the Andes from the farthest reach of the territory of Santa Cruz through all of western Argentina, even beyond the broken dream of Huaytiquina, including Mendoza, San Juan, La Rioja, and Jujuy.

2. The precordillera is a fragment of the planet from the second step of creation. It begins in the south amidst dense shiny fog that

envelops the world of shadows in a film of leaden transparency. People and things have a phantasmal and chimerical vagueness. The center and the north are more clear but equally arid. Within the cordillera are geosynclines, which preserve a lost ancient atmosphere in the midst of the newer. In the very center of the mountains, the Notohyle provides a nucleus of trees similar to the jungle of Misiones: in a bosom of stone is a longitudinal woods, a humid, narrow belt from which emanates a benign, prehuman climate. It is a ribbon of gigantic trees from the thirty-eighth parallel to Tierra del Fuego; these old trees are contemporaries of ancient fossil forests.

The cordillera of this region is constructed on a different plan than the rest. It really has no plan; it consists of stone heaped in disarray. This fragment belongs to the Antarctic continent and it is a stem of the South Pole inserted in the cordillera and running up to Mendoza, covering an area of more than thirty thousand square kilometers. From there to the south the whole cordillera remains as though it still were in the hypothetical glacial epoch. In no other region, except the polar, has the world preserved intact this phenomenon of ice and snow which had its period of domination 500,000 years ago.

All the rest is continuous pampa and continuous mountain. The landscape is divided into three essential parts: tree, stone, and plain. But each one of these elements has been isolated and differentiated into three expanded categories. The plain, with few exceptions, has neither forests nor mountains; each element of the panorama forms a bloc, the concentrated characteristics of which, alternated and divided, would have formed landscapes and nuclei of settlements. But none of these blocs is a landscape—only an element of landscape multiplied by itself.

The desert advances from Patagonia, passes in back of Tucumán like a Sahara cloistered in stone, and another of its arms dies out in the gloomy Puna de Atacama. That puna is depopulated, with only one inhabitant for every thirty square kilometers; and it is possible that it will evolve into a totally uninhabited region. Man—even the Indian—is very much a newcomer to attempt to inhabit these places which preserve themselves as they were when on the earth neither animals nor plants existed. Nor is there water there; the altitude produces endemic sicknesses that conspire with toxic herbs to reduce any inhabitant to idiocy. Only the native son of the soil can bear, as if asleep, the telluric forces of the environment. Great salt flats, sandy wastes, and high, bleak plateaus destroy whoever tries to reside there. Nonetheless, that is where the greatest metallic riches are: gold, copper, silver. But that wealth is defended by solitude. Herds of goats and impoverished shepherds vegetate promiscuously above these mines. Women superpose their dresses, beginning with the first ones they ever used. In the end, they take with them to the tomb that accumulated winding sheet which they always wore. Man, not being a Silurian animal, could not resist labor in the mines of gold, copper, wolfram, and borax; and transportation costs more than the metal.

3. Primitive nature is volcanic; the vegetation of volcanic lands is aggressive; a plant does not know how to adapt itself to an aggressive land except by imitation. The thorn eventually becomes a mimetic phenomenon. Thus the botanical world was modeled to the image and likeness of the earth and not in accord with man's scheme, although there is a common plan in all that lives. Instead of fruits there were dry stalks, metallic leaves, and poisonous thorns. Life in these neutral zones which separate us from Chile is harsh, hostile, without sap or blood.

The native has gone to take refuge in the depth of a nature refractory to man because it does not belong to his epoch; it is arid and rich in metals: primordial wealth in unusable form. Ignorant and poor he lives, with the rural code in mind, so that tomorrow they will not take away his handful of goats and his land, which may represent a fortune because of the gold existing a thousand feet below his hut. Who covets that gold? One would have to renounce the advantages of civilization and the benefits the earth offers elsewhere and bend all one's efforts to fertilizing this rock. It would be an abstract struggle for wealth in which a whole lifetime would be misspent. Each day's work is a pea-sized gold nugget; a year is 365 grains of gold ingots. It is not worth the trouble to extract it from the earth to sell it at that price. To undertake the conquest of the wealth of these parts is a total renunciation of life. It only has been possible to wrest land from the steppe forming a homogeneous continuity with that of Patagonia and that which goes beyond the mountain range; this land consists of but a few irrigated plots maintained in artificial fertility at a cost of huge sacrifices in lives and fortunes. Livestock grows sickly and insubstantial; man becomes harsh and unproductive. These are oases that, like the tunnel, must be maintained against the cosmos. Neither the locomotive nor the plain has the strength to cross these topographic distances; what is needed is the pressure of two vigorous and consummate peoples. Any attempt that would do violence to nature's decree will place itself at the service of that nature; and, instead of uniting, it will divide.

4. Chile was called to disappear from the concert of nations: terrestrial and oceanic currents dragged her to the center of the planet; for that reason she wanted to make herself strong, without realizing that all that desperate energy was weakness—like the digital tentacles of a plant born between two rocks. She made herself into a warrior by believing there was danger from the other side of the Andes; the real danger was in her copper and nitrates. As in the case of Paraguay, she imagined that her strength would be in her army; and she was destroyed by it, morally and materially. By shaping citizens in the school of suspicion she created the third ingredient for her own isolation. When her wealth and patrimony, consisting in copper and nitrates, had favorable markets, she armed herself until she possessed the most powerful fleet and armed forces in South America. Whether by the inclination of her brave and vigorous people or by the bad example she may have received from the Argentines who emigrated to Chile during Rosas's dictatorship, she turned her ideals toward the power of armament. It cost Chile dearly to uphold that defense on a war footing as taught by German instructors. When copper and nitrates did not yield their former gains, the people, who had neither unity nor strength, because they believed that the army had assumed both, disintegrated and fell into a chaos of misery and violence.

The collapse left Chile isolated, confronting alone its geographic problem, the root of all its difficulties. Thus, the closing of the tunnel was a fated consequence of the desperate attempt to triumph with determination in a world where material things were against her. If we were not already on the downgrade of an analogous regression proclaimed by the same symptoms of the decomposition of a fictitious power and of a prosperity based on the prices of meat and bread, our copper and nitrates, we would be able to see the omen of imminent ailments. Other countries launch themselves into absurd wars as though heeding death wishes or obeying the organic energies for dissolution that spring up from the primitive world. The vulnerable parts that have not yet healed are the first to be wounded in any incident. Among the causes of the Chilean economic crisis, which produced a disaster, were operative circumstances due to nature and not to men, to industry, to capital, or to labor. Vegetation, metals, and climate are the true protagonists of the wars and uprisings with which our countries destroy themselves.

Our crisis, which is in part an echo and in part a logical result of our authentic backwardness, persuades us to defend ourselves with nature's weapons and to seek rationalization in the social and political upheavals. A revolution may cover up an embezzlement, but it brings to the surface the hidden forces that work toward the erosion of mankind.

Our other neighboring nations are at an equally telescopic distance from us. Even the accidents of geography, such as rivers, which always act to unite peoples, separate us. A form of nature contrary to that of our West breaks in at the North. The Chaco, Formosa, and Misiones form the pelvis in which are joined the dry land and the hostile stone, fecund and virginal. The jungle that extends southerly from Brazil cascades with its oceanic wealth; but it shuts itself off like a pelvis, in repugnant chastity. And that wealth of forest and fecundity is jungle in a geographic sense; it is isolation, unscathed nubility. Among great clumps of trees it chokes the architectonic rubble of an effort to conquer, molded in titanic proportions but contrary to life and the valid forces of the world. The wrought walls of those constructions will always bring to mind the best organized attempt to develop an emporium with universal implications, though the effort was defeated by nature and by solitude. In those ruins is more philosophy and more history than in all the books written to explain America.

5. Even the rivers go no place when there is neither desire nor necessity to go. They are converted into impassable cordilleras with empty clay, floating islands of vegetation, and snakes.

The Bermejo, the Pilcomayo, and the Uruguay are mountain ranges of water, deserts of water, chasms of water. The Paraná River pours into the Río de la Plata thirty thousand cubic meters of water per second and deep-draught ships navigate it; nonetheless, it is a sterile river. The Paraguayan nation has bled itself white because of the river; and the two thousand kilometers of the river's banks have nothing more to show than Rosario, which rises above its hydrographic destiny, while Santa Fe and Paraná are undercut by it. Because this river separates them from the other parts of the Republic, Corrientes and Entre Ríos are the least Argentine provinces. Our South American rivers are wider, carry more water, and are more extensive than other rivers of the world, but never will they have the significance of the Ganges, the Euphrates, the Rhine, or the Danube. Those are rivers of struggle, of civilization, on which the destiny of gods and men depend; but ours are rivers of distance, isolation, confinement. We have no roads because we have no human necessity for communication; nor have we studied the rivers from another angle, for even those which are navigable, such as the Bermejo, are not highways but frontiers. Even though he might have known of it, the Indian did not navigate, because he usually traveled to flee from other tribes and not to forge links with them. The civilizations of America were born under the shelter of stone, not of river banks. They let the water secure their isolation as sure as stone. The Paraná River and the Uruguay, which, according to Sarmiento, unite symbolically in the Río de la Plata estuary, have a tragic history from the founding of Santa Fe as the obligatory transit port of the viceroyalty. Paraguay wasted herself through her rivers; their movement toward the east and drainage into the Atlantic are symbolic and tragic. To defend her borders from the rage of these rivers, Paraguay wanted to make herself strong with armaments, like Chile, yet by that immense effort she destroyed herself. Now Paraguay is struggling with another country that also wants to defend itself with arms against the fatal pressure of geographic forces: she struggles with Bolivia, which violates reason and nature for the very causes that gave birth to the latter. For Bolivia was born of South America's divisiveness and lack of mutual understanding. That struggle does not move or impassion other nations, and from a distance of seven thousand miles it lacks all meaning and is judged to be ridiculous: "En Europe, ce conflict endémique prête à sourire."

The soldiers die covered with glory in the swamps, starving and malarial and with no weapon other than their own machetes. Victory and defeat mean nothing because the warring countries do not participate in an existence of historical context. Our sympathy becomes hate and our compassion becomes circumstantial and humiliating, because with the coming of peace these countries will again be forgotten.

6. Nor does any feeling of unity tie us to Bolivia: her people are the farthest removed from Europe. Dismembered from a teratological body, we replaced the land connections with a rail line, and that sufficed to free us from any concern about whether Bolivia existed or did not exist. More than to unite us or to put us in communication, the train has a bureaucratic function, like the streetcar that carries the employee to his office: a diplomatic function because this type of relationship in South America pertains to the functionaries of the Ministries of Foreign Affairs and Culture, who live abroad. Everything else that may be said is rhetorical or in bad faith. We do not have extended contact with that country or with any other neighbor, and even the international mail trains arouse dispute; at the point where the rail lines link up, the correspondence is despoiled: this much is known in Berne. That branch line does not yet represent for Bolivia the danger that the tunnel poses for Chile, and there is no need for her to be disturbed even though it does exist. It is Bolivia's obligatory drainage to the outer world;

she believes that only by looking to water as a substitute for iron can she defend herself. But a river or an arm of the sea will no more unite Bolivia than those two fibers of steel. Beyond all sentimental and diplomatic reasons, Bolivia is an absurdity. Like Chile, Peru, Ecuador, and Colombia, Bolivia could only exist in a mind that labored at incandescent heat, by virtue of an interfunctional and unitary concept of America. Once this live, passionate, feverish unity and function was smashed, its existence was that of a useless appendix. With Bolívar dead, San Martín exiled, and Latin America eternally fragmented both in mind and in fact, the continent found itself besieged by Tertiary forces that emerged from the world surrounding her. If Chile focused upon herself, Bolivia desperately sought an outlet to the sea; her anxiety to pour herself out is in itself a suicidal impulse, as is that of Chile in attempting self-isolation. Bolivia never attempted to establish extensive contact with the neighboring countries where her fellow men were suffering an identical destiny; by having large neutral zones along the borders she became isolated. The movement toward the remote is the death wish that she has carried from the beginning, for even to reach the sea would be for such a country to follow again the highway of loneliness; it would be another link in the chain of the land.

Nor can we say that Uruguay is nearer to us, or that we are separated from it by fewer obstacles. Rivalries that have not slacked off for a century keep her thousands of kilometers away from us. Sports separate us; the identity of rural labors separates us; blood, culture, and material differences separate us. Uruguay is as remote from our national economic system as our provinces and territories are from Buenos Aires, Entre Ríos, and Santa Fe. Uruguay should for many reasons be closer to us, to the region we describe as the Argentine Republic, than San Juan, Corrientes, and Salta, which are without any doubt remote; notwithstanding, it is Uruguay that is farther away. Governments and beliefs that well up from the depths of the soul, and that are much more powerful than geologic, economic, or political unity, oblige us to remain at a vast distance from each other. Such concepts of imaginary remoteness are more understandable when applied to Uruguay because they are at the root of her independence, which was inevitable a century ago, and even done in the style of the great ideas of the liberators. This independence now has its own reason for existence, in the same manner as La Plata becomes distant and anonymous so as not to fall into a situation of becoming a suburb of Buenos Aires. She would be wise to deepen her provincialism and withdraw psychologically to avoid being assimilated and lost in that vast body of such greater size and lesser vitality. Fortunately Entre Ríos and Corrientes, cut off by the Paraná from the rest of the Republic, deepen and widen the currents of Uruguayan life.

The other South American countries are plunged into a Balkan-like chaos. Although they differ greatly among themselves, the sum of common characteristics comprises an undifferentiated geographic and cultural territory, similar to an immense Hellenic-Turkish peninsula. The fundamental characteristic is ethnic: Ibero-American; from this, other characteristics are derived relative to the technique of governing, obeying, living, and being free. All that we understand to be unity is Spanish or Portuguese; that which differentiates us is nothing compared to that which makes us similar. The capricious drawing of boundaries has ended up by making nature take on in those parts a desolate aspect—unpopulated, sterile, unhealthful, dangerous. All is indifferently encompassed by cordilleras, rivers, and jungles.

Discontinuity

And the same occurs with what we call historical facts. These states were born of a dismemberment, and they remained with capricious boundaries in no way related to true national territorial necessity. Colombia, Venezuela, and Ecuador were a single nation; and Argentina, Bolivia, Paraguay, and Uruguay should have been one. If any petty forces had parceled out the map in some other fashion, the divisions would have always been capricious. The interfunction that never existed could not have been established between the separate members; they would continue to be amputated segments of a vast body, which during the colonial era also lacked unity.

Although the people of South America have a great affinity for each other, the final configuration of their countries does not show it; thus we have large countries, such as Brazil and Argentina, and small ones, such as Uruguay and Paraguay. The people of these countries could exchange places and only a small difference would be detected. Only those whom Frank calls "the stone people" keep their telluric soul. The life of such people within such extents of land surface is precarious; they live a kind of cosmopolitan life and are incapable of making an adjustment from their person to town, from town to province, from province to nation, or from nation to world. There is a kind of ethnic, somatic, and mental South American universality that gives a similar atmosphere to half a continent; nonetheless, nothing unites these nations which lack the high ideals that confraternity creates. Thus it is that even their wars have a certain aspect of being revolutions, and that their revolutions are, despite their frequency and uselessness, the incidents most charged with significance. But no episode has a far-reaching projection, and its area of influence covers only a few kilometers and a few days.

Events are limited by that neutral planetary nature which interposes itself between country and country; the meaning of each event is exclusively local, determined by the frontiers. Each nation has its hero and each hero his personality. Except for military chieftains who obeyed limited influences, everyone labored in the bosom of a formless world in imitation of their models. In the manner of gods born out of dissolution, they endure to defend their heritage. Localities, states, and entire provinces are linked to episodes of our history like words in a dialect that is no longer understood in the neighboring region. From province to province Urquiza, López, and Rosas change appearances; Sucre, O'Higgins, Artigas, and Alvear signify nothing beyond their own lands.

What they did accomplish concerns their region and their epoch. They and their deeds passed by in the dissenting march to forgetfulness. Lives and achievements disconnected from the whole did not gestate in an amnion rich in vital and organic substances. In the plains the man who moves is an imperceptible point. The event is isolated and frozen in the vast, shapeless, and solitary areas, without receiving or transmitting life. One sees them moving about, going here and there, without their actions being of interest to more than a handful of men who follow the chief; today they are sketched in the anecdotal appendices of history. Occasionally something of value would occur only to be sealed as tightly as an oyster. The entire merit of the historian is reduced to the exactitude of his facts, to the work of a mere naturalist.

The forces in play lacked global significance, and the event did not transcend its intrinsic merit. Under the pressure of terrestrial and demographic forces that the men of the conquest thought were their own, the history of the South American countries offers in its totality the same archipelagolike aspect characterized by a map of the continent: disunity. History is not made in every place inhabited by man, although something may happen that resembles what history itself has conserved in its pages and documents; ethnography is also produced. The history of each South American country up to now is a separate event—and by no means the happiest. If the accident of battle to which this history reduces itself had been slightly varied or even opposite, we would be neither less nor worse off than that which we are. Neither Cuvier nor Goethe could have uttered a word contemplating these loose pieces. From two antagonistic points of view, Cuvier and Goethe surveyed their surroundings with the gaze of those who know how to differentiate that which is "once again" in the trail of life and that which is a leap out of the ordinary.

It is necessary that there exist a state of historicity, a complete historic form, in order for an event to have living meaning and not to be merely circumstantial and complementary. In such a historical medium whatever happens is irremissibly history; there were places and epochs that used to create history simply by existing, by representing absent humanity. These places and epochs kindled interest in true historical events, those whose outcomes define our destinies. These events and individuals embody the remains of eras past, and they link distant places and epochs.

Those events and those men cannot be imitated without one's

appearing to be ridiculous. What our heroes accomplished, as can be clearly seen by contemplating the medium in which they acted, was an episode of their lives. It would not be possible to reconstruct the whole with loose pieces out of context. Belgrano and San Martín were for Mitre the essence of Argentine history from the proclamation of independence to its realization. Mitre, who was the logical continuation of Belgrano and San Martín, captured in both biographies the vital elements of Argentine history; that is how he titled it: with two names. One should reflect on this because it is the most meaningful foreword we possess to penetrate the true meaning of what our national life has been and is continuing to be. The lack of history in the landscape, the enormous superiority of nature over its inhabitants, and the supremacy of environmental forces over will: these isolate events and force them to float unrelated, surrounded in a halo of irresponsibility. Technically, in those regions there was no one and nothing happened. That which moves our nationalistic sentiment is indifferent to the dwellers on the other side of the Andes, or of the Bermejo, Pilcomayo, and Uruguay rivers; that which arouses emotion in others we take for boasts of individual feats. None of this is America; none of these sporadic gestures even mimic the development of a unified drama. If the life of the Indian is clandestine, the history of South America is apocryphal or means something different than we presume. The wars of independence are episodes in Spain's history; only passions and biographies belong to us. What we judge to be the prologue is only the epilogue in a series of maneuvers that close the chapter of Spanish domination in America. In retrospect, those glorious events are not even history. They have remained in the domestic obituary, as dead as in the ethnographic graves or in the doldrums of present-day towns. In the immensity of this empty panorama, Tucumán and Caseros regain pride in their heroic deeds. Whatever the intrinsic value of our battles, they are disjoined from the genealogical tree of history. Proof of this irrelevancy is the disillusionment that overcame the protagonists when, nearing their ends, they bitterly contemplated their own deeds. Napoleon is an entire chapter of France even if he does break the rhythm and style of history; Ayohuma is only a bad day in the life of Belgrano. In Saint Helena, Napoleon wrote down the history he made; in exile, Belgrano wrote his autobiography. Paz did the same.

Therefore, nothing new has happened in this old land without a human past. We have reproduced with individualistic variations many forgotten histories, as if they were stories omitted in the world chrestomathies. The geographic past of this part of the continent, with the vicissitudes of the people who inhabited it, forms around man a hiatus and breaks his ties with the international community. Events shape themselves to the configuration of the land. The dividing lines on the map—mountain, desert, jungle, ocean—are the limits that cut off man from the continuity of history. Because of this isolation the South American nations cannot develop their lives with true independence; inter-American understanding is progressively more difficult, and it is easier to shut down the tunnels and to turn inward on a search for roads to illusion. South America is still a subsidiary European episode, but it has an American soul: closed, mute, solitary. South American history is to the world but a few pages of statistics. The dead in the land of nothing have yet to be buried, and they constantly fight against all that is foreign, wishing to again be alone in their nothingness.

Dismemberment

Regardless of size, these republics of Celtiberian America are shipwrecked on a territory much larger than they should occupy by reason of their culture, their wealth, their production, and their population. There is a surplus of land. Depopulation and desert are a function of the excess of territory. The configurations of the masses of inhabitants should be symmetrically superimposed on the geographic structure; any barren interstices are ignorance and misery, zoology and botany. The ailment of true nations is the vastness of the land, and this vastness can only be understood in terms of distant withdrawal from the world. This is the relationship between the planets as expressed in Newton's law. As the land becomes more encircled by water and is more distant from the hemisphere of compact earth, its dimensions increase and only quantity matters.

A nation is only great when it is populated, since area only makes sense in relationship to man and his regularly functioning institutions, which act as live organs. A populated nation has many uncivilized areas, and they are useless. These lands are isolated because they are empty, and they are empty because they are confined between two oceans. People rest on them without settling down and they do not truly occupy a place: they fill space, and between them is solitude. The physical and psychological spaces between individuals are empty and changing because one cannot think about space without thinking about the soul; the unpopulated lands are a regrettable truth: solitude.

The latifundium, the despotic form of government, the fear of the unknown, the extensive cultivation of grain, of cattle, and of intelligence are geographic, economic, and psychological needs that could be explained with the mathematical equations for gravity. All these small barren islands of the mainland Antilles form something they do not wish to be and which they deny being: colonies and dominions. They could not be anything else even if the written laws attested otherwise. They are colonies and dominions that revolve around incandescent nuclei of financial and industrial interests. Independence deprived them of the unity provided by Spain and implied voluntary economic and cultural servitude. With autonomy came isolation. The great dreamers of a free and united America saw in the unity of the whole continent the only way to break the colonial condition, which was self-contained in the vastness of the territory, in the distances, in poverty, and in barbarity. They knew that without this unity, freedom would be a lie. But the planetary and racial reality shattered forever those beautiful dreams, and those who followed did not have the strength to confront the cosmic current that America poured into the Atlantic and the Pacific, and they behaved like the day laborers of an anonymous society.

The empty land requires both men and capital in astronomical quantities. Men and capital are usually concomitant energies, but

they never form a partnership unless they arrive together. Between
a group of activities encouraged by profit and another group of activities fomented by life, there are voids impossible to fill because
of the disagreement between ends and means: the patterns of enrichment become incompatible with the patterns of living. The natural equilibrium between these groups is disrupted when capital is
revenue instead of work, rental income instead of circulatory movement of wealth, action, and joy. Each group becomes transformed
into an independent organ that tends to create a pseudostructure
around itself and to assume a function that should be divided and
correlated with the whole. Capital comes to South America from
far away and creates centers of wealth unrelated to work: these
generate a cycle of activities that produce dividends in the form of
raw materials for export. Banks, industry, and commerce work in
function of the unknown lender. His activity is ruled by the degree
of profit and not by the public need, the internal needs of the country. The revolving around a remote center is in the style of a satel-
lite around a planet, or of a colony around the mother country.

The worker is here but his salary is fixed abroad. He suffers a decrease in wages equal to the interest and amortization received by
the banker, who is not disturbed that his money is in America; in
addition, the worker's income is dented by the gains of the intermediary whom we suppose to be the owner. Work is unable to create nuclei of strength and remains weak and individual as capital
becomes more concentrated; one can even say that there are no
class struggles or social problems.

All South American countries are subjugated by centers of economic energy located in the Northern Hemisphere; the system operates in accord with the demands of foreign markets where the
South American goods are sent; conversely, the foreign centers export their excess products. The South American countries cannot
be the regulating centers and, even though they produce basic foodstuffs, are unable to control supply and demand. They have to be
by necessity the marginal zones of foreign consumption centers
that need certain products we are forced to cultivate. In the same
sense we are nothing but factories, colonies, and dominions because

we produce what they want, and they want us to produce what they cannot. That foreign constellation of interests destroys the guilds and the cooperatives. Each one of these republics has a dilemmalike internal problem of organization and of interchange: that of internal commerce and internal culture. It is impossible that they begin to participate in a system of international relations before solving those problems. As long as the solution to these questions is dependent on a foreign will that has no interest in solving them, these countries cannot directly communicate among themselves, because their union would mean a true independence. The lack of understanding between the South American countries is the effect of prevailing conditions between North and South.

The republics become isolated, without love and without hate, by an adiabatic band—no longer composed of frontiers of stone, of water, of deserts, and of jungles but of Europe herself—that is interposed between those republics. Since all these countries were born untimely, none of them could have achieved a greater degree of liberty by the manipulation of the rigid social mechanism; but apart from differences in degree, of a bit more credit or a bit less land, their destinies are identical. The price paid for the barbarity present from birth was the mortgage now burdening them; it allowed for emancipation but also produced anarchy. Since capital was organized from outside, work was dispersed and the system did not produce artisans or skilled laborers. Each worker would become his own little capitalist—probably his own worst boss. The crude forms of the obvious and dangerous barbarism were followed by the dissolution of the national soul, of the collective ideal, and of faith in the community, all under the predominance of humiliating gold that was the caricature of prosperity.

The distancing between the republics, which exist in nominal sovereignty, eliminates all curiosity and human interest to the spectacle of their being. We barely notice wars, revolutions, epidemics, earthquakes. We do not know each other, but we understand each other. We all produce the same raw materials, we all fulfill the same function as Europe's suburban real estate, we are all defending the owner's possessions while intoxicating ourselves with the clandestine liquors he sends us: gold, magazines, movies, weapons. We are interested in Europe, but we are copying from her what is already America there. An extensive telegraph service every day dumps on half a continent the residue of a life that throbs to a different rhythm and functions in a different temperature. Our heritage does not interest us, because we still hold a grudge against what we really are. What the telegraph transmits to us is the surface and the shell of the social, political, and artistic phenomena of Europe. The intellectual life of each state in the South American archipelago is directly related to the abundance of news. The state of culture in each nation is judged by the consumption of cablegrams. We overlook the essence of those images and our incorporation of forms without substance—from dress and laws to flirt and sport—are only grotesque imitations. The figures are refracted through seven thousand miles of water until they appear to coincide with ours. The inward, which is what we do not want to be, continues its enclosed, deliberate, and imperceptible life. It is doubtless that true freedom, if it is to come, will arrive as previously: blind and barbarous from the back country to sweep away slavery, intellectual servitude, and the opulent lie of sold-out cities.

5 DISTANCES

Space

    The eye is the organ for distances and as such
the most subtle tentacle for apprehension. The clearness with
which another town may be perceived from one's own fixes a sentimental position, and when we contemplate our neighboring village we are in part residing in it. Thus one rests from the march of
life. In areas populated for centuries, the towns are separated by
arable lands, by trees, by yoked beasts, and by roaming animals; as
in the old paintings, spaces are filled by figures that take up an
ample sector of the perspective. Today they exist exactly the same.
Sentiments of intense rivalry may be generated between them, but
we know that these are emotions parallel to love and the normal
result in the contact among human groups. Society segregates such
ferments. These rivalries represent Anteros, the opposite pole of
love. As a result of such struggles, man is able to identify with fellow man. Rivalry and jealousy are aspects that end up fusing themselves with the great torrent of sympathy. However, after residing

a while in these old towns one notices that the prevailing mood is one of reliance on order and mutual protection, as happens in the city homes and old people's asylums. This situation, born of closeness, with time creates affection, and grudges take on the role of common misfortunes in the human drama. Men die with their hate, but people continue to work for friendship.

It is much worse to be isolated. The inhabitant of our towns knows the names of his neighbors, but he does not see them; the fields and the sky do not offer a resting point for the eye or soul.

The unit of measurement between isolated villages is not based on eyesight, on love, or on rivalry; it is the geographic measure: the mile, the kilometer, the league, the traveling time. A unit of measurement that is foreign to man occurs, and it warns that man and world are constructed to a different scale. They are only in concert as to position: man is within. That space does not surround or contain him. It does not even attract him; it rather expels him, forcing him to march. The disparity that thus results translates into distance measured in leagues, in kilometers, in hours. What was always understood to be Mother Nature, from the times of the Vedas and Homer, is precisely that relationship of child to womb, of fetus to placenta, which should exist between man and landscape.

A town grows by a process of aggregation; the key element is the position occupied by the following generation when it becomes independent: the size of its herds, its capacity for work, and its degree of cooperation. Even in those towns which grew by military occupation, the sons were always within range of the umbilical cord. The strength of today's offspring depends on their degree of independence; to overcome the umbilical radius the children need distance and economic independence, not love.

Hippodamus and Aristotle fixed the numerical limits of a town. By conferring on Agamemnon the epithet "he who governs from afar," Homer indicated a judicial power that exceeded its immediate surroundings, a clear hierarchical power. Plato set as the maximum population of a city the number of people who could live within the radius of an orator's voice.

That is also why the systems of weights and measures patterned themselves on human proportions and based their units on parts of the body. The foot, the yard, the toise, the pound, all take as their standard arms and legs, instead of a unit based on one ten-millionth part of the distance measured on a meridian from the equator to the pole. Beyond a certain magnitude, distance is a matter for geodesy rather than sociology, useful for planning itineraries but not for daily use. Man's physical endurance is not sufficient to overcome the challenges of distance; he needs the alliance with power and speed provided by machines. But if the machine does not cross or fly over new villages, it is merely a device for transportation, not for union. The traveler turns into the machine's conductor. That same wise and healthy reasoning which produced weights and measures gave towns an intermediary space, measuring and counting them in the census.

Even if modern life characteristics impose new ways on living environments, they can never be superior to the exigencies of the spirit, whether in love or in reason. It is true that old cities are of Neptunian form, while the modern ones take a Plutonian shape; but in both cases their location obeyed the demands of man's organic law, and not of solitude. To take a recent example, North America became populated with the scum of a sedimentary race who found it also necessary to fight against nature and savages. This struggle required certain methods, since those settlers knew the difference between winning by assault and winning by the application of constant pressure. Man fought with wife and son at his side. He cleared forests, laid bridges, and worked, always bearing in mind his socioreligious unit. He expanded concentrically with his property and his first-born; to recede meant to unite, not to separate. The pioneer became fierce because he was an explorer who asserted his life; the circumstantial weapons were the tools of daily labor. Sarmiento thought that God himself would be moved to emotion upon seeing how the towns were being laid out: all along meridian arcs forming a harmonious and geometric net.

When the struggle is undertaken against the settler instead of against nature, with the weapons used as tools in times of peace, the resulting sketch cannot be pleasing to the eyes of a good geometer.

The Settlements

On a trip from one village to another, there is nothing in between except the clean, white bones of gleaming skeletons off to the side of the road. These skeletal quadrupeds sleep intact as if liberated from life; only occasional birds perch on their cagelike shapes. The horse senses the true meaning of these remains and rises up in terror on its hind feet—instinctively wanting to gallop away.

The road in itself is not interesting. It is space to be covered and one tries to pass to his destination as soon as possible. In order to be compatible with man's life, loneliness must be full of human substance. The pleasure is in arriving, not in traveling. The inn is preferable to the road where the traveler deeply feels the message around him: the stillness of the plain, the desolate and ephemeral flight of the bird, the inert, putrid flesh.

The difference between the voyage and the voyager is infinite. It is very difficult to achieve cohesion in a country where the population resembles birds settled after disbanding, because two-thirds of the population is in the cities, and the remainder is confined, without contact, in the country. The closest point is the distant city. One leaves a village and enters another, erasing the steps behind. One travels without remembrances, and it is easier to go ahead than to return. The traveler never looks back; what attracts him is beyond the horizon: the point of arrival; all that he remembers is the point of departure. Every plainsman is a native of another place. Not even the tree of the plain, the *ombú*, is indigenous to it. Only the tree's roots are in accord with the landscape; that tormented and partially bared root is testimony to the plains wind. The branches give the tree an appearance of a jungle dweller. It is easy to see how it springs from a hilly and uneven land. Like a lonely traveler, it has been advancing from the north; for that reason it appears as loneliness amidst the solitude. The *ombú* brought part of the jungle with it; huge and without equal, it needs the new environment of the desert to attain its capacity. Perhaps the tree's southward progression is the result of its need to extend roots; these may have been strengthened by the violent winds. The root would have framed this tree into an ascetic specimen. But we know that it was disseminated by a lesser wind within the range of its climate; dispersed slightly farther to the south it would have died. It spread its roots, as extensive and powerful as the wind, and it was transformed into a lung under an immense sky of thin air and of light.

The *ombú* is a tree that only provides shade, as if designed to serve the traveler in his rest but not in his stay. Its strong, thick, and low trunk is a useless, spongy lung. A perfect instrument of the wind, it breathes the earth through its plant parenchyma. It is impossible to salvage wood from it, and Vergil would not have sung its virtues in the Georgics. It is not possible to manufacture from it ceiling beams, or table boards, or spade handles, or plow handles. It does not contain wood; rather than a tree it is shadow: the shadow's body. Its leaves are poisonous, but the root at times offers shelter with its grottolike caverns. The *ombú* is the symbol of the plain, the physical and spiritual embodiment of the pampa.

After a long journey, the first village we fall upon appears to be the last one, as if nothing were beyond. We are invaded by a feeling of sorrow as the initial joy is dissipated by the depressing appearance of the village: flat, colorless, and made to mirror the appearance of the countryside. The streets are wide and made of earth, and the unplastered brick houses are separated by untilled lands. The village grows horizontally by overflowing on all sides. There are huts made of adobe or of metal sheets. The settlement surrounded by the countryside is the loser in the struggle against loneliness: besieged by the countryside, it is subdued and reduced to a kind of curious mimesis.

Weeds invade streets and fields. The weeds are harbingers of the countryside's slow, tireless invasion. They are constantly being cut, yet they always sprout again from the dirt floor or from among the bricks. The countryside overflows into the courtyard, and the courtyard spills into the bedroom.

The houses are not really small, but they appear flattened by the immensity of the perspective. Their littleness is an optical illusion caused by the pampa. The passerby in the streets strikes one as being smaller than normal because his size is judged in relationship to things that are dwarfed by the pampa.

Those villages look like aerolites, parts of inhabited heavenly bodies fallen on the countryside. Upon arrival, we may think that the village we are entering is the one we just left and that the entire trip has been a dream. People smile when we ask for the name of their settlement because they think of it as "*the* village"—the only place with a name in the midst of a nameless area. The settlement is totally dependent on the countryside and there is no difference between the two. The village lies where it is, but it could have been born slightly more to the right or to the left, or not been born at all. It exists to supply the countryman, who occasionally wanders in to stock himself with provisions and to drink without moderation. Loaded down with supplies, he leaves at the end of the day with a sour taste in his mouth to once again return to long weeks of solitude. That village does not possess an independent life, because it did not appear and prosper through indispensable demands made by the land on which it is anchored. The settlement exists only for the benefit of those beings which appear from small isolated farms and melt back into them. On the one hand, the village is tied to those men who raise foodstuffs and do not even know each other; on the other hand, it is dependent on Buenos Aires, or some other city, to which it ships crops and cattle. Once the products of the pampa have wandered halfway around the world, they return to the village by way of Buenos Aires, or some other city, in the form of manufactured goods.

Night is a fitting time for those still, sleepy, quiet villages saturated with lewdness, greed, and rancor. The lights of the remote houses and huts flicker like stars at a telescopic distance. Even beyond those lights, one can hear the whistles of mysterious and nonexistent animals: delicate and subtle sounds that bathe the ear like a soporific drug. The plain, which did not seem to exist during the day, at night breathes a convincing but removed and toned-down life. It becomes so rich and seemingly inhabited that it is difficult not to believe in grieving souls that rove in the darkness. Those hypnotic voices beyond are of dreams and shadows, which invite us to sleep and to die. They are equivalent to the nocturnal creaking of furniture by which we come into contact with the world's unknown forces, but in a much more delicate and penetrating way. It is a delight to absorb and distinguish the clear notes emanating from solitude; in this way solitude acquires its true meaning.

Even with the coming of dawn, fear of the night endures in the houses. It is easy to comprehend their sadness and hostility when one grasps that the day is but a parenthesis, a rest for the fertile night.

A country house is plain, flat, and earthy and conceals itself against the background. It is a simply arranged dwelling, without inside or outside adornments. Our villages are extensive and flattened; they occupy a larger area than they should in accordance with the number of people and buildings. Therefore, the houses are not as tall as logic might dictate. Every village seems disjointed by the centrifugal force of individual plots. The separate pieces of land are disbanded, crumbling, and without intimacy. A physical and psychological neutral zone has been created along the boundaries of the property lines. Those families seem to have secret emotions that isolate them: fears of guilt, of taking a false step, of contagious diseases. These feelings create in the entire village an atmosphere of seclusion and enigma. At the outskirts, silent and with closed jealousies, is the Big House. That house is the repressed thought of others: the bad house, the taboo house.

Well outside the mud walls of the village is another hamlet: shallow, silent, dead. The two settlements are different worlds. In the country the cemetery is oblivion and abandonment. It is far away and not even visited on the days given to devotion. Occasionally people go to watch over crosses and memorial stones—exposed in the solitude to sacrilegious theft. There generally is a watchman who takes care of the graves and serves as gravedigger. But in the small villages the job usually falls to the person in charge of well digging, who also works as a carpenter. He erects houses and constructs tombs. The cemetery is always carefully proportionate to the size and needs of the village. The merchants and the rich laborers erect vaults for the dead, but the common arrangement is a simple grave with the name carved on a wooden cross. Grass and weeds grow in the paths and soon invade everywhere; the cross disappears. To die is to be cast into oblivion. Time can be measured by the sinking of the ground; the wealth of the deceased may be gauged by the amount of weeds on his grave. People think of the graves as separate entities, as if they belonged to passersby whom the night accidentally surprised in town.

The countryside surrounds the cemetery and encircles the town. The same nightfall descends on both and the same sunshine illuminates them. The town has some of the cemetery's sadness; the house of the dead is very similar to the tomb of the alive. The population vegetates and it seems to nourish itself on the houses and on the earth itself.

At the outskirts are the huts, the poorest and most isolated houses. Women and children almost never go to the village. They vegetate farther away and take their time to greet the traveler, who in his sulky stops at their doorstep. First come the dogs and the children. The older people spy and groom themselves a little before appearing. When the traveler leaves they return to their huts. The women do not care about the town and are not oriented toward its life. Those huts are always halfway between the town and the cemetery. At times the children ignore the name of the closest river or railway station, but they are always well acquainted with the closest road. The names of unseen towns that lie farther along the road, however, are mere abstractions. Those people of the huts have not even reached their own towns, or else they have tried and have been rejected. A few have managed to penetrate, and along the streets we can see their houses made of such coarse materials as zinc. They all have the identical layout and the same somber loneliness. They are cells of a shattered and dispersed cloister where one engenders children, resides, grows old, and dies.

The habit of visiting the neighbors becomes slowly atrophied and friendships are never deep. Certain parties are well attended but each family seems to retain the same place as their house does in relationship to the town. The party is the meeting of the town reduced to its people; the same distances are conserved as between houses. If there is dancing, the couples are attentive to the beat and do not speak. However, they must communicate something, since love has no other opportunity. Women sit in a row of chairs in a distinct sector; men group apart and they drink and tell jokes. When the orchestra composed of violin, flute, and guitar begins to play, the men go toward the women and they are together for the duration of the music. Immediately after it stops playing, all return to their places: women to one side, men to another. The poor women are accustomed to being submissive and to being happy with very little. From this fleeting, superficial, and physical contact sometimes is born the fertile love that begets children. The courtship takes its initial step in a barely perceptible manner; it is curious how women can surmise men's desires in spite of the haughty male demeanor. We could say that the engagement is the most natural result, a necessity inherent in the nature of events. Woman and man love each other from that date, and neither engagement nor matrimony will present major complications. Even adultery, if it should occur, will be a simple incident. Passions, along with virtues and vices, are natural forces. Inside all, and above all, is nature: that unadorned, monotonous, and eternal space. And the human being lives on its surface a two-dimensional existence until death takes him from one village to another, from the house to the earth.

The Physiognomy of Cities

Cities differ among themselves by their climate and their age. An exception is Mar del Plata because of its cosmopolitan nature and proximity to Buenos Aires; it is formed by the prolongation of Florida Street, which extends itself until it is dissolved into waves and hills.

Cities resemble man in life span: fifty years is a long time, to be celebrated as a golden wedding anniversary. But the characteristics imparted by the span of time are reduced to buildings and inhabitants. The architectural styles age prematurely and acquire a certain taste of antiquity, as can be observed in the construction burdened by door frames and railings as well as by fixed standards of size. The soul of all these cities is identical. Spain remains inside as if she were abandoned household goods. Her presence can be felt in the abundance of churches and in the sites occupied by the plazas, the municipality, and the episcopate. Her pervading presence can also be sensed in the spiritual darkness of the nights that submerge all in an unremitting silence, in the taciturnity of people's faces, in the harsh inhospitality of entrance halls, and in the passerby's insincere greeting. Life does not circulate along the streets: it remains encloistered in rooms behind furtive Venetian blinds. From Buenos Aires we go to Rosario, from Rosario to Córdoba, from Córdoba to Santiago or to La Rioja, or to Catamarca, or to Jujuy, or to Salta, and the impression is always that we are seeing Buenos Aires in retrospect, smaller and younger. This same feeling of retrospection is experienced when we travel to La Plata, or Bahía Blanca, or Mercedes. Any city of the interior, stagnated fifty, a hundred, or two hundred years ago, bears a striking resemblance to any other city of the same age. The cities lack soul and authentic expression; instead of searching inward, they direct most efforts toward imitating Buenos Aires. This goal is visible in businesses with oversized premises, in bars at certain hours, in the styles of dress, and in the appearance of buildings. All these are nothing more than stiff tracings of the borrowed, yet they serve as a mold under which squirms uncomfortably a local psyche. The original contribution of those cities, based on environment, on heritage, and on the life experiences of its citizens, is negligible. The loneliness of the fields has penetrated the cities and soaked into the dwellings and men's spirits. The cities have devoured everything around them to assert their existence, and now they are a mixture of suburb, village, and ranch.

The likeness that exists among those cities, even between Tucumán and Santa Rosa de Toay, can be attributed to the soul of the pampa, which weighs over the flattened dwelling, over the lazy pace of the people, over the cautious curiosity so noticeable to the stranger. Every outsider is discovered at the most unpredictable time from imponderable data captured by avid eyes. For the traveler there is no difference among cities except for the change of some external signs and perhaps for the different location of businesses. The width, stone pavement, and infinite perspective of the streets, the color, the faces, the pronunciation, the layout of the city, and the height of buildings are almost identical everywhere. The voyager may notice different states of poverty and varied degrees of attempts to hide it. In all his voyages the traveler will feel like a foreigner in his own country. The people from the south do not regularly travel to the north, and vice versa; very few have become acquainted with their vast, sad, and dear country. Generations of men usually remain confined to small areas. The newly arrived will take many days to establish basic contact with those around him. He is considered a stranger; it is difficult to brush away a reticence of centuries. If the outsider has no money, people will try quickly to get rid of him; after all, those who travel from Buenos Aires to the interior have the obligation to be as rich as those who travel from America to Europe. Even distant relatives view their guest in disgust if they cannot exhibit him as the pride of the family.

All these harsh and insignificant cities where people read day-old papers from Buenos Aires, and which have but a superficial tinge of culture, possess unsurmountable redoubts, shrines with bone pieces from Spain. Not even the bourgeois is allowed into the so-called social circles in which people fill their brains with such preoccupations as genealogical charts. Those circles have been since colonial times sacred enclosures for what is known as "the society." As in Molière's plays, each city has its aristocrats who carry the proper lineage and who direct local politics. Their families owned country estates for generations, but the land was first mortgaged and then lost. The only possession of this aristocracy is their names, which adorn many properties and tracts of land. Any city more than a century old, such as Paraná, Salta, or Córdoba, has in its heart this lofty nucleus which regards the common people with disdain, who in turn show no respect and exhibit no jealousy. Since everyone is engaged in approximately similar pursuits, the men with aristocratic backgrounds may mix together with the populace in business and jobs; but their families do not associate or marry outside their own derisive kind. "La Comtesse d'Escarbagnas"; or, better yet, "George Dandin."

To comprehend the cities we must penetrate the countryside where we may observe them reduced to the basic elements, whether in the form of a provincial town or of a backward little village. These places are cities on a smaller scale where we can see how various currents and feelings crystallize, and we can observe the circumstances that forge the future city and its citizen. The various stages of the growth process are clearly visible in the country's interior. The urban dweller has no great difficulties to overcome if he wishes to become wealthy or prominent; intelligence is a hindrance he quickly learns to ignore if he does not go to the capital. The forces in play are very simple, but for that very reason they are unmanageable for the man who does not consent to be their docile instrument. The countryman is at the physical center of the system of forces, in the midst of where they germinate before gathering momentum and spreading everywhere.

Pioneers Who Halt

As uncomplicated as the countryman may be, he is more complex than the simple world surrounding him. He may not amount to much, but in his environment he is a demigod. Within himself he finds powers that help him subdue everything around him; as occurs with a child, he judges on the basis of values of existence, of being or not being. At the top of his scale of values is life, then wealth, and then power. Even the most uncomplicated being, when transported to this primitive environment, awakens his dormant personality and develops astonishing powers of conquest; but the conquered matter and the tools cast aside are always incorporated into the swell created by the exercise of very restricted qualities. The countryman is an entity that lives and wants and is able to influence the immediate environment. It is a shame that his aspirations are limited, because instead of bursting forth in a quest for immortality, all he has achieved is to become the most adequate animal in his surroundings. By collaborating with the environmental forces he temporarily dominates them, but they eventually swallow him because he is nothing more than a toy.

Feelings analogous to the ferocious and uncastrated ego engender in the hills the characteristic love for a piece of ground, for native tradition, and for heroic myth. The plains incubate a self-esteem that is projected toward all possessions, a rebellion against order imposed from outside and against the law. The town's rich man is always cunning, and with secret liking he adopts the brawler. His dissidence with a purely substantive context prepares him to defend all that he fancies against an intrusion into his world, where he maneuvers without obstacles. He surrounds himself with forces related by affinity and is inclined to disperse those of an opposite electric charge. As a catalytic agent, he changes a certain number of social components and nullifies the action of others; in this way he has the support of the whole town and he is the representative man.

At the beginning it was necessary to fight by means of one's labor against a medium charged with hostility. The town and its inhabitants kept inside them the virulence that was lost in surrounding things. They vanquished solitude by saturating their homes with loneliness and anchoring their souls to despair.

The mountaineer has surrendered and lives in an absence of everything; he barely has sufficient will to go on day after day. Since he lacks everything, whatever he possesses is sufficient. Through his senses, he is only conscious of a bare existence; and he survives by believing in a superstition embodied by a scapulary and an image of the venerated saint. On the other hand, the dweller of our plains, where the fortune as abundant as sun and water acts as a magnet for the bravest, lives with the tension of a spring and the strain of a cocked trigger. Our plain is the levigation of the old mountains. The plainsman has put life in his own hands, and we already know that the hand is one of the oldest weapons. Solitude directs the individual into the center of that infinite circumference of the plain and converts him into the key of that absurd firmament. Solitude produces in him a diastolic feeling toward that which lives immersed in his ignorance and a systolic movement that halts him by representing coercion and demanding discipline. In identical situations, he may hide and crouch or run away, depending on the mixture of imponderable psychic molecules. The inborn curiosity of the animal of prey is latent in him; a strong desire to explore and prevail inclines him to search for details by which to gauge and measure the strength of forces he sees and hears. He leads an alert and unblinking existence. He is interested in the number and size of things, ideas, precautions, and risks. His only motive when inquiring into the life of a neighbor is to invade and penetrate a world he suspects is similar but that impedes him by its mystery. The meekness with which he inquires is the same primary movement of insurgent vitality that in the child crops out simultaneously with the stereoscopic capacity of vision, when it is able to isolate bulks in planes of distance and attempts to grasp them. The childlike soul of the mature man of the Argentine countryside, and of others similar to it, reaches its limits and halts, transforming impulses into a curiosity complex often mistaken for an ingenuous self-surrender. He is as curious as an animal in solitude; when he appears to become interested in insignificant points he is scrutinizing us, and the timid eye that looks at our feet is in fact carefully exploring us.

Because of his disposition and the need to establish relations with the world, he has a tendency to live inside other people's dwellings and bodies, in a manner of speaking. All the attempts to establish a deep human relationship become frustrated because he is a solitary entity. Even what is beautiful becomes transformed in his subconscious into imaginary dangers that require defensive or offensive maneuvers. The question "What are you doing?" is a depredatory tentacle that is to be dodged with the answer "We are getting along."

But that subconsciously defensive social reaction is not impregnated with love, since his fellow being is only of interest as an unknown. To the contrary, it provides new variants for the theme of distancing, such as the exaggerated distrust evidenced in a natural mutism of the countryman and in a lack of respect shown toward any intimacy. The personality offers a harsh outward appearance when it is attacked in a head-on assault. The plainsman is as skillful in hiding his personality as he is in marking an incision in the joints of cattle. The brawler is representative of this medium.

The Brawler

The brawler is the people's atrophied organ, a summary of an epoch and executor for the Indian. He floats without being influenced by any of the forces that condition the existence and govern the succession of beings. He is made up of the past and the future. He extracts from within himself reasons for acting, and nothing that surrounds him teaches or modifies him. He withdraws into the skin of his temperament, and in the manner of an animal or a philosopher he obeys his own closed cryptogamous system. Lacking in any didactic or conventional ornament, he may appear to be close to the schematic type as, for example, a dry tree may represent the essence of the tree itself; without doubt he possesses a superlative dose of maleness. Lacking flexibility and ambivalence, he does not contain even a trace of the marionette that lives in all of us. Hence proceeds the irremediable seriousness of his gestures. He truly lives his own drama, conceited, as if he were its author.

He is a roaming bandit, without affiliation, without accomplices, reconciled to tolerate up to a point the conventional order of things; and from every angle it can be seen that a male logic governs his person. He is fearless by inclination and has no relations with society, only with himself. He does not participate as a member of any group and is not responsible to anyone; he is a fellow man without fellow men. He is masculine, totally amputated from the

feminine and infantile; he is not influenced by the world nor does
he work for the world. That is why he is called the male—the
macho.[1] As a consequence, he is a sterile being that does not engender and that consumes itself by its own action, independent from
the context of social activities. He could well exist on any island.
An individual and not a representative being, a symbol and not a
man, he incarnates an idea and not an ideal: Hagen rather than
Siegfried. The hero follows a parabolic trajectory, and, just like the
wild beast with its ineluctable central solitude, he concentrates his
movement in a siphonlike whirlpool. Since his actions lack social
projections, he overwhelms all with his body. He knows of no way
to influence others except by physical coercion. He kills and causes
fear without trying; his language of actions ignores premeditation
and repentance. He is never satisfied or fulfilled, because he does
not become impregnated: it is as if he started anew with each deed.
An unquenchable itching spurs him to graft himself onto things,
since he knows no other method of interacting. He considers the
woman as simply another being; he does not pity her or scorn her
—he uses her. Material possession excuses him from paternal responsibility; his passionless marital act has no transcendence. He
is a cruel and passing ghost and an inferior being because he does
not project himself. If in addition to the zoologically pure quality
of braveness we could combine a social awareness, a purpose of action, and a notion of duty we would have a chief, and in old age a
patriarch. But nature has deprived him of organs to relate to and to
comprehend what forms the vital horizon of the carnivore.

The brawler is a solitary being, the only-begotten of the bad
gaucho, the man in a beast's territory, surrounded by his own figure. His natural habitat is the small town where he is a force from

---

[1] As with all other facets of his personality, the brawler's courage is of a
sexual essence. That is to say, there is contained within the brawler a condition of virility, which is organically expressed in the language of men. The
event by which courage proves itself is less a heroic deed than simple manliness—it usually refers to the conquest of a woman. Thus, courage acquires
the ferociousness of a clawed animal in heat.

the countryside. He circulates without greeting anyone and does not attack if he is not provoked. Wickedness is in him a natural state, just as abundance of hair or foul smell are a normal state of nature in a mountain animal. He has the absolute responsibility for his acts. Everything he does is irremediable and could not have happened in another way: it is fate. He deserves respect, as does anything that cannot vary regardless of what transpires. In the secret liking with which he is looked upon, there is a certain esteem for the inexorable powers that have settled in him. And there is also the secret sympathy for the destructive.

In a badly constituted society or one constituted with discontent, the antisocial element represents a large part of the repressed feelings of the society: the latent society. This is why the brawler's badness sometimes acquires a heroic and an appealing character. This wretched being provides an outlet through which the people take out their vengeance. With his courage and open violence and with his silent gait he imparts to the honest mass of people their own reconquered sense of power and protest, stifled by the sentiments of order and justice.

In almost all towns there exists at least one of these men, a specter of a dead yesterday. He is a fugitive from justice but walks about in freedom. The stay of proceedings negotiated for him voluntarily by the chieftain converts him into a personage whose function is made official, and he is surreptitiously integrated into the public administration; he circulates with the endorsement of the tribunals. Although he does not brag about his killings and dislikes to talk about them, he is above the law, above leniency and fear.

Naturally, he is poor and knows only the occupations of the countryside. Often he lives off a loose woman, who above all admires in him the male soul. He is reduced then to a parasite of the bawdy house, where his jurisdiction is indisputable. The prostitute takes upon her this financial and social burden, thereby freeing the decent people from it; the money with which she maintains him would have proceeded from commerce in the form of tributes. That beast has enough to spend on food, dress, and vices; he rarely demands payment in cash. However, he is provided with a line of credit that he uses prudently by taking only what he needs; he never settles an account.

The police can do nothing against him, and, paradoxically, they imitate him in all that is possible, since he is considered a model of integrity, of righteousness, and of absolute authority without ostentation. His predecessors were some old Indian chiefs, and Moreira is his literary and romantic replica: *Don Segundo Sombra* is his *Cantar del Mío Cid*.

As an inborn product of a small town or of a rapidly growing new one, he requires the proximity of the countryside and an outlying ranch where he can live. He degenerates in contact with submissive beings. In the cities and larger towns he decays into a rhetorical, political, and bureaucratic protector. And he is no longer the son of the bad gaucho but of the poor foreigner who longs to find the village in the city.

Hostilities of Solitude

The vast plains are dotted by small settlements accidentally peopled by beings of diverse origins who eventually come together and have children. These settlements, instead of becoming more cohesive as they grow more compact, ferment sentiments of dissolution, which by their superficial nature do not create long-lasting hates. But the pampa is a place of dispersion. Because solitude is a stable and constant state contrary to all will, it prevails over work, which is a precarious state and not profoundly coordinated with any social, unified, or mystical plan. A house is erected to serve as shelter for the duration of the task, but water and wind are eternal. The plain does not provide solid building materials, and the people who agglutinate in towns are there in the hope of enriching themselves quickly. Instead of making a fortune, they leave children; the children abandon the town and it reverts to the same type of inhabitant. Of all the elements that integrate the vital formula of these towns, the only common factors are the egoism and disaffection of its inhabitants. In this sense, our towns are psychological fortresses. The forces that previously were alert to outside dangers have now subsided and withdrawn and are used against the core. By no means would the inhabitants wish to eternalize the present and to begin anew. They are there because they coincide in what they are looking for, and their common purpose is to remain until they are able to reap the reward. They manage to accumulate a few material possessions and thus become fixed in an aimless drive in search of something. They are trapped by property while their uneasy souls float like ghosts between things and beings. They constitute live archipelagos surrounded by indifference and hostility, masters of a fortune that isolates them by casting suspicion and arousing envy. They live like guests in their own houses and their children pursue a morally emancipated life, as children of solitude do. They engage in studying and then remain in Buenos Aires, ashamed of their parents and their names. The native views with disgust the lowliness to which the foreigner stoops to enrich himself; the foreigner does not understand that the native may enrich himself without feeling despoiled; poor and ignorant, the native is still a descendant of conquerors and colonists. He judges that his passport was the license to triumph.

Those towns are extremely sad and man's acclimatization is inconceivable in conditions of such spiritual celibacy. There is no need to single out any town; they are all identical and differ only in name and number of inhabitants. Their configuration is the same, and people and houses remind one of birds resting after a long flight. As soon as the newcomer acquires material possessions, the door shuts behind him and he cannot escape the jaillike confinement of the town with its walls of countryside. Old people leave or die and are displaced by the new generation. People barely know each other by name but they are well acquainted with each other's wealth. They keep up a process of renovation as if each generation had to begin anew; nothing lasting is transmitted from the past, not even memories.

Rancor and conflict saturate those towns of floating beings, and it is difficult to unite people in spirit and, in fact, to create a solidary achievement. Businessmen manipulate funds to ruin their neighbors; the sudden fall of a rich farmer brings a ray of sunshine and a fresh breath to those dark souls. They are not worse than other men—they simply are the way they are. In these places one certainly should not hope to find an artist or a good writer or any type of idealist or even a bird lover. The souls of artists sink in miserable bodies and lives. All those towns have a share of useless people and of hopeless drunks who swear and exhibit their genital organs to little children. At times we see them leaning against a wall, wasted by alcohol, and attempting to sing a tune from their school days. Such is the deformation of the spirits shown by God in the song. As soon as some hidden clarity crops out in one of these creatures and his spirit suffocates in the excess of coarse sordidness, he takes flight as would a poor disconsolate bird, never to return.

In the towns one still lives with a weapon at the waist. Disillusionment, weariness, resentment, and want weigh heavily upon the souls; a diffuse uneasiness guards against something invisible in expectation of imaginary aggressions. The political parties inflame the spirits to the highest degree; the electoral struggles are for those minds mere calisthenic exercises and nothing causes astonishment, to the point that murder and suicide are commented upon in a jovial tone. Crouched, scenting the secret news that spreads with fury, they seize upon scandal to sink fangs into their victims. In this way they earn their daily bread of raw meat. Politics has in them a total and vital meaning.

Rivalry becomes a permanent state, normal and unnoticed; the naming of a doctor, of a commissioner, or of a candidate for some post is a mere pretext under which the muffled beast manifests itself without scruples. However, so much cruelty and so much hate doubtless result from an inclination toward congeniality and toward justice that finds its path blinded. Hate is only withered love. Because of such an allotropy, to assume someone's defense is to fire a weapon: and joy is almost always declared by firing off shots in the air. Many groups are formed, such as development societies, athletic centers, and cultural circles; but they all degenerate in committees or dissolve completely because rivalry is more powerful than the desire for solidarity. Newspapers are founded that are at the service of discord, since they are children of solitude. Poorly written, born of rancor or of ambition, these papers do not entertain their readers with informative material but instead charge the columns with useless dynamite. Their virulence is the lack of exercise, a language of constant opposition. It is useless to search for anything other than diatribe in these newspapers composed of four or eight disreputable pages. They defend the interests of the town and their editors live sentenced to death. The editor ignores how to defend without attacking, as if political parties existed only as adversaries of an ideal. The men in power take advantage of those cavalry charges and use them to defend their persons and not the ideals, which they lack, because they are also children of solitude. When the verdict is carried out and the editor falls gunned down, the national representative arrives to assist at the burial, where he delivers an infectious speech so that the wound may never heal. After the large newspapers publish the story, oblivion sets in slowly. The deceased formed part of a guild; he was not a leader of the press but a journalist, an isolated member of a body of organic unity. Because of all this, his sacrifice was, as a deputy said, "a tribute rendered to the cause of civilization." He fell in the town fortress, fighting against the specter of the Indian.

The animal is much more resigned in its isolation. It lives enclosed by the skin, and its blood lacks the perverting germs of altruism and congeniality. It fears or attacks without expecting aggression at every moment, without silently and laboriously plotting vengeance. During heat it couples, defends the litter, and then returns to solitude.

The remoteness of the towns and the violent emulsion of passions are fragments in the imagery of the plain where the Indian enjoys a posthumous victory over the ethnically weaker anarchic force that displaced him. Those new forms are redoubts against old violences that infiltrate through the porous earth walls. When the force deep within lies dormant, speech is timid and imprecise. When it awakens, the questioning is ringing and charged with purpose as it reaches the depths of the soul.

Distrust

The inhabitants of those towns which I have
known are ingenuous and distrustful. They distrust because they
are ignorant, and in their appearance and gestures there is a tinge
of unpleasant aftertaste from the hostile solitude surrounding
them. Their courtesy is cautious and they use ceremonial formulas
for greetings and farewells in a manner that must have been in use
for centuries. They are incomplete beings without a precise psychological shape, with only completeness and unity in their bodies.
The soul is full of sterile zones, of wild vegetations. Even what they
know is ignorance; even honesty is an adornment out of style.
They do not live in the fullness of health if they are healthy, or in
the plenitude of intelligence if they are intelligent, or in the abundance of wealth if they are wealthy. They lack the full development by which molds are filled to their proper size and robustness.
Generations ago they were cast upon the place where they now
live, and they seem to hide a secret rancor. They look into us for a
secret motive for mockery; they examine us until they find the vulnerable point and then return to the tranquil conscience of the
plenitude of their being. All that we know, all that we morally are,
all the effort we expend to show without shame the little that we
have—all this means nothing.

The inhabitants lack precisely what the complete being has in
excess: the only part that leaves a favorable balance when we compare what we should have been to what we in effect have become
in spite of everything. This positive value passes unnoticed. They
lack well-being, comfort, generosity, forbearance, a feeling of
achievement, and the understanding of united and harmonious
groups. They developed without experiencing all the modulations
in loving and living. They know many things that the men of the
cities have already forgotten; they believe in what no one believes,
and they distrust because of the same motives that induce them to
love. They remain as dauntless as that nature, as that countryside,
as that animal which they keep, as that town in which they live.

The inhabitants want to enjoy themselves and do not know how;

they want to love and are grotesque because naked sex is apparent even in the most delicate feints. Solitude has defrauded them and taught them lies. They confuse names and dates and any answer satisfies them. They read newspapers and magazines and are more or less up to date on what is happening; but they lack the feeling of continuity and do not grasp the harmony of the many voices that transmit information, thereby confusing the news. They know how to speak and they only think words. Because of this, events that transpired two or three days before have for them the same distance as does for us a page from Thucydides, which we believe we understand but no longer do. Radio brings them the disconnected sounds from the throats of modern cosmopolitan cities, and the dress they order is of a style long ago. They admire what is detestable and they ignore the rest. The big newspapers publish whole pages for our country people and devote special sections to them. It is for them that the committing of crimes is repugnantly described in full detail; it is for them that we distill powerful alcoholic beverages and write and declaim shoddy verses. In that way the great city collaborates with the pampa; ideas spread, in spite of the immense distances, and become diffused in the process. The author may forget about his provincial readers and the musician may believe that they do not exist; but they arrive silently from the countryside, stand at their sides, and demand the payment of tribute to the land. Images become deformed through the distances, and the identification with the language is not sufficient to assure the identical meaning of words; in this sense language keeps us separated.

The Poor

The circulation of false coins that are minted for the interior constitutes spiritual poverty. The rich voices of music, the emotion of plastic arts, and the art of clear thought have there a lesser value than false money and cheap jewelry. The poor man dreams his rich dreams. Solitude is poverty. Even if they should possess land and cattle, they are poor; even if they should own businesses and properties, they are poor. Those goods signify the sacrifice of their entire personalities and the withdrawal into a distorted medium where feelings, ideas, and values are deformed. Their fortune is not a key to penetrate the world but a fortress to become isolated. They have withdrawn with their prey deep into the interior where they lie low, afraid. That fortune which is only wealth, and is not evident in art and superfluous luxuries, isolates them from others. It is not a means for allowing further development but an excess that inspires pity. The poor man who sleeps on a park bench is immensely richer in comparison to the wealthy rancher whose money has the sign of solitude. When the rich man comes to the city, people spy on him and scheme to steal his money because he is not worthy of what he possesses. A surgical operation deprives him of a chunk of the filthy pile of gold that he amassed; a lawsuit sweeps away with leagues of land; a friend takes away the rest. His wealth is uncomfortable in the presence of the poor and of the truly rich. He could enter the world and the world would be at his feet, but he is unable to do so. Everything around him has its fauces opened with covetousness and mockery. He cannot spend that fortune which is the price of his life and that of his wife and children. He has devoured everything and that is why the world threatens to devour him, to recover what was removed. Naturally, there are also the real poor, the poor who have nothing, not even the security of their poverty. They also have their vague hope, although it is subdued by misfortune and indifference. We have cast out poverty into the interior so that it will not deface the city streets or interrupt a cinematographic dream with its vehement cry.

Poverty still somehow provides security when everything surrounding the poor is firmly bound to the ground and constitutes the miserable community of one who possesses nothing. In the old Catholic countries the beggar hides something from God; here, he used to ride horseback and solicit with the exigency of the chosen ones, without bothering to dismount or to thank.

We could define the poor man in the metropolis as a citizen who uses the whole city as a house. We could also say that an old man in his hut is the desert itself. Isolated poverty is worse because it is reduced to itself and lacks even the social assistance of crowded buildings. The poor of the interior are beings isolated by solitude and by what they do not have; the ties that unite man with fellow man are broken. Among us, the poor man is a deserter, a fugitive who causes shame and has no right to be the possessor of nothing. He is our father who has worked for fifty years and owns nothing, and we are ashamed. Remember those other poor who leave behind their homes and families and, with a bag on their shoulders, wander from one town to another, following roads or trains. They are searching for work. They are not vagabonds; they are workers. They do not have their poverty, because they are laborers without bread—hungry with calloused hands. I know of nothing more solitary, more gloomy than these wanderers of the pampa who cover enormous distances and pass one by one, distant, removed. They camp at the foot of embankments and then it can be seen that they carry in their bags leftovers from home: kitchen utensils, blankets to sleep on, plates to eat off. They sleep together like animals because the night is too powerful for the soul and the grief; but next morning they leave quietly, one by one. It is as if God is lacking in their persons.

In the country, poverty loses its aspect of social failure and appears to be individual incompetence, the punishment for a mysterious crime. Since there is no guilt, society is exempt. What do the small farmer, the field laborer, and the fruit gatherer have to do with the poor man? They give him shelter, and such is the distance between the haves and the have-nots that it is unclear who should reproach whom when the poor man leaves. The indigent in our interior is much more similar to the animal than to the rich man. The animal is poor in a true way: it lacks all that is superfluous, both outside and inside. It does not have anything; it does not ask for anything and does not worry about death. Poverty in the open air is a personal accident and therefore an unknown, a threat. It cannot be perceived how poverty or wealth was produced by pressure of the surroundings, according to the functioning of a mechanism that segregates success and failure. Those poor country people, who live on tea and biscuits, breathe and procreate poverty. Since there is no concern for them, they are becoming more numerous and isolated. When these people lived in their solitude they developed a system within the environment without being able to relate to a better state. Distance maintained them cut off from the rest of the world. Yet they were close to everything because the points of reference to which their life threads were tied were the hut, the tree, the well, the dog, the horse, and the family. But when the village and the hut, the tree, the well, the dog, and the horse joined with the great distant city, they became part of another large system; everything was put in motion and tranquility vanished. Distances and differences between the local world and the immense outside world increased the solitude of the poor man. Everything that serves to unite, such as telegraph, trains, and cars, separated him more. The metropolis began to drag the country to itself; and the poor man was placed farther away with each passing day, on the boundaries of the primitive world.

6 SOLITUDE OF WORLD AND MAN

World and Man

Except as a curiosity, the tombs and ceme-
teries in the Río Negro or in the valley of Calchaquí or in Campana
that attest to prehistoric cities tell us nothing. The Indian is par
excellence the man without history. Remains of cities and of cemeteries have stayed united to a place by terrestrial signs and not to
time by vital marks. The Indian has no past, because he has no future; dead or alive, he merely occupies the space filled by his body;
like the animal, even in a developed society he carries on a life that
does not surpass the limits of his senses. He is born and he dies clandestinely. The cemeteries, the few remaining ruins of dwellings,
the vessels and utensils, the weapons and adornments, all of which
had names, belong to archeology; they are simply a fixed past.
They form the epilogue of another series that no longer holds interest and that is left on the margin of history, outside its net as a
branch of prosimians that develops at the fringes of humanity.

History takes note when man works and operates coordinately

and especially if that coordinated work and way of operation are in general accord with man's style of working and operating. Therefore, history is what acquires independent life in man's hands and what exists so strongly it forces man to continue his existence, taking into account the social suprastructure. The lateral beings, who do not collaborate in that unity of forms, fall into the realm of ethnography: they and their remains are nature. They lack that power of effortless evocation which in its intimate sense resuscitates and revives the past within oneself. Neither can the fossil tell us anything, since it belongs to another order of existence even more removed, although in the same tangential direction. The fossil tells us the history of the earth and even the age of the earth rather than the history of the disappeared species. In its quality of fossil it is an atomic fragment that is of less interest for the phylogeny of its species than for natural history in the broad sense. It is a fragment, common or unique, which by itself only has meaning for paleontology. It tells of a victory of the all-powerful forces of nature over the weak and fragile forces of life, whose meaning is in the struggle with nature. There was a fracture in favor of the earth and against the vertebrate. The animal that disappears with the total extinction of the species supposes a parenthesis in the definite control of the unconscious cosmos. This is exactly the opposite of history, which not only is concerned with happenings and changes but also wishes to salvage from the evolution an eternal quantum, to outlive itself. Through the fossil the earth shows us its brutal victory over a being temporarily at variance with it. Such a being was a fleeting episode in the large monologue of matter accidentally alive. And as in the stone tier of the building in ruins, man's will is affirmed against the horizontal force of nature; so too in the petrified bone is affirmed all the inert weight that has crushed him. Nature has defeated all resistance against its laws and the zoologic remains are a matter of position, worth less than a cadaver; they are joined to earth by their capacity as heavenly bodies. The fossil is a heavenly body.

In the evolutionary process there were deep ruptures between those beings and the ones that live today; these disruptions left them isolated and without bonds in the present living world. They are solitude in the bone of stone. But those fossil species which still have at least one representative enter into the history of life and save their ancestors from being submerged into the history of the planet. The Indian is a participant of history although he is closer to the geographic and planetary condition; he forms the history of the bastards, or the apocryphal history. His cemetery is an erudite and ethnographic remainder. Its logical location should be in a museum showcase. He fits into the chain as a chapter in the biography of the veterbrate. The ruins of the Aztec and Inca empires and those of Guatemala and Colombia tell us less than the most modest countryside cemetery and much less than the handwoven fabric. It is not the distance in time that matters; it is the resemblance of our destiny to that of those who lived here. The other matters are the province of science and erudition. History cannot be for us anything that is outside the trajectory of the meaning of our existence. On this soil without human past we are the first settlers of the world.

That loneliness of the landscape implies another solitude from which it is in part derived. Even the most infertile land can give the impression of being rich and habitable if it had been so in another time. The natural aridity is joined by that barrenness felt only by the soul, but felt very deeply, when under one's feet there is nothing but the physical support of the world. The solitude that spreads through the soul with unmotivated anguish and subtracts human interest from the spectacle of panoramic beauty exists because of a lack of history. In those regions nothing has happened that speaks deeply to man, and consequently man goes unnoticed and, as Spengler imagines, always impelled forward. There, a man is alone, isolated as if he were in the field of vision of a miscroscope or a telescope. Whatever he does, he begins for the last time. In the Colorado, Frank used to feel the vibrations of three vanished and superimposed civilizations. Barrés also expressed that uninterrupted contiguity of the prairies of Santa Odilia as the "silent will of its dead." When we cross our fields and our villages with their inexpressive names, we feel like transient beings without a past and we are even disgusted by the ostentation of empty and insignificant names. The names of our forefathers and of historical events still cause them to be recent. In other parts of the world, men carry toponymic names of places, cities, or things; but here the towns and villages acquire the names of persons. In many cases they are anonymous towns, unbaptized, with only a nickname.

Almost all the names of those towns could be exchanged for others and they would still continue to be equally adequate or equally inappropriate. When we read the town names on railway station platforms or see them in catalogues, we realize that there is no spirit of linguistic or moral unity. We may see the surname of a foreign soldier who conducted campaigns and who does not even appear in the history manuals, yet his name is dragged around. Or we may note a name, of another origin, that belonged to a peddler who became rich and received a decoration from his country. Still another name may express something in Guaraní or Quechua or Tehuelche, but we do not know what it is nor do we care—it is only a word. The names of those towns are like abstract numbers because their designation does not arise from an inner force or from the depths of surrounding life or from some geographic peculiarity of the land.

Our fathers knew those people now evoked by the signs in railway station platforms and mentioned in guidebooks: they were the same as they are today, dead from death itself. The owner of the plots where a village was being started would give a hectare for the square, a thousand square varas for the church, a square of suitable dimensions for the cemetery, and the stretch from semaphore to semaphore for the railroad. With this he would acquire typographic immortality at a modest price. But the inhabitants rarely know whom the signs commemorate or what the names signify, and they do not care. From one village to another there may be thirty kilometers, and two different languages may be spoken. The inhabitants never visualized another way; they remain far removed from the lives, the works, and the geographic accidents that may unite or separate peoples within a nation or between two nations.

With the name permanently affixed, the village remains anonymous, since it is nothing more than a conglomerate of houses and a number of people psychologically in transit. Inhabited and maintained in high tension by passions, hates, and feelings of dull unity, those towns are the same as the archeologic remains that we now consider as detours in the path of humanity, although less authentic and less reliable. If any seismic catastrophe were to bury them, they would be left as ethnographic fragments in a vast common ossuary. And their name would be given to them later.

Ancient Solitude

Our territory is very old and very new; the primitive world of solitude is ancient, and the recent world is the present one of greatness and servitude. The present world may be circumscribed in the zone of heavy rainfall or the zone of cattle and cereals. From the borders that which belongs to the white man and human conquest begins to decline until it penetrates into the untouched planet, the tomb of the Indian. Within our territory we also have the extreme orogenic accidents, ranging from the most ancient, such as Puna de Atacama, to the most recent, such as the Andes.

Puna de Atacama and the group of brasilides are pre-Cambrian, contemporaries of the Canadian shield, of the Finnish-Scandinavian shield, and of the Siberian bulk; we can precisely locate on them the vertices of the tetrahedron of Lowthian Green. We can touch there the dermis of our heavenly body with its tectonic and ecliptic mysteries in the deposition of huge masses and in the folding of slopes. With the gondwanides and the patagonides we reach the Paleozoic, almost in the style of a pure Cambrian-Silurian. Wind and water have eroded the summits, but the eye inevitably reconstructs the broken line of the sides and then outlines in the sky the profile of sidereal times. The Andes, which reach into the Cretaceous, were seen during their formation by eyes as complete as ours. The center and the north sank as far as Brazil, and the flooring of the pampa was formed.

Between the mountains and the plateaus, which are the dominion of the Indian, and the plains, the dominion of the white man, intercede entire periods from the Tertiary era, just as India, Egypt,

China, and Europe are interposed between the aborigine and the white man.

The ocean that once covered almost all of the continent's area has left traces in various spots: wavering dunes that invade arable lands and extensive salt beds that are scattered throughout the territory. The working tools are dulled and the arm softened by the territory still within the realm of the ocean. With the mixture of salt and sand the landscape acquires primitive and biblically lugubrious overtones. Teasels, opuntiae, and numerous specimens of halophilous flora defend their solitude from imaginary enemies who succumbed many centuries ago. The prick of a spine evokes the sole leatherlike skin of a gigantic edentate that no longer exists. In those wastes rose biblical cities; they were founded where the pasture overcame the nitrate: San Luis, Córdoba, La Rioja, Catamarca, San Juan, Mendoza, San Rafael, Santiago del Estero. In the end they became surrounded by the desert, and it is necessary to work and irrigate tirelessly to prevent the simple phenomenon of osmosis by which the desert becomes aroused from centuries of sleep and penetrates the streets, leaving the houses submerged in salt and sand.

The foundation, the basic scheme, is the mountain. Below the pampa is the mountain reduced to plain. Chaco and Misiones, which seem to submerge their roots into the mud of Genesis, have a rocky base. The very ancient continental nuclei of Brasilia subsided from the north as far as the Colorado River; the centers of Patagonia dropped from the Colorado River to the south. As a result of these sinkings, prior to the Devonian period, the immense stone platform that almost constitutes the totality of Argentine territory remained under water during the Oligocene and under loess during the Quaternary. The sinking of the Chaco gave the pampa a continuous structure as far as the Patagonian plateaus. The wide mass of Atacama remains, and the Puna de Atacama breaks the cortical geologic unity. Together with Patagonia and Pampa del Monte, Atacama is the land of the primate. When the intruder occupied the fertile plains, the Indian was exiled and he ventured into those lands. When the Indian was definitively repelled, he sought refuge in the vast neutral zone, in the bosom of a world that had not experienced life. Europe penetrated to the very edges of the sedimentary lands, and that is where the frontier between America and Europe is delimited. In that other zone lie the oldest known fossils: petroleum deposits, metalliferous mines, and ancient xerophilous plants. Now it is the world of the Indian and the refuge of primitive forces whose breath spreads imperceptibly throughout the cities, demolishing walls and scattering weeds in preparation for the advance. The Indian confined himself in these regions to die because that land is death.

Seventh Solitude

To contemplate a map of the world is to look into the depths of oneself, to see the outline of man's history. It is to see Earth's skeleton. What one takes notice of is unutterable, meaningless for thought and sensibility, tucked deep and far away in the recesses of the spirit. The intuitive understanding of our land on the map extricates the mind from the context of reason that binds us to the world in our condition as spiritual beings. This diversion of the mind produces the dread of solitude, never felt through voluntary isolation or by means of imaginative ideas. He who does not experience that organic and cosmic sensation of fatalism while examining the terrestrial globe as a heavenly body, with its solid masses as a foundation for an olympic race and life as a momentary phenomenon in the existence of a heavenly body, cannot understand the true destiny of the world and of man. Nor can he understand the working of biologic forces as they determine the regions in which life will flourish or become stagnated forever. That glacial impression which penetrates through the eye, which is the organ for feeling space, is sharpened when we pass from the Northern to the Southern Hemisphere. To travel is somewhat akin to being in the same place occupied by the body, but to have the sphere in hand is to look at it with God's eyes. The Northern Hemisphere appears as a homogeneous map of life. The Russian steppes and the desert of India and China resemble scaly formations of the planet that are intercalated in a thinking and aching pulp. Everywhere else, especially on the borders of the Mediterranean, in the warm area of the northwest, and in East Asia, life is rich and lively; compact existence abounds.

If we draw a circle using as a radius the largest possible quantity of earth, we include Europe, Asia, Africa, and three-fourths of America; the island of Dumet would be the geometric center. The first men and women appeared very near, at the banks of the Mancha canal. Inverting the sphere, we would have a hemisphere of nine parts of water and one part of land made up of Australia, New Zealand, New Guinea, the Sunda archipelago, and the remaining fourth of America, with Argentina and Chile in their entirety. Its geometric center would fall close to the Warekauri islands in the middle of the Pacific Ocean. This hemisphere of water is the planet's oldest, the Silurian world. Europe is the human foundation; there are nineteen probabilities in favor of and one against the chance that for a solid point on the planet there should correspond an antipode of water. On the other hand, the Tropic of Capricorn closes a morphologic cycle; in its band lie the most copious fossil deposits; some specimens of species older than these fossils are still alive. Patagonia, which until the Eocene formed one territory with the polar land, is in geologic concert with the south of Africa, Tasmania, and New Zealand. There is also a surprising identity of structural forms between parts of the pampa and certain areas of British Asia and regions of South Africa. The bone structures of beings that populated the tropics are in correlation. Analogous forces have worked in accord and have exerted their influence on the beings of the land and water hemispheres. The tracks of Neptunian work are still evident; the hernias and scars may still be seen. The struggle between man and world is more difficult here than in the earthly hemisphere, which is what we feel deep in our soul.

Patagonia, particularly as far as Río Negro but including the entire plain we know by the Indian name of Pampa, is also the bed of the ocean, although it is uncovered, harsh, and bitter. It is an extremity that begins to submerge from Tierra del Fuego and that very possibly was united to the antarctic mass. Later, when the waters that covered most of the territory receded, there were more species—now extinguished—in the thermal zones than in any other part of the world. The climates changed and they must have emigrated through Arquelenis, if it existed, or they may have followed the ecliptic, still unfixed. Other species, the Cetacea and the Pinnipedia, survived by adjusting their organisms to the oceanic forces that still predominate: the foot changed into the fin.

Throughout these lands of the Atlantic and the Pacific it would not be possible to contemplate the map of the world without feeling ancestral chills along the marrow, which is where the geologic ages have left inscribed the episodes of the human form. The eye comprehends better than the brain that this part of the world, over which shines the sky richest in stars and nebulae, is at the boundaries of the planet. The men who inhabit the southern extremity of the globe live in Ushuaia. It is a penitentiary; the heavens are its closest neighbor.

The Dominions of Water

From the Atlantic to the mountain range, Patagonia climbs in expanses of land that form the "arid pampas," with deep valleys that descend as much as one thousand feet. The raising of these lands was intermittent. During the Eocene, the masses of water that receded from the west clashed with those which the ocean nudged upward. The Santa Cruz formation begins with alternated layers of marine water and pluvial water. There still remain a few lakes with brackish water, geological reminiscences of a long oceanic period; these impart the basic inflection to the southern and western parts of the Republic. Those accidents which characterize the struggle of the waters in the peculiar southern topography preserve in the plains traces of the convulsion by which, farther away, the Andes rose from the sea. Deep hollows, gorges, and ravines are vestiges of that frustrated attempt at insurrection. These remnants show the losing posture. They subsist as scars that are so fresh the present seems fused with another epoch. At the bottom of the canyons lie the river beds of very ancient rivers that ceased to flow thousands of years ago, much before the hominoids sought protection from the icy winds under the shells of glyptodons. Going upstream along the course of those diluvial and extinguished rivers, we reach the central plateaus of Patagonia, sterile and interminable. The littoral, in ample strips of beach that separate the ocean as it awaits reprisal from the forces that defeated it, is made of sand and saltpeter, like the salt pits of Pampa del Monte.

Life in those places demands a sacrifice that perhaps an individual could fulfill in actions of supreme resignation, but the species has to reject that land which belongs to the ocean and not to man.

On those plateaus there are no large birds, or large animals, or trees. The beings that populated these areas have been absorbed, incorporated into the land where they lie. The fossils indicate that conditions favorable to Quaternary life ended many centuries ago, and life has become invaginated in the Cenozoic. That landscape, which is now more or less as it was in the Eocene and upper Cretaceous, conserves its fauna inside.

There also were birds, enormous birds, with skulls more voluminous than those of horses.[1] They had already disappeared when the *Homo pampaeus* emigrated. Today no birds fly across the dense skies dotted with invisible knives that wound the flesh with incisions of cold air. The total absence of noise creates a vacuum that covers the eardrums with a film of deafness.

The Forces of Solitude

1. On this Eocene world there blows a wind that seems to emanate from the depths of geologic eras. It is a persistent wind, very severe, charged with cosmic ozones and chemi-

---

[1] "Non-flying birds and birds of prey, which tested their strength against the biggest mammals of the time" (Ameghino). There were giants whose names evoked mythological monsters: Brontornis, Eucallornis, Liornis, and Phororhacos. They were birds with short, thick, and unfeathered wings that were useless for flight and only served for balance during a run. They were like those other giants from the pampas: megatheres, mylodonts, toxodonts, and the solid glyptodons, which were contemporaries of *Homo sapiens*, and of *Homo ater*, and perhaps as domestic animals they followed him in his exodus through the jungles to the north and to the east through the hypothetical

cally pure oxygens in currents similar to atmospheric gulfstreams. No one can resist them today; perhaps they forced the emigration of the Placentalia. It is an empty wind of the reservoir and of the glacier; it drags away mountains, particle by particle, eroding and filing them down as in prehistoric times. It impels avalanches of fine dust in eddies and clouds that blind as they uplift bodies with their powerful forces. That air torrent is the aeolian machine in all its primitive power, in its full erosive work, constructing Quaternary lands, sharpening shrubs until they have the aspect of coils of barbed wire. That wind is still performing the mechanical task of the Jurassic and for that reason bestows a primeval aspect on this part of the continent, containing the progress of time. The Pampero is no more than a mere arm that wanders away from the main path, and the Zonda is a mere aerial brook. The wind does not allow man to exist and if he should persist in resistance he is driven insane. The wind pierces the skull and produces an ardent desire for escape, a neurosis of solitude, a panic that impels to tireless flight or suicide. The passage of cars and trucks is impossible; the wind erases the tracks of vehicles that have passed and cleanses the ground of tire marks or of hoof prints.

Those winds blow from the west and southwest so violently that no farming is possible; there is no root capable of fixing a tree, and there are no trees; entire herds of animals die out. Only the sheep resist the rough weather. The wind is the perceptible body of solitude. It is compact like the one Dante envisioned in the second circle of hell so that lovers could not hear or join together, or like the one that separated the flames from the bodies of Eteocles and Polynices according to an old legend that Aeschylus did not know. It is the wind as sterile as the sea, the wind of the sea, the sea as the wind.

The animals have a presentiment when the wind is to arrive; they lift their heads and become restless. With only occasional res-

---

Arquelenis. They were mammallike birds, with solid jaws, prolonged to a tip bent upward at the extreme; the solid and triangular beak curved downward to furnish a formidable hook for attack.

pite, the winds commence in spring and prolong themselves into early fall. They race at speeds that reach ninety kilometers per hour as they travel from the Pacific, cross all of Patagonia, and finally drive deeply over the Atlantic.

2. That same direction is also followed by the waters. The rivers flow into the Atlantic, as the winds do. It is the march of dark forces of the Center and of the South: from the mountain range to the ocean. There are no currents with much volume; the true hydrographic center ends in ramifications absorbed by the dropsical earth, which continues to be a sea bed, eager for water. It almost never rains and thirst is another invisible enemy. This is not the region of fresh water and of juicy fruits but of saltfish and undrinkable water, of chemical and hydraulic water, or perhaps of petroleum. The wells that are drilled do not search for water veins but for the deep pre-Cambrian flow. And yet, thirst made their discovery possible. Man does not even perform the drilling; it is done with powerful electric drills. Fabulous capitals manage those enormous steel structures. The brute power of machines, only comprehensible in abstract numbers, drills those artesian oil wells which are the water of that landscape.

The mineral bestows fertility on that primitive world. The world forces of engineering and of stock companies utilize it, while man is a mere tool that deteriorates in an enterprise where capital and subsoil form an alliance.

3. It is surprising that man would even venture into these regions of the first didelphian; he goes in search of fortune. His body and reason are put to trial by the difficulties of climate and the harshness in the struggle for life. He is an individual without scruples or ties of love; he goes alone. He fights mercilessly against a pitiless nature. By wagering his life he wishes to test luck. If he should fail, he returns undone to the city for a final attempt with his remaining forces.

At other times he is cruelly defeated and is destined to live out a vegetative existence as a shepherd among flocks of reindeer and sheep. In such a man, deep and ancient appetites awaken that gush with the power of deep and ancient life from an oil well. He is reduced to the bare elements of existence, distended through thousands of centuries. He feels in his flesh the roar of sexual ardor that leads him to all imaginable disorders. In those places are also women who, attracted by the fever of making a fortune, surrender their bodies for the price of a fruit. Hideous or beautiful, old or adolescent, they all mean the same in the desperate commerce of pleasure: women. Man does not require them to be anything else. His instinct to last long and avoid being cut down in his prime is manifested through an insatiable eagerness to perpetuate his person. Solitude incites and removes the brakes to his carnal appetites. Fear of total and anonymous death pushes him toward that act symbolic of life. Sexual frenzy is the fever of the cold and arid plains. Another fever of that climate is alcoholism, a balm against solitude. Alcohol offers a way to escape isolation and to jump to another world; sexual appetites permit one to remain in this world, to penetrate it, to possess it. That man who with all his animal forces wishes to procreate, with all his human forces wishes to die. By means of both intoxications he removes himself from a reality he longs to destroy and submerges his person into the hopeless course of the future and of life.

Entire towns live in a somnambulant state of free love and of drunkenness. Such are the ravages of solitude. Whether they are miners or shepherds, those men are a danger; when they rise in rebellion because of starvation, or because they form a sufficient number to rebel, they hurl themselves in attack upon towns and herds in the manner of escaped convicts. Then it is necessary to shoot them down, using the army if necessary. They live and die like wolves.

4. The perpetual drought lends to that region the characteristics of desert zones and gives it the appearance of ancient panoramas. It only rains in the winter, very heavily and for a short period. The river beds swell and the rivers flow, gyrating like snakes over the permeable earth, which soon absorbs them. They are extinguished almost at the start of their violent rush. The west wind, in accord with the anhydrous earth, hastens the evaporation of water. The river is but a dream.

The geological lapse of time between the lower and upper Tertiary sprinkled the ground with boulders. From the time of the Miocene, violent torrents falling from the mountains scattered these chunks of mountain which were finally dispersed by the fresh waters. They constitute the soil from the Strait of Magellan to the Río Negro. This destroyed mountain range has beneath it still older layers. In that stony ground grows a suffering flora composed of stubborn plants. The Argentine steppe is so similar to Siberia that even the suffering human being is not omitted. The noxious flora, sparse and bitter, extends from the precordillera to the Neuquén. Then it penetrates through Pampa del Monte and reaches the sierras of the pampa, a still more ancient portion of the planet. The plants are those of dunes and saltpeter beds; they are dwarfish, without fruit, without wood pulp or flowers, flattened against the ground, and of a reptilian color. With their leathery leaves they resemble metal Arachnidae and Crustacea; it is a vegetation like that of the circle of suicides. Behind those plants hid terrified souls who were to be found there by evil people seeking to destroy them. In the midst of those plants man sometimes dies, pursued relentlessly by terrible diseases. He dies alone, like a dog that bites its liver or its peritoneum.

Certain shrubs stretch to a height of four meters; they are always the same austere plants with woody and deformed trunks, filled with thorns and sharp points. Their combustible wood evaporates in fire as the rivers do in the air. The "black shrubs" are covered with poisonous stilettolike bristles, have a barely ramified trunk, and terminate in a lancet. At times they resemble sea urchins. Cylindrical leaves, sharpened like gouges and surgical instruments, grow in infinite expanses among the rocks. Only in the valleys, where the water concentrates and forms humid slime, or in the canyons, which are somewhat similar to the fossils of ancient torrents, does vegetation bunch together with the solidarity of an abandoned herd and does it peer forth with kindness at the sky. These are the oases where animals and men go to search for Quaternary soil and a shelter against cold and air; they are more than a hundred million years old.

All that dominion of nature, enclosures in which land defends its intact minerals, flora, and fauna, are the boundaries where the son of the plains was cast out and where he will be extinguished. The rest—the flat land, the central pampa, and that of the littoral—is Argentina, the land of Europe, the white man's land. But between the new fertile pampa and that dark ancient world is the son of the white man and the Indian woman. He has to choose, but for hundreds of years his decision will be delayed. Everything is left in suspense until such a day.

III·PRIMITIVE FORCES

7 TELLURIC FORCES

The Molds of Earth

The more the man of the pampa coveted, the more he was enslaved and confined in a circle of barbed wire. His ambition was not born naturally; it was a tumor that entangled his life. The man of the pampa has a restricted concept of the world and he is a captive within the limits of that concept, in the jail of his horizon. He believes that he dominates a sector of reality over which he perhaps exercises domain, and he is converted into an instrument of reality that is cut off from the world. As a result he is unhappy.

The surrounding medium was shifting and varying and had the perfect shape of the formless. By fighting against such a changing medium, man acquired the conditions of instability, of insecurity that by reflection he transmits today to the plastic medium surrounding him. Since he left an imprint on things, the surroundings express his natural idiosyncrasies. However, he is the maximum exponent of the medium and has already acquired the perfect shape of the formless. This form we may call a circle of barbed wire.

All molding is a new beginning after many centuries of what has already occurred thousands of times: the raw struggle of man against a primitive world.

The primitive world imposed its forms on primitive man. However, at the same time it yielded with great ease to the modeling by his hands. The molds were still fresh and man's hands sufficed; it was later that he created complicated tools. There is nothing here that corresponds to the design of a machine, except the anonymous forces that oxidize it. For example, the gaucho is not a being in process of formation, but a completed type that has acquired the forms of nature. He is not a new source of anything, but a being already invaded and shaped. The soul, the weakest and most malleable part, yielded first in our world without mechanized structures. By raising animals, the artisan became a shepherd. He grazed, sheared, skinned, and sold livestock for profit. He lived next to the animals as if he were trying to understand them. When Azara saw him, he gambled and drank; now he trades and views himself with conceit, which is to do the same. As long as the cows and sheep continue grazing, he will carry on gambling and drinking. After many years he has become converted into a being of limited will with a one-sided preoccupation with cattle; if he really conserves any kindness it gives the appearance of a herbivorous virtue. He does nothing else; he knows of nothing else. But the predatory animal does not submit to the herbivore and becomes invigorated by the meekness of the ruminant.

Live cattle, which constituted the foundation of our large fortunes, were the tendon of civil wars, the skeleton of the nation, and the stone of scandal of the governments. We conducted lives limited and ruled by cattle hides.

Whether cattle are dead or alive, they lend a style to the manner of conducting commerce, to ways of entering into agreement, to marriage patterns, to being melancholic, to loving, to dancing, and to a manner of looking at things. There are close similarities between government and the operation of a ranch, between the public official and the foreman, between the cities and the packing houses. All these were formed at the same time, with each species differentiating itself from the galaxy to compose constellations shaped in the same zodiacal sign: Taurus. While our peregrine fathers thought they were shaping this world, it was the world, with both its well-shaped and ill-defined forms, that modeled them in its own image. The process of formation of a temperament, of a personage, of a chapter of history, or of the predominance of a race consisted in a condensation from a Milky Way of agriculture and cattle. We have an example of this process in the surrender of Buenos Aires to Santa Fe. Dorrego, López, Rodríguez, and Rosas did not realize they were attending a symbolic act at the height of the age of rawhide. As is known, the capitulation was made explicit with the delivery of 25,000 cows, which Rosas guaranteed to deliver and which he exceeded by 5,146 head in a delicate display of opulence; thus, he remained a victor for thirty years. It appeared in the capitulation clauses as a compensation for damages caused to Santa Fe, but in fact it was a booty and a masterful stroke. Rosas, much more skillful than López, in addition to inflicting on the latter a moral defeat by making him accept the poisoned gift, added for him a feast in Los Cerrillos. In this act are intermingled politics, economics, art, America, prehistory, and diplomacy; otherwise it would not be a symbolic event. For the payment of the stipulated compensation in kind, Rosas had to resort to the subscription of other ranchers because his own flocks had been plundered by the Indians and decimated by drought. He bound others to an act of honor in a chieftain's maneuver that was in accordance with the policies set forth in his own *Rancher's Manual*, a true code of Hammurabi and basis of our law. This contribution was common, and the interesting aspect was the strategy employed by that great man of the pampa in whom the formless took perfect shape. The Pact of the Cows was a typical episode for Rosas, although handled in a more masterful way than usual and with a greater feeling for the essence.

Men fought for cows, against cows, and because of cows. Indemnities were paid and moral damages were compensated in this specie; a few soldiers would be dead on the balance sheet. However, the forces in interplay were eternal; they came from beyond the protagonists and dragged down everything within reach. Men and institutions perspire a georgic vapor that arrives from the settled plains and is penetrated by a millenary chill that sets sail from the Indian's tomb. Civic life was being shaped by the live substance of the pampa; men, things, and events could have been represented in the allegorical form of medieval bestiaries. In the manner of a guilty person who is tightly bound and then exposed to the sun for punishment, the state wrapped itself up in coarse, crude leather. The smell of fresh blood and the odor of fresh and distant alfalfa fields impregnate politics, finances, the exercise of jobs, education, literature, and friendship. As Ajax did from the back of an ox, institutions, societies, centers, and clubs extract their strength from the pampa, from the suspicious fear of the herbivore.

The flat country contributed its wealth to the maintenance of armies, and the first lesson in law for the cattle hunter was the wire fence. The horse herds and cattle stockyards supplied the army with provisions and stores. The tanning industry, the salting place, and the saddlery—the latter among the best in the world—prospered in the shadow of the civil wars, as in the good decades of Rome. Regular militia bodies had been established to defend the ranch owners from Indians and from rivals. The rancher contributed in species to the support of the militia, and these cattle were later used to wage a war of seizure on other ranches.[1] Civil wars, when divested of historical finery, are no more than organized cattle thievery resulting from a lack of military discipline. This was the final state of the troops of Lavalle and of Rosas; in addition to cattle, the expeditionary forces of Alsina and Roca obtained land. Finally, the foundation of the Faculty of Philosophy and Letters implied the prior creation of the Faculty of Agronomy and Veterinary

---

[1] "The cows, threatened by the Indian, necessitated the existence of an army. Each owner sacrificed part of his herd to conserve the rest . . . which is as if the cows defended themselves" (Sarmiento). He could also have said that if the cows maintained armies so that these could attack opponents, then the cows attacked each other. This is the second proof. In our own times we witness merchants forming groups and acquiring weapons for protection against assailants, thus seconding the police.

Science, without which the former would have been considered an entelechy.

The shepherd was already a soldier and the soldier a shepherd. For a long time there was no difference between the hunting of animals and the hunting of men, between feasting and everyday living, between polygamy and religion. The hunt was a type of war carried out against beings whose possession was sought for reasons of utility, of security, or simply of superstition. War developed that same spirit of dominion over fellow man by the occupation of territory or by the spoliation of property or for superstitious reasons. These three motives receive in some histories the pseudonym of politics, but they merit more modest names in ethnographies. The nation of hunters that marauded in no man's land in pursuit of cattle was a nation of warriors that naturally took up weapons upon acquiring the notion of power or of wealth. Our Hyksos of the pampa waited for an opportune moment to carry out a daily war of plunder against the herds of cows, of horses, and of sheep. Unintentionally, they formed a clan with a collective spirit and with somewhat well-defined forms of totemism. Guided by topographical characteristics, they clustered in districts to constitute a precarious society much inferior to the Indian tribe. But they were of one spirit and were capable of solidarity against their neighbors. Any remnant or resonance of civilized life sufficed for that accidental, warlike, and bucolic grouping full of clan spirit to attain the pseudostructure of an army and the ideals of a party. Then, the instinctive and geographic forces sublimated themselves in undertakings of a heroic, commercial, or juridical nature. The three primitive motives stir in the background.

The religion of such groupings, even if spiritual restlessness be grafted upon them, is usually fetishism and totemism: the garment, the cult of courage and freedom, and the knife—the object of work and of armed combat. The beast they used for riding, the animal they ate, and the one that accompanied them became noa, the propitious spirit. The enemies of the herd were taboo. Initially, the enemy of the herd and of freedom was the cattleman; later it was the owner of salting places, and, finally, the rancher. The three

governed in turn. For this type of religion and politics the aborigi-
nes had a natural inclination that was doubtless sharpened by the
corpulent and resistant animals the first conquerors had brought.
In a medium so openly predisposed toward transferred totemism,
the Jesuit missions exacerbated the tendency and deflected it into
artificially opened channels. Totemism and fetishism, still latent
in the gaucho, flowed through loopholes and revealed themselves in
the veneration of things tied to the earth and of images translated
into concrete living beings. The credulity in totemic amulets and
a blurred and soiled idea of religion and of free government, on
the one hand, and the missions and Indian labor systems as coun-
terideals, on the other hand, produced a totemic-commercial aspect
in the rancher and the cattle thief, whose personal and economic
powers increased tangibly with the slaughter of cattle.[2] Mounted
revolutionary groups and the Mazorca Society, Rosas's arm of terror and enforcement, gathered and shaped the prime matter. Once
throat cutting is converted into a regular task and the knife becomes part of common law with its own proficiency and technique,
they transmit to the executioner their mystique of reason, of freedom, of strength, and of fortune. Those religious instincts, complicated by economic instincts, can only be transferred; Sarmiento
calculated at least two hundred years of purgatory for such of-
fenses. These primitive forces still act obliquely. Today in Mendoza
and San Juan they are incarnated in the mobs handled by totemic
politicians.

The clan, with its agglutinating ability, clustered the rural
masses. These groupings, through an automatic need for defense
and coordination and obeying an idolatrous urge, erected chieftains
from their own ranks. The chieftain was the man-symbol who de-

---

[2] An example of the viciousness of those prehistoric times is the ostentation
of the enemy's head as a trophy. War was often waged among those primitives
to acquire a given number of trophies, a number of heads. The inventory of
human heads signifies for a warrior people the same as the inventory of heads
of cattle for a pastoral people: victory and booty. Peñaloza, Ramírez, Aberastain,
Avellaneda, Cubas, and others were decapitated. In those crimes and in the
capitulation of Rodríguez with López we may see two aspects of the same force.

fended the clan's interests. Today the politician is the paterfamilias-symbol who defends the home and the rights violated by public officials.

More curious is cattle stealing and its development. Until a few years ago, it was a lucrative industry in the cattle provinces, and it still is in Patagonia and the northeast. Cattle stealing and contraband were forms derived from a legal system of commerce before the days of the Independence.[3] At the same time they were surviving but atrophied forms of totemic leadership and faith in its propitious spirit. The tribes would elect those chiefs who possessed the most cattle or the cattle of the best quality or perhaps the richest saddle. What is commonly understood in committee jargon to be politics, democracy, and universal suffrage is part of that primitive process—not better and not worse.[4] Electoral law is the mythology of the city victors in whom lie incarnate the demons from the plains.

The trail guide and the scout are representative of this period. We can see traces of them in the leaders of multitudes and in the improvisers of knowledge.

The Trail Guide and the Scout

The trail guide possesses fine organs of orientation and has the qualities of a spiritual medium. Through him, the earth seems to express the secrets of its forms, colors, consistency, and distribution. Each accident of nature is registered in the guide's mind and unfailingly linked with others, so that he need

---

[3] The traders between the Río Grande and the Banda Oriental were bandits. "There were young men of good families who because of idleness and depravation—typical vices of a country without industry and without political life—sought out that epic style of life. The military provost sought them out with lancers and dragoons. The chieftain who could defeat one of them was held in high esteem" (V. F. López). In 1880 they were called the Indiada and in 1910 the Patota.

[4] According to the works of Waldemar Bogoras, the position of leadership among the Siberian Eskimos and the Chukchee depends on wealth. Among the reindeer Chukchee wealth is measured by the size of herds and among the maritime Chukchee according to the potential for constructing a ship covered with hides (R. Lenoir, *Sur l'institution du potlach*).

only survey an extremely limited piece of landscape to construct the whole picture. He is blessed with a gift of thinking logically, according to the configuration of the plains, the forests, and the mountains. He intuitively feels the proximity of water, of trees, and of beings. He is possessed with divination, rhabdomancy, and an infallible stereoscopic memory that orients itself with barely visible clues. The guide is not even conscious of many minute details. Without thinking, without remembering, he knows which trail to follow; and at night he moves with the sure-footed certainty of a somnambulist.

In the wars of independence and in the civil wars, he was the tactician and the topographer. His word was worthy of blind faith. Rivera was a fortunate military man because he knew the littoral like the palm of his hand; Facundo and López were equally well acquainted with the plains. The generals, including Güemes and Paz, had to abandon themselves to local trail guides. Without maps, strategy in unpopulated lands remained subordinated to knowledge of the regions. Ramírez, Hereñú, and Ibarra maneuvered in their districts, as sure of the landscape as bandits. Dorrego was defeated at Gamonal because López's tacticians led him to poisonous pasture grounds, and the horses died. Rosas knew by taste the pasture grounds of the forty ranches within the province of Buenos Aires. All those men were closer to reality than those who studied it. They knew where to find water holes, farms, or fresh horses.

The trail guide does not need to have passed many times over the same place; he may never have seen it. But guided by his experience of the grasses, of soil colors, of remote peaks, and associating omens with infinitesimal insinuations, he ties the piece of field or jungle before him to the immense totality stretching for leagues and leagues. He knows the fords of rivers and the time of the year when waters descend; he smells out the storms ahead of time; with the clarity of a neurotic, he is aware of dangers several days before they occur; he calculates distances with the precision of a theodolite and his judgments are infallible.

He is gifted with those subtle organs of insects and of birds that allow him to register the sightest vibrations on his nervous system.

Without a doubt, all his mysterious knowledge lies in the province of magnetic sensitivity. Instead of being an expert of things exterior to him, he is attuned to nature's secret of modus operandi; with this key he can solve any problem. It is something similar to a bloodhound's sense of smell, only on a more intellectual level, more complex. If questioned, it would be difficult for him to say why he chose a certain bearing instead of another or why he suspects the existence of a river ten leagues away. Such reasons as he may give will seem to us ridiculous and captious. Yet, he hits the mark: along the path he chooses we reach our destination, and ten leagues away there really is a river. If he wishes, he takes shortcuts through unexplored paths and knows when forage plants or towns will be found. A few musical notes or the rhythmic diagram of a phrase suffice for him to comprehend an entire symphony of hills, rocky folds, and swamps. With only a femur or a tooth of that anatomy, he reconstructs the skeleton of a landscape whose sections join before his eyes with unequivocal naturalness.

The scout is a twin of the trail guide. The scout has his antennae in the optic nerves; the eyes are for him everything. While the guide is an intuitive discoverer and rhabdomantist, the scout is analytical and logical; like a bird or a fish, he only requires a barely perceptible clue as a reference point from which to deduce the logical scheme of orientation. Sarmiento describes him as a serious and cautious personage who was convinced of his miraculous capacity and of the authority of his word. His figure and his dignity are etched forever in Calíbar. Darwin has also told of the scout's extraordinary feats. The eye is the supreme organ with which to touch, to smell, to think, to listen, and to imagine. Nature has endowed him with a wise and cerebral eye. He knows the difference between a grass that withers alone and the one that withers by pressure of a foreign body. He sees in the tracks whether the beast goes tired, satisfied, or hungry; whether it is lightly or heavily loaded; whether it is male or female; whether it is directed by a firm hand or an inexperienced one; and whether it is guided with or without haste. He looks at the ground and is able to distinguish whether the arrangement of dirt is caused by the wind or the waters or someone's passage. Like a detective, he can infer a whole history from a hoofprint: the march unfolds before his eyes like a map. He will find attached to branches impalpable and invisible particles of a body that brushed against the tree; he will note another imperceptible sign in the leaves. It is not possible to lean with impunity against the trunk of a tree or to cross a river or to advance by climbing from branch to branch for long stretches; in each place he sees the fresh trace that remains for many days. He applies the magnifying glasses and lanterns of his pupils, and without any waste of time he knows which way to proceed. Nature is stained and withered wherever she has been touched. It would be impossible to disintegrate that instinct which is so close to magic, to the art of divining from animals' entrails, and to divination from dreams. And yet, everything is clear and logical.

Inclined Planes

He who proposes to make money, and is without a past or a future, has limited goals and may triumph. What he cannot do is fulfill a destiny with money. The pursuit of wealth as an ideal demands that sooner or later that which does not exist must take the shape of gold, just as gold assumes the form of that which does not exist. We all know those deserters from human values in whom the greed of old age is cloaked in picturesque aspects of altruism. The present treasure hunter is our pioneer, the owner of the pampa; he subverts values and he rules the emporium of adulterated possessions.

Everything the pioneer of the pampa appears to desire intensely, such as the urge to acquire possessions, to be loved or feared, to excel, or to gain knowledge, is nothing more than an unsatisfied appetite for material objects. There is for him only one concrete, positive, and desirable good: wealth of any type. The concave shape of his poverty matches a voracious appetite; the anxiety to possess deepens the hollowness that yearns to be filled. Enormous is the emptiness that the man of the pampa feels within himself when he yearns to annex immense stretches of land, a multitude of buildings, unaccountable herds of cattle, titles of written works, women, and positions. What he searches for is a pretext; what he needs is something with which to fill the emptiness. He hopes to attain a spiritual ascendancy over material objects, but at best all he can accomplish is a multiplication of what he already possesses. The accomplishment is a substitute for his hope, and it leaves him unsatisfied and with a greater thirst.

He lives in a diffuse state of inquietude, even of restlessness, because of something he does not have. He ignores what it is or what it consists of, yet the need for it incessantly gnaws at him from within. He searches for one thing and fixes on another. It would suffice to have peace at home and an intelligent son; instead, he stores bushels and bushels of wheat, sells sacks and sacks of sugar, and builds a city. He experiences all of what is lacking in the social order and all of the collective needs as his own trophic faults. All that is no longer nourishing in the atmosphere in which he and his loved ones breathe ceases to feed the vital organs; these become impoverished and search out substitute food. He is not provided with those imponderable elements which help one to live, which make death less severe, and which allow one to view the world with joy and without rancor. As he triumphs in the order of material things, larger fees, income, fame, goods, that part of his being which remains unsatisfied, which does not assimilate, and which does not become strengthened, forces him to desire more of what is accessible. What he secures becomes overvalued in relationship to what he could not obtain; he is proud of what he acquires, extolling the merit of his achievement. And so, automatically, the unsatisfied ideals, the desired goods, the enjoyments looked for in vain, are devalued and in the end are considered as antitheses of ideals. Little by little, acting like water that carries particles down a slope, he shifts from the difficult to the easy. He aspires to be rich, without thinking of what use the fortune will be to him; he aspires to become president of the Republic or a trust, but nothing pushes or sustains him in his eagerness. Investiture or wealth achieved in this manner are a fiction and the cadaver of a misspent life.

The beam of his vision divides to reveal the most resplendent colors along the lines of power and wealth. Both bands appear to be the whole prism only when the vision of the world and of values is incomplete; the eudaemonistic values of the world are not located in reduced bands of the gamut but in the total clarity of light; the rest are reverberations. There is a great hidden misery in the eagerness to progress blindly and indefinitely. It is somewhat like the fantasy of the servant in the movie house. There is no road to reach those extremes; the logical progress might then take the form of a sudden jump. The fever of desiring much may be a reflection of hunger and of thirst.

While those objectives, which advance like the horizon, have not yet been reached, one lives in a perpetual journey, traveling for days in a criminal expanse that attacks with fists and elbows. Life is a bother when it consumes itself with an overall disposition strained toward the best and the most. In each two-dimensional or cinematographic dreamer there is a suicidal subject murdering himself and his dreams in a cowardly manner.

Those places along the journey are steps on a ladder of hierarchy and power that are climbed toward a humanly senseless peak: senseless because it does not lead toward the collective good, or toward man's betterment of living conditions, or toward the prosperity of all, or toward the advancement of art and science, or even toward egotistical satisfactions. Life itself becomes a machete with which to clear the way in a jungle of men. The individual, propelled by a suicidal force, passes like a catholic ray through the scale of human, intellectual, and economic values. He produces around himself a psychic whirlwind of fear and perhaps one of admiration, because a certain intimate resonance disturbs the living matter he comes across and agitates. His bold trajectory is that of a projectile passing through the intermolecular spaces of gaseous social matter. But in synthesis he is not a speeding bullet produced by the same intermolecular forces we have called spaces. The restricted ideal of the dreamer of power and wealth is a mental figure of that world of interstices that surrounds us. The danger that lies in wait for the individual consists of institutions without cohesion, of lax morality, and of the need of a superior and heroic context. Finally, longing for the best, with all scruples unleashed he falls, a dazed victim of his own staged dream.

Erosion and Oxidation

In the immensity of the territory, still three-fourths unpopulated, it seems easy to live, to struggle, and to triumph. Unlimited possibilities unfold as if this formless world could cede to human will. But that long and wide world, unpopulated, has a shape as impenetrable as stone; its will, ancient and certain, opposes the invader. It permits movement but awaits in ambush. Sooner or later difficulties arise that seem to be born suddenly, beyond all prevision; then, the formless and static will affirms its slow and unlimited power, coordinated with astronomical, climatic, and geophysical forces, equally imperceptible although always in action. He who struggles appears to triumph; survival is in part a victory. However, looking closely we see that man serves as human forage for the hidden forces. Because it is erroneously assumed that something not formed in the image of man must be formless, nature appears treacherous, with extended and impalpable nets. The native of the country already knows it is too risky to force nature; he is content with his hut or his job. The reverberation of the plain continues to produce mirages of silver seas in the eyes that arrive burned by the aridity of European fields, similar to cinerary urns of labor and time. In the towns the newcomer is submerged in those seas of reflected silver; he undertakes a task, falls, and rises again; he does any job, stifles his conscience, and finally dies leaving ingots of that mirage. This world is freedom, a lack of human order in the imperceptible forces; it is a whim, a lack of recentness in what already functions autonomously; it is a possibility, a lack of intimate feeling and direction.

The immigrant who beholds the passing leagues as he goes deeper into the interior feels that he is undertaking a journey left to his own resources and that he is taking the road to the withered antipode, without species of household gods on his shoulders. Ideas and feelings of joy invade him in the melancholic vision of solitude. If he does not think of the cities he is free because he has broken with a world that observed and watched over his every step, enchasing him in the pincers of a regulated and mechanized life. He identifies with the fields: limitless, formless, fenceless. There he can manage any task that offers an immediate gain. To prevail is to fight hand to hand, without self-control or self-imposed restrictions—for that we have the laws. To accomplish is to build, to create from the formless a form of likeness, such as a son. But that apparent lack of shape, structure, and strength of the field, the town, and the inhabitant which governs from methods of cultivation to the way of looking at people is an incommensurate placenta of the formless. The germs deposited in her are gestated and developed according to her disposition. One has to live many years and then be able to leave and examine from afar to comprehend that the flesh and soul have been molded in the womb of the formless.

This medium, without its own physiognomy and apparently without plastic energy, absorbs and communicates its rustic substance to the individual. Its plastic strength lies in its ability to break down and reshape character. Whatever falls into the vastness of the plain drinks from the soothing juices of the formless.

The feeling of impunity from actions, that recondite notion of being alone which one has in the pampa, crops out from the crevices of the personality like the excretion from sudoriferous glands. What is seen and heard does not inspire respect; it is new, it does not mesh with our nature, and it is not a quantity of life, of science, or of faith; it is not a statue, an arch, or a plaza before which time slowly passed, leaving its shreds.

The medium lacks its own life, regular function, substance, and energy; man cannot provide these. Before the infinite parade of things and events, the individual is an unknown full of hazard, of error, or cruelty, and of egoism. He maintains himself upright and whole as long as he can, but when the deforming and erosive forces commence their action, he falls corroded and undone.

In the bosom of such a state of indifference and disposition, even the most noble feelings, such as love, friendship, and altruism, are converted into reasons for dissolution; love does not impregnate beings to their depths but is localized in erogenous zones; friendship is a pretext to deprive the stranger of his rights at the benefit of his accomplice; altruism is an abstract formula that only applies to the closest fellow man in the struggle against poverty and injustice. Even the impetus that takes man beyond his personal interests of family, of class, or of nation is not sufficient; his interests bend and fall, beaten down by the lack of expression in anything long-range. Love is a contact, patriotism is a uniform, and humanity is the horizon in which a person weakens; that is to say, all those feelings without which the species cannot exist even if it procreates are reduced to the skin of the soul, to the epithelium. The thoughts in the plains, like the boomerang, come to rest at the foot of the thinker. At no moment do we walk surrounded by the ample waves of congeniality, of eternal projects, or of imperishable ideas. Outside of immediate contact, those zones are cold and sterile; that is why one must live alertly; we are our own best friends and censors. Society does not take care of its interests; it lacks that which makes ants and beavers similar: the architectural form of instinct. Beings are together because they occupy neighboring places, as if they lived on the train or in the theater; they are not in neighboring places because they live together. Farther away from us are the true judges, powered by codes in a hermetic world that bears no relationship to the norms of common existence; and on the other side, far away, are friends moved by their own autonomous impulses in a space that reflects their own images. Although that defense may be useless, we carry it as Siegfried did his corneal skin, and it is through the skin that we enter into contact with the world.

Useful Tools

To penetrate such an inexpressive nature we should previously have an adequate configuration, one susceptible to deformation, to flattening, to becoming wide, long, and savage, if it has not become so already. The infinite possibilities of being successful at anything quickly prove to the adventurer that he can only do one thing; that is the moment to surrender or to begin.

Our land has an owner: it is property and not freedom; the owner is also a hidden force, far away. From afar he imposes on the adventurer a way of working, of existing, of resigning himself, and of accepting, even if it may appear that from so far away he cannot see or hear, or dispose of the land, or shape it in any way. The newcomer will earn little at first; he might be a hired hand or a day laborer. He will be the vassal of an absent lord whom he does not know and who makes arrangements according to numbers. He will be the prisoner of freedom, the slave of whim, and the pawn of a game. The second letter he writes will say different things from the first; with the passage of time he will write no more and the door at his back will close forever. Often, the shame of having been mistaken leads to an insistence in the error; but it already does not matter whether he triumphs or fails. The land's absentee landlord orders the collection of rent and the payment of wages; neither loves the land: it means sacrifice for one and rent for the other. From far away the master makes and unmakes; his foreman receives instructions, watches over the property, collects rent, and evicts the tenants. The foreman does not love the master's possessions, because he feels his own independent life is being interrupted. The field laborer and the day laborer someday will have to depart, with bags over their shoulders or with pesos in their pockets, marching over this triumphant land with which they have not established meaningful rapport, as if they had never lived. They depart, a few years older and with many cancelled mistakes behind them. The loss of will may be considered as the first symptom of invasion by the plain, the preliminary step for all mimesis; the last phase is the departure, without looking back. The earth already has no secrets: it is pure, simple, uniform. Whoever lives on the land has very possibly left behind, far away, a world beset with intricate and difficult forms, which perhaps were not worth as much as this simplicity; but the two worlds are different: they cannot be the same. He surrenders or becomes angry and resists. He digs in his heels and says no; if there is a difficulty he tramples it with audacity. No one knows who he is or what his name is or where he comes from or what loved ones he left behind or if he is

alone. When he has to halt, he halts; one has to be defeated to triumph and he surrenders without reserve at the tip of the fishhook.
He plays to win. In the end he triumphs after having sacrificed
everything; he has achieved his inhuman ideal, like a Brand without a heart and without a brain. He is defeated, shattered; the
pampa rises to his scalp, penetrates his insides, rules his voice, flat-
tens his look. He is the pampa, covered with the pampa when buying animals, sowing, selling, signing contracts, or being feared.
Later, with his aim achieved, he returns to the nothingness and
submerges like an unwound automaton in the anonymity of the
world. And around him nothing has quieted down or settled; there
are more houses and more people; the old impalpable forces push
from outside with the rain and the wind, they fall on the roofs,
knock gently on the walls, silence the throats, and sharpen the eyes,
whispering advice of a vast, incorporeal rebelliousness.

It is better to stay in Buenos Aires, to penetrate the city and to
confront it. The illusion of the countryside and the poetics of gold
have lost their hypnotic force and now repel the immigrant. An
immigrant who arrives today attracted by a sonorous name—what
program does he bring? None. Anything is better than what he left
behind; he is a fugitive. He arrives late, when the territory is populated to the maximum, when even in the cattle and the cereal provinces there is no meat or bread and one has to go to the authorities
for protection of his life. This is worse than what he left behind because it is open to all possibilities. Did he bring along a plan? He
came to try his luck.

As he enters Buenos Aires, an unlimited eagerness awakens in
him; he feels possessed of an energy he did not know in his native
land or in the ocean crossing so propitious for idle dreams of power.
Every possibility is generously open to him. He recommences his
heroic life, as if he were penetrating into the jungle. He came ready
for anything and now he understands it well. Perhaps for the first
time, among beings who do not consider him strange or inferior
and only regard him with cosmopolitan indifference, he feels equal
among men. There are no barriers, no classes, no places he cannot
enter; no examination of his ability or his honesty is required, and

there are no norms of living that impose any form of capitulation. He enters into Buenos Aires, the great gambling house, and he remains. If working conditions are bad, he has no objections to accepting a lower position; if working conditions are moderate, he lowers them by offering his muscle and brain to the highest bidder. He agrees to surrender temporarily and later takes vengeance from any position to which he may rise.

From the moment he understands, the newly arrived is a formidable adversary. That man from the exhausted land and miserable neighborhood, who left everything behind and chose adventure, disowning his destiny, comes determined to conquer even if it means reprisal; he has ancestral insults to avenge. All the city activities, the telephone, the theater, the public administration, the factory, and the leasehold are weapons he wields because he is the same as all strangers. He ignores the conventions within whose boundaries we adjust our ways of living and prospering. We have renounced, as he had in his native land, many freedoms when we submitted to the city, to the state, to the home, to friendship; the city adapted us for its uses and we function as one of its parts. He ignores what renunciations we have made and only sees expeditious ways and open doors where we have agreed to erect walls and gratings. Within the city he sees the village, which we do not. He finds the fissures, which we do not note. He identifies himself with figures on pedestals, with the effigies on fiscal securities, and with the plaques indicating street names because he only sees the truth that is far below the buildings, the vehicles, the property, and the positions. To move within his limits he only needs to find out the frontiers of tolerance. He glides along the fringes of the forbidden; and the dark, unseen world shelters him with secret liking because he is a destructor. If he cannot arrive at once to any position of importance, to the directorate of a company, to Florida Street, or to a remunerative job, he will arrive sooner or later regardless of the departure point; he only needs to possess the master key: money.

Man and woman can risk any adventure; if they wish, they may use an assumed name because the true personality is abolished. From the scaffold and the jib of a crane the stranger looks upon us with contempt. Incorporated as an anonymous member of a sect that detests whatever demands patience and pulchritude, a full-fledged member of the group upon cementing a few friendships, he has on his side all the endocrinal work of the city. If that world which he measures by his own stature and which he contemplates without modesty were essentially superior to him, he would succumb; and yet, little by little, he triumphs. We see that he outdoes us, that he pushes us down, and that he is right. His limited soul is expert in a narrow range of values singularly well suited for struggle. He has understood the softness of this world in which we look for peace and quiet. For those beings the world is displayed in accord with their organs and senses; the magisterial aspect of the city has not fooled them; they have taken possession of its public lands. They demonstrate to us that we were not as strong, that we were not as united, and that life was not as complicated as we thought.

Upward movement is obstructed; at first, spiritual values are negative forces. Downward movement offers infinite, tempting, and attractive possibilities. That is why we float like phantoms for thirty years and he adapts himself immediately; there exists a universal, special relationship between the ordinary man and the real world, which we do not see. That which demands special ability, resolute aptitude, moral acclimatization, control of technique, dependability, completion, cleanliness, and transparency begins much, much higher.

8 MECHANICAL FORCES

Adaptation of Instruments

The defective version of the North American Constitution, acclaimed on May 25, 1853, under the dictatorship of Urquiza, in reality signified less than any of the preexisting pacts. Except for Buenos Aires, which was of more import than all the other members of the federation, all the provinces were represented in Congress by prominent men that today would be impossible to find. A religious ardor for peace and order encouraged their hearts and their intelligence. But the provinces continued to be governed by the same chieftains as before Caseros, and the body of the Republic lay mutilated in scattered fragments. What could not be achieved in practice was instituted in theory, and 107 articles of Las Bases were the Nation born of chaos. Neither the landlords nor the merchants could have faith in a poor paraphrase and a State composed of Three Sections and a Preamble. But the chieftains declared themselves satisfied with the model that was given them, and they continued in power.[1]

Much before the existence of a State that assumed the direction of law and of ecclesiastical, juridical, military, and economic relations, there existed a state with a small *s* which operated more or less in good faith and in accordance with the preexisting pacts based on common law. The constitution created a State within another state, and it left out Mitre and the Republic of Buenos Aires. Religion, law, commerce, and militia from that moment would obey theoretical norms, while even contraband and cattle stealing retained their empirical clauses and their ethical imperatives. But the Confederation, in its role as a central body regulating and censuring those relations, dissuaded all and placed them on guard. A new danger was rising from the ashes of another, and that theoretical State to which the provinces had inadvertently delegated their autonomy and vitality was a leviathan with 107 joints and three fauces.[2] The contraction of faith led both the poor and the rich to place an exaggerated value in what was first sheltered from the Indian and then sheltered from the leviathan. A defense had to be

[1] "If we were to make a present of our constitutions to the South Americans, it would be necessary to send with them a sufficient number of our countrymen to make them operative and to teach their function" (Brackenridge).

[2] "Our first government was called Junta because that was the name given to the ones established in Spain to govern in the name of Ferdinand VII; but, after the idea of independence took root, the names adopted by the French Revolution were preferred. Our first legislative bodies in 1812 and 1813 were called Assemblies, after the French Constituent Assembly of 1789 and the Legislative Assembly of 1791. The executive power was established in 1811 with three governing members and three secretaries in imitation of the three consuls established in the year VIII of the French Republic; in 1813, the Supreme Executive power was denominated a Triumvirate . . . The name probably echoed the alliance of Robespierre, Lameth, and Barnave in the Constituent Assembly and of Robespierre, Couthon, and Saint-Just during the Convention, without excluding the possibility that the name could have been derived from Tribunat—created in the year VIII of the French Republic. Finally, in 1814 the executive power was invested in a Supreme Director whose authority lasted until the national dissolution in 1820; undoubtedly this designation was inspired by the Directory—composed by five members—which in France followed the Convention" (Carlos A. Aldao).

organized against that product of chaos which wished to feed on chaos by taking refuge in the customs house, behind enormous buildings, or next to the Republic's drainage into the Atlantic. That State, with only citizenship to offer, had neither tradition nor solvency of any kind. It was a foreign stepchild that was entering into full possession of three million square kilometers of unpopulated land.

To aggravate the natural distrust, its initial acts were extortive and violent. It despoiled the peaceful possessor of his goods; with futile pretexts it forced land properties to change hands; it termed a barbarity the period that it capriciously ended on February 3, 1852; and it labeled the new chapter as civilization. The exiles returned to their fatherland, and new exiles departed. If the panic did not result in complete exodus, it was only because of the difficulty involved in leaving the country: it was as arduous to leave as to enter. The moment was arriving when the law, the order, the economy, and the culture organized in the Magna Carta and in the souls of fifty extraordinary men would take reprisal against Rosas and his era, against barbarity.[3] Rosas exercised total public power; he was an instrument of the anonymous forces. Already in exile, the governors and the legislature delegated to a foreign organism all the addends of public power; still, they continued in the role of

[3] Rosas exuded Argentine life and represented it through his acts and his temperament. It would have been absurd to erase and to suppress as barbarity all that Rosas signified; that is why, skillfully and with only slight alterations, the existing system and the internal, visceral methods were left standing. The tactic consisted in strengthening to the greatest degree possible the ideals of the proclamation and of the edicts by calling them law, normality, and government. Urquiza possessed the necessary clairvoyance and sagacity to ensure that the theoretical body would not grate against living organs of the pre-existing reality; he left in power the chieftains of the deposed regimen and designated them constitutional governors. Then, he erected a colorless counterpart of himself; this mute personage, by the name of Derqui, played the role of an ornament. Urquiza himself aroused natural misgivings. He created someone and something that certainly was not Rosas, but neither was it his rival; meanwhile, Mitre embodied the sentiment of rebellion, a transfigured Rosas. Mitre realized which interests and unbridled feelings had been wounded. He rose at the head of the formless, of what existed even before Rosas, and he triumphed.

anonymous forces. Everything that until then was valued in terms of power acquired a tangible value with a price. Land ceased to be a feudal estate and became money or a basis for transactions; it was bought or sold as a bond payable to the bearer. Proprietors and farmers, in need of money during harvest time, obtained usurary loans at 12.5 percent *monthly*. The lender was an intermediary between the bank, which gave him credit at 7 percent per annum, and the farmer, who would take it at 5 percent per month. In addition there was the stipulation that payments would be made in products whose price was fixed by the lender. But the wealth generated in the bowels of the earth is more gradual than that produced by spontaneous generation in the usurer's hands or at the merchant's counter. The speculators became rich rapidly; the farmers and the ranchers sold their products with ease, and by monetary means they acquired power. Before, the acquisition of power used to demand strength and cunning. The government was converted into a speculator that obtained loans abroad at high interest rates and invested them in so-called works of improvement; simultaneously it possessed the machinery to issue money. The army and the navy made certain that paper money would be legal tender; meanwhile, they served as institutions of peace by responding to the demands of the farmer and the worker. Fields, houses, tasks, and goods became secure by federal action after Pavón; they acquired superlative values and were won and lost as in a gambling house. The annihilation of the aborigine and of the aboriginal forces, which used to give aleatory values to landed properties, signified strength for the State and security for the landowner. As the dangerous force diminished, the patriarchal strength of the State increased; the new value was paper money engraved with the effigy of the State. Powered by the fuels of barbarity, the leviathan constructed public buildings, health projects, trains, and institutions; however, the force extracted from the earth was weakness. The problem of land easily gained was coupled with the problem of land easily lost. The dangers and the evils inherent in the feeling of pervading insecurity or in being abandoned to chance gave way to other dangers and evils arising from a contradictive style of living: security in the future and the ability to obtain anything with some patience and skill. Existence was inverted. Whether one possessed wealth or not depended largely on whether one was favored by those in power. Friendship or kinship strengthened anyone's possessions, just as friendly relations with the chieftain did before. In its guise as booty retrieved from the Indian, land passed in immense tracts into military hands, to the heroes of the campaign and to the semiheroes of the desert: simultaneously it was the spoils of war and an offering of peace. Although it did not contribute to the formation of a landed elite, it did help to secure a military caste representing order and guaranteeing property rights; the military possessed jointly the power of weapons and the authority of proprietors. For the new landowners, who had obtained land under the pretext of reward and decoration, the fatherland meant property. Therefore, the ideas supporting property were closely allied to those in defense of territory; each owner of a few hundred leagues of security grafted upon the concept of fatherland his sentiment for a piece of land, for a fief, for law, and for progress. The original force of confusion metamorphosed into the primordial force behind juridical precepts and the authority of the State. With this transformation, the new goals were reduced to the defense of the frontier, the consolidation of internal order, and the stabilization of the status quo. From that moment the clear vision of a parabolic destiny for the Nation became clouded in the eyes of the landowner and the military man; they did not visualize the need of mobilizing that which remained rigid; confusing our fields with those of Europe, they saw no necessity to divide into lots those vast extensions of lifeless land in order to improve production. The Nation meant an expanse of land, a quantity of cattle, a census of population and of goods, a number of functionaries capable of sustaining the march of public administration, buildings, and statistics of exportation and importation. Cattle raising and agriculture, rather than the provincial governments, had delegated the management of their interests to the federal government; national interests would therefore take the shape and direction of the land. Although they had none, the rights of colonists and workmen were guaranteed by perfect codes of law. Indians did not bring cows or crops and they did not serve as mute tools in the hands of masters. The colonists were mere tenants, beings abandoned to their own initiative, to break their backs and their souls to scratch the earth in pursuit of the only real good: fortune. A thousand misfortunes and unique circumstances increased the value of arable lands and pasture lands; money did not compensate for the inhuman toil and the tribulations of a solitary threatening, dark, and loveless existence without a real home or lofty ideals. The National Confederation was as vast and untilled as a latifundium. It was powerfully supplied by the arsenal of sabers and rifles that the provinces had reserved; however, it only exercised the powers of fear and censure over souls. Because it resolved to assure the general well-being, the Confederation multiplied the value of whatever could not be uprooted and dissolved, as if well-being were the possession of real estate; it left homeless and uncultivated whatever could not be used as a tool or as a weapon: everything that appears useless but is eternal. Statistics demonstrated that we export what is engendered in us and we import what we cannot produce. A child of the latifundium and of chaos, the Confederation loved magnitude and confusion; this fondness arose from having assigned an intrinsic value to money, which was the first item stabilized in a world of fluctuations and catastrophes. In short, the latifundium had given strength to the Nation, authority to the government, and gold to the public treasury. The landowner and the State bought the farmer's land and the artist's intelligence with miserable salaries, and both ended up in the wooden hands of their master. By its very position and by means of mortgages, the State acquired its strength from the desert, from the no man's land, and from the fiscal land until it possessed as an inert force almost half the territory; it exercised tutelage over thought in its universities, over devoted newspapers, and over political patronage. The price of society's goods and the value of the intellect could be quoted on the market as easily as could be the lands liberated from the dangers of disorder; politics gave and took away according to whether or not knowledge and conduct could serve as flesh for the three fauces of the leviathan.

Integration of Intangibles

National unity was the ideal of exiles until
Buenos Aires obtained its victory over the Confederation and in
turn became the Confederation itself, settling in the fields an old
problem of federalists and centralists and annulling a clause of the
political code. National unity was lacking among the masses of inhabitants, and it was not planned by those who brought it about.
Urquiza's feat in Cepeda and Mitre's in Pavón signified an accidental victory for forces that were not included in any clause of
the political code. In spite of the efforts of opposing bands of patriots,
of the free port, of the gap between Melincué and Río Negro that
divided the plain of the white man from the region of the Indian,
and of the wagons and boats, Red Cap and the rural teacher were
forming the Nation with God's help. The federal government absorbed in its cells the danger loosened in the countryside; it sufficed
for the interior to have a task with which to occupy itself in order
to give rise to that body torn into fourteen pieces. The fall of Rosas
was of more import than the five presidencies—except two—during the period from 1862 to 1880. The destruction of Rosas appeared to be the rise of civilization. But the fact is that Rosas fell
when he was incompatible with the state and form of the European
nations; Europe's troops, ships, diplomats, and gold could accomplish nothing against the valiant knight of the plains, but they
could accomplish everything against Mitre, Sarmiento, and Avellaneda. The plan of the latter coincided with the plan of Europe;
with armaments, ships, diplomats, and gold they reconstructed the
nationality that the barbarian had wanted to uphold with only
American resources. What Rosas had achieved with land, they constructed with bricks and iron; what Rosas gave as the capitalist of
an enterprise, they gave as agents and administrators of the world
banking system. The immigrants made a day laborer out of the
gaucho; justice, commerce, and public education were organized;
life and property of the inhabitants were respected according to the
written laws. But the Nation did not yet exist. The victorious entry
of the invaders was couched in the form of loans: private capitals

that took root amid ample guarantees. They waited fifty years for the propitious hour.

Rosas was the pampa; the Confederation was Buenos Aires. A municipal type of government succeeded a pastoral type. The fourteen provinces that had destroyed each other were assured of their autonomy and thus were surreptitiously reduced to fourteen suburbs of the federal municipality.

In this manner the State came to be the integral of all the forces, the sum of public powers, the arsenal of violent impulses retired from circulation. And yet, it lacked strength and mobility. It did not stimulate life but tamed it by paralysis. The State was created to oppose a dynamic chaos with a static mass, to unite and to fill with health a shattered body. It could not be done. That State, which was the coveted dream of order and harmony infeasible in reality, entrenched itself in the metropolis and closed its eyes to the truth of the countryside. The State could do nothing: it was a slave of its own grandeur and power achieved by foreign gold; it could not budge. It maintained immense armies of employees and of soldiers; it manufactured university graduates in the same way as it did paper money: without control and without solvency. It split the budget in two parts: one to support those who supported the State, and the other for the functioning of government. Its apparent strength originated with the State's weakening everything to make itself powerful. But it has no blood, no muscles, no movement; it is like a machine that manufactures death and nothing more.

Molds of Steel

With the loss of centralized power, the viceroyalty was disjointed into autonomous segments because it had never been a unit. The army assumed the responsibility of serving as a focal point for unity in the political dissolution. All the weight of the immense task fell on its shoulders: to destroy and to create. Armies were organized and headed by generals who in civilian life had been professional men or businessmen; urgent duties forced them to abandon the toga and the store to wear the uniform and to

experiment without errors. Because of the failure implicit in improvisation, this type of leader fell ten years later during the civil
war. It was the salvation of the independence; and, though it was
the most efficient way to dismember an organized nation, it was the
only way possible to avoid the moral dissolution of a rootless nation
and to create a central nucleus for the dissolving interests. In the
absence of national unity and of real war, the skirmish and the
active force of the armies were to contain the masses under the
military discipline that served as a substitute for an identity based
on customs, ideals, or common interests. The absence of a preexisting geographical nation and of a schematic disposition of the
inhabitants toward society and coordinated division of labor led to
internal dislocation followed by a personalistic struggle for individual gains. Only by the spilling of blood and the plundering of
homes could the national conscience be achieved; only thus could
be realized the respect for magistracies and the comprehension of
patriotic ends—not even clear in the thesis of independence. No one
believed in the promised wealth, and the nonbelievers had to be
forced at bayonet point to search somewhere for fortune. Levies
were conducted by force, rooting out gauchos and workers from
their jobs and diversions to convert them into soldiers. Dressed in
uniforms and adorned with a simple distinctive mark, which at one
time was a piece of red cloth or an ostrich feather and in another
age was a pair of yellow flannel trousers, and provided or unpro-
vided with weapons, they formed regiments. These were corporations superimposed on other growing institutions but not bound to
them by differential functions. They formed a body but it was a
teratological and all-embracing body, whose decisions could not be
appealed. The battalions were used to save the lives of the traders
and farmers and to erect from the chaos a tribunal invested with
the attributes of strength and justice. As an emblem of order and
security, the army recruited the most capable men, who were brim-
ming with the best intentions. Those who aspired to participate in
the dawning state of affairs enlisted in the ranks; later, the military
career became the occupation that was embraced by necessity but
that evolved into the most honorable profession and the only one

with a practical and noble end. The army developed alongside the structure of the State, parallel to the political and civil development of the State itself. The political and economic State arose from the army's fissiparousness; the army modeled the institutions of order in its own image and similitude. It imparted its adult shape to larval forms; it curbed excesses with excesses; it compelled legislatures to function, congresses to dictate constitutions, and the executive power to govern. The advocates of a despotic organization declared themselves monarchists and centralists; those who longed for the dichotomy of powers called themselves democrats and federalists. The latter recognized the necessity of founding a new order; the former thought that the remaining pieces of the old society could still be utilized. On this was based the divergence of the plans of Moreno and Rivadavia. Moreno wished to deny the continuity of time by clipping the present from the past. Rivadavia wanted to organize institutions as if a mature nation had existed in theory and in fact. There was only one reality facing all the utopianisms of the disciples of Story and of Montesquieu: the army. Still today, even the organizations copied from capitalistic models or cast in a popular mold lack character and physiognomy when compared to the army; they appear like orthopedic devices in the living flesh of the Nation. Only that body which possesses the form of the country is endowed with structure, unity, and logical meaning and function.

The South American armies were formed before the South American peoples; they were composed of such a heterogeneous conglomerate that we can say that life in that out-of-the-way region was integrated into the armies. The realization of being a free country materialized in each free country with the first victories of arms, perhaps in direct proportion to the vicissitudes to be overcome. During periods of peace there would be such a state of laxity that life seemed slavery, disorder, and adventure in comparison with the army's well-formed and well-disciplined society. The worst war and the greatest dangers were in the fields and in the cities; the man of initiative and good will had no other choice than to settle on a career of arms. The best men joined the militia from whence emanated the patriotic forces that were to fill the empty alveolae of the civil institutions. The military and the clergy were the first classes to jell, pure and unadulterated, and to assume the direction of the movement; they became enthroned in the high ranks of politics. In all South America it was a natural phenomenon to have governments by proxy, presided over by a civil regency of the dictatorship.

In our society, the army's intromission in government is not an act of strength consented to by the latter but an act of weakness imposed by the former. We only have to lift the civic film to expose the metallic framework of military structure. Beneath the pampa, the subsoil of rock.

The offices of public administration were installed in the barracks; everything from culture to the guarantees presented to foreign capitals was subordinated to a state of force. The municipal councils were barracks, and the barracks were consistories. But that army which served as an example and an archetype for society and institutions was only strong for lack of any other national force —religion, culture, love of land, economics, politics, fellow feeling —that would part from the depth of consciences or, at least, from the disposition of objects in space and time. The army was not an entity born of the superabundant strength of the people; it was an existing force occupying the empty interstices and destined to shape the people and to inculcate in them the notion of their rights and duties.

That force has only one logical application: war. When reduced to police functions, it overflows all its superlative power like a fiery liquid. The evils of peace were worse than those of war because they meant the oxidation of idle arms. If war has been South America's endemic plague, it should be considered as a derivative of the soldier-professional, of the soldier-patriot, of the soldier-financier, and of the soldier-judge. At first war was a machine hurled against the continent and its autochthonous population; later it was utilized against the last vestiges of barbarity; finally, it was turned against civil governments when they were prone to disorder and antimilitary postures. From Pueyrredón's time until today, the army acted in peace and was as a government of appeal because a concept of leadership separated from the concept of arms was inconceivable; equally unimaginable was the notion of investing capital in industry and commerce without the assurance that the existing well-organized force represented the word of honor, good faith, and the law.

The force of laws followed the force of the armies, which since Caseros and Pavón gave cohesion to a hostile medium; in pacification and in political order, the laws carried out the same coercive mission as did the armies. Once the peril was removed, we returned to the toga and the store. The laws required the army's help to become operative; and, although the two were in collision and discord, the law had its adventitious sway; the army, which was solid and united, kept a watchful eye and controlled the functions of the three constitutional powers. That incommensurable force had been born from terror, and now it represented peace, security, order, and justice. But a State that affirms its power through successive battles and then enters civilian life equipped with all its military tools is forced to struggle, like the hero who always slept armed, against its dissolution rather than to struggle for its growth and betterment; it exists under a hanging sword and a sentinel's eye. Also, compelled by the power of law toward unity and order, it has to fight more against its moral dissolution than to struggle for its improvement because it is not controlled by society but by the sentinel who permits it to sleep without anxiety or a sense of guilt.

All endemic South American revolutions carry the stigma of their original sin. The governments, even in times of abundance, are derivatives from the preceding time of agitation; their apogee of health is the state of siege. A latent state of belligerency persists in a people conditioned by the habits of the sword; their peace takes on the aspects of a bivouac. We possess all the powers—judicial, legislative, executive—that are required for the theoretical organization of a modern nation; but we lack an economic state, a religious state, a cultural state, an ethnic state, and a moral state, which should be implicit as prior postulates of our organization. The schemes of the institutions are clearly drawn, but they obey the profile of an ideal nation and do not possess the shape of true reality. To achieve those theoretical structures we have resorted to the most noble, vital reserves, as did Bernard Palissy when he threw into his smeltery the silverware and whatever art objects could be found at hand.

Conversion of Values

The historical vicissitudes that gave birth to the State endowed it with a power equivalent to that which it was commissioned to overthrow; the model was the politico-juridical organization taken from texts and treatises. It dragged into the sphere of constituted power the forms that were valid in the fields of battle, absorbing in its precepts the rural forces that might be of use in practice. The same recourses used by the chieftain, the provincial governor, the military leader, the rancher, and the store owner served the people governing during the era of constituted government. What before were simple individuals and simple entities became complex individuals and complex entities; what was before ruled by will and by strength became ruled by law. The technique with which the ruler attacked the solution of State problems was identical to that of previous years, and the experiment made in the countryside provided a table of proverbs for the magistrates and public officials. Economically, the State was born poor and with a specific inheritance: debt. Indians, wars, and local chieftains took a great part of the funds destined for public works. The management of income had to be improvised; for a long time the funds were limited to the proceeds from the customs house. The public treasury assisted in all necessities; everyone would attempt to draw on it for concessions, subsidies, and positions. Everything was the same. It was thought and pretended that the Nation born of chaos was order, and that every failure in the struggle for life merited fiscal indemnification. The public lands had been an inexhaustable mine to assist the neighbor at hand and to balance finances. The issuing of money without backing and the stock-market manipulation at the risk of the future provoked crises that exploded in the official banks and in the national treasury coffers.

Economic prosperity obliterated reason, and reason demolished ambitious and imprudent works. The government ended up as a charity institution, with its lottery and its asylum for invalids.

Occupation of Precincts

While the still cartilaginous social structures were taking shape and solidifying, the State and the army together reached the plenitude of their strength. The State was born equipped with keen defense weapons to face a disseminated danger that existed, but no one knew where. In synthesis, the State was no more than a resting place for the army, its winter barracks. And the army was instituted as the custodian of law and order. They were both dimeric-somatic bodies amid chaos, a fortress with thick walls and wide gates where the citizens sought refuge during a storm; it filled with fugitives, and wherever arose a nucleus of necessities a new office was installed. Proclaiming a liberal welcome to all men of the world, it covered with its attributes and swords the life and activity of the resident and the transient.

The State promised much, but it could only deliver by resorting to acts of coercion; that is why it began to display its power without running any risk. In a world lacking in shapes, the patriarchal army-State possessed a perfect form; where the ethical, mercantile, and religious brakes were lacking, it was a model of order and a guarantee of the future. Public administration, with its elastic budget perennially unbalanced, offered a monthly stipend to those who came under its protection. The public treasury meant a good crop, one's own house, and respect. Merchants and landowners searched for a remedy to their ailments in the State's pharmacopoeia; the State dispensed benefits and was the indirect cause of disasters. Capital was not risked unless it was somehow guaranteed by the State, which was made a copartner of every doubtful enterprise; it was as if one were assured of God's favor before attempting a feat. Private initiative was shattered by the State; whatever was being born and ossified remained under its auspices and conformed to its image and similitude, like paper money. The executive power exercised an all-embracing patronage over the provincial chieftains

as was demonstrated by the sixty-two federal interventions realized
from 1862 to 1916. The men of talent revalidated the patronage in
the governmental bureaus, in the universities, and in the courts of
justice; the politicians, as apostles of science, art, and faith, sermon-
ized the gospel of the promised land; the least gifted put themselves
at the service of the State in the lowest jobs; finally, the administration became the popular receptacle of Argentine manna from
which the initiates extracted extraordinary powers. But a State
constituted as a juridical and patronal entity, backed by the militia,
has no strength. It might serve as a dam of containment and as a
correctional jail, but it is undermined and is a fragile toy at the
mercy of its servants. A handful of men can overthrow it, even a
handful of virginal adolescents. It does not exist in the souls. However, such a State is to be dreaded. Fear and ruin lie outside the
orbit of its power. It is not known where its power ends or where
its weakness begins. It manufacturers turbulent men and it jails
them; it incites to depredation and forecloses the mortgage of the
unfortunate farmer; it crowns the artist and insults him: with the
right hand it pays tens of thousands of pesos, and with the left
hand it threatens to take his bread away.

All that which is made dependent on the State is what oppressed
races made dependent on fatality. Whoever is not entrenched within the public administration is not strong, because power is concentrated in arsenals and bureaus. The possibilities for a respectable life are in inverse proportion to the distance occupied from the
center, until on the boundaries of the State's dominion there are
only wide avenues leading to the desert.

Mechanical Functions of the Law

Decomposition was implicit in the theoretical
formulas for national organization, in the suffocated protest of the
masses, and in the forms silently procreated by the pampa. The
juridical organization of the State aspired to make a civilian, bureaucratic, or university recruit out of each citizen; lacking symmetry, it commenced to operate with the capricious and antisocial
functioning of the masses; its dispositions, obeyed until the secret

management of institutions was discovered, took on the character of disciplinary acts against which men were potentially in revolt. The interpretation of Article Thirty-seven of the constitution led to Pavón, and the reality of national unity came from a feat of arms; Article Six led to the murder of several governors, to the trampling of the provinces, and to the ill will, which was as old as the viceroyalty, of the interior toward the capital.

The provinces agreed to a dismal system for their freedoms and interests; although it was theoretically perfect, it was not in agreement with ethnic and geographical necessities. In actuality, the centralist ideal had triumphed under the misnomer of Confederation. If Buenos Aires had declared its independence when the province reached the strait and the mountain range—as Mitre and Del Carril had wished and planned—Argentina would have encompassed that whole span. The rest, allowing for the natural secession of Corrientes and Entre Ríos, would be another Bolivia without a way out.

Subconsciously, the masses understood that the tribunals were ruled by precepts foreign to life and to the nature of things; though they yielded and adjusted to the demands of that vast omitted reality, the primary forces produced invisible dislocations in the system. Those masses were also a people, the same people invoked in the Preamble and the national anthem; a people in an embryonic stage, they lacked the potential to transcend the individual, so typical of the order Hymenoptera where it is the beehive rather than the individual that imparts character to the species. The people had a function, free and uncoordinated. They had laws, traditions, and customs, although free and uncoordinated. All those heterogeneous ingredients constituted the artificial society, the legal society, a whole constellation; superimposed was a life of urban codes and barracks ordinances. It was an intrusive State with resplendent attributes of yet unripe severity. It did not have the form of a biologically based society; instead, it was geometrically contrived, which is why it proceeded contrariwise to the evolution of living organisms. The law will never be able to create in the individual a moral conscience of justice, which is so easily learned from maternal lips in children's stories. The law will not produce beings respectful of the rights of others or of common interests. It formed, among us, beings who examine the codices to determine how far fellow man has the right to be respected; at the same time they maintain themselves at the margin of the law. In a people who are not acquainted with children's literature or choral chants and who do not dispose of time to occupy themselves with useful things, life, which is more like a novel than an allegation, has to feel uncomfortable outside its habitual laxity; the way to express discontent when immediate interests repress it is to await the proper moment for revenge. In this way a juridical tendency and a revolutionary vocation are created. Meanwhile, in the apparent forensic peace of the cities and in the indifference of the countryside, there proliferates, subterranean and entangled, an arabesque of procedural forms, a labyrinthine and eristic manual of procedures, of ordinances, and of decrees learned by heart so as not to be transgressed. There emerges a fictitious state of cohesion, of respect, and of harmonious life symbolized by the inhabitants of Puna de Atacama: miserable shepherds who know by heart the rural code.

The relations of a society thus constituted by logic and juridical convenience forfeit all that is generous, ample, disinterested, and trustworthy and are transformed into redoubts or into plans for attack, into daily cerebral litigations that dissolve before the judge like cases of conscience. And while the judge and the commissary are not scorned, everything that represents justice and authority in the book of moral values is ostensibly or hypocritically abused. The jurisdiction of the father is denied; the overpowering primacy of talent is disregarded; the invincible power of honesty is ignored.

If the institutions do not have the maturity and fairness to oppose the overflowing of ancient impulses or if the law as it is spelled out does not establish a psychic order of interrelationship with the individual, then the idea of justice and all jurisprudence are simply an inconsequential, artificial mechanism.

There does not exist a people who could progress while demanding promissory notes and receipts from brothers and friends and at the same time disdaining obligations and moral sanctions. The subordination of conscience to rules signifies the annihilation of the soul; the law is the instrument of corruption. In this sense the optimistic dreams of our best men have indirectly caused us serious damage. Rivadavia and Sarmiento may be viewed as diabolical geniuses. And Vélez Sársfield's work contributed toward our belief that we are constituted according to civil law and that we are socially organized; thus, we relaxed our consciences: the code became our character, and our initiative was limited to efforts for extracting grants from the State. We felt preserved from a danger that, although it had been contained, had not disappeared and could well assume the shape of the civil code. If knowledge of the law is always sufficient, if the perfect law is an automatic mechanism, then the model is converted into fraud and the law injures and inflames.

A way of life has been developed that appears orderly, peaceful, and without serious dangers, because the danger that previously was in what was being done is now in what we know cannot be done.

Distribution of Labor

Each public official is a live cell of power and embodies in his person a fragment of authority. The first magistrate produces the administrative body by mitosis. All the functionaries free within themselves peculiar forces of dominion that are put into play through the position they fill. Therefore, the result of the totality of those cells is an executive, judicial, legislative, and administrative body of a volume greater than the sum of its parts. The deputy has his privileges, the policeman his uniform, and the usher his livery; they are a piece of legislature, a piece of police, and a piece of tribunal. That division of power diminishes the strength of the State although it may appear to be a superior arrangement, mingled with everything. Represented molecularly wherever its functionaries may be, the State is always found everywhere, like a god without shame. But it only exists as a trustee of the armed force and of personal interests. It is a macerated leviathan that fills everything with the particles of its dissociation. From the sum of functions exercised by those who make use of it, the State acquires the structure of an external skeleton, like that of an arthropod, measuring three million square kilometers. But inside it has no life; it is a receptacle for gas corpuscles. The public operation has no servants, and it only gives strength to the citizen who knows how to make it his own manna. It suits everyone that each person's strength be universally respected. People would not be respected in weakness, and the State would be affronted daily through its servants. The State allows excesses in its officials in order to maintain its equilibrium. The policeman knows that when the infractor forgets that he is in the presence of authority he must somehow enforce that authority and take him to jail. In the presence of a judge one notes there is something above the law, and before a high-ranking public official one senses the weight of power. Something special stands out like the tip of a knife underneath the shirt. A State separated into its components and disseminated throughout the visage of the territory is redoubtable, but it lacks the force of cohesion. It can protect or despoil; it can invest 100 million pesos in a development project or 120,000 pesos per year in the promotion of sciences and letters; it can accord subsidies, suffocate riots, and put 100,000 men under arms. But it is no more than a phantom and a source of fear; equally informed it might do the opposite.

When the citizens aspire to a lofty position and to wealth, there is no value in intellectual capacity, in virtue, in quiet work, or in investigation. The spirit and its poor accessories are worth nothing; they have to be filled with another substance that simultaneously represents the ideal and the well-being. A position in the administration, in the judicature, or in teaching denotes money, competence, power, and honor. The State grants salaries as subsidies and administers knowledge, respect, fame, and honesty. The chosen individual visited by the god of fortune and called to fulfill a sublime destiny functions as a tool and not as a wheel in a mechanism; the position he occupies represents the sum of his aspirations. He knows that corresponding to his name is a position that he may imprint on his calling card; he also knows that he is responsible for his acts before the friend who named him to his position, like the chosen one before his god. Once the office is secured, he automatically obtains impunity that is inherent in any type of prominent position. Impunity means to be above ordinary sanction, ratified in power by the silence of those who aspire to the same. The race toward power is the race toward impunity, toward the expansion of individual forces whose march has been contained by society. Since he is always assured of his subordinates' esteem, he frees within himself some of the collective ego. Without that arrogance, which surpasses by a few centimeters the strict orbit of his action, he would betray the ideal of multitudes: to make a fortune and to command. Everything that might impair one's reputation contributes to enhance prestige because it appears as a capacity for power that is denied to others. The public official who does what he wants, perhaps in the belief that he is carrying out an obligation, embodies a certain cloaked and capricious power that has to be attracted and conspired with. The simple performance of duty would make the position inappreciable; fraud and immodesty are signs of strength because through them we have proof of a man more powerful than his function and therefore more dreaded.

The scenic pomp is a basic value in this comedy of high positions with its primary characters and primitive plots. The dignity of the position purifies the official of personal misery precisely because it is placed at his personal disposal. That dignity which differs from the customary and the normal is multiplied by the categorical affirmation of the arbitrary act; thus is demonstrated the capacity to exercise the function and to exceed it by an unexpected factor. The common people consider the national employee as a being who has the privilege of using public service for his own ends, one who causes alternatively their hope and their fear. Therefore they pay homage to him. Without that arbitrary act, the power would seem common and diminished and the usufructuary would appear to be a servant. Now it is clear why the public official who invents, who wishes to innovate, is the most dangerous among us: because the innovation consists in introducing his own person into a new operation.

The subordinate possesses a recourse to the same fraudulent nature that allows him to win disputes. This is the unexpected factor also present in his superior. If he considers that he has been unjustly injured, he appeals to another strange power even more powerful than the public official. The power is a hidden functionary of unknown potential: the politician. To resort to the politician is to call on the body of privileges and demand justice for that which was injured and, simultaneously, to carry out vengeance of a transcendental order by paying tribute to the collective ego. And yet, the usurpation of institutional power by personal power and the absorption of public office by the individual sometimes contribute to the glorification of the public position. The judge, the legislator, the public official, and the policeman who enforce respect for the investiture by the addition of the personal factor speak to the incredulous in a way that he might understand the meaning of an investiture. In the aggregate of forces there is a certain compensation that balances personages and functions. In this comedy of equivocations and *quid pro quo* interludes, eventually everything is lost except honor.

The nature typical to the functionary and the public employee, which Agustín Álvarez knew so well and despised so much, is a sublimated variant of the *compadre*. The *compadre* is one of the typical characters we inherited from the colonial period. He abounds in Spanish one-act farces, although not overly gloomy or perverse. In the gallery of barbarous figures, the *compadre* is perhaps the most common. His type is widely dispersed and may be found under the most unexpected conditions. He is worth analyzing because his area of action is vast and his meaning very representative.

The Compadre

On the calibration scale of human characters, there is, between the brawler and the insolent, ill-bred personage, the octave of the *compadre*. He approaches certain characteristics of the brawler, that brave, upright, and solitary man; on the other hand, he may appear as a variety of the *guarango*, that ill-bred and insolent personage who is a man without character, factitious and incomplete. The octave of the *compadre* ranges from the playboy who goes to dare the washerwomen by the river to the bully who strikes old night watchmen, from the bushwhacker of Indians to the public official who successfully exploits a regulation as a privilege of his rank. He is characterized by a sense of personal worth; consequently, he depreciates the value of others. He stands out, as does the *guarango*, by his essential contempt for the external values—in the broad sense. This contempt is offensive because in this case he makes immoderate use of another force not in play. Because the flat aggression of those who excel him often involves a danger, which his bravado or which his position does not allow him to face, he resorts to the expediency of discharging his fury against the weakest point. He oscillates between the brawler and the *guarango*, between the type who takes no account of society and the one who reacts because of society. He does not appear to function in the bosom of society, an individual excoriated by the concrete and polished forms of urbanity.

Primarily, the *compadre* and the *guarango* are poor; their natural environment is poverty, but they are not so destitute as to lack bread. "*Compadre*" was the form of address among low-class people, and it meant the equivalent of friend or comrade. Likewise, "*cuñado*," or brother-in-law, is a familiar form of address that in the countryside is lavished by people of the same class. The *compadre* used to be poor, but it has been some time since the rich joined into that immense family of the common people, into that spurious bond of character. The word qualifies a species of individuals boasting of plebeian lineage. We could not say of the *compadre*, as we licitly could of the *guarango*, that his germs of decomposition and discrepancy from the environment are antisocial. It is more accurate to consider him a retarded being with respect to the firm march of the social body. His defiant and hostile attitude harmonizes with the manners of one who begins to have a clear consciousness of the fatidic unevenness between his stature and that of the average surrounding humans and things. He knows that the environment has changed and moved forward and that his anthropological relationship with it has been strained.

A being of untimely arrival, he is possessed of such total pride that, instead of reaching out to things and people, he expects them to come to him. Although he is intellectually unable to conceive the inferiority in which he is mired in relationship to reality, his organic consciousness perceives that he does lag in the march and so he attempts by inverted efforts to put himself at the flanks of the vanguard, of that reality which outpaces him. He refuses to become defeated but he ignores reality while invading it with his person, and he looks down on fellow men and the values of civilization: these are his manifest characteristics. By attempting to annul the distance, he is exposed. In this movement there is not a plan or an artifice: these are simple organic forces, which through word and gesture manage to apply a cold chisel to the vulnerable points and thus to shatter the lock of the external. He employs a picklock to penetrate society; society has not shut its doors to him: they are open on the other side, which he does not see.

Being a *compadre* is also an attitude, a formula for resolving incompatibility problems with the environment by reducing them to conflicts and fights where the solution is arrived at by fists: a false key because it provides beforehand the solution to any problem. We should note with care: in every act of being a *compadre* there is a fallacy of people and events.

It is also a form of resentment. The difference between what one really is and what one believes himself to be raises a wall outside of which is the world and inside of which is the man. Scheler says, ". . . the great repressed internal pretensions; a great pride coupled with an inferior position, are singularly favorable circumstances for the awakening of the feeling of vengeance." To the above and to all that could be said by exploring the subconscious we could add this: the countries that pass very rapidly from a savage state to a civilized one march at a faster pace than the human being. Man accompanies events; the human being requires time to acclimatize himself to progress. Civilization, which is above all a burden, is perhaps already incompatible with the normal physiological state of the human being. Culture and civilization are states of conscience as much as mastery of techniques. The resentful man we find in the *compadre*, whose accidental definition is given by Scheler, may well be a normal man who is developing normally in accord with a conscientious physiological process of civilization. Perhaps the lack of equilibrium between his ethical-mental metabolism and the development of things does not prove his lack of adaptability as much as it does the injustice inherent in wishing him to incorporate, with excessive urgency, the elements of the social state, which is itself the result of the rash haste of conventional forms. In our environment he would be the man who proceeds correctly as opposed to the man who skips the intermediate stages. He errs in the reaction, but he is not responsible. The *compadre* as a resentful man opposes himself to a language of forms, not to a language of substances. We have to at least recognize his right to barbarity when such a state is justified by an invisible, impalpable, and intramolecular context. The spontaneous verdict confirms it when he exclaims "it is a product of the environment," or "the father and the friends are guilty." That is why he is always so generic and representative.

The *compadre* yearns to prove that he is unadaptable; his mistake lies in the excessive urgency he applies to his endeavor. He employs a greater degree of force than necessary to dominate while "saving his honor," or while attempting to terrorize or to ensure that he is left alone. He is inexcusable because he indulges in excesses and boasting without proportion, as does a person who jumps from the twentieth floor when less than half the height would have sufficed. Arrogance does not result from his commentary about events but from his muteness before them. Verbal braggadocio always crowns a formerly corporal attitude.

The glorious soldier of the Sicilian theater and of decadency and the stepdaughter of the Latin farce are advanced characters of this embryo—dialectic characters; the state of being a *compadre* is similar but antedated to action, reduced from an imaginative and a psychological element to a corporal, biological element. Rather than delighting solely in the concept of merit for a hypothetical action, the *compadre* prefers the pleasure of announcing it and executing it, even if it is effected behind one's back. He is inclined to use coarse language when asserting something certain and veridical, some defenseless exterior point; what is normally screened in the satire and the one-act farce takes the shape of a verbal dagger.

Perhaps aggression and provocation are persuasion's last resort in the absence of language that is proficient to produce a convincing argument. In this light the *compadre* is a being of minimal and deficient language who appeals to action for the lack of that valve which gauges precise phraseology without beating and allows one the internal satisfaction that the word has already discharged a blow. There are senators, for example, who from their benches, won with obvious fraud, appeal to the conglomerate of civil *compadres* to save their positions, while they themselves have no explanations to offer their accusers. The *compadres* perhaps represent a complementary language.

The blusterer who requires the sword and pierces the hat is a national and theatrical variety of this authentic character who admits no possibility of pretentiousness and who becomes a public spectacle by turning into a spectator of his own posture. The *compadre*, as well as the blusterer, is not a psychological but a social type; his soul is that of a multitude. They both need a large audience but one from the circus crowd and not from the theater public, because their show is performed with real beasts and weapons. The *compadre* appears in a certain medium as the product of moral class, of a caste of moral Sudras where the theater is still a degree of representation superior to the social exigencies of the ego; he performs for that society which applauds in silence. That is why the blusterer that we find in literature, although undoubtedly related to the one in real life, actually has nothing to do with the latter; the blusterer is impossible to transport into fiction because he is only a specific case and lacks intellectual and theatrical meaning. Anomalous beings have their place in the warehouse where they do not disfigure the monstrosity that is the essence of their art —in the warehouse, which is everything opposite to the theater.

9 PSYCHIC FORCES

Stylistic Unity

It would be difficult for one of us today to clearly perceive the substantial analogy of values, of techniques, and of styles between the events of 1830 and those of 1930. However, those last hundred years of world history span more profound alterations than other periods of the past. Our century consistently advanced with its destiny, developing what had been imported. The year 1830 is a moment in the dissolution of an order that had been ruling by inertia; it is the instant of exhumation of an immortal body and soul. So is 1930. But we can see that period from a distance of a hundred years, reduced to its scheme. We contemplate the present period through the passage of the days that form our age; it is apparently more logical and more continuous and, without a doubt, possessing a greater quantity of moving matter. Bones speak of events past, but we are living what history omits. The stylistic unity of a people is perceived late and from afar. It will be necessary to wait for the present to lose its character of biological phenomena and to await its conversion, like the past, into a synoptic diagram. Then, we will be able to understand that the present in which we live is a chapter of the same work and that, by the theme now being developed and by the characters now on stage, it is most similar to that work which appears to change plot in the middle of the nineteenth century. The years in which we live are in no way superior to the past, although they are seasoned by outside events that enter into play accessorily through the telegraph, the transatlantic liners, and the airplanes. What end do they serve, what genuine forces do they put in action? What we believe to be a greater, overall measure of well-being and what we take to be phenomena of culture and wealth may appear to be symptoms of decadence and backward motion when we disappear from the stage and the events stand unencumbered, with only a theoretical meaning, without flesh and reduced to bone. The year 1830 is judged by us in relationship to a universal date. The year 1930 will be seen later in comparison with the new present.

The protagonists of the historical period in which we live are not more numerous or any better than those who acted at any given moment in the past. As before, they are no more than twenty, but today they operate under the disadvantage of having lost a national vision of events; they proceed to track from the shore a complex aggregate of forces already mechanized. The men of the past forged a state of affairs; the men of today are dragged along by a state of affairs that escapes their comprehension and skill. In days past, our civilization did not present inferior values unless it was compared to others; today it displays inferior traits within the concert of elements adjudged to be desirable, even by national standards. Those heroes without stature and without character whom we see participating in public life and whose acts seem trivial, routine, confused, and even insensate—will they perhaps be the heroes of our grandchildren as for us are those other men full of passions, cruelties, and brilliant observations? The grandchildren will see the curvature of descent, the identity of historical matter and the gap that to us seems filled. They will see that the leaders have been imitating the past and are not capable of handling a system that overcomes them with its complications. Without a past rich in experiences, they unconsciously devote themselves to it; lacking a program, they improvise. These years should perhaps be considered as the penultimate chapter of the colonial period. The year 1880 will appear in the awakening of new blood as a less authentic and less Argentine year than 1930, the year in which history is once again welded to previous eras in a continuous plane of feeling.

Approximation Curves to the Normal Vector

What we understand as the progress of the last sixty years may be characterized as the megacephalic growth of the seven cities in which more than half the population is concentrated; also included should be the increase in the price of land. The contemporary level of what we understand to be the intellectual and moral state has descended as sharply as has risen the production of material values. The ascending curve corresponds to the traffic of international commerce, and the descending curve to the yield of what is properly Argentine. The larger has been the growth of what corresponds to the history of Europe's dominion in America—political or capitalistic—the lesser has been the intellectual, poetic, and emotional output.

The greatness and the decadence of a people are measured by data other than those indicating the mechanical expansion of wealth. They result from an exhaustive balance of resources and consumption; an inventory should list all those elements impossible to enclose in the thick statistics of importation and exportation. A plus on the balance sheet results in greatness, and a minus signifies decadence. These processes are not visible to the spectator; whoever forms part of a system that is progressing or degenerating is saturated by the changes, which are operative even in him. What happens to him was described by Poincaré in the tale of the inhabitant of a hypothetical world that at night symmetrically expanded or shrank in all directions: next morning everything seemed unaltered because both the inhabitant and the measuring rod had expanded or shrunk in the same proportion. Those processes are comprehensible from a distance; then it can be seen that the decline of moral values during the expansion of material goods has been along the line of a vertical drop. A surplus slowly accumulates on the plus side, revenue not strictly needed: the reserve fund. The same occurs with the deficit, which accumulates and must be covered at the expense of high-quality substance. In new peoples, a hypertrophic growth of population, of immediate yield, of mechanical instruments, and of superficial forms of knowledge may conceal the deficit by drawing on reserves of vital substance. And, even if in absolute terms a nation's curve of material growth should on balance be positive, it may have a negative result when compared to other growth curves. Does Argentina signify more today than she did in the concert of nations in 1870 as measured by intellectual production, state of organization, and economic potential?

The monstrous growth of Buenos Aires since it was constituted as headquarters and mirror of the Republic has placed the interior in a negative position with respect to its growth. Each skyscraper that rises in the center of the metropolis makes poorer, more ignorant, and more unproductive the piece of land lost in the provinces; and it imparts to the fiscal deserts of the ten territories, which are public lands of the metropolis, aspects of solitary remoteness.

There is an accumulation that pertains to man and his spiritual good; there is another that refers to material things, which in a manner would seem to exist, to grow, and to multiply independently of man. These two factors are usually in opposition and even in declared combat when the sum of the force of things surpasses the sum of the capacity to dominate them. Then it is necessary to appeal to the foreign capital, professorship, and technique and to bring professors, specialists, and fiduciary fuel. These are culture and civilization, soul and body, the forms of thought against the shapes of the cranium, and, in summary, the moral deficit in relation to the material superavit. We cannot speak of an improvement and of a fundamental change in the political, economic, and artistic life of our country by only taking into account the adopted use of the latest forms of humanity's advancement. We have become the dumping grounds for civilization's products. The telephone, the press, the radio, the automobile, the movie house, the fabrics, the books, and the tobacco are susceptible to taxes and they increase revenues; but they can have dissolving effects when used and not assimilated. In a sense we may say that man routinely accumulates, multiplies, and reproduces as a mechanism that has its unexceedable limits; it is as if the things, the tools, the machines, the buildings, and the goods that acquire life in his hands were the ones that create, innovate, and vary. Man is converted into a vegetative being before the creation of that world of objects which is born, grows, multiplies itself, and dies. Civilization means the proper use of forms created by it. We have to judge how the use of those products contributes to real progress; the products are instruments that the country ought to utilize effectively. It is possible to make a rheostat from a wire. Alberdi used to say that the telegraph and the printing press could be vehicles of barbarity. Let us view the province of San Juan as described by Sarmiento, or Corrientes as seen by Echeverría around 1840, or Salta in 1800, or Santa Fe in 1780, or Mendoza in 1900. The San Juan tradition of political crimes, of abuse, and of exactions is at present in its fullest bloom. Corrientes, which initiated colonization on a grand scale and of which Pellegrini in his speech against the federalization of Misiones could speak in high praise, has fallen into ignorance and poverty, regressing more than a century. Entire towns never taste meat; children eat manioc, oranges, and maté; three-fourths of the population is illiterate; the percentage of men exempt from military service in La Rioja, Catamarca, Salta, and Jujuy due to thoracic insufficiency or endemic illnesses is frightful. Licentiousness obliterates whatever is left standing by misery. The story of riots, of regional hates, of malversations, of the systematic persecution of acknowledged intellectuals, of scorn for what is not oriented in the direction of pecuniary fortune, of the army's hegemony as the only institution of order and of power, and of the subjection of education to politics demonstrate that a parenthesis is closed after a century and that history returns to its regular course. We may use as a comparative index the journals of the legislative chambers, the newspaper publications, the speeches that are proclaimed, the books that are read, the theater plays that are in vogue, the popular music, the prevailing spectacles, the sports, and all the other expressions of the authentic reality and we will see that the moral and intellectual level has not reached today's lows for fifty years. A political depravation without precedent and the enthronement of ignorant, egotistical, and fanatical masses replaced a system that was perpetuated in fraud and ineptitude. After the fall of the so-called democratic government, power was recuperated by the real owner of an older claim to rule and of less debatable rights. What we had been calling barbarity had not disappeared; it had taken refuge in neutral zones, awaiting its propitious moment. It makes its appearance everywhere: in privateering, in assemblies, in stadiums. The economic crisis resulted in a resurgence of banditry, of contraband, and of bribery; aggressiveness was cloaked in groups and in leagues. The Córdoba seen by Funes is the same seen by Nicolai; it was suffocated by high salaries and by the freedom with which everyone exploited his lucky streak. We only have one great city left, a fortress against unforeseen disasters; what was before divided among the provinces is now concentrated in Buenos Aires. But the city has grown without varying. The big village of Lucio V. López is the factory of Ortega y Gasset. It is described by J. A. Wilde, Hudson, and Cunninghame Graham although without subways, without electricity, without telephones, and without a coastal avenue. The provinces, with their cooperatives, silos, automobiles, bank branches, and shops, have not prospered or advanced more than Buenos Aires.

Love

        The grandchildren of grandchildren were burdened by a soul laden with all the ballast of the past.

Time was on the side of those who waited. Man's flesh grew old and returned to the original dust. The humiliated woman, in whom man wants to erase all feeling of dignity, retreats a step and exercises her vengeance by the very meekness with which she surrenders and resigns herself. Captured, used for pleasure, she leaves on man's soul the material destiny of her body. Man's soul was prostituted simultaneously with woman's flesh. Fraud, greed, scorn for what will not perish in spite of everything, lack of enjoyment of today's work, no hope for a better tomorrow, and an anxiety to fill with money, power, and appearance the holes that cannot be filled are the spiritual legacy of that long affront to woman, whose human significance is mystical.

Such a past is best forgotten but there is no way of avoiding it; it is covered with the latest conquests of science and art, and it rises like a ferment to disarrange everything. The grandchildren know nothing of their origins. Time seems to have erased iniquity, and we hear it from the schoolboy's lips when he is angry at a schoolmate, and we see it in the adolescent's smile that betrays at a distance some allusion to the feminine taboo. Bloods may be mixed; the offended drop is immortal. New men arrived from other parts of the world and imported new customs. The transfusion was slow and was diluted in the circulatory torrent. The new human contingents, impelled by the same incentives, possessed by eagerness and urgency, did not contribute love or kindness—which is never absent among partners who understand each other. They brought no love and could not find it although the fire lit in their scourged flesh may have ephemerally illuminated them in the great splendor of an uncontrolled passion. Their children joined with other children who labored in molding a formless and cold reality.

Pellegrini narrates that during the Paraguayan war women accompanied the troops as in the civil war and the campaigns against the Indian: Corrientes has lost that war. From the possessed women who served only as domestic beings were born children who would be raised in regularly constituted homes; in each family there were at least half a dozen children, but whoever possessed more raised more. Santos Ugarte, in *The Ombú* by Hudson, is this type of man who populated and depopulated the countryside; Entre Ríos had its own type. The subrace born of such disorders, the sowing of pariahs on a scale unknown in world history, produced the gaucho, who respected no one. Women hated men who in every respect were their inferiors; when they kept silent and surrendered, something inside them gathered strength and prepared to raise its voice.

Between the time of spiritual separation and the somewhat

guarded union that followed, there existed a neutral zone, an untilled land like that which so commonly separates farms. It was a
psychological distance that with time became a physical one, as can
be seen between the husband and wife who go from the fields to the
village and from the village to the city. Man and women walk
through the streets as if they were ashamed to be seen together, perhaps because the sun never surprises them joined together. The rural chores, which tie the woman to the home and carry the man to
his task, leave them only the cold night of solitude when, tired, they
lie down to engender children and to fall asleep. These are customs
and defenses of dissociated beings, which may equally be discovered among immigrants. They appear to be disoriented as they
blame each other for nonexistent faults that could not be confessed.
The man goes ahead; the woman and children straggle behind. He
walks along with the air of a lost and an astounded man scrutinizing indiscreet insinuations—which do exist—as if those who followed did not belong to him; and they are his wife and children.
To the natural scorn for the woman, whose position in society was
inferior because of a complex of circumstances, was added the ancestral Judeo-Christian disdain, according to which she was considered the source of all evil; the incitation by Eve and the fall of humanity took on proportions of theological evidence. In the Catholic
sphere the woman is the instrument of pleasure, the handiwork of
the devil, and the sin by antonomasia; if life lacks the organic
strength to eliminate the virus, it captures and vitiates it. That religious idea, divulged without resistance from the status quo actually based on love, infused language and life with a special tone;
the perverse idea hid itself in lewdness, in allusions, in gestures, and
in a state of mind disposed toward such synthetic judgments of lowliness. On the outside, an excessive rigidity proscribed even the most
innocent erotic feints; on the inside, laxity and dehiscence. From
such a breach and such a censorship, the constrained and asphyxi-
ated sexual life had to be transformed and to emerge with morbid
virulence: on one hand in the public house of pleasure, and on the
other in the home resigned to a life of suffering without love. Everything faintly connected with a sexual origin was covered with a

layer of austere repudiation: a layer as solid as a transparent cornea through which was viewed the world of sin. No compassion was extended toward woman; the most elaborate traps were set for her and men lived in the expectation of defaming her. Camila O'Gorman, executed while heavy with child, is one of the poor martyrs of the public censor's inclemency. The confessional and the furtive look from behind the jealousies were the terrible prosecutors of that life enclosed in a capsule of hypocrisies. There were only two extremes: immured chastity and prostitution. In the classic Spanish theater without mothers, without children, with wives as lovers, and with maidens of brutish virtue, there are abundant examples of what was exalted and of what was reviled. Sex remained always concealed, but it wreaked havoc in the souls, corroding, in the spirit, portions equivalent to those which could not be nobly satisfied through the bodies. We find a picturesque evasion in the heavily veiled women of Lima who covered their faces to avoid jeers; another example is to be found in the masks of our carnival. The most curious forms of licentiousness occurred under the disguises of the most refined integrity. Outside her home, the woman remained exposed to taunts and insults that waylay in Buenos Aires after ten o'clock at night. Love was reduced to forbidden places, as it was limited to the bedroom in the classic Spanish theater. The dissociation of a unit that was indestructible created a population without love that also feigned love; it produced a cancerous growth in society's diseased tissues. For Bertrand Russell, South America is one of the last areas where prostitution continues to be a social and municipal problem; he ignores that it is a moral problem, as all our problems are.

The banishment of instincts to the confinement of bawdyhouses did not diminish the virulence of the dilemma; the problem worsened as it became more feigned and more taciturn. Those places were disseminated through all the neighborhoods of all the towns, yet they were isolated by a halo of spiritual quarantine; the somnambulists who frequented these establishments acquired loose and insolent habits that contaminated homes and children. The adolescent stood in the whorehouse, his vigil of arms for admission to knighthood in our Middle Ages. Woman projected an abstract image, and, basically, she occupied a fictitious position and was not respected. She was looked at with the malice of one who from early boyhood is aware of her anatomical secrets and her generic functions of menstruating and giving birth. Old and young demons alike viewed nubility as a physiological humiliation. Sexual matter was displaced from the sphere of feelings and it fell, like a shooting star, into the orbit of matter; the genital was the sexual and the sexual the sensual. Voluptuousness and emotion were fixed in a corporal place; hence, the parody of love in the houses of ill repute. Genital inflorescences were the spices that seasoned the chatter among males. They form an integral and a parasitic part of language, or ideas, and of the common background of thoughts and images; when they are excluded, the effort of their elimination is quite noticeable. Life revolves around what one avoids saying: a Milky Way of allusions forbids the use of numerous words and grammatical constructions. Even the most inexperienced woman has great subconscious agility to interpret the most veiled insinuations to sexuality. Suspiciousness winds through prohibited meanders, and even children in their games mix obscene terms with gestures whose meanings they ignore. Sexual matters were reduced to the recesses and to the suburban zones of conscience, and they did not occupy the places that they should have. Under police and religious vigilance, the problem of the libido produced phenomena of moral disturbance. Normally simple and free of neuroses, the libido is saddled with laws, secrets, and ordinances.

Faith

The religion that was brought to these lands of myths as ancient as its plants and its beings was, at the time, a very complex instrument of dominion. It lacked all contact with life; it was a machinery intended to function in the bosom of nature. The Jesuit order was an engineering system designed to convert the raw materials of a savage world into fuel for apostolic strength. Those in charge of inculcating the doctrine of Christ did not bring with them charity or hope; they came to recruit spirits and bodies for war, to carry out the most daring plan that a despairing cynic could have engendered in the mind of a fanatic. The doctrine that Machiavelli conceived for politics was the consolation and the resignation that would be preached to the children of solitude by their adversaries.

Catholicism, which, except as a coalition against the Arabs, had not captured Spain until the time of Ferdinand and Isabella, takes on its Hispanic shape with Saint Ignatius of Loyola. From the moment of his appearance, Catholicism was consubstantial with his life. The saint discovered the way to regroup the religious forces of primitive harshness, which had been weakened by the Renaissance, and to transport them into a new era; thus were preserved the mystical contents of Spanish medieval life. Jesuitism was Spain overflowing toward lands in which to battle for faith and for domination. The brilliant idea was to convert Christ himself into The Crusader; in this way love for Him could be transformed into warfare, and prayer and ecstasy concentrated in hypnotic discipline of a barracks. The absolute truth of the dogma was indisputable, and theological debates were useless. There was only one truth, faith, and only one way to impose it, the army. With the Company of Jesus, Spain found the way to strengthen herself by becoming the fighting arm of the Church; she placed her courage and her ignorance at the service of the dogma, and she annulled the distance separating her from Europe. Religion left the cloister and interned itself in the jungles and deserts of the wild world, carrying its soul on the cross and in the sword. America rated with China, India, Poland, Lithuania, Russia, and Africa. Saint Ignatius's idea was to substitute in the people at the precise moment their need to reason with the need for faith, their need to command with that of obedience, their need to be ordained with that of enterprise. The company was born to save Spain from an imminent danger by providing her with substitutes extracted from her own essence to replace the advanced culture to which Europe was becoming adapted. Spain found how to persevere without abandoning her ferocious nature, without compromising with the Modern Age. The arrival of the order made possible the continuation of the conquest whose purpose was at a dead end; the Jesuit had a plan and the "settler" did not. The order assumed its character at a time when Spain's power was increasing and she was basing her international aspirations on the strength of her armies. The armies of preachers and missionaries found a propitious horizon for conquest in these latitudes. It was easier and more meritorious to subdue the Indian than the peoples who had embraced the Reformation. Once again a chosen people appeared on the eve of Catholicism's failure and provided the Church with a refuge. In those militias the Church had a force that could not be ignored at the time of treaty and alliance making.

Among the shapeless promises that America held out to the limited spirit of the sixteenth-century Spaniard was the possibility of carving an empire and amassing a fortune. America would have its justification: the levy of a formidable army for the defense of the faith and the exploitation of a native race for the pursuit of wealth. The missionaries were a complement of the armed invasion; their purpose was not to legitimize despoilment and slavery in the eyes of the pope and of the king but to secure a safe and peaceful reign for dogma. The evangelization of Spanish America was an ecclesiastical enterprise, not a religious one. A catechism and precepts that were artificially exaggerated were introduced instead of the Gospel and the Epistle. The priest was the incarnation of a combatant Christ. The empire was to expand according to a plan that would make it eternal and impregnable; the headquarters would be located in a strategic point of the holdings and the subsidiary organs would obey the disposition of the whole—something not understood by the conquistador, who settled without a plan and ingenuously served in the plans of others.

Misiones was the place where the building of temples and the recruitment of the soldiers of Jesus began. The clergyman was a man of conquest, of domination; he took the aborigine under his tutelage and made him work; he promised the native a paradise after death in return for his servile effort on earth. The clergyman and the magistrate occupied prominent positions; while the magistrate had as his province the guarding of frontiers. the clergyman watched over the integrity and discipline of spirits. To appeal to the savage's soul and to put within his grasp a simplified and materialized belief it was necessary to hyperbolize what was picturesque and touching about religion. Catholicism returned to primitive forms, to the doctrines of Paul, and, insofar as they were compatible, consented to the infiltration of elements of autochthonous mythology. If the Indian was not to reject all religion with the indignation of an Atahualpa, some adjustments were necessary. An enervating, tropical type of drug was elaborated by a combination of the new cult and the old superstition. Theology and canonical law, which were the principal subjects of instruction, were unrelated to that inverse process practiced by the friar, who was progressively benumbed by a mythical Catholicism, adulterated by the parishioner's ignorance. His last recourse was to abandon himself to politics in a search for the strength lost in the dealings with the subject peoples; this quest included parliaments, cloisters, pulpits, and homes. The religion administered to the catechumen was deformed; and, when the subject accepted it, he further disfigured it. The symbols and the rhetoric of mysticism had to be reduced to the level of that infantile intelligence. Very quickly the spiritual part of religion disappeared and what remained was the ornamental ritual to be used as an instrument of torture and dominion. The architectural forms replaced in the Indian's soul the legends of martyrs and saints. Francisco Solano had to lower himself to the condition of the errant Indian in an attempt to resemble him as much as possible because the native was incapable of rising to his level. The effort to convey to the brute the mysteries of the Trinity, the Conception, and the Eucharist led to a materialistic form of superstition that the Indians themselves rejected in the long run in order to return en masse, purged, to their ancestral cults. If the Indian is taught about the mystery of virginity, the end result is a phallic cult. The priest as a man enjoyed the highest prestige. His worth was measured by the amount of hell at his disposition. For each Santa María de Oro and each Mamerto Esquiú, we have ten of Castro Barros and of Aldao and Monterroso, classical exponents of what became of the priests in the countryside. The tonsure would disappear under the growth of hair; the spiritual and physical signs differentiating the priest from the layman would be slowly erased. The priest led armies, incited them to combat, and compelled them to plunder; he gambled, he courted, and he blasphemed.

Religion found no refuge in souls and thus sought shelter in the temples and the barracks. Saint Ignatius and Corpus Christi were the recruiting points in the conscription for faith and work in the terrestrial empire; Córdoba, elected to be the center of colleges and congregations, radiated scientific justification for the enterprise as a work pleasing in the eyes of reason. Asunción, the central key, was the last head to envision that dream. Córdoba constituted the soul of the order as much as Saint Ignatius made up the body; it had the university, which worked in conjunction with the seminaries to deepen the conquest of souls. Both arsenals occupied strategic places, taking into account the area of the viceroyalty and future plans for extension throughout South America. In Córdoba, the umbilical center that would absorb Chuquisaca, the heavy artillery of theologians and jurists was prepared. In Misiones, which was to absorb the Río de la Plata, rose the industrial, mercantile, agricultural, and cattle emporium that put conquest at its service and furnished, as the Lubeck of a barbarous Hanseatic League, the Church's coffers and troops. They were two fortresses constructed without doing violence to nature and to the fundamental lines of communication; always in mind was the ideal map of the empire of the invading armies of colonists, soldiers, theologians, and merchants. But religion was excluded from this Machiavellian tactic. It was negated precisely at the time of the diffusion and the domination of that egoistical fanaticism which had intended to use the victory over the savage as a point of departure for victory over the European Catholic world—a world slowly withdrawing from the Church. The renewed instruction of those forces for their deployment in Europe brutalized the undertaking: the means became the end. The idea of Saint Ignatius of Loyola found its arm in the Council of Trent, but America lacked a previously irritated state of Catholicism sufficient to permit the unperverted accomplishment of that formidable fabric of cruel reasoning and chemical logic. The conversion would be inversed, since the instrument for dominion was infinitely weaker than the matter to be dominated. Preachers and soldiers would end up at the service of America, utilizing the lessons of their experience to reject a military liturgy that, however, was destined for ordinary souls.

The medium in which Christ's captains and generals were to develop their activities was hostile—refractory in every imaginable circumstance. Blind faith requires the draining of reason and demands the conscious suicide of the capacity to create, to doubt, and to search for the innermost path. This blind faith reaches the spirit, distorted and undermined, after many years of searching the inner abodes with sterile anxiety. When blind obedience is preached as dogma, the acceptance of the absurd, accentuated as a virtue of merit, concludes by bursting and overflowing in destructive waves. The armed troops, for the first time at liberty to think and to love according to their own judgment, felt themselves to be God's cohorts. The rebirth of the unbribable faculty to think without coaction provided an arsenal against the emancipated conscience itself.

The first claudication of the missionaries consisted in their submission to the primitive condition of the savage in an attempt to catechize him. They began learning tongues linguistically unrelated to any known languages; they learned Quechua and Guaraní to teach those peoples the catechism and the prayers. It was the only recourse possible for transmitting doctrine to the catechumen in his mother tongue, and in this lay the first victory of the Indian. Grace would reach him in his own language. With the change of language the purity of doctrine became corrupted, regardless of the catechist's intelligence and of the good will applied to the task. A religion is inseparable from a language, as is shown by the adoption of Latin for liturgy. Through the usage of an inappropriate vehicle, the subtle components slowly evaporated and the substantive ones became desiccated, material, and didactic. Those peoples, who possessed a soul similar to that of a European only by reason of a papal decision, were in no way predisposed toward anagogic disquisitions or toward the concept of a supraworld of philosophical categories. It was necessary to give them coarse examples and to consent to the interpolation of entire selections of their theogony into the Christian legend. Preachers and missionaries corrupted their own language and ended by definitively proscribing it from speech and from the euchologia. The Spanish language in the missions and the Latin in the lecture rooms suffered, by hybridization, the same deformations as did the religion that spoke to a people's stupefied fantasy instead of their heart. To comprehend minds and hearts it was necessary to close one's eyes to the past and to the present, both of which were being destroyed by the very existence of those incomprehensible structures. The credulity of those teachings was affirmed only by the power, the style, and the infula identified with the preachings and the lives of those men of a different color, who seemed to carry with them Truth and Strength. They believed in men.

All that sacrifice of patience, of perseverance, and of reciprocal accommodation had a secret, nihilistic motive. Gently, inadvertently, the titanic task led to the edification of a Temple, of an Emporium, and of a Barracks. And with no less imperceptible gentleness, the Indian attracted the perseverant worker toward his landscape. He was forced to work and to manufacture without leaving a trace of joy or of love. Two worlds were in constant struggle: in the food they ate, in the manner they dressed, and in the way they used the land. In this struggle the Indian was subjected to rural and manufacturing tasks and reduced to an enchanted servitude full of canticles and images. However, he was silently in rebellion against a task whose universal meaning he did not comprehend and against an ornamental liturgy; slowly, the Indian began to dominate the Jesuit by transmitting to him the native inborn superstition and the ways of working, of thinking, of feeling, and of paying homage. Both sides fell into the adoration of amulets and into the fear of black magic, catechized by ignorance and ingenuousness. The saint regressed to the category of a totem, and the glitter of a universal empire became dulled in the gluteal pleasure of material power and the excessive pride of a victory harshly won. From then on in those lands, the Catholicism of the Franciscan and of the Jesuit was to be a new schismatic sect, with all the external pomp of the cult, but without the strength that true religion inflames in the believer's soul. That spurious Catholicism could not have been preached, understood, or accepted in any other part of the world. Ultimately, it had to be destroyed by the expulsion of the priests who disowned the language and paid no homage to the king, as if they were haughty heretics.

The pious Fray Luis de Bolaños and the saint Francisco Solano, who spoke that spontaneous language which God miraculously let them understand, had to resort to other methods of persuasion. They created a method where the philosophers had created a system. In addition to their divinely endowed understanding of the Indian tongues, they were blessed by being understood. Francisco Solano, in the manner of Francis of Assisi with whom he shares parodylike similitudes, used his hand-built violin instead of a branchlike lute to attract the Indian. He modulated his improvised musical compositions and melodies, and song mixed with the rustic tone of his angelical instrument. Once again art served as a language of domination, more powerful and efficient than weapons. What he accomplished, alone, the entire order did not do. He performed marvels and left souls who still venerate him. It was the only way to reach the recondite parts of the spirits and to show them the light. But for this he had to reduce himself to a transient of the desert, a singer for the hordes, and a violinist in a natural state. His miracles are as plain as his poor life; and in heaven, even next to Francis of Assisi, he is probably ashamed of his rusticity and of the proofs of God's existence he gave, under divine inspiration, to those peoples of the uncivilized land.

Not all followed the road of sacrifice and defeat; some preferred the other way, more related to the incitements of the environment and to their own motives for going there: to daringly fight next to the chieftain. It was easy to change loyalties. Quiroga considered his enemies as atheists; Aldao and Bustos called their political antagonists "dangerous innovators" and also "atheists," which was the satanic word. They had hypostatized themselves as a hybrid

Divinity, even usurping a Messianism of which they had no clear idea. And the new sect replaced the Virgin with the Holy Federation.

Religion had served to maintain obedience while no laic institution existed; within religion were polarized all desires to suffocate the adversary and to erect the will as the foundation of an invincible government, for the greater glory of God. Andrés Lamas narrates that in Entre Ríos a Franciscan monk "had been administering civil and criminal justice, even imposing death sentences." Since the environment had been hostile to the absorption of mystical or even religious food, religion imbibed by a simple phenomenon of capillarity the customs and sensual and hedonistic forces of the horde and of the horde's government. It was impossible to carry out any innovation without having it judged as sacrilegious by the tribunal of the Holy Office, which also would consider it as opposed to divine law—that divine law which had trampled other laws of nature and of reason. Don Nicolás Oroño secularized cemeteries and instituted civil marriage in Rosaria before it existed anywhere in South America; he also planned to found a school of agronomy on the grounds belonging to the convent of San Lorenzo. Such impieties unleashed against him the revolution of December 22, 1867. Rosario was sieged by forces arriving from the north of Santa Fe province under the command of Major Nicolás Denis, the national chief of the border garrison; his forces were joined by those of Colonel Patricio Rodríguez. People and armed troops traveled through the city shouting, "Long live God!" and "Down with the masons!"

The priest, who was definitively defeated by the surrounding barbarous forces, joined politics and war and put himself at the head of outlaw gauchos. It was not possible to transform a violent and stubborn world by persuasive means; it had to be subjugated and branded by fire and iron with the supreme truth of religion. The most astute priests formed part of municipal councils and congresses where, after exhausting all reasons, they thundered with reproaches from the Apocalypse. Sarmiento lost his faith while hearing the sermon of an energumen who had been a congressman in 1816. From his parish, the priest would incite the faithful or publish infamous diatribes as did Father Castañeda, who inaugurated our ignoble journalism and initiated impudence in our literature. The religious soldier was converted into a pulpit chieftain; when his personal influence waned he resorted to the hidden force of intrigue and defamation. Expelled in 1767, he discarded the ecclesiastical robes, intervened in government, and proliferated in Argentine social life, like a system of ganglia. All the religious practices and exercises were reduced to the cult, to the material presence in the temple, and to the observance of religious holidays. Having discarded the ecclesiastical robes, he assumed innumerable disguises in teaching and civilian life. Religion became an external liturgy and an ostensible instrument of faith. Naturally, the theoretical mystic and the substratum of concentrated devout believers, so common in religions other than the Catholic, did not exist. Everything that had been spiritual exercise became political and bureaucratic militancy. Like a spider that weaves its web, the schools continued to prepare invisible armies; not a single mystic was produced, not a single great man, but religion became secured by the law and by the budget, which allowed it to lead the decorous life of a crafty unbeliever. The intimate fervor of the heart touched by grace flowed to the outside as can be seen in the extroversion so typical of the conquistador and the trader. Tied to the administration and the army, religion lost its essence and became converted into an external cult and ostentatious piety. Without roots in real faith, it changed into another false structure. Its material symbols are the demolished temples of Misiones; only blocks of their façade, covered by vegetation, remain to betray an architecture overloaded with stone ornaments.

The sumptuous temple hoards cold riches that are envied like a fortune in bad hands. The cathedral and the seminary of Catamarca, whose construction cost three million pesos, store riches greater than the province's wealth. Wherever they are, basilicas and cathedrals are symbols of material ostentation, not of spiritual life. The new and unartistic temples have been constructed according to ancient and artistic plans; they were financed by repentant sinners and built by workers who cursed their own fates; these temples, false even in the manner in which thin coats of marble cover huge cement blocks, are enclosures that bring together Sunday multitudes who then leave to once again harass each other. From the pulpit, the parish priest imparts electoral instructions or blazes sermons in the style of an incredulous fanatic; his fame as preacher spreads, and he is meekly accepted although not believed. No temple speaks to faith or conserves venerable ashes. Sculptors have not beautified them, and painters and engravers have not dignified them; the word of God has not begun to appear in their aisles; and the sad man's soul, more solitary and despondent, once again returns to the street to join a life as cold and hostile as that temple without God and without madness.

Language

It was the language, rather than the customs, that embodied the race's sum of experiences. It quickly spread to the world's confines and was spoken as in Spain. The settlers brought with them a language rich in concrete forms, which through many vicissitudes conserved its Peninsular strength. Although during the colonial period America's temperament found no avenue of expression through a foreign tongue, the past century produced in Sarmiento the language's greatest prose writer and in José Hernández a talent capable of adjusting the language to the usages of Argentine life. It was a struggle to get rid of the dead weight imposed by language on ideas. Language adapts itself under defective conditions and does not serve as the soul's real language outside its landscape and lineage. The words brought by the conquistador did not correspond to the American reality; the absurdity so obvious in the nomenclature of autochthonous plants and animals—based on European models—has its parallel in concepts and feelings. It is curious that the Spanish language had been conserved with relative integrity in regions so remote and so removed from the boundaries of its source. The loss of a number of terms is part of the deformation process; without a doubt, languages change in proportion to the volume of words in daily usage. The relative

integrity of the language could be partly explained by its inflexibility in the expression of complicated states of the soul and by its
adaptability to very low stages of culture. It is interesting to in-
quire whether that integrity could be attributed to the imperfect
alignment between the verbal and the psychological elements; in
that case language would be a system that does not suffer the variations of life. The words with the most correct flavor disappeared
from common usage, as is the case with those pronounced with a z;
it could be no other way. There were profound observers of reality
who, although not expert in linguistics, proposed the adoption of
Guaraní or some other language; in this and in the altering of
orthography there is nothing more than a movement of resistance,
doubtless born from the same depths in which language has its
roots and from where it surfaces through the conscience and the
voice. More silent and concealed was the resistance of the soul to
the employment of an instrument that had to be utilized from necessity. Although language conserved its relative purity much more
than in certain regions of Spain, that vitality, always reduced to a
lexicon of practical use, arose from the impossibility of destroying
something that formed an integral part of life itself. The philologist
could investigate to good advantage whether those words which
are linked to the appraisal of Hispanic qualities, to peculiarities of
a distant existence without meaning, or to valuations on a spiritual
order have radically disappeared from the tongue. Because of the
lack of time and spiritual energy, language could not be destroyed
or altered. Later it was lowered by being converted into a tool and
a specie; the significance of language on the level of ideas and
forms generated by the spirit did not surpass the meaning of language employed for tasks and transactions. The use of the latter
sufficed. In the provinces, language maintained a certain respect-
ability with an extensive vocabulary and a phonetics altered by the
vicissitudes inherent in a region of pronounced topographical characteristics. In the coastal cities and in those of a marked cosmopolitan physiognomy, language was bastardized and became impoverished. All the words removed from habitual use died under the
violence of racial and environmental factors; these words, sheltered

in the redoubts of writing and of cultivated and erudite speech, provoked a contemptuous smile in the populace. Such words have died of ridicule and they have been supplanted by others of varied origin, more adapted to the rules of the souls although not to those of language. The proscription of certain words and the plebeian intromission of others, obviously inferior, are clear semantic signs: the result of repressed hate for things Spanish. This may also be seen in the crystallization from the Salzburg branch of certain anodyne words that are tinged with sometimes surprising irisations and phosphorescences.

Above all, a language is not so much an instrument of the mind as of sensibility—both organic and subconscious. It is the oral form of life, and it is perishable in proportion to its identification with life and change. The languages that live long, until they are eternized on papyrus, are those whose use is not totally removed from the psyche. We do not speak thinking but feeling; therefore, language, which has a tendency to retain qualifying terms in preference to the substantive ones, is first an organ for esthetic needs and, second, one for logical needs. Even abstract thought operates in support of a vital organic substance, susceptible to conversion into ideas but also into acts or songs. From the days of Horace to those of Darmesteter, a comparison has been made between language and a living entity, two parallel metabolisms: the truth in this comparison is that the existence of language is physiologically related to the activities of the soul. The modifications and the adulterations of coarse words, which can be perceived in the short history of our spoken language, have the fresh trace of violence and repugnance. For the same reason it is not strange that those among us like Sarmiento and J. M. Gutiérrez or like Lugones and Banchs, whose language is typical of self-made intellectuals, wield a richer and more substantive language that is simultaneously more concise and temperate than the one employed by the best poets and prose writers from Spain. The peasant is voluptuously pleased to sacrifice unacclimatized words, and he prefers others that are bastardized and barbarous; the cultured person seeks to evade that same uncomfortable tutelage by insufflating language with a new life of special quality, which bears no resemblance to the original. Knowledge, detailed and erudite studies, a precise understanding of grammar, and a personal enrichment of the lexicon cannot replace the loss of live substance, the internal secretion of the ample and habitual language that operates with the naturalness and vitality—perhaps somewhat neglected—of the glands.

Psychologically, something worse can happen to a language than its subdivision into dialects: its crystallization into tedious forms as it is limited and amputated. In the dialect lives the local soul, the vernacular landscape; in the extended and superficial language the word grows weak and, as its numbers decrease, the surviving words acquire a holophrastic meaning. Synthetic phrases and judgments are superposed on words, in a paleological regression. Functions and organs are inactive; complicated operations of the differential calculus of images are not performed; the conscious acquisition of words and the solitary exercise of language through the dictionary and composition do not dress words and ideas with the resonance and perfume of an active life. The noble part of every language is that which rises above the exact meaning to stir in a superior atmosphere, in a region of beauty and accuracy. The rest is the crust and, whether erudite or coarse, does not truly nourish.

It is still common among Argentine writers to reject the pure and correct form because of instinctive incompatibilities. Quiroga's style, shrewd and austere, is a good example; the cold correction cannot signify anything to a man who thinks with all his nerves and blood, and who pursues other superior ends. He is a master in spite of everything, and that is why we must look at the common writers. We write poorly because secretly it shames us to write well; incorrect models are adopted because one does not wish to submit; the natural forms of spoken language are disdained because what we wish to express corresponds to another untamed substance, from here or from other parts of the world. That which is anastomosed to language causes disgust. He who writes badly, if he is not merely torpid, is discontented with his lineage; he who writes or speaks a language poorly, tends to concede it only a conventional value; exactness, elegance, and fluidity are supplanted by vagueness, slovenliness, and coarseness. At this point language as a tool is transformed into language as a weapon. It is necessary to ignore all demands that make public the deliberate desire to capitulate; the search for originality frequently covers up the eagerness to flee from the atmospheric pressure of language and its natural forms of being. Below that plan is the defiant attitude of the *compadre*, the insult, the neologism of the ill-bred jargon; these are vindictive, keen, and secret forms of wounding. In the formation of spurious words there is something of ignorance and laziness, but there is much more of rebellious intent. Those words which victimize and bury other words spread with ease even in upper circles because they arrive as the breath of an anonymous vengeance. When there is congeniality, the commutation acquires another character and words appear as pivotal points of harmony.

The hidden rancor against a tongue of paternal filiation, which is not present at birth, may have led to two typical forms of writing, of speaking, of reading, and of hearing. Among the common people, whose instinct directly opposes things with less evasion, this phenomenon is simply manifested in an immediate inversion of the language rather than in its slow deformation. A person who unintentionally speaks the wrong way, exhibits, aside from incapacity, a pathological form of hate. Unable to speak another language, yet disdaining its use, the people are forcibly compelled to employ it in every type of social and intimate conversation. Since they lack the means for another mode of escape, they choose to invert syllables within words; thus, language, although apparently the same, is the exact opposite, the inverse. This malaise is generalized and diffused through very ample and delicate mental and emotional zones because it is not limited to mispronunciation of words but saturates an important sector of psychic life. Among more cultured people this inclination takes the form of reading in another language. It is natural that a high state of culture demands the introduction of other climates into the soul, but it is also natural that it constitutes an evasion. Through the reading and speaking of foreign tongues, we leave a world of inflexible forms and penetrate into another. What allures one even more than the insight into something new is the escape from the old. Aside from the benefits to spiritual life, for many it is a movement of repugnance toward the native tongue; the same tendency may be observed in the man who, discontent with his parents, makes use of the pseudonym and is fond of names with a foreign structure; Rosas changed the z of his surname into an s and it sufficed. These forms of secret resentment, which on the personal level may lead to suicide, on the social level may lead to the collapse of fundamental sectors of culture, of progress, and of order. However, unfortunately, the soul possesses other means more expeditious and efficient in this destructive design and it has at its disposal other weapons of greater range and steadier stroke.

IV · BUENOS AIRES

10 ARGIROPOLIS

The Nation and the Municipality

It is not new that everything considered to be a national problem has been studied and resolved as a municipal problem. Nor is it new that finances, government, politics, art, culture, and everything that refers to the whole and its digital values, have been viewed as a problem of Buenos Aires. With the advent of independence, Buenos Aires replaced the mother country. Once the viceroyalty was separated from the king, Buenos Aires supplanted the monarch in the defense of Hispanic privileges, in the administration, in the army, and in the archdiocese. Independence was born in the municipal councils; for this reason it was an urban and municipal phenomenon. Buenos Aires drew up the preliminary plans for emancipation and later became converted into an enemy of republican, federal, and representative ideals. Until 1862 Buenos Aires remained apart from the constitution and outside all agreements; from 1880 Buenos Aires encompassed everything. At one time it embodied centralism against democracy and the littoral

against the interior. The city that sparked the revolutionary movement subsisted as a piece of Spain in the viceroyalty, because its
interests did not go beyond free maritime traffic or beyond customs-
house policies. Instead of totally detaching America from Spain,
Spain was only loosened; Buenos Aires remained as a fragment of
the mother country.

The interior has always looked toward the metropolis as though
beholding the mother country: their nationalistic plans have been
antagonistic and even disjunctive. Buenos Aires has been the center around which has revolved Argentine life, national organization, culture, and wealth. Alberdi used to say, "They are not two
parties, they are two *countries*; they are not *centralists* and *federalists*, they are *Buenos Aires* and the *provinces*."

The city grew up in rivalry with the Republic. Our clear-sighted
men saw that it was not possible to stabilize a system of government by taking the great southern capital as the base for the federal
headquarters. *Argirópolis* says it clearly, and it was the opinion
sponsored by the Congress of 1862; Mitre and Tejedor could not
perceive the problem with clarity, because for them Buenos Aires
was Argentina. In the old centralist-federalist or the Mitre-Urquiza
dispute what we have is Buenos Aires on one side and nothing on
the other; but it was a nothing that aspired to be half of everything.
The province-republic stood in opposition to the city-nation. Real
federation, or union, and progress were impossible to achieve with
a rich province located on the sandbank of the delta and the desert,
and a monstrous city in the fluvial center; a formula was agreed
upon in the weariness of repeated revolts. In a struggle of ports,
Buenos Aires swallowed the previously opulent Asunción, whose
weakening began with the creation of the subsidiary port of Santa
Fe. In like manner, Buenos Aires absorbed the whole Republic; it
is the breach by which the Republic, flowing through rivers and
railroads, hurls itself into the ocean in the direction of Europe.
Buenos Aires assumed the direction of the emancipation movement: she wished to replace Spain. This ambition is the root of all
imcompatibility between this free and capitalistic Danzig and the
rest of the country—condemned to servitude and labor.

We should carefully examine the urban aspect of the Republic to clearly understand the Argentine problem and to discover the rip in the mysterious veil, where the spell of illusion is undone. Once the postemancipation violence had ended, the residual elements of reaction took refuge in Buenos Aires. Although apparently defeated, the urban influence was a danger to the federal constitution and it managed to impose its preserved geographic, demographic, and plutocratic reality; it stood for centralization of economy, of public health, and of education; it maintained a feeling of greatness against the political regimen, which was a false structure.

However, the interior continued to be the reality. Buenos Aires, which affirmed its hegemony over almost three million square kilometers, was the federal district, which served as the ideal for a "better life" to fourteen provinces and ten ministries. There were attempts to create an artificial union with Rosario—under the name of Rivadavia—with Villa María and with Fraile Muerto or Villa Nueva. But in no place could a center be formed in a void.

So Buenos Aires remained as the center of a circle formed by the settled and cultivated points of the interior. All these points are at the same distance; they are the periphery, and the capital is the center. Europe became the closest point to Buenos Aires, although the city was but an out-of-the-way place for Europe. In a special spiritual, historical, and economic sense, which is what really counts, Paris is closer to Buenos Aires than is Chivilcoy or Salta. There is a greater difference in human climate and in chronology between our monstrous polypary and stationary towns, such as La Rioja, San Juan, San Luis, Catamarca, or Jujuy, than exists between it and New York. The external structure, the amplitude, and the appearance of a busy and heroic life make of Buenos Aires a universal, cosmopolitan, and wealthy city with a great destiny. But from inside, in its blood and style, it is more similar to any forgotten town like La Rioja, San Juan, San Luis, Catamarca, or Jujuy than to any European or North American city in its category: Buenos Aires is the federal capital of the Argentine Republic.

The city swelled through the deposition and congregation of large contingents of immigrants attracted by a fantasy; after the ocean crossing they did not dare to proceed in the march to the interior. The immigrant who stayed in this focus, dominated by fear, enlarged the metropolis together with the immigrant who from inside searched for its populous streets; the city was made into a place of rest or of evasion: "the other city," "the certitude of greatness," "the ideal headquarters." Growing to excess, it was the measure of the truth of an empty and hostile interior that not only was incapable of attraction but also was repulsive and frightening. Whoever believed in Buenos Aires and entrusted himself to it automatically negated the interior, the Republic. The federal capital has always been the province, the city, and the nation. A disproportionate greatness also implies a disproportionate smallness. We wished to avoid the truth by sticking our heads into the sand. The characteristic and essential movement has been to create taboos out of unpleasant things; this practice was creating the fetishism of appearances and of false values, which were converted into the ideal by those who lost hope. The polarization has also been between the State and the country, the desert and the truth. That disproportion has not varied but has grown worse as it became more ineluctable and a part of reality; it was more difficult to remedy what was idealized than what was rejected. Werner Hegeman, who as a technical expert studied our ideal city, could only find three extreme solutions to correct its vices of conformation and development: "a huge fire, a great revolution, or an enormous earthquake."

The Gordian knot and the aorta were cut in 1880. The victory of Buenos Aires determined the death of the interior. The hypertrophy of Buenos Aires may be explained as the hypertrophy of a city, and the metropolis may be considered as a nucleus for absorption of the timid immigrant and of the best provincial talent. However, this does not tell the whole truth. The opulence of Buenos Aires was a bank deposit placed there by other cities and by the countryside. The entire life of the Nation consisted in the pursuit of something immensely good, easy, and glorious that could not be found. The hopes of the pioneer were being disappointed in the ratio of an arithmetic progression; but the power of the citizen was increasing geometrically by virtue of his possession, through politics and the advantages of civilization, of the central keys to all activities. Buenos Aires is Trapalanda. Its growth was the accumulation of the objects and goods of a coarse dream. Now we can look back 130 years. The intended goal of post-Independence was to convert Buenos Aires into Spain and that is why it appeared reactionary to the hordes of Artigas and of Güemes, the generals of the land, of the plain, and of the mountain. From the moment that independence ceased to be a dream and became an irrefutable and indelible reality, Buenos Aires discontinued contact with the interior and became its antagonist; decidedly foreign, it embodied a mercantile and bureaucratic ideal of subjection, of dominion, and of the Crown. Thus it was possible for Buenos Aires to be ruled by Rivadavia at one time and by Mitre and Irigoyen on other occasions. The municipal council acquired an unexpected power; it was the Nation. Rivadavia, who was attuned to the city, seemed even to Groussac to be an administrative functionary. From that time, no ruler has considered the Republic to be anything more than an enormous city of almost three million square kilometers with fourteen useless plots in the middle and with ten deserted squares in circumvallation.

Pampa and Rooftops

The almost 189 square kilometers of the city of Buenos Aires are in direct relation to the almost 3 million square kilometers of the Republic but not in terms of their position or development. The Republic's territorial immensity and the residence of over half the population in seven cities resembles the map of the Pleiades. Buenos Aires is the capital of a land with a density of three and one-half inhabitants per square kilometer; it has approximately nineteen thousand hectares framing its perimeter, although in fact the area is more than seventy thousand hectares. By a generally centripetal movement, the suburban towns have invaded the metropolis and amalgamated themselves with it. It is not that Buenos Aires has spilled into Témperley, Quilmes, Morón, or Tigre, but that these penetrated into the city before it could be edified in a compact form. Within the boundaries of what is referred to as the urban zone, there are many areas of idle lands much greater than those found between the capital and Avellaneda or Vicente López. City and village have been joined, leaving sterile lakes in between. Nearly three million people inhabit those seventy thousand hectares: one-fourth of the total population; 50 percent of the commercial establishments are installed there and 40 percent of the industrial ones. It is an ample and a flattened city: a pampa of low houses, with an extended population. Neither Mendoza nor Garay would have supposed that Buenos Aires would become a viceroyalty, nor could a merchant in 1770 have imagined that 24,000 inhabitants would multiply one hundredfold in a century and a half. Only the administrators and the councilmen—since these calculations fall within their province—have foreseen in building ordinances and regulations a city of 31 million people. The intendant of Buenos Aires has always been the master of ceremonies of this metropolitan spectacle.[1] When the dream of these aediles of the pampa will be fulfilled, the interior will have returned to what it was three centuries ago. Only by depopulating Buenos Aires will the country recover its lost equilibrium. London and New York are symbolic metropoles on two islands; Buenos Aires has been engendered, conceived, and superimpregnated by the plain. Surface: that is the problem word. Surface is the essence of the city that lacks a third dimension; surface has the function of the plant's vertical root: it anchors man in place. A city is not such until the citizens exist as an entity: *urbs* and *civitas*. A coralline pew of houses is not a city. The universal cities of the Middle Ages, as well as imperial Rome, were superposed strata of dwellings, in the manner of castes that sort themselves out and settle. The skyscraper of American origin is a means of hurling depth into empty space. That piece of beehive is an apparatus applied to the capitalistic industry; it is a wealth-manufacturing machine. The soft flooring of Buenos Aires

---

[1] The regulations authorize a population density twenty-five times greater than necessary. Hegeman comments: "This calculation proves that it is not necessary to pile up the inhabitants of Buenos Aires like cattle at the entrance to the slaughterhouse."

speaks of another agricultural conception of the urban machine. The magisterial contrivances create an industry not only of housing but also of life itself. An immense construction and population factory does not provide a small town's firm place of residence: it is an anchored transatlantic ship cruising to the spot where it already is. The town is a tomb, and the house in the city is a factory. But it can be a vast horizontal warehouse for the storage of products and species generated by the countryside; these goods do not exist as objects and as bodies but only as dreams and entelechies. New York is all front; Buenos Aires is all rooftops. From a bird's-eye view the city appears to be a map in relief for the use by the blind. Only by walking in the streets can one notice the fronts; the show window is in place of the grating. And except for Florida Street, which is not a street but a state of mind, the front—including the apertures—is the wall and door of Tintagiles, which separates two worlds.

Compared to Buenos Aires, any other city—Bahía Blanca, Rosario, Córdoba, Tucumán—is a mere countryside of rooftops on the horizon of the pampa. A peasant air pervades the streets and crushes against the façades; without whistling it glides over the buildings: the silent wind of the pampa. Everything transpires of a rural aroma: the broadcasting programs, the speed with which vehicles move, the color of garments, the manner of casting furtive glances, and the habit of not yielding to anyone the right of way. No city is more than a prosperous village: none has taken the step by which a village vigorously shrugs off its stupid rusticity and acquires the easy and polished manners of a city. It is useless to search in those hypertrophic towns for a peculiar and distinguishing soul; like herbivores, they are sad, silent, and of one spirit. The street outlines and the house plans, Gothic and Vandalic through Spain's influence, are ways of evading the problems of perspective and of the broken, undulating line rich in family motifs—natural to a race of horsemen. The shape of the drawing board is correlative to the plain and to the spiritually uncomplicated man. Only an inexpert eye, unable to perceive the shades and the tones of panoramic symphonies, could tolerate without displeasure the coarse sincerity of the perpendicular street and the edification of entire blocks of one-story houses through which the plain invades. The Gothic outline of the streets and the slablike appearance of the city blocks give the impression of a tedious geometric-administrative figure. The roof tile resembles the paving tile; the undulated zinc is formed into water spouts; the roof is the same as the floor. It is a symmetrical monotony typical of cities with horses and carts: Pompeii. The streets are designed to spy dangers, to see far away into the horizon and not to display architecture, fronts, and the aspect of affairs; such is the case with Rivadavia Street, long like a telescope. The countryside flows into the cities through these infinitely straight avenues, through these troughs; the cities flow into Buenos Aires and finally, following the direction of rivers and railroads, they all empty into the Atlantic.

For the inhabitant of Buenos Aires, to look toward the interior is to look outside—abroad. For him, the interior is Europe. He knows that to intern himself in Argentina would mean to dislocate his person from the unit to which he belongs; he would have to be faced with different events, to be confronted not with the adventure but with the ashes of the spent adventure. The interior does not attract him, as in years past, with the promise of fortune or of freedom. The interior is already purged of illusions: it signifies work, illness, ignorance, and oblivion. Nothing there interests us. The landscape is empty and far away; the mountain is a mountain, the lake is a lake, the forest is a forest. The forest is not William Tell, the mountain is not Juxthausen, the lake is not Wordsworth. They lack the dimension of life. It is impossible to escape through these straight streets, as surely as water cannot flow uphill.

The Polypary

The apartment-house owner is merely a possessor of real estate; he is a juridical entity, not a moral one. He buys, rents, sells, and shuffles tenants in and out, but he is not tied to the fate of his property or to the destiny of his city; neither is he bound to family or religion. He possesses an instrument of speculation whose value fluctuates; he takes advantage of the tenant as much as possible. The homeowner considers himself his own ideal tenant; his property is also an instrument of speculation with a varying price. But to possess a house in Buenos Aires is to have achieved a foothold in Trapalanda. Buildings and land can rise to unexpected worth during the commemoration of centennials or upon the arrival of princes. Residential property may also become a general instrument of speculation, since housing is one of three productive industries in a land without industry—the other two are food and clothing.

The families who rent space in an apartment house are at the service of the landlord; they all work for him. The house devours 25 to 35 percent of their salaries; the owner's handsome profits arise from the exaggerated values attributed by the lords of the city of Caesars to their necropolis. Consequently, while the house is for the proprietor a machine of the housing industry, it is for the tenant a source of anger, of indignation, and of inconvenience. Many people are forced to obtain additional jobs to defray the cost of housing; the individual sags under the burden of excessive work. The streets and houses teem with disgust from a life without joy, and they emanate that look of sadness which is copied so well in the pupil of the ox; it is the valve through which we perceive the loss of life.

It is possible that a virtuous life could arise from this mercantile-industrial state which does not respect or love the dwelling and which shows contempt for the owner and his property. But neither peoples nor civilizations endure so as to witness how defective forms convert faults into virtues. It is as if rogues were to be, for centuries, larval forms of superior beings; the experiment is not worthwhile for humanity or for the history of morality. Meanwhile, a city of tenants and of housing-factory owners is tearing at all moving parts. The tenant is a hermetic cell. The house is as isolated as the inhabitant. Everything conspires against harmony, from the high rents that establish a hierarchy according to place of residence to the baseness of language that makes men defensive. To speak well is to communicate without useless precautions; to establish differences between one street and another, between one house and another, one-third of the salary is spent on rent.

The bus is the symbol of the individual's isolation: society and closeness mean nothing. The apartment house is the symbol of the isolated dwelling. Each apartment is a family, but taken together they are much less than a family. When misfortune strikes, the doors are hermetically closed; an elementary duty of courtesy is fulfilled by discreetly inquiring with the doorman as to the magnitude of the event. Everyone must depend on himself; the neighbor's proximity lacks social significance, and the mutual respect that consists in ignoring one another's private lives is converted into the most ruthless indifference. But man cannot remain indifferent: he loves or he hates. He may love without knowing it and hate without realizing it; passion could assume the strangest disguises in curiosity or in the difficulty in remembering names.

The suburban house, which communicates with those adjacent to it, conserves an equal degree of hostile reserve. The fence made of wire or of plants delimits the owner's psychology. From the time of betrothal, the dream house emanates from the ascetic ideal of withdrawal from the world and from the romantic ideal of a castle on an island. The wall fence is the dividing frontier between the property and danger. But that rim does not enclose each family in its lot; there is an aggressive invasion of looks, of voices, and of living attitudes that leaps over the fence and penetrates into the most recondite intimacy. There is a need for neighbors, visitors, friendship, and cordiality; if these are lacking in civil forms, they assume shapes of assault. When the houses are close together, it is unavoidable to enter into the neighbor's dwelling; if the front door is barred, one penetrates through the rear window. The need to know certain secrets of the surrounding area, which one ignores and therefore supposes to be plentiful, is what encourages gossip. The gossip acquires characteristics of a captured secret that has been rooted out and is now exhibited. The gossip is the clandestine visit among those who do not visit each other; it is the theft of goods that robbed one of sleep; by dragging others through the mud, gossip becomes the miscarriage of a spirit of sociability that cannot be born by force.

Face and Cosmetics

Buenos Aires can appear as a beautiful city in the eyes of an observer who contemplates it as a huge mass quickly erected in the solitude. There is nothing like it in the Southern Hemisphere. It offers a certain attraction for the outsider if he has not imagined the city to be possible; the interest quickly evaporates after the initial impression. For the native born, or for the one who inhabits it from childhood or judges it within a known context, the city is of no interest by itself or as a world wonder. Buenos Aires is a city without secrets, without viscera or glands, without deep convolutions or caries. Everything is in the open; once the city is known on the outside, it ceases to interest. It lacks a yesterday and does not possess a true shape; when it stops growing and developing, it might have an entirely different configuration. Today it possesses the beauty of youthful bodies; the limbs have acquired their definitive size but have not as yet defined their function or achieved the robustness of maturity. Its defects may well be blamed on factory blunders. But this undoubtedly grandiose city, is it related to the area in which it lies, to the Nation to which it belongs, as Paris is related to the other French cities, and as Berlin, London, Amsterdam, and Moscow are related to theirs?

The city is beautiful because it sprouted while overcoming enormous difficulties pertaining to its outline, its area, its location, and its inhabitants. It is beautiful precisely because against all those difficulties it embodies a will more powerful than the will to build and to populate; it is a vigorous assertion in a landscape that conspires against all things exalted. Whatever its faults, it will remain famous as a monument to an aspiration. In the first place, it suffers from improvisational defects, and they are most difficult to detect by those people who are themselves improvised. We are disgusted and indignant whenever we witness a structure that will not be able to stand tomorrow, because we see it as an unnecessary squandering of power and someone's autonomous will, whereas coopera-

tion would have produced a more desirable result. The marvelous
aspiration is full of crevices. Next to finished pieces there are others
barely sketched; within the finished pieces there are others that are
provisional or unfinished and other incomplete parts impossible to
finish. This defect is particularly true of those sections which are
well hidden, such as the back part of Congress, the interior of the
Tribunals, or the drainage of the main Post Office. These hidden
sections are the digital impressions, the factory's stamp of incapacity, and the differentiation between a project in which the entire city has collaborated and one that has been erected treacher-
ously. Buenos Aires is ugly if one views it as a city and not as an
effort. It has been conceived with beauty; the attempts at beautifi-
cation, wastefully and very expensively done, produce ugliness and
are the ostentation of the provincial parvenu. Beauty cannot be arbitrarily placed in various artificial locations of the city, such as
corners, monuments, and promenades; poverty also can be beautiful in a city where even ruin speaks of life and of forms of existence and not of the hastened pace. Along one block, the different
buildings speak assorted languages of time, of economic eras, and of
styles, allowing us to see, as does the earth, in its strata, the various
cataclysms suffered. Unfortunately, that diversity perpetuates the
precarious, the fortuitous, and what has already past, and not what
is everlasting and protected from catastrophes under the assurance
of an already successfully tested formula.

Next to the one-floor houses are the two-floor houses; between
them are the empty lands and the skyscrapers of twenty and thirty
stories that rise with the predominant ambition, like a personal triumph that annuls the effort of others and proves the omnipotence
of the empty plot adjoining the skyscraper. A skyscraper located in
a block of low-lying buildings, next to pasture lands, indicates the
same—but just the reverse—as a cave-in: the fracture of a piece of
ground on which everything is settled, on which is built a city that
does not oscillate or change. The empty plot is correlated with
three million square kilometers, and the skyscraper relates to adventure and to the dream spoken aloud. The smaller houses are the
older ones; the new ones have been erected when the economic out-

look of Buenos Aires has improved—although not the architectural
outlook. The earlier city was made up of one-floor dwellings; over
these constructions is rising a multistory city. The buildings that
are above average height are like the old one-floor dwellings that
looked down on the ground, the oldest flooring of Buenos Aires. Today's one-floor houses are yesterday's empty plots of land. At the
beginning, construction was sporadic and was erected directly on
the soil; today, the first floor is used as the ground, and thus the
one-floor houses are the idle lands in comparison to the higher
houses. Buenos Aires has the structure of the pampa: layers form
on top of layers, resembling the sand and the loess that cover the
plains. This process has not been even and homogeneous, but fractured and selective. The diversity of styles and elevations indicates
the difference in methods employed in the conquest of fortune and
demonstrates the malleability of the medium to the impetuous attack of events or to unforeseen disasters. Although at some time
houses may become stabilized at a certain height as they are in the
old European cities where the ordinances, the economic capacity,
the architecture, and the mayors' talents are well balanced, there
will be a lack of harmony in the growth, in the styles, and in the
ages that will be immediately perceived. The materials age quickly,
the styles are outmoded, and the sojourner outlasts the buildings
and watches them crumble and be demolished. Each building is a
cement shape that pays for itself and triumphs in an easy victory.
The styles are as independent as the buildings; they are quickly out
of tune with the general taste or with the passing whim, which
inflates certain values in the market of triumph and of defeat. The
buildings age in their ornaments, in their adornments, and in their
cornices before their masonry becomes old. The houses of Buenos
Aires, although relatively new, have a withered face; they are experiments, provisional houses to occupy the land and to increase its
value. They will not remain long; they are merely part of a passing
Buenos Aires. Neither the wealth of the proprietors, nor the faith
in the future, nor the architect's love for construction has conspired
to make these houses last indefinitely. A city like Florence, where
mansions built five hundred years ago still stand, is an honest city;

but the portable fair of the gypsies is the swindle and the flight. Although Paris and Berlin may perish as soon as New York—the architect's taste, the administrative regulations, the constructor's city built to last thirty years—they have the stamp of eternity. The experience, the orientation of activities that enriched the owner, the glance of the passer-by, and the care of the artisan give a look of eternity, of stability, and of symmetry to each house in relation to the city, to each building in relation to the whole, and to each family in relation to its home. In that which wishes to endure there is the gaiety of life; in that which must perish there is the sadness of the fleeting moment. "Only gaiety desires eternity."

The man who conquered the plain, who made money in the plain, who bent the plain's defense with his tactics and methods, and who came to the city brought with him a rural breath that may be observed not only in the general flatness of construction but also in the manner in which, suddenly, that flatness is shattered in hand-to-hand combat and the jewel of economic victory is shown off. As far as Torcuato de Alvear, the northern part of the city was not an aristocratic zone; the opulent physiognomy arose from the success of export businesses, and the age of a whole neighborhood coincided with the age—why not with the forms?—of that prosperity, that eagerness to trade wools for architecture. The southern part of Buenos Aires is at present, as it was before the economic outbreak of 1880, more authentically Buenos Aires, as Argentina was more authentic in 1860 than in 1932. Whether in the northern or in the southern part of the city, the one-floor house will yield to the two-floor house; irremittably it will become the foundation. The city grows over the palaces and the miserable huts.

Urban Image of Rawhide Wealth

Among compact constructions, amid the massiveness of buildings struggling for every centimeter of light and air, suddenly, the magnate opens a tennis court to show off his millions—like a yawn. As if he were tying a horse to the palisade, he introduces a fragment of latifundium into the city, and in a piece of forest he affirms the nostalgia and the resentment of the pampa. To open his park, he has probably demolished some houses that, in a painful twenty-year encroachment, have barely cleared one-fourth of a hectare. The passer-by scorns a vanity that over-does itself when aiming to arouse envy; the city is wild in its empty lands and ill-bred in its palatial parks. The countryside's influence on the city is evident in the egotistical conduct and in the whimsical manner of edification. To build a house to one's taste implies the rupturing of social unity and coincides with the desire to impose one's personality on the world. It is the affirmation not only of the ego and the fickleness of exhibited wealth but also of an unpolished rebellion. The proprietor has no intention of submitting to the architectural canons; his personality lacks style because he imagines that respect for esthetic values is equivalent to individual submission. For this reason, the ordinances have taken into account the fancy of the lord of the pampa, and they adjust to his uncivil judgment. The proprietor is always able to find an architect who shares his opinion and who knows how to reflect the owner's personality in the façade so that people will not be able to say that the house does not resemble him, like some child of suspected origin. Those owners conceive of the dwelling as a salting place or as a silo; their idea of beauty is like that of a rubric they can barely sketch. It would be useless to try to make them understand that the acquisition of a good style is in good measure related to the style of others.

Each house in the city represents the magisterial and architectural shape of a fortune; in turn, each fortune stands for a way of life. That is why we have such a diversity of styles, of elevations, and of colors, which causes each building to appear isolated, in the heterogeneity of the whole, as an unsociable personality with a temperamental idiosyncrasy. Nowhere in their façades, floors, or overhead views do the houses breathe the collective spirit of the city; they loathe to integrate into a similar group or to form one of the same age, and so they agglutinate into a chaos of unconnected fragments in which we can easily perceive the economic differences from decade to decade.

The people who own the houses differ in their long-pursued

goals; contrasting systems of life, of morality, and of comprehension of reality have delivered into their hands the wealth with which to erect their dwellings—which will condense their biographies. Each house is more similar to a unique dream than to the city. Vestiges of individual struggles endure in the physiognomy of frontispieces. Each house takes advantage of another not only by sharing a common wall but also by infringing, as much as possible, on the neighbor's air and light. Whoever obtained more suffocates whoever procured less; a ten-story building proclaims to all winds the barely muttered ideal of the two-story house. The eagerness to possess real estate tramples respect for the laws of style and of edification that make a great city the collective home of millions of people. The ostentation of power reaches its apex in construction, and, since the housing industry provides—together with the food and clothing industries—the safest investment, the ten stories assert the ability to edify. The building represents a capital invested to the utmost; the mortgage usually starts from the sixth floor upward. The last four floors correspond to the disproportionate ambition and to the confidence in a successful outcome for that type of business.

The effort of the poor man who writes, paints, or plays music is not enough to absolve the city from the judgment, so richly deserved, that renders it barbarous; the city has grown at a time of maximum wealth but has paid no heed to aesthetics. Fifty thousand structures that proclaim fifty thousand surly wills fashion a formless city, a mosaic of souls who operate against the harmony of the whole: a cosmopolitan and polyglot city. A room in a house changes into the prison cell of a captive spirit whose most anxious desire is emancipation. The totality of souls constitutes more than an architectural people or a necropolis; it is a multitude compounded of brick, iron, and wood, without unity or spirit. The city is invaded by the pampa on all sides; the ranches and fields are sold or leased and transformed into buildings. At the end of the street we once again meet with the horizon. Except for the skyscraper, which scrambles over the aggregate like a ram over its flock, the only variety among low-level constructions is provided by the balustrades devised for the upper stories. The roofs are not at one level and the fronts are not of one style, nor has the material acquired the patina that results after prolonged exposure to bad weather. If the houses are designed to exceed one story, they almost always have a balcony as an entablature: the balcony of a nonexistent upper parlor, similar to the dirt square in front of humble dwellings, which is kept in reserve for better times. The owner's project went beyond his means, and that second-story fragment, that balcony to the sky, oppresses the house with its nonexistent weight. A whole family lives in expectation of the floor that is not yet there. The sky's temporary habitation rests on bare hands and shoulders; often, the house must be demolished before the upper story is completed. It is an imaginary floor, with the mystery of an attic seen in a postcard of a city that will never be visited. It is an aspiration, but it is also a hole through which disappear, in a vain attempt to fill it, many things essential to life. The floor has its own preexistence, like a child who begins to rule from the first months of its gestation: everything has to revolve around it, submit to it, and be at its service. To labor toward the dream means to suffer deprivation, ignorance, hostility, and many lost years that float by as mere phantoms of an ideal; each year is a small unpardonable fault, though solid as the bricks piled on the stumps of amputated walls to encase the sky with nonexistent walls. It sometimes occurs that the long-desired dream is achieved. It may have cost ten or twenty years of sacrifices, of slavery to ambition. The head of the family is happy: his house, instead of one story, has two.

11 THE IMPOSING VILLAGE

West against East

Corrales and Mataderos used to be the con-
fines of Buenos Aires: the Mediterranean shore and the borders of
man's habitation. The metropolis was contained within this perimeter for a lengthy period, the river at its back. It was a formative
period for the urban soul. Until then, the city had been an indistin-
guishable mass.

A long time ago, a latitudinarian Buenos Aires was enclosed by
the river, by the Entre Ríos and Callao boulevards, and by Inde-
pendencia and Viamonte streets. They were the bounding lines beyond which the villas, the pasture grounds, and the summer resi-
dences extended as far as San José de Flores or Belgrano, and from
there into the pampa. The city was concentrated within such
demarcations until it conquered the dike of stone sidewalks and
spilled into the municipal fields. Boedo and Pueyrredón remained
as boundaries for a long time. The configuration of the teratological body varied not only in size but also in shape and structure, as

does a fetus; at a given moment in its development there occurred a total change. Jujuy and Pueyrredón marked the maximum radius for our fathers; beyond that lay the pampa. Boedo was a suburb when Corrales and Mataderos filtered the pampa that entered and settled at the city's threshold. New confluent routes were opened through Alvear Avenue, San Juan, Patricios, Montes de Oca, and Canning; the stone masonry was constantly expanding its limits and overflowing from one boulevard to another: through Triunvirato, through Parral Avenue, through Warnes, and through Cabildo—contained by the river. A typical shore population was encrusted on the sand bank: intermingled and roguish.

Those avenues not only fixed the limits, in terms of the municipal configuration, of the public lands and of the census, but they also were the edges on which crowded a peculiar form of life with the characteristics of frontier flora and fauna. Along those routes of containment was grouped a population whose character varied with each epoch; but whether yesterday or today, in Boedo or in Alvear Avenue, people fell in step with the new pace and left behind the sidewalk of the pampa.

In the Alvear intendancy, north and south used to be as much alike as a poor sister and a rich one. Later, the gap between the bourgeois north and the proletarian south widened until the two were entirely dissimilar. From Alvear, everything that is magisterial rises bejeweled; the homonymous avenue is the summit from which all urban things begin to decline. The opening of the Mayo Avenue deepened the division between the noble and the ugly: the avenue was a deep incision that rooted out a portion of the Cabildo to connect Plaza de Mayo with Lorea Square; Congress, the Casa Rosada, and Parliament would hence be viewed from the channel of patriotic multitudes.

The unconquered pampa stretched west and south. It was not dislodged by the construction and the extension of suburbs; the pampa hid itself, and the avalanche of houses spilled over it in a movement of reaction.

The *compadre*, with his knife and scarf, was typical of the men who lived on the periphery; eventually, the *compadre* judged him-

self to be a member of the city's community, demanded his share
of rights, and affirmed himself as a frontier being. The pampa was
irremediably invaded, but the man of the pampa was trapped between the city's expansion and the countryside's resistance. As a
countryman, he was a misfit in the city, and the construction
passed over him as easily as over the pampa. The suburban commercial establishments faced the empty and abandoned lands. Although movie houses, fashion shops, coffee shops, jewelry stores,
and establishments that sell tobacco, postcards, and dream books
are only part of an ethnic expansion, they take on the aspect of a
social revenge. The embroidered scarf is the symbol of the plain's
assertion; its voice can be heard in the contempt for the stiff collar.
Today, the provincial rancor is transformed into multiple disguises;
it may be seen through the gaucho and the half-breed of Palermo
and Boedo, in the businesses that compete against those downtown,
or in the literary schools that conspire with the villains in a civil
war against the center. Once the centrifugal forces are absorbed by
the city, they reappear after a long subterranean voyage in the poetic defense of evil and in the practical exaltation of the *guarango*.
It is the neighborhood against the city, the countryside against the
metropolis, and municipal nationalism against snobbery. The reasons for revolt are proclaimed in archaic dress and gestures and in
bastardized forms of language; if someone declares himself to be a
Bolshevik, it is because he is profederalism and anticentralism.

Boedo is a boulevard as wide as a river, whose banks are lined
with low houses of a vivid appearance. It seems as though the avenue were stripped of everything but mere vestiges of façades and
perhaps an excessive animation visible on faces and sidewalks. Outside, the movie house exhibits enormous prints of the current film;
women and children crowd the show bill as they dream about the
plot and anticipate the heroine's perils. The protagonists may once
again be seen in the lobby. People swarm over the wide sidewalk
while a bell rings continually, announcing the show's imminent beginning, whereby repressed dreams will be bathed in light. They
wait. It is difficult to comprehend the bright showcases, the people,
the automobiles, the perpetual bell, and the posters after having

crossed blocks and blocks of darkness, of hermetic doors, of silence, and of pampa. Boedo pretends to be the Florida Street of the urban desert. It has the Parisian glitter of Florida Street but reduced to the peasant mentality; the same objects are sold but of a lower quality: glass diamonds and adulterated gold. However, Boedo is more authentically Buenos Aires than Florida. What transpires in Boedo is more easily understood; it is more logical although not more sincere.

There are many avenues similar to Boedo in every district. They have in common a frontier atmosphere that may be detected in people, in houses, in trees, and in automobile speeds. The center and the north wish to emulate France, southern Riachuelo wants to be Italy, and the suburbs as far as Tigre aspire to be England. Those areas, which until recently ruled the pampa and which have been formed by a gradual triumph and not by an act of decision, possess a certain visible softness of the veins, as in a tense forearm during hand wrestling. The ancient and the national appear in new places; the aggressive spirit of the interior against the metropolis is latent; and the old, unresolved litigations are once again renewed.

Florida Street will not resist with the years the advancement of the legions that are incubating in the frontier districts; she will remain, glistening in electric signs and lights, more false than the force that readies itself to recover a lost city. The means for assault are being provided by the lyrics of the tango, by the bludgeonlike criticism, and by the neglect for what is beautiful and universal. The application of new aesthetic theories to throwing tar bombs proves that in the dampness and darkness of areas discontinuously edified the new force is being generated. The melancholic dreamer outside the city paves the way for the gaucho's revenge for the battle he lost together with Tejedor against Avellaneda.

The Guarango

Although he may be found in the middle of the city, the *guarango's* habitat is on the periphery.

The *guarango* originates from the same matrix—although more worn—as the *compadre*. He paraphrases his older brother but without daring to put into effect a full-scale, inflamed, and perverse attack against society. The *guarango* operates at his discretion in an ample sphere, with an unrestrained expression, and in perpetual invasion of places forbidden to others. We may observe in him the characteristics of a fool without culture and of an actor who improvises without genius, as if he resented some deprivation—of which many people are guilty. He is not satisfied with his lot, with his authentic role; and he seeks to compensate by bothering other people.

The *guarango* needs a larger radius of action than the *compadre* and a greater public to triumph in his aggression, which always takes the form of a sociable and sinister jest. Only when people are willing to witness *guarango*-like acts can there exist a *guarango*; rudeness acquires the category of a *guarango*-like feat when projected into a theater lobby, a railroad car, or a party room.

The *guarango* offends urbane conventions, not social ones. He is uncivil, coarse, and without the polish and attrition that society imposes on man's pantomime; he is an equivocation through which—as in the malicious joke—a forbidden and inadmissible perspective may be discerned at a distance. When a *guarango* crosses paths with a man who lives in the center of a system based on courtesy, on moral conventions, and on respect, he evokes a paleolithic vapor and leaves the bitter, unpleasant aftertaste of a mountain animal. He announces that he is in possession of the secret of man's dark background to which he may appeal as a last resort. He is an ignoramus who falsely interprets reality, as does a barely literate person who can decipher a text without understanding it. The *guarango* introduces his ego, not face to face as would the *compadre*, but obliquely, as when crashing a party or bringing along an obnoxious friend. A perversity is present, but it is a perversity typical of an inferior being who has lost the sharp edge of aggression and whose atrophied sting conserves a poison that barely smarts. He is a primitive man who proceeds as if he were acquainted with civilization's rules, and he acts as if he obeyed them and understood their intent; but, he only feels comfortable in deceit.

His first movement, the volitional, which can only be judged by

God, is the insult; but the intention to offend is covered by the grin-
ning pretense of innocence. The public *guarango*-like act is like a
formal theatrical performance; the rehearsal takes the aspect of an
anonymous telephone insult.

The *guarango* also wishes to be a hero; he wants to be an important person who attracts attention. His incapacity leads him to the
mistake of tactless bragging that later turns against him. He makes
the same motions as the great, powerful, strong, and loquacious
man, but without the greatness, the money, the courage, or the elo-
quence. The *guarango* suffers from dulled senses; he lacks a feeling
for the opportune and correct, for the civil and cultivated. Psychologically and clinically, we should perhaps consider him to suffer
from no more than a case of prepuberty insipidity that is retained
to annoy adults.

The *guarango* is not a moral degenerate, though by preference
he leans toward the offense that has a hidden picaresque meaning;
he is simply unconscious of courtesy, of literature, of eurythmy, of
pantomime, and of opulence; instead of investing time to learn
about these difficult topics, he impudently improvises. In the mockery and scorn for fellow man, there is a sad reflection of his own
personality. The *guarango*-like act is a vengeance cloaked in the
outward show of moral irresponsibility: it is the insult of the poor
man who attributes his moral, financial, and intellectual shortcomings to another's well-being. Since the *guarango* pretends to
gore with his behavior as if by an oversight, he takes precautions
to avoid a direct confrontation. It is the *compadre* who faces consequences with his body. The *guarango* attempts to cloak his coarse
intent in an anonymity of gestures and words to hide the true aggressor; he unfolds two personalities, so that the part reaching the
victim seems to come from afar and in spite of the aggressor. That
is why *guarango*-like behavior is not spiritually rejected against
the *guarango* himself but against the family, the neighborhood, the
technology, or the whole country in which the *guarango* takes his
inspiration; the *guarango* is literally a fraud in a subhuman
comedy.

The propitious stage for this clown, for this rascal without pedigree, is the place where many people are gathered. Also, he usually requires the assistance of one or several witnesses who can shield his impunity; he feels uncomfortable without accomplices. Faced with the same danger, the *compadre* asserts his crude and impudent ego but the *guarango* cowers, apparently harmless. Slander and flattery are his favorite stabs.

Generally, the *guarango* presents a neutral, absent-minded, and innocent face and attitude before the person who reacts to his behavior. He may excuse himself as an ignorant or distracted person; he may appeal to either excuse without detriment to his personality, because he perseveres in the role of deception. He removes his true self from the mask and hides behind his automaton. A being detached from everything, like the mask, in disguise he acquires a new personality exempt from obligations and responsibilities.

A vocation for carnivallike things can be observed in the *guarango*. He is usually a mask even after the carnival's end; he carries his triumphant unmasked character to other neighborhoods during workdays. His face has the immodesty of the mask and it is inexpressive—a hard mask of rags and paper. In the *guarango*-like act, the theatrical, the false, and all related to the carnival partake in equal parts. That untimely festive instinct is the dirty and arrogant attitude of the Latin ruffian; it appears as a dodging grimace in an ignorant being with dreams of glory. After the *guarango* follows the monkey.

Florida Street

1. Florida Street is a state of mind, like a temple or a historical shrine. Within Florida it is only possible to think and to see in a certain way; while we are inside, Florida infuses us with its spirit. We pass through it with a special disposition; there are dark days during which we could not walk along it without feeling a sense of guilt. The street is endowed with a commanding personality because it is a temple, a rite, and a dogma. There, we walk slower than along other streets; thought is calmed, becomes reflective, abandons the solicitude to Divinity, and undergoes all the peripatetic influences.

It is a street of old vintage: in 1823 it was the only one with stone paving. In those days it was the only clean street; garbage was usually thrown out in the streets, and in many localities this practice produced a spongy flooring that causes today's asphalt and pavement to cave in. Florida attracted rosary-reciting peregrines; they had previously paraded on Victoria, where the Marcos Sastre salon presided over the fashion of letters. Florida is the street of bookstores, of shops, and of dressmakers; there, we dress in the English style and speak in the manner of the French; it is the fashionable street. The stones in the pavement are very expensive because the pampa is stoneless, but it was the stone pavement that allowed people to walk along the street until today.

Florida is the city's façade and the pedestrian's apparel. It is an open-air salon where one may silently socialize by walking up and down. The people who promenade are not going anywhere; they derive pleasure from the walk—to sit down and to converse would fall into another category. The street is a salon of urbanity and sympathy where no one knows or bothers anyone else. Florida is a memberless club because it satisfies the need for social intercourse without making any demands. It satisfies the elemental need for company but without the obligations and bother of friendship. Such is the temple that, without obligations, unites spirits and beings. Florida is not even the living room, that favorite place of the Argentine home that faces the street. It does not create ties of fellowship or of solidarity: it is a fair of gallantry and composure. Indistinguishably, all the social classes parade under the appearance of well-being. The only requirement is to be acquainted with the rite and to believe in the dogma.

2. Dress becomes the uniform of the militia in which both rich and poor enlist. Florida's pedestrians seem to be readers of fashion magazines; thus, the bookstore and the clothing store together crossed the threshold. Dress, whether it is worn or is displayed in a showcase, acquires the meaning of a fetish. The dress is the person and also his amulet, but one so perfect that it lacks the person's folds and wrinkles. It is a person's dress, without the wrinkles, which enriches the physiognomy.

The lack of an orientation to life, of a resolute will, and of a spiritual civility leads to the well-kept dress, which stops being a generic skin and becomes a uniform. A well-dressed people is not so much a people that has solved its economic problems, but one that has no wrinkles or internal problems. A correctly dressed people may be living in the ethnographic time of tattooing, which is its equivalent.

To be indebted to the tailor in order to dress well is to ignore the problem of values. The dress is for others; it is not a safe-conduct for circulation through the streets, but a feast we offer outside our home for the passers-by. To exercise extreme care in dress, at the expense of other needs that eventually vanish, is to live for the street. It is clear that the Argentine descends from men who have lived for centuries in the coffee shop, which is the collective gathering place of the poor. Dress is the dwelling that we wear; to enhance its worth until it becomes the most important factor in life, to the detriment of human values, is to live in a disguise. That is the other meaning of Florida: a luxurious disguise. The dress should be in accord with one's economic state and his manner of thinking; it should not merely keep pace with other dresses. To dress well, one does not need to be a living advertisement for the tailor's shop.

Florida is Buenos Aires's Sunday dress that is worn everyday. It acquired the quality of a fetish in the days of Rivadavia and Belgrano, who wanted to transform our habits on the basis of dress. Fetishism is the religion of that temple in which we march. There are politicians, professors, and descendants from the fathers of our country who could not change their clothes without abolishing their personalities, losing converts, or denying their surnames. They are condemned to their dress: they have become parasites of their clothes. But we all dress well, so clothing is an inexpressive clue. Rich and poor alike, we march faithfully, displaying our second nature.

The worker's smock, the office worker's lustrous coat, and the working woman's elegant apron are the attire used during the hours of breadwinning. Harsh destiny and, therefore, the task end with the smock, the coat, and the apron. They remain as masks of a fiction; the street clothes carry one into the reality that is presumed to be more desirable: the other life. An almost religious aura can be felt on Florida. But dress conceals the true situation of the smock, of the coat, and of the apron; specifically, it conceals the depressing poverty that is left locked in the closet. Thus, dress is a real disguise because it is what robs, by artful means, the essence of tragic destiny. By removing the smock and the apron, the workers forsake their true roles and live in the illusion advertised by the splendid multitude. That is how theater originated. The figures communicate the fiction of theatrical personages, and the illusion is universal because everyone believes in it. The dress hides the tragedy of destiny and promotes the protagonist to the category of a dreamer.

3. The merchant who installs himself on Florida establishes his hierarchy. The roaming population considers itself the darling of the showcases, which are the spiritual fronts of buildings. The merchant who exhibits his wares on Florida possesses the materials of people's dreams and he displays them as icons of the faith. The showcases are also dresses: the dresses of the houses. The showcases are everything; the house fronts, probably the ugliest in the city center, are not seen. The showcase does not allow us to perceive the front. The front is the surface that the house wears for the street; it is the main detail of Buenos Aires's dwellings, but on Florida it yields priority to the showcase. The small, grey, old buildings do not exist, and if they do they are overwhelmed by luminous signs through which the dream of heaven begins. One looks no higher than eye level: whatever is higher is of no interest. Reality reaches as far as uncovered heads. To look without raising the eyes gives things a familiar perspective and the limited and intimate scope of a living room. Florida is perhaps Florida because of its compactness, which prevents us from stepping back to view the showcases at a convenient distance, unglued from the fiction.

4. As in the movie house, one dreams of fortune and of love. The luxury of the showcases replete with jewels, artistic objects, silks, perfumes, books, radios, and projectors makes Florida the showcase

of our ambition. The real owner has in one locale all the things we wish to possess; they glitter like symbols of an opulence that borders on waste, as happens in dreams. Florida is like a movie house: through its magic we settle into multimillionaires' palaces or into poor, hygienic rooms of ideal seamstresses or into little country houses free of mosquitoes and stagnant waters; we share the adventurous life of men of the world, of industrial barons, of bandits, and of artists; or we achieve at thirty a love that we dreamed of at eighteen.

Those showcases also offer us by reflection the goods that are beyond our means and outside our destiny. The public roams at noon and early evening, and it dreams at night or during breaks at work; all those dreams which are concentrated on the diamond, on the beautiful woman, or on the famous book are as accessible on Florida as on the lights and shadows of a movie screen. The Jockey Club is there: Florida's internal showcase; that is the place to dream of genealogical trees that have produced a thousand cubic meters of wood this year, of the live Golden Fleece that has dropped in price in Liverpool, and of gambling—which is the machinery of hope. On Florida are the bars that artists dream of, the jewelry stores and other shops that women ogle over, and the book shops that writers long for.

The astounding part of this grand fiction is that everyone deceives himself without purpose; everyone is partially aware of the secret, but he passively accepts appearances as reality. If someone thinks, as in the church or in the theater, that everything is a lie, he does not say it. So, Florida continues to exist in the souls of the faithful.

5. Once the fiction is accepted, as with a film, all that occurs is perfect, logical, and veridical. For example, when children play and pretend to be princes, generals, and bandits, it does not cross their minds that none of them is a prince, a general, or a bandit. Perhaps one word of frankness pronounced on that street would destroy the illusion, if it is possible that a word could sometimes overcome a tradition of one hundred years.

In any case, those transitional moments, like the hours that float by in the movie-house lobby during the show, are impotent to offset the effect of the movie. That dream of opulence, of abundance, of luxury, and of a good salary or dividend—stimulated by the ground floor of buildings that really have no other stories or any need for them—is what we dream of by contemplating an island of reality that we have agreed not to awaken or to submit to an examination.

Florida has a festive atmosphere even on a working day, and our state of mind reflects it. The conversation topics are conditioned by the environment: we speak of projects and not of failures. Our topics are dictated by the street: Florida is a concave mirror that reflects an enlarged image of what we think we are and will be. It hides what we unfailingly are today and gives us confidence in what is unavoidable. The surroundings are optimistic because there is more light than in our homes, because the people are not hostile unless they go in groups, and because no one seems to be thinking about real things. The intoxication of success and of fame accompanies the people leaving the bar or the book store; accessible love appears with the women leaving the shops. Everyone entering the street is invigorated by new possibilities. Everyone is suspended over reality. Even words that are not shameful are whispered. On Florida, conversation is also part of the dress. It suffices to enter from any other street to realize that people speak of other topics and that preoccupations are no longer trivial but become grandiose in an intrepid atmosphere. It is a promenade of giants. Florida has been such an entity for over one hundred years. On that street, which detests a sincere voice, have been born the utopian dreams that have stimulated so many illusions of wealth and of culture— illusions that are still with us. The main plot of the comedy we dream is unfolded in the most elegant and ornate of settings; at last, some greasepaint rubs off the face of the poor man who returns home to once again face life.

The Night

In the early evening Buenos Aires is impregnated with a bucolic melancholy, which, with the arrival of night, fades into sorrow. Buenos Aires does not have a night, except for the one that arrives from the immense pampa. It seems to penetrate the city from the suburbs, through the interminable streets, in the manner of a sleep that commences in the extremities of tired limbs. It is a night of the fields: taciturn, concentrated, and lugubrious. The lights and noises of the city center are not an integral part of that calm, peasant night; they are spasms that attempt to shatter darkness. Night is crushed by the street lamps, the showcases, and the luminous signs; but the residue, powerful and intact, stretches to infinity.

Buenos Aires lacks a night life. Only the cabarets and coffee shops stand watch and make conspicuous the city's impeccable bourgeois sleep; they are the dreams of slumbering, repressed appetites. People retire early and seldom visit each other at night. Each home recovers its hermetic isolation, and, through such a zodiacal quietude, the imposing village recuperates from the day's treacherous drudgery. At ten o'clock, night penetrates the homes and offers the body and soul a material rest. It is a monastic repose for beings who have few intellectual or moral sins; it is a purifying repose that the Divinity accepts in place of the ancient prayers at those hours. At night it may be observed that Buenos Aires is a virtuous city and that its evil is reduced to the minimum imposed by life on anything living. There are no complications of intellect: it is the holy sleep of a tired beast. It is a sleep of cement, of iron, and of a conscience without reproach.

The sinning souls gather around the coffee shops: those coffee shops which now have a dancing floor framed in a superfluous space with a small orchestra interpreting the tango, the music of sleep. They wish to plunge into an adventure of which they are ashamed. That is where the unemployed women begin their Via Crucis and practice the profession of libertines.

The cabaret is a coffee shop of more importance. It is a salon where people are afraid to be recognized. They seem to be restrained by the fear of being discovered.

People go to the cabaret to dance and to drink; so they dance and drink for want of something better to do. The women carry out a task that does not amuse them: they gain their bread by dancing and drinking. They do not have men who support them; and their lives are harsh, especially if there are children to feed. There is no reason for them to be happy. The men do not amuse themselves either: they simply go to have a good time. Everything has the indifferent aspect of objects being bought and sold. There are women with the vocation of a courtesan: one who enjoys for enjoyment's sake and envelops life with her sexuality. Words and laughter emerge from the surface of beings who have erred along the way. None of them has forgotten her dolls or renounced the hope of a happy home. They incite to virtue; and almost always the unwary young man asks them some impertinent question about their private lives, about the details of the false step. The lyrics of the tango revolve around these vulgar and cruel themes. By being suggestive dancers, they earn their bread.

During such diversions, the young man does not totally give of himself either. In his mind he combines the worlds of home and of brothel; from this superposition there results an equivocation that makes an unpleasant impression. A certain respect, a certain coldness, and a certain psychological repugnance impossible to dissimulate give the spectator the impression that the young man is dancing with his sister. They are beings unacquainted with each other, and it does not appear that they find pleasure in being together. However, we must not imagine that it is their purpose to beautify the environment or to infuse that farce with chastity. Love, compassion, and modesty are substituted by the incapacity to courageously accept reality as it is.

Some get drunk and fall into the extreme opposite of taciturnity: they become bothersome or aggressive. It is not possible to be tipsy without having to demonstrate one's courage and importance and to insist that it is reality and that the state of drunkenness is merely accidental. The protagonist may exercise enough self-control to avoid a commotion, but he is a dangerous and hostile man: a man who is outside the party and has not been penetrated by it.

That is why the cabaret is a sad place. Even those who act happily are acting out an artificial gaiety. Those who go there lack the habit of committing themselves, of plunging into life as into water; they suffer from the modesty of a person who never disrobes before others and who never learns how to swim out to the open sea.

The women understand their obligation and do not forget that they have been hired for that barely licentious farce. They know that love—which is serious—has nothing in common with that image resulting from intoxication. Love is not for those women, or for those men. Sex presents no complicated problems outside of what is already tacitly agreed upon by reason of the surroundings. Both man and woman are autonomous redoubts that have no recondite relationship during the dance.

Domestic virtue has taken refuge in homes and the sleepless man is in the streets. The woman who walks arm in arm with her husband, her father, or her lover receives a direct challenge from this man of the night. Night is the time for secret societies, and each passer-by behaves like a member of a sect of people who do not go to bed at ten o'clock. The woman who goes arm in arm with her man perceives, in each male she passes, the impetus—controlled with great effort—of coarse expression or of the intentional brush. The anonymous male is not a faun or a member of the underworld, but he cannot resist showing that he is at least as much a man as the husband or the lover. He believes that he cannot pass in silence or in respect without renouncing a right that belongs to him: the joint ownership of the woman.

The streets of Buenos Aires are hostile because the night of the city is the night of the invading countryside, and things take the appearance of a darkness without shelter. The honest women who retire early implicate those who do not. The open doors proclaim the chastity of closed doors. If men go out, they leave their wives at home and join their mistresses. And the mistresses, so believes the man of the night, belong a little to everyone.

In the passer-by beats a wild soul that is stimulated by that night billions of years older than the city's first house; gradually, the unrestrained spirit has been shaping night life. In order to avoid any responsibility, if he should indulge in an excess, he feigns to be happy or to have drunk too much: two things easy to excuse.

The tango, the nocturnal music, saddens those places of entertainment because it carries in its rhythm reminiscences of an abject past and of the suffocated voices of a rejected life. It was a
result of the black man's journey, uprooted from his land and deposited on tobacco, sugar, and coffee plantations. It encloses in its
cadences the compulsion and the will to submerge fatigue into
flesh, until it is converted into pleasure.

The Tango

It is danced from the hips to the feet. From
the waist upward, the body does not dance: it is rigid, as if the
lively legs carried two bodies asleep in an embrace. Like matrimony, its merit lies in the daily, unbroken repetition.

It is a monotonous and expressionless dance, with the stylized
rhythm of coupling. In contrast to other dances, it lacks the feeling
with which a suggestive, plastic language speaks to the senses; it
does not arouse in the spectator's spirit feelings of joy, of enthusiasm, of admiration, or of desire. It is a dance without soul, for au-
tomatons, for people who have renounced the complexities of mental life and seek shelter in nirvana. It is to evade the world. The
tango is the dance of pessimism, of everyone's sorrow: a dance of
the never-changing, enormous plains and of a subjugated and burdened race that crisscrosses them without end and without destiny,
in the eternity of a forever repeating present. Melancholy originates from that repetition, from that contrast which results from
seeing two bodies, built for free movement, subjected to the fatidic
mechanical march of a beast of burden. It is the same sorrow we
feel upon seeing young horses tied to a hoisting machine.

Previously, when the tango was only cultivated in the suburbs
and therefore had not yet experienced the city's smoothing and
polishing, it did have certain steps in which the dancer could display his ability. He could introduce improvisations, such as hip
and leg movements, rhythmic pounding with the heels, cuts, bends,
half-moons, and the strategy by which the subtly deceived woman's thigh was trapped in all its length by man's thigh, firm and
rigid.

The dance was prestigious in the bawdyhouses. It was music only, a lascivious music without the lyrics that would appear only after several years, when the masses found their popular poet. The chords could be heard at night on the outskirts of towns, escaping from the brothel like a vapor through the always closed jalousies; it would fade in the countryside or shatter in the deserted streets. It carried the lukewarm breath of sin, resonances of a forbidden world outside. Later, it acquired its citizenship when its tunes were played on the streets by the beggar's organ. It clandestinely infiltrated a world that denied it access. It reached the cities under disguise and triumphantly entered into the parlors and homes. It came from the suburbs, where it had arrived from the whorehouse. There, it lived its natural life in the full glory of its filigrees: the syncopation signified something infamous; and the musical notes, prolonged by the pipe organ's throat, reverberated an erotic languor. The music combined with the breath of cheap perfume, the heat of tired flesh, and the alcoholic evaporations.

In the family atmosphere, the dance was of a "clandestine" interest when performed with all the ornamentation, unctuous and lubricious. It was then endowed with sponsorship and its peculiar identity; now, it is lost, and in its place has appeared the verse that incorporates, as does the satirical drama after the tragedy, the ritual and the phallic element. Even today, the lyrics clearly betray the tango's lineage; they speak of the loose woman, of the despicable act, of elopement, of concubinage, of sentimental prostitution of the wailing singer. The purest girl has on her lectern that scrap which previously was the dress of a venal body. The innocent mouth sings the lament of an infamous woman but does not redeem her, although she may ignore the meaning of the words. Her voice rings a woman's humiliation.

But it is now that the tango has achieved its just expression: the lack of any expression. It is slow, with the feet dragging and with the pace of a grazing ox. It would seem as though sensuality robbed the dance of the grace of movements: it has the seriousness of the human during procreation. The tango has the fixed earnestness of copulation because it seems to engender without pleasure. In that sense it is the most ulterior dance, the consummate dance; the other dances are only premonitory symptoms. Everything in the tango belongs to the reign of the vegetative spirit, from the waist down. At a given moment, one leg remains fixed and the other simulates a step forward and one backward. It is the moment in which the couple remains in doubt, like the cow that looks to one side, then another, and behind; its elemental faculties of thinking and desiring are in suspense. Then, the tango once again resumes its own march, slow and tired.

The tango is stylized by being reduced to the simplicity of a lament that consists in modulating a single musical note that is polished or enlarged by the pressure of one finger sliding on a cord. It has something of the spasmodic, submissive moan filled with anguish. There is no need to search for music or for dance: both are images. It does not have the alternatives of other dances or their excitement provoked by gymnastic movements; it does not excite by the accidental contact of bodies. The bodies are united, fixed, and adhere to each other like coupling insects. But flesh thus intertwined is dulled in its ardor after a few movements; there is no flush or unexpected contact. In the tango, all contact is agreed upon and stipulated beforehand. The tango's movements do not imply a possession fraught by resistance, doubt, and reticence; on the contrary, they reflect the security of a legal act in which the possession is agreed on and paid for. Rather than being a betrothal, it is a concubinage that does not upset social conventions.

It lacks the exquisite courtesies of the other dances, which are implicit in their structures. Man and woman do not stand out, do not conserve the peculiarities of their character or a certain elastic distance. The tango is the uniformity of the sexes; it is the already known, without possible surprises, without the curiosity of first encounters; it is the ancient possession.

To dance with a partner can be inciting and sensual, and can constitute a Freudian transference; but the tango is the act itself, devoid of fiction and innocence, and without neuroses. It could be viewed as a solitary act: the lamentable music is reminiscent of rumination; the mandolin, this propitious instrument, emits the sounds of a moo. The second phase of the tango's stylization, whereby it is reduced to its essential scheme and to its unadorned substance, is the finding of the proper instrument: the mandolin, a portable substitute for the barrel organ and the pipe organ.

From another point of view, the tango is a humiliating dance for the woman, who submits herself to a man who does not direct her and does not force her to be attentive to his fickleness, to yield to his will. It is humiliating because the man is as passive and as bound as she is. In almost all other dances, it is the man who leads in the movement; and one has the impression that, at times, the woman is lifted up in an invitation to fly. Those dances offer the possibility of an escape. But in the tango the partners move with one will, as if each one possessed one-half of the totality; they yield to the mechanical motion of walking and of breathing. It is the mechanical act par excellence and has the isochronism of blood circulation. It is a dance without will, without desire, without adventure, and without impetus. The woman seems to carry out an act that is for her annoying or senseless, one in which she finds no pleasure. Nothing about her hints of grace, fragility, fickleness, or shyness. She is flesh barely alive, unfeeling, unafraid. She is sure, submissive, heavy, moving slowly in a straight line as if following the route of a beast of burden. We do not fear for her; it cannot be said that her desire is controlled, step by step, by a decision that governs her imperatively. She yields consciously; she is agreeable. For this reason, she does not incite one to stealing her from her partner. She is not desired, and her body is far from ours when she is dancing: it is anastomosed to her partner. They belong to each other and are one being. Therefore, we do not identify with her partner's role. To desire her would be to commit adultery. She is fulfilling a painful rite without aesthetic value: the conjugal act of surrender and the everyday act of walking.

On the other hand, we can observe that she forms a unit with her companion, and if she were taken away by force, a part of the man would remain with her, as does part of the husband in the abducted wife. They form one body, with trunks immobilized; four legs perform as one will. It is a body that thinks of nothing, aban-

doned to the music's rhythm—guttural and distant, to be reached
by the orientation of the vague homing instinct that tugs at them
through the music.

Perhaps no other music is so apt for fantasy as that of the tango.
Like a narcotic, it enters and takes possession of the whole being.
To the beat of the tango it is possible to arrest thought and to float
the soul in the body, as the fog wafts over the plain. The movements do not have to be forcibly produced; they are automatically
born of that music which is already carried inside. The will, like
the image of an object, is disintegrated in the fog, and the soul is a
plain in peace. Vaguely, the woman accompanies the dancer in an
almost inarticulate skidding. The dance's spell, in its sentimental
sense, lies in the obliteration of will, a state in which only deep
feelings of sensitive and vegetative life are awake. This mystique
meshes with the feelings evoked by twilight on the prairies and
with the vague sadness observed in the eyes of a contented animal.

Once the dance is over, it is impossible to forget the woman's
cold act, in which she has been possessed like a mollusk, in a reciprocal sexual intercourse. A vapor of affliction and of sin, something
clammy and viscous like the echo of her movements and of her
surrender in a trivial dream, surrounds her body. She has not been
possessed by her incubus but by her own celibacy.

Carnival and Sadness

To study what has been called the native sad-
ness, which is a very complex state of mind, undoubtedly containing elements of real human sadness, we must first understand the
carnival. The carnival is the festival of our sadness.

The carnival's psychological center does not precisely rotate
around sadness; rather, it revolves around the need for joy. A zest
for life is not apparent, and the colors of dresses take on a somber
appearance. The new has been so quickly erected over the debris
of the old that the thirst for joy is a potential movement, ready to
explode under favorable circumstances. The inclination of somber
spirits toward explosions of joy is a universal law: witness the
chained dogs that are let loose at nightfall. The deep need to rid

oneself of the grey and taciturn noose of an oppressive world through which circulate magnetic currents of indifference and distrust puts the citizens in peril of bursting with gaiety at the advent of night. Any pretext suffices for a party or for laugh-making: thus originate the *guarango*-like act, the fear of being exposed to ridicule, and any type of demonstration with placards and cheers. Any kind of popular celebration is given a carnival atmosphere by the masses. It is a contained gaiety, a joy not shown in its nudity; these are the feelings of people who have not established frank sexual relations with women and ignore how to satisfy them—they seek the din of a crowd. Such is the real nucleus of sadness: what is called carnival by the calendar and is in effect a psychoanalytical treatment.

The strained merriment unleashed on diverse occasions is cruel, desperate, and hostile. The carnival lacks songs or courtesy; it requires the street, the multitude, and the intoxication of urban masses, because the rest of the year is so sad and abject. It is difficult to enjoy a cloistered existence complicated by problems too serious for our social state. The organic necessity to laugh and to enjoy such an existence becomes concentrated, and, saddened by the weight of unbearable formulas, it ignites in a boisterous reprisal against the inborn seriousness of everyday existence. Argentine sadness, which has been described by everyone, totally surrounds and saturates Argentine man. What should be studied is Argentine gaiety because it holds the key to somber humor, with its patriotic, political, and sportive festivals, with its picnics, and with its theater unmerciful in aggression and wanting in tenderness. The carnival as a feast of impersonality and anonymity, belonging to the discontented and the oppressed, is the allotropic state of sadness—its mask.

The Indian, the naked man, adopted the carnival many years ago in the country's interior. He immediately liked the appearance of the carnival of colors, of ornaments, and of noises: the crazy dress of the white man, the dressed man. He first adopted the showy garments: weapons, many-colored clothes, beads, and plumes. To this he added alcohol and his own feathers, thus elevating a coarse and humiliating reality to the level of an absurd fiction. The bitter truths were packages like capsules. Alcohol and color were lewdness and gaiety: the counterreality. In the future, reality would not change. Catholicism joined carnival to Holy Week, as Dionysius combined tragedy and comedy; it was liturgy and theater.

Lugones described a carnival in La Rioja. Nine costumed people mounted on burros wandered through the streets. They sang and produced unutterable sounds with bladders. Hearts full of blood were employed as water bags to be thrown at random. All this occurred at the time when the pharmacist Cranwell manufactured in Buenos Aires the first flasks of perfumed water.

Carnival and theater are alike, and they will always exist as a counterforce to work, to orderliness, to logic, and to honesty. They are the triumph of repressed forces: of idleness, of madness, of rejoicing, of absurdity, and of sensuality. In the theater we witness imaginary scenes that could have been but were not. It is a revenge for what was lost forever when life veered onto alternate paths. What remains unblemished of man's ideals, of his intense comprehension of destiny, and of his emotion for virtue, beauty, and pain are here represented, reduced to a set shattered by the forbidden imagery of what could have been but was not. Theater is the triumphant performance of life's wasted years; it is the resurrection of the soul's lifeless matter; it is the retaliation of absurdity that had in its roots a bit of reason—just as the brief manumission of Horace's servant allowed him to voice long ignored truths. Throughout the struggles in which the powerful impose their patterns on the weak, the carnival, like the dream, is the theater of repressed acts.

A people that is unhappy with its destiny and that dreams excessively about heroism, saintliness, and health is a theatrical people whose suffering is imprinted on all its festivities. The carnival is the standard feast of the Latin peoples, a Mendelian variety resulting from the grafting of goat and grapevine. The suffocated sexual phenomenon provides raw material for the combustion; the fallen pride, the aspiration limited by ignorance and impracticality, the bacchanalia of the wounded and the slaves, in short, life, theater, and carnival mix together indistinguishably. Our theater as a stage for a crepuscular life, which is conducted in secret, is tragic and of a carnivallike appearance. It copies topics and characters from the carnival, but on other occasions it is the source of inspiration. But carnival and theater harmonize with the real, serious, everyday life and for this reason the carnival is the national feast, and the theater is a public spectacle performed on the proscenium by jobless actors. The truth is reflected through those caricaturelike and Dionysiac types: it is a one-act farce transforming itself into an oral judgment where reality is metamorphosed into offense, without losing its character. As Athens could be studied through written works, Argentine life could be analyzed through the one-act farces that copy a thoroughly despised sector of reality, which cannot be ridiculed at home. It remains to investigate to what extent, by inversion or by transfusion, the street life develops in terms of the stage life, and to what degree we live by parodying the stage. Theater is more carnivallike than life, and the carnival is more alive than the theater. Throughout these three stages, a grave soul, discontented with its destiny and uncapable of frankness, confuses the weekly and annual festivities with the comedy of ordinary workdays. An intense gaiety or an unusual situation in which serious interests are in play throws our man into a theatrical stance. Buenos Aires possesses only one face for all the popular festivities: the same used for revolutions or worn upon the return from holidays in the country. The municipality can only visualize one way of decorating Mayo Avenue and Mayo Square: it hangs the lights and entangles roofs with small lamps. It suffices to exchange grotesque faces for names of heroes; the framework for the entertainment is the same and only the serpentines are missing. The spectator assists at rallies, religious processions, and Ninth of July parades with the attitude of a person who wishes to have fun but lacks the experience of gaiety and the training in happiness. He expends the same kind of thirsty glee on all ceremonies, in the manner that he wears the same garb in his home, at work, or in the coffee shop. The dates change but the spirits do not. Even during burials there are unmistakably theatrical elements, and the comical can unexpectedly appear from the lugubrious region of the subconscious; laughter is a misfortune during pathetic moments. The sense of the ridiculous, so sharpened and extended, can be the vigilant sense of an act whose development we witness. Everything that may appear to be a tendency toward humor or to be an alert critic's distrust is actually the same reaction to situations that require a varied response.

The same technique applied to the joke and the jest by our native fool—the *guarango*—may be seen in the torpor of the neighborhood troupe, where everyone sounds alike. The ingenious phrases sometimes circulate for years. The Latins are inheritors of the farce, the Slavs and Germans of the theater of ideas. The comical part of our people is a tragedy as serious, as natural, and as transparent to the destiny of the race as the tulle mask that covers the face.

That everyday carnival which explodes at given times is somber, aggressive, typical of a workday. The contained forces spread out, not by accident, but because the carnival is embodied in our character. We are temperamentally theatrical and we cannot play with mockery or with love. Sarmiento describes an incident in the provinces where a man was burned alive when someone struck a match to his carnival costume. He was carbonized in the tumult. Then he was buried without anyone denouncing the crime. Approximately twenty years ago, on Defensa Street, a citizen of a somber humor, who was on his way home, decided to have fun by making others laugh. He covered his entire body with serpentines. Then, someone threw a lit match and the costumed man was on fire; he ran in panic until he died in flames. The city game is the same one played in the provinces one hundred years ago.

The sensual part also acquires characters of violence and of exhibition. It is not the hidden need to love that leads the disguised people into the obscene joke, the pelvic brush, or the pleasure of lust; rather, as in the spicy compliment or in the ingenious phrase, there is a hate that, beneath a veneer of courtesy, carries the intention of wounding.

Our carnival does not have songs; it has insults. We no longer play with perfumed water or with flowers. Stories are not told nor are weddings performed at dances. The serpentine, thrown with a smile, carries the venom of a maliciously aimed stone. The carnival is grotesque and serious, offensive and lubricious, with all the sadness implied in what we desired but could not have.

12 THE NATIVE CITY

Passing Through

The race that peopled us had no home; it was ancient and it resided in stone houses where no ideal existed. The ideal was lodged in the church and in the court. A father was not a paterfamilias; he exercised his authority like a lord over his serfs. His wife and children were his honor and his victims. Only God and king were more powerful than he. His country estate had the inner appearance of a monastery. When a new house was erected, it was so planned that each room would enclose the role and the drama of its dweller: wife, children, and servants. The living room was used to receive guests; conversation would be carried on in a fixed manner, in accord with ceremony. The arrangement of the living room, the bedrooms, the dining room, and the servants' quarters never varied, nor did the spiritual perspectives differ. The house was a redoubt for resting; within a variable cosmos it could not affirm any fixed ideal. The materials used to build the house— whether clay, straw, wood, or zinc—were correlated with the dweller's soul. The precarious and transitory elements have today been reinforced: the residents have rendered the dwelling unstable. A home is constituted by two beings of different bloods and tastes who had previously followed separate paths; with their union, they give origin to an entirely new entity. Life demands irreparable sacrifices from man and woman. They have to adjust to the exigencies of struggle; if no stone is available, they must build with clay in spite of ancient instinct. The lessons taught by everyday events tend to destroy and to change. Work in the countryside led to the terrible habits of destruction and change, and dwellings were constantly being shifted. In a city of the plains, such as Montevideo, Buenos Aires, or Santa Fe, the dwellings—initially made of rawhide—served as shelter, not comfort. Love, equally adventitious, roved about the beds like some nocturnal phantom. Love is more serious, firm, and gyneocratic in houses of solid walls than in huts. Love made in a hut has a dishonest flavor; it requires the eternity of the surrounding world, as if the whole species were to inhabit the home.

It never occurs to us that we may die in the house that we occupy in passing, as we never conceive that we could die while traveling. We are on a journey in our own home; we fear death, but do not visualize dying at home, which proves that the house is not seen as a tomb with definitive and perennial characteristics. The brick walls endure less than we do. With glee we will watch them be demolished, we who are so fragile. At first, the furniture that we put in the house is in style; then, it quickly grows old; we endure it with coldness and finally exchange it for other models, equally obsolete. The furniture provides us with sufficient strength to face the world, but it does not receive us with friendship. It only is useful when we are tired. Even when the house is our own and we try to decorate it forever, those objects and that furniture can only have a superficial relationship for us. Tomorrow our luck may totally change and perhaps we will vary the conformation of our dwelling to the amelioration or to the deterioration of our soul's habitat. It would be different because we would have changed completely. We live in the expectation of such a change, and we grow older and die during the wait. The same occurs with the wife and the children; they have suddenly appeared and have their own plans and destinies. Neither the wife nor the children seem to be meant forever, here in this land where everything seems for today.

The House Plan

The old house, the poor one, is laid out just as it was 150 years ago. It has not varied in its arrangement, because the structure obeys vital and organic reasons, in the manner of the disposition of organs throughout the body. Those houses have a function that is manifested in the life of the occupants. The distribution of rooms corresponds to the family's need, to use, and to the definition of comfort. The consecutive arrangement of rooms imparts simultaneously a taste of jail and of monastery; each room is an individual cell, even if it is intercommunicated with others by interior doors. Passing through all the rooms on one side, we reach the poultry yard, the bathroom, and the kitchen; passing through the other side we reach the living room. The rooms are isolated and only make lateral contact; the contact of friendship and of love, in conversation and in frank social behavior, is face to face. The architectural conception corresponds to the vastness of space, and the house is designed with only a ground floor. Its model is the ranch, which expands horizontally. Constructed from scarcely resistant materials and according to the most elementary and empirical laws, it rises uncurtailed in an abundant land. Thus, it possesses a lateral and linear disposition. The house with little front but great depth—ten varas by sixty—has the layout of a ranch. It offers a minimum of exposure to the outside, and it guards the internal life from the stranger's prying inquisitiveness. It begins with one room to which are added others, one by one. The house does not grow by expansion of the whole, but by partial additions that are juxtaposed. The story that is later built on top of the ground floor is simply another ground floor superposed. The movement that generates growth is that of a line that prolongs itself and separates in two: one direction goes to the street, the world, and the other to the bedrooms, the secret. The farther a room is from the entrance hall, the more pronounced is its monastic character and the more it acquires the decorum of a single woman's bedroom. The room in which we accumulate inexpressive objects lays bare the utensils that we use daily, and it is a history of our economic life. There is no attic in those houses. If the furniture, the objects, the garments, or the curtains should fall into disuse, they are not conserved. The renovation is total, definitive. Where there is no attic, life passes quickly; it passes with what is exchanged. The attic keeps in storage—in a new and capricious disposition—the objects that have been wearing away faster than we have; they are a reminder of time's passage. The attic is the house's and the family's archive where children learn unforgettable lessons of sentiment, of emotion, and of beauty. The indelible education is more profound than all of philosophy: rag flowers, a picture book without covers, or a broken toy. In those attics lie the dreams that are not forgotten; they are the sediments of our life, with all the good and bad alternatives, and with all the health and bitterness. In our old and poor houses there is no attic, no past, no leisure, and no childhood. The humble lodging implies that all is in readiness for moving and for a new beginning. It is necessary to live through this romanticism to enter into a complete life. The house without an attic is solemn, as is shown by the living room's austere affectation. People are also solemn, serious, or superficial. The attic is the immovability of childhood, the nape's eye, and the pathetic remembrance. Musicians or poets are not produced by those cold and severe houses, neither are inventors or sailors.

The Floating City

Poverty and ugliness cluster at the doors of Buenos Aires, like beggars at the palace gate. The cans and wood splinters mix with the trash and greenish ponds; these are the metropolis's wastes and the rubbish piles of dreams of opulence. Here lies what does not belong to the city and remains stubbornly rebellious outside the municipality; at the same time, it is a force that rejects solitude and that crowds in from the countryside. Such sordid and ugly dwellings are simultaneously two things: city and countryside. With close observation, we may note that they are huts that have slid from the depths of the plain to pile up at the edge of the modern world. The zinc house that crowds the entire family into one or two rooms is the old hut reconstructed with new materials: metal substitutes for clay, as previously clay substituted for rawhide. Metal sheets have replaced adobe, and the dwelling is now less stable. The heterogeneous materials are refuse that has been painstakingly collected to fill the interstices and to offer an appearance of solidity. The truth is quite different: the provisional and portable hut can be taken apart sheet by sheet and transported. Like a toy to be assembled, it is capable of alternatively serving many purposes. It continues to be, as in the days of the gaucho, the home on horseback, the home with an unpredictable base. The man who there resides suffers the instability of his dwelling; while he lives there, he waits. He is passing through, living in expectancy. He wagers his hut: either he will improve his lot or be reduced to nothing. His economic situation has not yet crystallized; while the wager is still in effect, the man occupies the shelter where he sleeps and procreates. But a house thus constructed is not for permanent residence; it is a refuge, not a home.

That poor lacustrine zoophyte scarcely furnishes his house's interior with only the most essential pieces of furniture and household goods. Outside grow the plants and the weeds: what man planted and what was indigenous competing in a silent and persistent struggle. He does not embellish his house, because it is merely a tent temporarily pitched against bad weather. The man is not a mollusk but his own house's tenant, its irremediable guest. What should be purposefully spent is saved or invested in house improvement. With time, this becomes an ideal. Whoever lives in such narrowness cannot allow himself anything superfluous or conceive of fondness for useless things. He is in a hurry; his own life is a necessity and not a luxury. The ugliness is embodied in a face ravaged by the disgust for life. He is a human being in urgency, who wishes to quickly leave his surroundings but almost never can. The house grows old before he does. It deteriorates and gets out of order; the ordinary materials resist less than man's organism, and the brick turns to dust before the flesh does.

He does not aspire to comfort: poverty is cruelty, ugliness, and rancor, whether toward others or toward himself. In that skeleton of a home, there breathes no eternal feeling; the home's fragility excludes sentiments of religion, of morality, of kinship ties, of paternity, or of property. There are no stones for the moss to cling to. The need for comfort is born from happiness or at least from the satisfaction of living; it is generated and grows from such happiness. To embellish the world is to repay it with merriment. But if that prisoner of an anemic dream should decide to adorn anything, it would be to deface and not to beautify: a cornice, the ill-suited paint, or an iron railing. All these grotesque adornments signify torpidity and eagerness to deceive. They are meant to increase the property's value; the clumsy hand that affixes a poor imitation leaves a miserable impression inspiring pity. The venal concept of property is also a hysteria arising from the realization of life's brevity.

The poor man is not happy, because he crudely dreams about what he does not have; and yet, the substance of his dreams is worth nothing. Neither the homeowner who is in a good financial position nor he who lives on a fixed income feels comfortable. They are unacquainted with the epicureanism of the home, so prevalent among the aristocrats and the bourgeois of other latitudes.

Buried Penates

1. The house is isolated: even its exterior does not disclose the frankness of an unprejudiced life. Even adornment takes on the appearance of defiance. The small garden, where someday will be edified the living room, has its flowers, its grass, and its ground brick pathways; however, instead of truly belonging to the house, it is more a part of the invincible countryside, which, with its weeds, will triumph if the wait is to be excessively long. In this sense, a plaza is an unconquered space, not a place to rest. Rather than being an open space in the center of a group of houses,

it seems that the dwellings are contained at its edge. The plaza is the fundamental part: the countryside. The park, which in European cities opens a parenthesis of trees and of birds amid the monotonous rigidity of stone masonry, holds in Buenos Aires—the plain's cosmopolis—the key to its undecipherable, peasant sadness. Palermo, Avellaneda Park, and the other smaller ones are urban outcrops of a still-untamed interior. The Rural Fair takes possession of Palermo, with its municipal concerts and its bovine competitions, with the same tyrannical legality as when in the plaza rises an equestrian statue.

2. The Rural Fair is the great Argentine feast; the palace it once occupied was turned into the Museum of Fine Arts, which, while it existed there, exhibited in its frontispiece the emblems of our abundance in cattle and agriculture. Our Bayreuth is there and our race track is there—the acropolis of a religion of hope without faith. Rosas's soul roams through the forest, and the champion bull and the champion horse are the idols of that excellent rider and ranch administrator. Sarmiento built a park, and the botanical and zoological forest completes the essential physiognomy of the barbarous politician. Later, Pellegrini, the last of the giant myth builders, founded the Jockey Club. The South American hero is embodied in the horse; the gaucho wears the racing colors. The horse races are our bullfights, our tragic feast of blood, as the soccer field is our circus feast. The hippodrome has three fundamental components: the aristocracy, which celebrates the genealogy of the thoroughbred, the nationals from the countryside with their totemic love for the horse, and the masses with their anxiety to tempt destiny with the wager. The rite is celebrated—as in the church—on Sunday, the day of the Lord. The discontented man, who struggles through the week and who vaguely aspires to do violence to the universal order, goes to this Delphi where the answer suffers from no amphibologies. The race track brings together the dreamers of fortune, those who enjoy showing off their presence and those who seem to radiate a dark American destiny. Men cannot renounce their deep emotions; when the energy that is consumed in art, in an intense life, in religion, in the search for truth, or in an authentic devotion

to social problems does not find its natural expression, it explodes in forms as curious as the gambling associated with a mystical, sentimental, and aesthetic sense. The beings that frequent the race track have not found the manner to channel their enormous forces, which are suffocated and annihilated by the environment, onto a loyal and meritorious path. They are beings of a thwarted vocation who resort to betting and to the visual pleasure of the race in the same manner as others, more inferior, take refuge in alcohol. Gambling and alcohol are two life preservers of the shipwrecked soul who wishes to preserve—even after his death—an immortal particle that finds no avenue of expression. He returns from the race track to once again intern himself in a world beset by inhuman difficulties, by a harsh, mechanical, and pecuniary world. He goes to the race track like the peregrine to the sanctuary, in search of a solution to an unsolvable problem stirring in the soul. Painters, poets, musicians, lovers, and apostles who have not been truly stimulated or who are latently incompatible with daily life leave at the track their children's bread or the wealth for which they were trustees. The idol who destroys the faithful is not as horrible as the Vishnu of Jagannath; he is an elastic figure, shining in the sun, nervous, with intelligent eyes, and tuned by countless generations practiced in this type of gymnastics; of princely blood, he walks by, exhibiting himself as does a perfect woman or an adolescent perfectly healthy and beautiful. When the idol is seen in the plenitude of an immortal work, eager to fly like Homer's lances, it is a moment of religious intensity. What happens then is a vertigo, more appropriately belonging to the realm of the conscience than to the world of forms.

3. The eyes on the outlook for an unleased and beautiful force fix with awe on the monument of the heroic idol. Whether in marble or bronze, the horse is something that belongs to us and whose true destiny we comprehend with a warm, fraternal sentiment. It was no coincidence that Paz stated that the Argentine captain always considered his horse as a partner in victory; nor was it in vain that the countryman lived on his back and was his friend. Here in this panorama, the horse, whether cast in bronze or on the

race track, acquires characteristics he does not possess in any other part of the world.

We the plainsmen, who dwell in the city of the pampa and who perceive the fundamental influences of the deep and surrounding objects, cannot view the equestrian statues merely with the eyes of spectators. To our intimate aesthetic emotion, man and horse form a unit independent of the pedestal that assumes its real place as a mere intermediary between nature and the work of art. The horse seems to be detached and to aspire to a vital union with the rider. The statue that depicts the horse rising on its hind legs presents a false impression, whatever the aesthetic and academic values may be. Such a statue is not artistic, and it offends the eternity expressed by the quadruped, whose equilibrium on the ground is that of perfectly mobile matter. The horse shown in an impetuous rush carries the authority of a main figure and relegates the hero to a passive complement. For example, let us compare the operalike contortions of San Martín's steed with the fatidic and sacred sobriety of Dorrego's. There can be no imposing and majestic equestrian figure unless the horse has four feet on the ground; in this style he gives a sensation of security, of equilibrium without compulsion, and of tranquility while simultaneously clearing the field of emotion to allow it to submerge in the figure of the rider. We can more readily observe how the horse in movement relegates the hero to the second plane when the hero's biographical data are sketchy in our historical and national life. For us, the horse is never the decorative support for the man; to the plainsmen, the horse evokes a piece of landscape, of life, and of destiny.

Nothing that concerns the horse is strange to us. The Spaniard can contemplate the struggle between the two animals in the bullring, and for him the bull will be the main element. The bull's vigor, strength, and blind and total rush place the blindfolded and tremulous horse in a miserable position, further goaded by the horseman. The horse can be a pathetic and even pious counterpoint to this theme of impetus. For us, the fundamental note in a bullfight is supplied by the horse; when we see the horse gored in the belly we are overcome by indignation rather than pity. That indignation is not common for all humanity but is the distinction of the plainsman. We immediately perceive an uneven struggle between a body that seems designed for violent attack and another that appears to be destined for loftier ends. Indignation, which eclipses any nascent feeling of commiseration, is what distinguishes us from the Peninsular African for whom the horse was a combat weapon.

The South American hero on horseback acquires perfect human and historical dimensions when thus depicted in a monument. The indifference with which we contemplate him in bronze originates with the failure of the sculptors—except for Yrurtia and Bourdelle —who have been unable to underscore the hero's emotional role. This secret valuation leads us to reject the statue of Lavalle that depicts the man so closely associated with the horse as a pedestrian. On the other hand, we are moved by the statue of Dorrego, which also is the only one sculptured in life-size dimensions; this statue represents by its noble simplicity and prudent size—at least to the historically knowledgeable—the maximum dimension of the Argentine hero. When the statues are exaggerated, as, for example, those of Mitre and Alvear, the historical figure is devoured by the pleonasm of stone and of metal, like the galloping rider who is devoured by the pampa. We are well aware of Paraná's repudiation of Urquiza's statue in which he rides English style.

4. The race track is the vocational temple for horse idolatry where the Argentine soul, in a Sunday rite, is placed in contact with underground divinities of blood. The soccer field is the temple of the man on foot, of the immigrant's son; the playing grounds are a cosmopolitan amphitheater—plebeian, and the obverse of the race track. The enthusiasm for the game embodies an aspect of politics rather than a tradition of blood.

Race track and soccer field are two political parties: the former stands for adventure, instability, ambition, centralism, and monarchy; the latter represents work, passionate struggle, committee disputes, chaos, and democracy. The Jockey Club and the sports associations support opposing trends and recruit antagonistic forces. Soccer has assumed the flavor of different ways of living; it is a serious game, freeing poisons accumulated in the muscles during six days of heavy labor. The soccer games are healthful valves for the players who need to exercise and for the spectators who need to purge their souls, which find no other escape to the world of action. The spectator attends a game to take sides; he has a personal stake in the outcome. The sympathy for a given team is a mean ideal when compared to the passion for horse racing. Victory or defeat become personal incidents; a tribal territorial honor is involved, and the game is the ordeal where secret rivalries are adjusted. In this sense, soccer is very similar to a collective boxing match. Any game should impassion, but in this case the passion seems to have originated the game, as if it were born from a state of agitation without escape. Nothing better resembles a committee than a soccer club. Soccer is the game for people who have finally achieved the goal of an eight-hour day. For man to take pleasure in this game, he must be fatigued and he must truly love the intranscendent substitute for his slavery. The idle brain also has its aesthetic exigencies. Soccer, as a spectacle and as a symbol of political struggle, is ideal for a brain that values things. That is why the workers during their free period play soccer, whereas students would spend their idle time by reading. They do not consider it an exercise (that would make it common) but a pastime. In the stadium bleachers, people dream and exercise a faculty of thought that is satisfied by passion and by the art of advancing an idea by means of the foot and the ball. That game is the plastic and corporeal form of the ideas of men who play and of men who watch. The spectator comprehends with all his body; he follows the alternatives with his eyes and involves himself in an extremely simple process of thinking and of acting at the same time. The demagogue knows that the electoral forces are in the stadium and that politics cannot run counter to the natural technique of the masses.

In each country, sport has taken on the peculiarity of the collective spirit. Among us, soccer means South against North.

The Gods of the City

The narcissistic decoration of buildings, the inhabitant's closed personality, and the active search for a motive by which to channel the energies of a self-made character can also be considered as style. In the large cities without history, religion has no strength; patriotism is scarcely a sensation of power and of ownership; neither race, nor language, nor tradition, nor geography brings souls together. And yet, a city cannot have 2.5 million inhabitants without possessing those basic sentiments. Buenos Aires has amalgamated them into politics, which encompasses religion, patriotism, and all other bureaucratic and cosmopolitan ideals. Whatever has difficulty surviving in the struggle for life due to the existing natural barriers falls into the bosom of primordial forces: politics. In its broad sense, politics encompasses the national tribute, which is unable to express itself under other collective forms. Any significant group manifestation takes on a political aspect. Such is the soul of the city, the underground drainage system, the subterranean electric cable network, the style of the whole.

Politics is integrated by an infinity of misunderstandings, by immature ideas, by illegitimate aspirations, and by an unconscious thirst for justice and faith. Impotent against the difficulties born of an intimate disorder, the soul surrenders to the fraudulent power and to the false impression, as if to magic and quackery. Politics offers to the indolent dreamer and to the hopeless failure a substitute for action and for competence. It ceases to be an aspiration to the concrete and well defined, but it concentrates energies potentially lost in a void or in a lethal blow. Whatever its intentions, politics substitutes what does not as yet exist, anticipates the improved conditions, and habitually performs acts of communal good or evil. Without lofty ideals, without entrenched convictions, politics incorporates ample cycles of action; instead of being a vehicle to somewhere, it transforms itself into a toothless wheel fueled by individual actions. If politics can become a dynamic tension in the more advanced phases of popular culture, where the collective conscience does not exceed individual instincts, it can convert its func-tion into an attainable end. When politics has no exit to well-structured forms, it projects its energies to the level of magic, of mysterious and arbitrary powers. Politics becomes the magic of secret influences, similar to quackery; the procedures are analo-gous to the sphere of economic well-being. The leader of Argentine multitudes acquires his prestige through the understanding of po-litical mysteries. Occult political power that violates the status quo without any apparent use of force vibrates in unison with affiliated wills that discover the formula to achieve what is forbidden by or-dinary routes.

In this aspect, politics is not only magic but also superstition; it sums up embryonic states civically conscious of well-being, order, and progress even though these may be frustrated by the technical complications of illicit activities. The practice of superstition is celebrated in committees, which are the residential bodies of frus-trated wills. Without those temples where the real men of power listen and discuss, politics would cease to be an abstraction; it would be shattered into as many molecules as there are souls, and it would expand through alternate means. If the committee as a living body of a sect seems to us to be worthy of divinity, it is be-cause we forget that the pragmatic divinity is hypostatized by rem-nants. Each spirit lives in the body that suits it best. The centers of frustrated action are composed of frustrated men of enterprise, ad-venturers who end by exchanging the ideal for an idol, which they eventually replace with themselves. Sooner or later, the schism is produced by fissiparity, and the ideal is shattered into as many fragments as there are dissenting nuclei of attraction. Even so, the heterodox remain faithful to the all-embracing abstraction known as politics, to that suspended force which reigns as the absolute re-ality. The schism is not produced by ideological apostasy, but by the condensation of interests in one leader.

The committee shapes the club, the association, and the cenacle; it incorporates its members and obliges them to participate in the dogma's sacrificial rites of art, of science, or of philanthropy. The committee is the home office of any corporative entity; it functions as the headquarters of a clandestine government that parallels the constituted powers and the autonomous institutes. As long as the group instinct is unable to produce free forms, everything that makes men gregarious, strong, and charitable will be stunted by futile efforts. From the artist's studio, from the academies, from the classrooms, from the trade unions, and from the clubs, the initiated migrate toward the committee, from the countryside to Buenos Aires. The committee attracts the skeptic who no longer believes in any mystical power superior to his will and to his existence, like the race track attracts the discontented dreamer who refuses to beg but surrenders to fate. The gambler is an atheist, and the skeptic a practitioner of magic. By joining the ranks of the standard-bearers, excessive aspiration is given an honest appearance; the victor is always converted into the infinitesimal instrument of an anonymous vengeance. It is very difficult to distinguish the usurper from the legitimate member. The sign with which the political divinity stamps the countenance of its initiates is scarcely visible; at best, the frequenting of the temples where tribute is rendered to the mysterious divinity leaves in their faces a mark of distrustful sufficiency characteristic of readers of black-magic books. If we observe them closely, we will note that they possess a secret power to penetrate through privileged doors; they behave with disproportionate arrogance, like fanatics who have their private god. We wonder if that is the aura surrounding all members of secret societies. The social daemon murmurs in its subconscious that, of all organizations in which the masses participate, politics is the only one among us that has achieved a closed, compact structure. Politics penetrates culture, welfare, and research. Its manners and jargon indicate its superiority because neither art, nor the search for truth, nor the apostolic spirit of teaching and of good, nor sport, nor friendship could subsist without the eventual incorporation of that magic, universal force which the wise have early recognized and paid their allegiance.

Politics was segmented into parties and names. No one has better embodied the will of the anonymous masses than Irigoyen.

However, Irigoyenism preceded the man and was superior to him. Although he embodied the transcendental and magic reality in his person, in his mentality, and in his acts as apostle and martyr, ultimately he failed to represent a sector of that reality. Although the latent tendencies of the multitudes were solidified in Irigoyen and although he became the champion of an ideal of limited perspectives, Rosas had already preceded him; the greater part of his work awaited the restoration of what had been damned and proscribed from the days of national organization. Unextinguished forces, aspirations conceived and gestated in darkness, awaited the propitious moment for their appearance. And Irigoyen, doubtless destined to assume his people's sins, represented them in the mob's nebulous conscience until it was elevated to power as the outcasts' revenge. Irigoyen succumbed; undoubtedly, Irigoyenism defeated itself. Those who subrogated it came into government by a short cut, impelled by a movement born in the womb; quickly they fell into the practices in force since the days of the civil wars: they assumed the representation of the sector eliminated from Irigoyen's government. Those who brought down Irigoyen had not only belonged to the ranks of the party that made and unmade him, but, in their mental conformation and in their basic vices, they had also obeyed the same plastic force; once they arrived in power, they turned out to be equally incompetent for the same reasons. The idol remained levigated in the amnion in which he had been engendered, but his ideals stood firmly. He represented a direction, and his adversaries represented another, like the river delta that will later combine; the year 1930 was welded to 1852 when, because of Urquiza and the exiles, history suffered a commotion and an eighty-year detour. Irigoyenism's two arms parenthesized those eighty years and hemmed in reality with two flanks. The forces that first called themselves anarchical later termed themselves political. Some governed with majorities and others by minorities always faithful to a superior will, to a nameless and formless divinity. Whoever is not in its full grace is immediately regarded as a traitor. Irigoyen has been not only the man of his people, but also his people's conscience and will. The idol's crucifixion was the sacrifice of his son, whom he denied in spite of his carrying the new law and his tragic destiny of bearing the blame for all sins.

The Politician

There are close similitudes between our professional politician and the quack, the sorcerer, or the midwife. Throughout time, this creature has been endowed with varied names.

No one who has been benefited by a job, tax exemptions, or concessions can entirely acknowledge the favor in public because there is always an unknown factor in the new being brought to life by the obstetrician. The untiring diligence with which the politician assists the birth and sometimes gives his name to the fetus is a surreptitious and professional activity: ostensibly, he confers upon himself the role of expert in what is known as the art of governing.

The first step in the career is to own a comfortable house. The politician's home is a public house with access for all. The devoted who suffer from some incapacity or some want keep on arriving in the living room. The hall and the reception room have the atmosphere of a clinic; a letter of recommendation is the prescription for the ailment.

The politician owes his existence to the committee, which is inseparable from his home; he is also indebted to his friends, who are the extension of his family. He knows that his mission is to serve and to give to the voter; when no one asks for anything he is restless, like a doctor before the patient who exhibits perfect health. When he auscultates, questions, and assists, he unfolds a manipulator's complicated psychology. He is a grand lord of the postulant populace, a ranking go-between who is in the cabinet wing and therefore with economy can furnish unpublished news in accordance with the posology for gossip. He lives in the midst of fresh news relayed to him by the followers as payment for the consultation. Later, if it should prove useful to his plans, he will make use of his information at meetings with other leaders; the midwife's art has its social exigencies. His role is to make promises, to speak of the future with the assurance of a prophet, and to have faith in something, whether it be the government or the fall of the government. He transmits faith. The magnitude of his promises varies as his power increases: councilman, deputy, senator, minister, and president represent positions that are like concentric circles from which gifts are distributed in larger or smaller quantities. But the true politician is not one who gives, but one who juggles the gift from one hand to another. When he reaches the highest position he acquires the aura of an idol; but it is then clear that he cannot give, whereas the magic pouch was inexhaustible when he utilized promises as a program and prescription.

The politician maintains his full prestige as long as he is able to employ ambiguous and abstract phrases, carefully chosen simple vocabulary and proverbs without risky, detailed opinions. He has to know how to transmit the faith to his followers. To accomplish this, he must show that he knows, however superficially, something of everything and that his most fervent desire is to improve everyone's lot. He plays his own ignorance to an advantage; his handling of names and of numbers, his intentional forgetfulness, and his evasions and circumlocutions make him appear as an easy victim in the scoundrel's eyes. No needy person believes for a moment that such a man could not be eventually maneuvered into anything. They are wrong and thus fall into the trap: the politician's apparent weakness is accidentally his strength.

The doctor, more so than the lawyer, has before him a horizon of successes because he deals in secret ceremonies; the control of an X force bestows upon him the prestige of unnatural talents. Jakob Larrain, when speaking of Rawson with the natural respect that the man deserves, discovers that in our environment the doctor has for the masses a dual personality, each a presumed cure. Many leaders are doctors, although they sometimes behave as magicians. Our ills are mysterious.

The Soul of the City

In comparison to politics, art is a sporadic and subsidiary manifestation, an exclusively Buenos Aires phenomenon within the metropolitan context. The spiritual anxieties germinate, flower, and wilt in Buenos Aires; culture should be considered as a special case of urbanism. The only road for talent is from the periphery to the center and from the omphalic center outward. Outside the capital, culture plods along in a parasitical existence; it must emigrate or succumb. However, as in the days of Rome's hegemony, talent does not originate from the metropolis. People do not read or write in the provinces; the immense plain is refractory to the intensity of any culture of the mind; the artists prophetically born there are burdened with the implicit, tragic destiny of being, in many forms, the plain's negation; they cannot acclimatize anywhere. Newspapers and books are printed in Buenos Aires with an eye on rural consumption. The ones published in the interior carry on their trivial and servile existence as the beggars of the provincial government; they are composed of the perennial four or eight pages of announcements interpolated with journalism's classically pretentious, common text, set with the typography of the countryside.

These newspapers should be considered as journalism's caricatures; no other form of publicity expresses with such ingenuous pretension the symbiotic fusion of politics and literature and of the written word with the graphic arts. What the provincial newspapers subconsciously reveal could be applied to the great city; we could observe what changes the urban gaucho has undergone with the growth of papers in number and size. Culture and politics are the same thing; rulers, pedagogues, artistic and scientific institutions, and authors are interconnected in a reciprocal web of rights and obligations. There once was a government that wished to be characterized by some august philistinism, precisely because it had its roots in the masses refractory to culture; it was involved in theatrical acts of patronage: for example, it distributed among the peasants a translation of the *Georgics*. The regeneration, the elemental transfiguration of the most authentic culture served to corroborate a plan for romantic urbanism; and, like the author of the *Comic Novel*, it produced its *Vergil Disguised*. Or let us observe the artistic and turf societies that protect the arts and letters as the representatives of organs of thought and livestock. Such is the lot of intelligence that flees the plain and is recaptured in the city by the eternal forces of the pampa.

No medium formed in the city to deny the reality of the countryside does in fact deny it. Even more than the government that was clearly inspired by the masses refractory to culture, it was the government born from the denial of that taboo that desired to consummate the devastating task of the pampa; it disowned the intellectual, it ostentatiously ignored him, and it persecuted him as much as possible. So, the government completed its program by depriving the intellectual of his legitimate rights and by herding him into a hopeless corner. And yet, Buenos Aires, the most extraordinary work of Argentine politics, attracts the artist in order to seduce him and corrupt him.

It is true that there are in Buenos Aires what could be called specific structures dealing with science, art, and the liberal professions, but they are not autonomous of the city. They exist because of the policies that erected the city, indirectly dependent on the public treasury. They are all municipal phenomena, ultimately sponsored or subsidized—somewhat secretly—by the government. If the intellectual wishes to clear a path in the jungle of interests monopolized by politics, he is obliged to offer his talent to the only bidders: journalism or public administration. Unable to derive benefit or joy from his work—which no one reads—he claims a subsidy, which automatically defeats him: he is but a collaborator of the plain's forces that took refuge in the village. Sham writers, artists, and scientists have occupied exalted positions by the conditional surrender of their persons. In possession of newspapers, of teaching posts, and of committee rooms, they defend their jobs tooth and nail. The apostates who bungled their faith are the apostles of the urban ideal, the sublimated heretics of the counterideal. Newspapers, universities, and salons maintain themselves by a complex system of interlocking interests; they protect each other, and throughout the entire chain flows only one blood and only one vital fluid: politics. The "chain" method discovered by the committee gamesters is ancient and continental.[1] The chain system, based on the serial complication, is the symbol of the licit activities founded on politics; everyone who is ambitious beyond his fortitude practices this system without knowing it. The honest artist is predestined to succumb because he is alone, and his rebelliousness or his renunciation contrasts with the embroidered canvas of the interests in play. The artist has no reciprocal commitments; he is a loose link.

The city is of a homogeneous texture although it may appear illmatched and cosmopolitan. Its soul is a solid block. The lonely workers are children of solitude. Twenty free men carry on their shoulders the Nation's prestige. If they were to suddenly die, the Nation would fall of its own weight into the austral darkness to a level even with the entire South American latitude. Science secludes itself in libraries and laboratories; literature offers itself to newspapers and magazines, and finally it dies in books. The State, which only believes in danger, acquires the books and paintings that no one buys and then distributes them among libraries and museums that no one visits. The artist's or the scholar's vocation is an antipode of the profound reality; the critic who silently passes over the works of substance and who sounds the trumpet over deceptions is unconsciously at the service of the dark forces of the pampa. The ivy of those who have failed climbs over those who remain until it covers them like pasture ground. The dead slay the living, as in the palace of Atridae. Abortive and monstrous forms, born of governmental copulations and engendered by the spermatic logic of politics, multiply by themselves in a pullulation of bacteria into complete works of thirty titles. Congress votes funds to acquire books or to have them written. They are rustic phantoms. The plazas are full of images in bronze and marble; the museums are

---

[1] It consists in each voter's sealing the vote he is given in an envelope and bringing another empty envelope, which is filled by the person behind him and so on until the end. This type of collaboration also implicates the victim, inciting him to the commission of a crime, after which he cannot even denounce the swindler.

stuffed with simulacra; the symphonic programs are loaded with ghosts. That whole world of immortal monstrosities is born from politics; it is the child of legislative chambers, of cabinets, and of committees. The public is involved in the chain system and it applauds; it fills the theaters and echoes the glorious refrains of the specters. But the public winks with sly malice at the lies and equivocations. People forget and await the real death. Playwrights, poets, musicians, and painters—they have died and are encased in the same continental tomb of oblivion. Yesterday's dead seem remote and ancient. Politics pushes forward with all its might; it weaves its cloths during the day and unravels them at night. While the defender of some specific interests is alive, while he can be useful or harmful, he is respected as a supreme politician; when he falls, he is forgotten. The government and the people are both complicated in the nefarious task of cremation and winnowing of ashes; they prefer the live impostor to the dead talent. The counterfeiters of culture feed on cadavers; someone's oblivion is their renown.

The lack of real states of culture is supplanted by fictitious ones; powerful publicity and news companies adhere to a policy of supporting standard literature. Curiously, the journalist's ideas agree with those of his superiors, and their ideas coincide with those of major advertisers. Thus the universal chain system adapts itself to the existing supply and demand; hundreds of brains work everyday at the same task of modeling and polishing to satisfy a journalistic precept of maximum consumption. The author's personality, even when he is allowed to sign his work, is dissolved in a bubbling alloy of lead; the whole wording is a grey mass of ideas and of lines set on linotype. But to starve is worse.

The writer's lot is still sadder than the journalist's. He must be wealthy or compromise with the readers of newspapers. The best writers are poor and live by some other means. They persist in their work because God wills it. The intellectuals freed of the politics of newspaper companies are eradicated. Whoever has money is famous: his books circulate under the protection of a banking firm of recognized solvency, and he can commit the greatest indignities without loss of prestige. Reputation is of indefatigable patience. The same reader who marvels at his favorite author's success wickedly enjoys clandestine editions, as if they were really forbidden.

The politico-literary committee and the public administration are just as tyrannical as the press; they receive with reservations the defeated man of action or the unflinching idealist. The author pays for his work's printing with the salary received from the State, and the State buys the book, returning the money. It repays the cost and recuperates the ideas, retiring them from circulation. Once the writer's fame is established, it is respected until death sweeps away everything. The chain is soldered among authors, editors, and consumers.

Once a good position is achieved, all restlessness ends; one can relax and wait for retirement or academic honors. And then, while one is still in life, immortality and death arrive.

V · FEAR

13 THE STRUGGLE

Panorama of Fear

The man came at age twenty and worked among strangers with whom he became related by marriage. He was inspired by a lofty will to triumph because he ignored the peculiarities of the land where he had come to settle and the moral labyrinths of the woman who would bear his children. Now he is rich; he possesses a fortune and he is old. It is not worthwhile to learn the details of such a common story, because a triumph of this type almost always includes the same incidents. If the man would ponder the past and see himself in a world that begins anew where he ends, he would feel that he has sold his life. At twenty he would not have accepted old age for all that money. He has lived subordinated to that money: he has deprived himself of joy, of sincere friendship, of tenderness, of the pleasure of gazing at the sky without praying for rain or for sunshine, and of living a life swollen with relevance. His fortune, whether he knows it consciously or subconsciously, is his life transmuted into gold. He cannot be magnanimous, generous, or altruistic even if he were eager to be so. He cannot part with a fortune representing the payment for a simoniacal sale; he does not understand that his reason for existence—to take—has another aspect of more ample and vital perspectives: to give. He is frightened; the lands he possesses, the wealth, and the property represent fear.

But often people reach old age without finding a bidder, without having Mephistopheles seal a pact exchanging life for fortune. A man may have failed, and in his old age he suffers from deprivation and abandonment. The children reproach his poverty, without understanding that such poverty is also the result of forty years of yearning for wealth, of work without pleasure, and of solitary struggle. The son fails to see in his father's face the tragedy of the fruitless search. He should look deeper. The man came to conquer a world that only offered riches; he was not attracted by curiosity, or by the desire to join the beings who lived there, or by the resolution to join a society that could repay his labor with the simple satisfaction of living. The poor man is psychically the same as the rich one; they struggle with determination toward the same ends, and the only difference is that the poor man has nothing. Perhaps at a given moment, like a gambler during a lucky streak, he possessed more than he expected. But, since there was no ulterior project in the undertaking and since accumulating wealth was neither a means nor an exercise, poverty crowned his error—not of detail or of capacity but of orientation, of organization. His spiritual situation is also identical to that of the wealthy man; he understands that the world is not ruled by immutable laws, that it is fragile and insecure; destiny is replaced by an unforeseen disaster, and he is isolated, without a friend's friendship or a son's charity. Then, he is overtaken by the dread and shame of one carrying in his blood a mortal and contagious disease. The true meaning of reality finally becomes clear to him; he feels by the sterility of his life's efforts and by the magnitude of the difficulties, which he improperly resolved a long time ago, a fear that he communicates to all that surrounds him. Anyone who is laboring to enrich himself within the poor old man's eyesight must appear unmerciful, ravenous, and stupid to him. The old man sees a chilling example: sixty years of life is the amount of the wager and the loser will not have lived—neither will the winner.

The fear that man feels is ancient, much older than himself. It is not felt for the first time; it is a state of mind produced by a new social condition and not an incident unnoticed within the context of existence. It is the same state of mind experienced by the conquistador and by the settler who followed him; far away from their homes, they were confronted by solitude, by the desert, and by strange men with an unknown past. The poor man among us does not have a right to his poverty: he is viewed as a being who defrauds and who transmits bad luck. With his presence he shatters, as did the naked Indian before the conquistador, the former hypothesis that explained wealth as payment for the risk undertaken. If the poor man is treated with apprehensive disdain, it is because he lives as an inopportune omen that destroys a dream. The poor man is the destructor of ideals; fallen and lying in a ditch, he represents the infinite death. For this reason, the poor man is always new in the bosom of a society that lives doing violence to its true reality. He forms part of a reality that people do not wish to see as such, a reality that is feared but that will be faced, sooner or later, by everyone not propelled by human motives.

Fear was awaiting the first soldier. Dread threatened him and peopled the solitude with phantoms. He brought with him a complicated image of nature, whereas it unfolded with simplicity. He saw a submissive Indian who adored him, and he killed the savage from fear; it seemed humiliating that one of his imagined dangers could cease so abruptly.

Not content with despoiling the Indians of their lands, with stealing their women and enslaving their children, he wanted to exterminate them as specters. He was fearful while crossing through virgin and unknown routes; with his gaze fixed on the horizon day and night, he tensed in anticipation of dangers and of monsters as if he were moving toward death. He prayed aloud. He had just finished an adventure and could not understand that it had come to an end. The adventure of the sea still resounded in his soul. The sea intimidated; after days of storm or when the longed-for coast could not be descried at a distance, scurvy wreaked havoc. Pedro de Mendoza and countless others suffered from horrid hallucinations; fever, syphilis, and bad nutrition combined to procreate ghosts that were thought to be incarnated in real bodies. The Indian quickly recognized the enemy and found he was defeated by diabolical weapons. He became infused by fear and was ferocious in his defense: the known things and the landscape that soothed him with its ancestral security were then peopled by furious devils. Henceforth, in mutual fear, there reigned the law of hate. It was the same to flee or to attack, as with beasts surrounded by fright and solitude.

The soldier resorted to equally fierce measures. His deeds, so simple, were a jolt to the nerves; fright gave him courage. To die in battle against the Indian was to perish without glory; but combat was for victory, not for glory. To vanquish was to kill without benefit.

Later came the difficulties of occupying a territory whose confines were for the newcomers as unknown and as vast as the sea across which they had recently sailed. This land was the end of the sea and the beginning of the true adventure. They brought war, whereas, if they had possessed it, they could have brought civilization. The Chibcha, Aztec, Incan, and Mayan civilizations were exterminated, and the seed came to naught, burrowed by mortal grub. Those primitive men, abounding with shortcomings, arrived fleeing. The Modern Age expelled them from Europe; and, recruited from jails and from hospitals for contagious diseases, they came to carry out their life sentences. They were deceived by the promise of a paradise they imagined to be like the one they had heard about, from childhood, in churches and plazas. They chose exile over jail. A fantasy of brutal El Dorado was incubating in the minds of those ignorant primitives during the ocean crossing. Ambition blinded them and overwhelmed the voices that instigated them to flee; on the other hand, flight was impossible. Ambition and fear were superfetations of poverty and courage. At the end of the attempted path they were once again faced with jail and quarantine, submission and shame. They decided to extinguish danger once and for all, and thus they created it even when it did not exist —thus chastising the hordes. The victory over the hordes distracted them from the truth; instead of rebelling against those who brought them to die, they rebelled against the native. The danger had not disappeared with the founding of the cities, which at first were fortresses. Danger lurked threateningly outside the palisades and later resumed inside, forcing men to live with their armor at bay, awaiting the imminent attack. Such was the city, the life, the home, and the mold in which would be formed the society of these oceanic latitudes. Such a state of mind endured for centuries; we could say that it was even experienced by our parents. The still night was peopled by remote and supernatural strains; the savage and the beast presented a homogeneous block of threats that, increased by superstition—the sublimated shape of fear—created a mental hell. Crime, robbery, vice, and frustrated ambition ignited by a desire for vengeance shaped the colonial man and the emancipated man. Some resorted to the protection of armed force; others took refuge in property or in political power from the fear of being annihilated. There were no gradations between the extremes of being assured against risk and being abandoned to any contingency. Everything was acquiring the aspect of an apparition: the clay-and-straw house barely visible above ground level; the fallen look of the gaucho, laconic and invariably crouching behind his voice; the acclamation of an organic letter; the possession of a numerary war fleet; the treasury's backing of government acts; the relentless yearning for a university degree.

Everything depended on chance: the adventure and also the law. The law could be bent, and the codes of law were full of cracks through which plunder and juridical monstrosities could penetrate easier than a camel through a needle's eye. Nothing was stable or fixed or even predictable. What was rewarded yesterday would be severely punished today. A great hazard had been born of a great chaos; the one common element left was fear.

Life conditions were the same as the conditions for struggle;

peace was impregnated with the horrors of exterminatory war. The captives were reduced to a condition of serfs not meriting leniency; the master treated them with bestial rage. The wars of independence renewed the rancor, and the towns became filled with insecurity and distrust. The forces organized for defense represented a danger as real as that of the assailants; the plunder would often be carried out by the defenders of the city. As we can read in the pages of *Facundo*, the abuses spread an epidemic of fear in some provinces.

Dysentery was the illness of terror. Those who fled and those who pursued were equally frightened. The history of revolts and murders describes the normal state of affairs from 1810 to 1820; it reached a peak of frenzy from 1820 to 1860, the period of Rosas's domination. The delation put brother on guard against brother; the Mazorca Society became the rural police and judicial organization, which after a summary trial would execute in the corral anyone suspected of being an enemy of the regime. The horror scenes related by the chronicles and works of literature from that period show that crime formed only an anecdotal element; the fundamental leitmotiv was panic. Families emigrated en masse to Chile and to Montevideo, an exodus of interminable caravans; those who could not flee remained to suffer the country's lot. The twenty years of dictatorship and the twenty that prepared it and continued it exacerbated family life in the deep interior and in the cities; from the latter began the cowardly persecution as a violent reaction to peasant hostility. In the southern part of the province of Buenos Aires, near the large drain that prolongs itself from Melincué to the Colorado River, one can still see the ruins of houses constructed by immigrants; half of the dwellings were sunken to resist the sudden attacks by Indians. The small windows would be placed at ground level, from where the tumult of cattle and Indians could be observed. The Indian would not assault houses if he could not bring down the mud walls with his horse's thrusts. It was his custom, imposed by experience, never to dismount. Even during attacks launched by the desperation of hunger, he observed this necessary precaution. The Indians only lit fires in their huts, like the driver under his cart. The children of those peoples grew up in restlessness, gazing at the horizon and listening for noises. They still spy the stranger's arrival. The merchant used to place a grating around his counter; he kept a revolver in the box together with the proceeds from the sale of herbs, sugar, and noodles. The gaucho, the peon, and the rancher's son all carried weapons to town. Some carried with them their entire fortune: a nest egg for the purchase of ranches and fields. Women would allow themselves to be seduced in the presence of their children; the hearth would remain lit at night; no one bothered with neighbors or thought of improving his house as long as he had enough to satisfy the needs of prehistoric man. No one would visit anyone else. The father of the family would construct his house far away, isolating himself in the isolation. His son was reserved, astute, and a liar because he was still afraid.

Life was carried on in such a state of nervous tension until recently, when the Indian was displaced and the land—the whole expanse—was liberated for agriculture and cattle. But the danger persisted even after the campaigns of Roca, Victorica, and Alsina; greed and hazard remained. Danger was eliminated by absorption, and now it imperils us all. The population was displaced toward the coast; fleeing from the empty countryside, it took refuge in the seven large cities that today shelter over half the population of a country that stretches three million square kilometers. In those cities lives fear.

Palisades and Trenches

The modern cities have been edified to protect their inhabitants from dangers; on their perimeters, crude battles are waged, and all the thunder of the campaign seems to have taken refuge within their walls. The inside agitation contrasts with the countryside's quietude; this internal tension does not support comparison with the pianissimo rhythm of life in the hut. The tall buildings, the malls, the accumulation of goods, and even the ostentation of power proclaim the courage with which they face the problems pertaining to society. The inhabitants take care of

themselves; but, before the city was a redoubt outside of which lay
the savage world, the vast region of barbarians. It was a meaningful fortress against the exterior, against the assaults from outside;
an invisible, solid shield surrounded it, like the stone and bronze
walls that surrounded Troy and Thebes. The wary look of the old
citizen is in the eyes of the Buenos Aires inhabitant when he contemplates the interior. The sentinels are on guard in the seven
cities, as before the seven gates of Thebes. Unpopulated, peaceful,
and immense, the countryside is uninhabitable; the conditions imposed on the living are very harsh when one prefers a salaried job,
a narrow life, and a known and respected destiny. The buildings
are wills raised to dominate a space they fill completely; but the
will is fixed and the dominion is exercised on a vegetative order. It
is a fortune of stone, of steel, or of brick; at the same time, it is a
sure revenue, a known and stable quantity. There is a relationship
between the city and the rural populations that responds to static
laws that maintain the equilibrium of production and consumption, of the typical forms of city and countryside. A deserted interior with a most fertile ground, capable of absorbing hundreds of
millions of people is not in equilibrium with seven cities that contain over half the population. There must be some reason why during a merciless struggle people deliberately take shelter in the cities
as crowded as in overpopulated countries. Outside the cities there is
no human climate in which man could live. Health is endangered,
education is at an inferior level and is finally weighted down like a
chain, and the conditions in the struggle for life recrudesce under
the influence of primitive forces; to these evils we must add the
certitude of poverty. To acquire security is to buy a lot, to edify
a house or possibly a skyscraper. It is something that always remains. The city is the State in which govern the laws of edification
and where all the inhabitants have entered into a collective contract for mutual protection. The tenants, the authorities, and the
beehive rules are in force and in harmony. Buenos Aires grew disproportionately with the arrival of the foreigner and of the native
who fled from their respective persecutors. The newly arrived, who
did not come endowed with sufficient courage, remained at the

edge looking at the country's vastness, without daring to venture a new conquest. Colonists would arrive from the interior, colonists who had lost everything after twenty years of toil. The children understood that the promised land was but a land of empty promises. The only prize expected in exchange for brutalization was enrichment; yet after the harsh labor, all hypothetical possibilities of acquiring wealth vanished. The children salvaged from the disaster the last thread of the will to live. Families arrive annually from the depths of the plains to seek the protection of some public position. Until recently it was common to hear people say that only the mentally deranged and the lazy renounced the future; but the pension is the last resource and now no one exposes himself to the hazards of farming and raising livestock. Whoever has something to lose takes refuge in the cities; without indigenous dangers, without violent death, and without wanton despoilment, the countryside is once again the unlimited province of fear, of poverty, of disease, and of useless effort.

Anxieties

Whoever gazes at the pampa can only see the immensity that lies motionless beneath all else: the earth. All that moves, operates, or passes over is uncertain. The cattle thief, the traveler of unknown intentions, the bird that scrutinizes the barren ground for putrid flesh, the hail, and the wind carry with them destruction and restlessness. Only the earth, which beckons one to rest and to die, remains faithful and unalterable. It incites one to contemplate it, the ultimate good, and to distrust all else. It plants parasitical notions in the field laborer's soul, so inclined to routine, to the perpetuation of the present, and to immovability. With the passage of time, the mystical forms of fatalism and shipwreck restrain the man and render him incapable of any concepts of dynamism and daring necessitating movement and enterprise. The peasant of the old sedimentary fields is linked to a cosmic sluggishness: the changes obey the rhythm of his race. America's fields suffer from all the uncertainties of the settler; his experiences as a laborer, together with the dangers inherent in an uncertain and unfixed state of affairs, deprive him of a passion for what is rightfully his. He is not interested in the country's production outside his own immediate property; he lives in the bosom of solitude. Heaven and earth are the two horizons that delimit his life. The events that disturb the totality of the march of life—with which he does not keep pace—determine what is to his benefit or his detriment. Whatever threatens the land, threatens his family. He hopes to increase what he possesses by intussusception and not by irruption; like a tree, he extends his roots and his branches. The landowner is the logical superfetation of the field laborer, because the land produces for a world that values its product without taking into account the sacrifices or the distances; the cultivation of extensive areas spurs the desire to possess. By extending themselves over hundreds and thousands of hectares, the peasants believe they increase their security and their future; but such a vast extension not subject to a solid economic foundation is a floating area, much easier to lose than a small farm that is supported by its surroundings—like the common wall between two houses. The basis for any scheme, for any enterprise, or for any evaluation is the land. What is quiet and off-limits to adventure is highly valued; the desire to increase provokes fear. Movement is always a danger in the plain. Everything associated with the timorous becomes threatening; it seems that the superlative values—which can hardly be taken away—are tinged with resentment by the lack of a stimulating community life.

However, we must look carefully to be able to notice the potential depredatory movement within a world that seems stationary, fixed, static. That open and flat land nourishes with primary energies whatever settles upon it; things and persons, seemingly still in the distance, move about and vibrate with infinite interatomic forces. What laws govern the concealed energy that transforms the hands and the eyes into dangerous weapons? The laws of chance and of fear. They are meteoric particles within a formless receptacle; they collide or unite, add or subtract, but an apparent equilibrium results from the totality of their movements. Fear impels one to stay close to the ground. Fortuitous causes dislodge what is not embedded, like a wind that suddenly starts up. It is necessary that the earth support, with its unequivocal immovability, what neither people, nor institutions, nor society has the power to conserve. Nature has not yet acquired man's habits, customs, or rules; she conserves historic resistances, and she shatters the malefactor and the rascal.

Hazards

Misfortune forms a part of any thematic development of prosperity and of happiness. Regardless of how energies may be oriented and what precautions may be taken, an unhappy incident can eradicate a prolonged effort. Intelligence and will usually construct a shelter according to theoretically correct rules: but a reality, somehow inclined toward the disastrous and the unforeseen, with one whiff may annul the most elaborate plans. The unsubordinated forces outnumber those indomitable ones which on occasion appear to ally themselves with reason. Juan Álvarez said that nature has turned the Argentine into a gambler; such a clearly trustworthy judgment unpretentiously expresses a cosmic front before which man's projects take on the character of a wager.

Whatever has recoiled from danger is enclosed in the cities—in very small areas of the cities; the free and circumstantial forces, in a ceaseless work, deform and abrade the embankments of containment. All that we have to fear, all that is unleashed, and all the infiltrations that we take for granted consist of ancient vapors that slither in from the corners of unpopulated lands and from the depths of the Southern Hemisphere; they impart to the struggle and to the conquered booty the characteristics of a telluric hazard. The friend's word, the chief's authority, the wife's fidelity, the edicts, and the customs are advanced on muddy grounds, and life is a march through a quagmire. Written and sealed documents, third-party endorsements, contracts, and receipts are the ropes to which we cling on our journey through this slime so fecund in vices and subterfuges. The man who here struggles, whether pioneer or follower, strongly desires order, but, without knowing it, he lives in accordance with a powerful disorder; if he is successful in this chaotic and formless world, it is only because he serves as an unconscious tool of disorder. The newly arrived best understands the technique of this world; he is the formless being without culture and without faith. I do not know if that is what Keyserling meant when he spoke of South America as a reptilian world. Whatever is organized and possesses a regular function encounters, without specifically realizing why, incomprehensible resistance, malevolent attractions, and a certain frontal breeze that benumbs it and makes it recalcitrant; eventually comes failure or a detour whereby the tactics of disorder and of hazard are accepted with daring. Not to have a rigid character or inflexible conduct and opinions and to only dominate the technique of a reptile that slinks and charms is to increase one's own forces with the external ones, like a swimmer who swims with the current to take advantage of the river's energy.

The trophies of that victory are not shown off with calmness. The man who has enriched himself and achieved fame hastens to safely place his wealth in mortgages, real estate, or academic seats of honor. It is as if he had stolen what he possesses, although he earned it within the law; however, it was a basically fraudulent law, and, if he does not embed his fortune in earth or otherwise affix it, the wind will come from the pampa and blow it away.

It can be affirmed, then: all that proceeds on a frank and resolute march, all that shows itself as it moves is exposed to anonymous risks; on the contrary, that which crawls, that which lodges in caves and takes on the color and the aspect of the earth is protected by transparent alveolae. All values renounce themselves to the static and thus wither in the sphere of the dynamic, whose infinitely more complicated laws only cease to be fearful in the serpent's eye. Like prehistoric man who hid in caverns to avoid ambush by the unknown, today's primitive man takes shelter in what could be called the stone caves of the dynamic world of culture and of wealth. He acquires mortgages, houses in populous cities, hectares and leagues of fields, national positions, and university degrees. All these are ways to shelter life from contingencies, and they signify the same as the purchase of real estate. From the house on Mayo Avenue to the mastery of a speculative technique, there is a degradation of meritorious values in a direct ratio to values of security. Intelligence is removed to a remote whereabouts, and it means the same in the stock market. The circulating capital of commerce and industry is invested in enterprises that theoretically approximate real estate.

On one hand, the speculation in articles of basic need guarantees a certain return because of the fixed minimum consumption; such is the case with flour mills, sugar refineries, lodging enterprises, shoe and clothing factories, and bread and milk.

On the other hand, there are huge capitals invested in packing houses, transportation, cereal companies, fuel, and other branches of primary social need that also can count on a market guaranteeing a minimum return. Commerce and industries that are not joined to these vital sources are left to flounder disastrously—together with intelligence and culture's useless products. In those areas, capital acquires its maximum extortionary power and obtains by entreaty the protection of the powerful. Even agriculture and the cattle industry depend on imponderable factors; the farmer and the rancher have not the vaguest idea of what will be the value of their possessions. As a ministry publication once indicated, the contracts for the lease of fields to farmers contained clauses characteristic of a gambling proposition; sales of futures and of commodities in general are institutions of cosmic hazards.

The relative security of businesses dealing in articles of primary necessity or in the production of raw materials involuntarily repulses capitals from those investments of doubtful success and agglomerates them around the inferior forms of production and of traffic. It is necessary to discount the absolute necessities of consumption. The more the market is assured for cow skulls, the less certain it is for muslin and cotton. The primitiveness of products is simultaneously accentuated with the primitiveness of the needs of consumption.

But a country where there are no incentives for initiative, for invention, or for altruistic boldness, and where thought and good faith are numbered among obstacles and risks, initially will be led

down the road of exploitation of raw materials and of speculation
in indispensable materials and then, immediately, it will fall into a
game of complicated banking and industrial forms, progressively
more estranged from the environment and subjected to world centers. Our people do not know how to produce, because they do not
know how to consume; the industrial, commercial, and cultural
problem is one of consumption. Fundamentally, production exists
because of consumption. Since we produce primarily raw materials
required by the international market, we live the life typical of
countries that produce raw materials. Walter Scott used to say that
when our gaucho repelled the English invasions, he chose seats
made with cow skulls over those of cotton and muslin. It would be
more appropriate to say that the rejection of the English invasions
was a consequence of the previous rejection of cottons and muslins.
The index of what could be termed the degree of civilization is that
which is wasted and squandered for spiritual ends. Food, shelter,
and clothing are common to man and to the lowest of animals.
That which is consumed in the sustenance of life or in additional
luxuries is listed in the thick volumes of statistics, which are the
official books of our political life. We produce this because we consume that, and vice versa. We own houses without paintings and
without books; the furniture is arranged as in the showcases and
advertisements; we take care that our clothes reflect the model until we are photographically identical; we cannot afford to buy an
art object or a good crystal because we have spent our lives and
have nothing left for the superfluous except rancor. It is the fault
of a whole commercial system based on the rejection of the muslin
and the acceptance of the cow skull that our rich have such an excess of inconveniences; their wealth inspires nausea and pity. The
middle-class man, trying to dodge open traps, lives on a disarranged budget; the poor man manages an embarrassing economy.
They do not know how to spend or how to save because they do not
live their definitive lives that end in death, but provisional lives
that end in the unforeseen.

Is it rational that such a man economize? When he dies he leaves
a house half paid for, a home halfway organized, sons halfway ed-

ucated, and daughters halfway married. Such a life imbalance, which leads to seeing with a serpent's eyes anything that flies, is a terrestrial lack of equilibrium: something similar to Foucault's pendulum. Whatever falls in the province of the unforeseen takes on such a configuration. Hazard, fear, and fiction are the three terms of almost all equations. In the last phase, deriving culturally from the lie, the lack of equilibrium produces a complicated and picturesque variation: credit. Credit is the latest form of commerce's evolution; but, it may also be an elementary form of speculation with an article of prime necessity: pride. Within each poor man there is a frustrated dreamer of wealth and an arrogant gambler who expects to gain advantages from the future or from God. He discounts a document that guarantees hazards; it is the way to collect beforehand some nonexistent prize of a nonexistent lottery. It all originates in the dream of a better situation. To buy on credit is to discount something that we believe someone to owe us: to enjoy on monthly installments a portion of well-being and comfort that belongs to others. The consumer who buys on credit conjectures that he is collecting a debt from the salesman who delivers what he does not possess; in this way, payments do not seem like payments, the product appears to be a gift, and sometimes these fictions are finally believed and no payments are made at all. Credit and deceit go hand in hand, and they form a circuit, a chain system, a system of freemasonry without statutes or headquarters, which involves the person who has and the one who does not have. In the background, the master of the lies, the one who possesses the lamp of our dreams and also the alarm clock, lives far from here. In this manner, business on credit—which together with the checkbook could be considered the ideal form of conducting transactions —is converted into a false structure of responsibility and into a somewhat legal swindle. It is the fear of sincerity, of showing one's true face in public that leads to these unworthy forms of well-being. The credit fanatics are imbibers of denatured alcohols; by becoming deranged, they flee their destiny. The true victim is not the supplier, who does not drink, but the friend who signs the document as a guarantor.

Collaterally, there are those who discount the future in a more exquisite way with false documents. The university degree, the administrative career, political ambition, publication of books, and what is basically a technique of serpent and of cow skull is applied to the exploitation of intelligence and of spiritual goods, both involved in the business of credit. At these levels, credit is transformed into the promise: honor circulates in place of money, like overdrawn checks and hidden forces—trade winds of the plains. The acquisition of a diploma confides a value that should be returned to society but is not restituted by the person who pawns property or honor. The first position resulting from the diploma is the downpayment of the right to eat in the prytaneum. The politician's candidacy concedes him carte blanche to operate with impunity in view of the position that is anticipated but not yet gained; if it should be won, salaries and allowances are discounted for the mandate's duration. The first book proclaims the genius who already writes overdrafts based on the imbecility of his fourth work. Meanwhile, life has continued, based on fame and respect on loan; it is quite natural to fall into the temptation of not proceeding with rectitude.

To serve such a system of commerce, a procedural system has been formed based on the requirements. Perhaps what christens a city a commercial establishment—more than its traffic, its use of credit, and its buying and selling—is its amount of concealed bad faith or the number of merchants of any type forced to come to an understanding. A commercial establishment is a place where one is always on the alert to speculation with fellow man's needs: that is business; in general terms, the commercial establishment is the place where sellers exceed buyers. A man who works there is a signature instead of a person. He stands for the authenticity of a signature and not for the prestige of an unstained name. In such a sense, a cultural society, a beneficent society, or a church could be a commercial establishment. It could well occur that assemblies, congresses, social gatherings, and parties become no more than markets in the agora. It is a question of scent whether money has an odor. By analogy, there is a radical difference between honesty and the exercise of a profession: honesty should not be negotiable, but virtue should not be made from the occupation. The forum opens to the distributors of adulterated drugs; the rascal who takes over his neighbor's field because he cunningly inserted into the contract a clause prohibiting the planting of shrubs and fruit trees, obtains money, buys a name with the money, and using his name as a picklock opens a respectable door to politics and the great world. A dry-cleaning shop may be born by the fermentation of a flask of Fierabrás balm to remove stains or from ox bile, soap, and water; a literary reputation may come from twenty leagues of countryside; political devotion may have its roots in mystery and glossolalia. These facts, the silent acceptance of these facts, and the jurisprudence of these facts impart to a city, a country, and a continent the character of a gypsy fair. The literary prizes and the pedigree awards are adjudicated in that fair: they are worth something until their owners take them home; then they die and no one remembers. The professional man and the intellectual man exercise their commerce with the avarice that the small merchant feels for money. A city full of such hosts, although it may abound in universities, tribunals, legislative chambers, and theaters, is a commercial establishment. In the majority of cases, it is not a vocation that impels the teacher and the writer—with the fatality that a bird is to his song—to earn a degree or to publish works. Neither is it the ladder structure of professions and of merits that inclines man to take one stream and not another in the delta of careers. He does not choose; he is attracted by the one with the most promising future: medicine or law. Son or grandson of that disjointed man of whom he is ashamed, he is propelled by a similar, eager desire to possess the future, assuring it with credits. His movements are inert forces, galvanic impetuses. The urgency lies in the concern for life's security, as in the middle of the jungle. The future is an unknown and there is no stable, lucrative, and honorary position where everything changes hands; the best is the firmest: whatever most resembles earth.

The rancher wants his son to study medicine; he suspects that the university degree is much like a property title, which he carefully preserves. He imagines that the degree is an amulet to triumph in life; he hangs it on the wall with the same reverence that he installs his patron saint in a niche.

That is why the son, whose authentic vocation and atavistic tendency is to stuff the money box, studies, earns the degree, and then, immune, allows himself to drift wherever he is lured by that stifling trend. With the doctorate he exercises vengeance in his father's name; he will be a rune inscribed upon the hilt of a sword. Medicine, engineering, law, philosophy, and diplomacy are instruments of a locksmith's trade. Ironically, veterinary medicine and agronomy are youthful brides. In spite of the university degree, the regressive forces push him in the direction of his father's youth. He is a doctor; he will obtain a teaching post, a banking position, a drawing-room or a bureaucratic position in which the State will pay him the interest on the capital invested in the diploma.

To shatter the ideal of fortune—the supreme memorial along with honors and attentions—would be to broadcast the error of a four-century enterprise; it would mean to proclaim the sterility of his father's life. If that fortune should represent debasement, then debasement will be respected: it will be dignified precisely because it represents the error. Intellectuals and merchants have been deceived by the demon of greed or one of appearances, and they have been led to the ship by the specter of a hero. As they endeavor to crown their efforts, they hear the songs of those who are not in a hurry and are not dying; it is too late to repent or to comprehend. They are all alone with the poor, sick donkey they have bought from the gypsies at the fair.

14 THE DEFENSE

Dangers and Fears

For a very long time it was necessary to lower the qualifications for the job in order to match the limitations of the man; the craft remained at the level of the apprentice. Factories and businesses had to be content with the workers and the employees who improvised as well as they could while toiling without relish for their task and while thinking about other matters. It was not possible to demand specialization where there were no specialty courses; everyone viewed manual labor as a contingent task, unrelated to his destiny. If he did not enrich himself quickly, he would abandon the job; if he did enrich himself, he considered it worthy employment. Men casually changed jobs; if a man remained yoked to his set of tools, he in fact renounced all adventure. Without artisans or operators, the tasks remained at a rudimentary technical level. Workshops and studies were the asylums for the limping; a formless, coarse, and miraculous hope hovered over the streets. Any job seems provisional until the advent of emancipation in the form of a winning lottery ticket or a public position. Work is basically an indefinite captivity; whoever accepts it with humility will not have his name included in the free drawing for money and for honor.

Each person aspires to a job where he can earn the most money with the least effort; the lucrative State jobs are the best positions to fatten on. Toil is hateful and shameful during the wait for manumission, like poverty on Christmas Eve, which is touched by haughtiness during the self-assured wait for the top prize in the lottery. The disillusionment resulting from the loss of hope for a better tomorrow is much worse than the worker's prophetic disillusionment. The reveille of vibrant ideals rouses the spirits, and a workshop becomes a rebellious barracks full of men crouching in ambush. Work, however simple, uses man; machines feed on his blood and his enthusiasm, devouring him piece by piece. Man is joyless because he still believes in the nearby existence of an unknown Trapalanda; he does not believe that his destiny lies in the rude necessity to work for a living; he refuses to join with others like him, as if the denial of his class would nullify its existence. The most persistent supplicants desert the factories, the yards, and the shops for an asylum in the administration. They ignore their function, but with the backing of a committee passport, they enter into a public position where there are no technical demands; public administration is the world of the formless technology and the ruinous rival of anything that is exacting. Each escapee from the factory is the most terrifying example of subversion of the strategic ordering of abilities; he unconsciously works against stability, against all hierarchy. Meanwhile, free intelligence and whatever signifies a form of independence beg for crumbs of bread in editorial rooms, in lawyer's offices, and in antechambers. Twitchings of rebelliousness smolder on the site abandoned by the fugitive, and they visit his new site of penetration. The mere possibility that anyone could become anything is not a democratic road for the betterment of the lower classes. Each worker who enters the world of formless technology is a traitor to his class, and he denies his own blood. The individual betterment accomplished through the school of indignity, contrary to the interests of the body, is not the triumph of society, but apostasy and treason. When those people who have not yet been redeemed by politics cluster for a strike or a rally, the deserters from their ranks fire upon them, frightened that tomorrow they may lose today's possessions. The caste system of superposed layers is less redoubtable than the liberal regime that is permeated from top to bottom with the eager desire to rule and to possess. What is everywhere understood to be the proletariat exists in the chaos of bourgeois ambitions but is negated by its own components. At the point of crossing over to the opposing ranks, the workers sell themselves; what makes them die in the plazas is the fear of renouncing personal adventure. In summary, what is understood to be the unlimited possibility for prosperity is a hidden scorn for the excellence of the superior man, an infamous promiscuity of appetites. In the absence of leaders who embody a human ideal, the electoral champions speculate with rancor; the masses eventually forget that their true manumission lies in not compromising and in fighting shoulder to shoulder. Bribed by promises, gifts, and salaries, the best leaders desert the struggle that does not pursue noble ends but becomes a guerrilla war for wealth or position.

A world viewed as a plain of unlimited horizons, where one may go anywhere, has no exit. It is a jungle where man preys on fellow man. Each apostate of destiny is a vicious person of submissive appearance who hopes to conquer and to oppress as soon as he rises above the lowest level. It is a world generous with alms, but terribly dangerous. What is actually learned in the experience of daily life is how to dissimulate the true personality and the ineluctable destiny. And yet, our strength derives from fear, as with the clawed animals.[1] There exists a climacteric fear, a tendency to

---

[1] Ortega y Gasset called Buenos Aires "the city of the anonymous." The anonymous, that written weapon, may also be discharged behind one's back through the telephone. Behind each curtain and in each shadowy corner there is a phantom aggressor.

play down categorical acts and opinions and to represent the role of a satisfied lion; at times, they take on the appearance of the simple truth. There is a wolf underneath the sheep's clothing. Mystery encircles events; the friend and the relative assault and swindle; there is a confabulation against truth, beauty, and good in which we are all involved and in whose development we perhaps collaborate like bandits who have by their crime realized the uselessness of justice. Man is the animal of dominion and hope. He desires to possess the present, and he conceives of his rights to the future in accordance with what he now dominates. His hope is to dominate the future. But, as the possibilities to possess and to conserve by the mere, mechanical function of living decrease, diametrically opposed feelings appear: impotence and fear. Those emotions are correlated with the consciousness of vanishing power or with the enslaving augmentation of whatever is opposed to his free and dominant activity. Likewise, hope and the desire for dominion usually emerge by reversion from impotence and fear—maintaining the semblance of superlative states. In an undifferentiated world, the possibilities for triumph are more ample but less intense —plural and aleatory. Man ceases to be the master of a circle that is subdued by him and whose management he is acquainted with, and he becomes a serf of a sometimes indiscernible complex of opposing forces. Capability and competence imply the need for self-control to achieve the desired goals. The area dominated does not have to be extensive, but within the radius in which the competent person operates, there should be no insuperable resistances. He knows, and to know is to be sure. In this case, the struggle has been circumscribed to concrete terms. Man unfolds his concentrated strength against the nature of difficulties; this behavior could be called competence, courage, and skill.

Man becomes hostile and cruel with the need to affirm himself in life and to avoid pitfalls. Such is the state of mind of those people who have not classified the surrounding difficulties and thus act somewhat blindly. They see danger wherever they are; since they are ignorant and disorderly, danger is in a dusty and diffuse state.

The finer stimuli are distorted into a defensive attitude, and then, will is not a solid directed to one point but a restless looking about, waiting for the vague danger to coagulate its threat at a concrete point. Whatever position may be reached under this pressure of fear is converted into an advance post, into a solitary excursion without the validity of conquest. The newly arrived sows confusion around him; concrete forms cannot be expected to arise from what he does or from what he touches; since he is not an organized force, he can only conserve his ascendancy for the duration of the status quo that made his arrival possible. He spreads restlessness whether he exercises a public function or achieves a fortune: he is alarming as a person and as a method. The aggressive force inserts itself into a structure and masquerades under the name of authority, of privilege, of hierarchy, of law, of mandate, of regulation, of authorization, or of power. But everyone realizes that the only truth is that of an insecure man who hides behind those concepts, like Bacchus behind Hercules's attributes. The chaos and the hazards that made him strong are more prevalent because of him. The specialist may be displaced by the improviser, the trained workman by the apprentice, and the honest man by the corrupter of minors. Knowledge, work, and dignity are mere tools of power and may be annulled by any substance that is part of the vague surrounding danger as easily as the father of a family may be wounded by a stray bullet. To meditate on how to triumph is to renounce all hope.

While one waits in the hope that tomorrow may bring some fundamental change in one's position, that tomorrow is already being shaped to include unexpected surprises. The total loss of what one possesses is unavoidable.

A world where it is easy to progress beyond all rational conjecture is a world full of dangers. In the same way that there is no rigid context of circumstances that would impede access to upper spheres, there is no rigid context of circumstances that impedes the fall to lower spheres. The hazard of attaining something is in conserving it; those who triumph increase the difficulties for those who follow them, because victory is not a conquest that passes into the common good, but the individual booty of a deserter who has erased all traces behind him.

Fortresses

The only solidified structure, the only segment of the sphere where the lands stand out from the waters is the public administration—the sandbanks of the State. Its outline and relief are clearly marked, and those who fear life may cling there; but, it has the mass of a floating island without internal consistency. It assumes the form of the chaotic components that integrate it; thus, it depends on the fortuitous circumstances that can undo it as easily as they gave it a specific shape. Adjacent to the constitutional precepts and the juridical norms are the indomitable will of the formless masses and the concupiscence and fraud of its parasites. Those who resort to the guardianship of the public treasury lack confidence in themselves and in their environment until the day that a massive shudder of the corpuscles forming that fallible figure radiates panic in centrifugal waves. A sudden change of government or the lowering of salaries and state pensions causes millions of tremulous men to quake; those who only have their hands or their savings discover that what seemed to be insured against chance is exposed to immanent contingencies. The State was the guarantor of personal security against such indiscernible dangers as the Indian, bank failures, and general conditions in the life struggle; the army was the institution of strength. The crumbling or the weakening of the State causes the fall of all the values based on the State's stability.

As the State increased its arithmetical strength by absorption of the most intellectually capable elements—and consequently of those most fearful of reality—the individual lost his vibrant and courageous energy. Once man was incorporated into the public treasury, he lost his initiative and his vigorous creativity; castrated and bored by having his competence and his entire existence subjugated under the governmental shelter, he merely became another functionary—not endowed with a free and creative thought. The presumed security within the ambit of public administration augmented the insecurity of what remained outside. The inhabitants locked out were subjected to the harshest destiny. Since the realms of intelligence, of action, and of technology were not liberally rewarded, any overtures by these areas toward the central focus of power were motivated by fear. Universities and committees taught the fiscal tactics of escape from the aleatory world outside the State and the methods of penetrating its ambit. Science became a safe-conduct to entering the circles closest to the center; knowledge was the vehicle to sinecures. In this manner, the State came to exercise a monopoly over intelligence, to sponsor it, and to stamp it with political attributes.

Outside the official façade—which showers money and honors —the scientific investigation, the ex cathedra philosophical speculation, and the lavish cultivation of the arts are today aberrations and idle gymnastics. If a remunerative teaching or administrative position is not available upon the completion of studies, those calisthenic activities which lack an application eventually overwhelm other aptitudes offering greater advantages in the coarse struggle for life. The professional man cannot resign himself to seeking his fortune from behind a counter. Those who squeeze into the most intimate circles of power or into the more ample ones that still offer fiscal security contemplate with haughtiness those who are excluded; the scorn for what is impartial and abstract, for what does not nurse on the swollen udders of the budget, is cloaked in fear in a need to shelter the possessed values from indiscernible dangers. The arts and the sciences are viewed as a bold renunciation of success, a conflagration of the spirit's good harvests; fear that mixes with mockery impels our youth to choose the only lucrative profession outside the realm of the State: medicine.

The leviathan that devours hearts and minds fosters a milieu of a rich and substantial life intrinsically lacking meaning. It receives security and transmits security. The cultural corporations seek out subsidies—their collective salaries; the commercial and industrial organizations obtain concessions and facilities for their programs; the great financial and mercantile enterprises are linked to the State by top public officials. Two-thirds of the most significant sectors of the population and of wealth depend on the State. Beyond, stretches the desert. The wealth assured by concessions and by privileges and the masses of public employees and their families set the pace for other activities. The apparent opportunities and guarantees for success offered under the State's auspices are eventually translated into chaos; the associated capitals, the politicians, and the public employees take advantage of the confusion; there is an alliance of frustrated action and submissive thought. The State, which protects the needy, the invalid, and the capital that will not otherwise be risked, exposes all to the worst enemy, to the indiscernible danger: the lack of organization and of solidarity among social groups. Corporations, communities, cooperatives, and institutes delegate their cohesive forces to the State, which thus represents cohesion and strength; but, all else is disorganized and without resources. The fear that first stirred the search for help is now the feared reality that debilitates and disperses. The dynamic ideals that uphold individuals and collective groups are obliterated by the fear of the immediate. Their role as postulants puts men in peril of taking the same refuge occupied by the public employee through the electoral process; a society of artists or of farmers surrenders its life to an entity that is only capable of disorganization because its strength is the sum of our weaknesses.

In short, what constitutes the power of the State to which everyone appeals in an evasion of reality? Why should one seek its protection if its strength lies only in its ability to weaken what lies outside itself? It is because the primitive fear, the one that gripped the first settler, the first rancher, and the first artist, had no opportunity to be replaced by security; death, ruin, and shame remained within the new structure as sentiments buried in the subconscious by overly vehement censorship and zeal; they are more alive than ever.

The Organized Defenses

Undoubtedly, the army possesses a defined structure as does no other organization; but it is so arranged and plotted that it is a formidable defense organism converted into a formidable organism of danger. Concrete, rigid, and omnipotent, it gathers prestige and power from the fact that it constitutes a caste, a nation, a guild, a state, a technology, and a religion. It is strength in the bosom of weakness, discipline and methodology in the midst of improvisation and chance. Endowed with the vitality that should be shared by the Nation's organs, the army assumed the functions of nonexistent or eradicated instruments. All Argentine history is a military history; the civilian and political histories are legendary chapters—apocryphal history.[2] Álzaga, who was a defender of minors, called himself a general; even Sarmiento took pride in his honorary title of general, equivalent to his doctorate from Michigan. The ranch administrators were commanders; the two wealthiest ranch owners, Rosas and Urquiza, were the two prominent figures in many wars and in peace. The military career replaced titles of nobility and land titles; apart from the prestige of the uniforms, which everyone embossed to his own taste, there were the advantages of promotions and decorations culminating in the donation of lands, which were the prizes in kind. The property titles, particularly those of the latifundia, harken back to the days of the Indian hunters. A rank could be attained by fighting under the colors of any faction; since the booty snatched from the Indian had no value, the State ceded leagues of its land. Thus, battles were waged for the country's territorial conquest; each victory cost the treasury the amputation of hundreds of leagues of territory, as if the country had been invaded. What was lost of its patrimony was converted into the equivalent of decorations, into a testimonial of courage and of money, and often into sale contracts.

Rivadavia was shattered by the army and by the clergy because whatever he attempted to renovate meant for both a despoilment of legitimate titles and disorganization. He really was disorganizing the only thing that was organized and attempting to replace the steel frame with the medulla oblongata. That is why Rosas and

[2] "Bad politics and war are the forces that reigned from 1811 until today [1898]. Whoever says that we have lived within the bounds of legality, tells a lie" (J. A. Terry).

Irigoyen, the two most genuine representatives of the people and the ones who wished to give the people an authentic style and physiognomy, to stock them with weapons, and to provide a gospel for their faith, found their defeat at the hands of the army. Without a doubt, their ochlocratical despotism originated from the armed populace; but the institution that watches over other institutions understood in both incidents that it was a case of concealed conspiracy against the dignity of the profession, and it undid them.

Because defense is the army's constitutional function, in the absence of real dangers it assumes the defense of institutions, more decidedly of those over which it has lost its moral tutelage. The army is established in the expectation of events that do not occur; in the meantime, it consumes vast sums on its maintenance that are deflected from other activities. It consumes as if there were a state of siege. A great army in a peaceful country is its pride and its ruin; each year of peace is lost economic battle. Everything appears to be helpless and poor in comparison with its voracity. To maintain that immense and onerous body, industries were abandoned to their own resources, the territory remained unpopulated, the means of production fell into venal hands, and transportation, telephones, electricity, and grain deposits answered to foreign interests. Once the causes justifying the maintenance of large divisions disappeared, the army continued on a war footing during peace.[3] It put itself at the service of foreign exploitation; and, by assuring the dividends, it assured progress. One-fourth of the total income is invested in the honorary bureaucracy of the defenders of principles; meanwhile, the farmers and merchants abandon the countryside and close down their concerns.

That army maintained for contingent defense needs cannot remain inactive; even those who are pensioned dedicate themselves to

[3] "In times of peace, the military organism finds itself in the situation of a means that cannot fulfill its end. Then, the army's technical structure is irremediably converted into the ultimate goal; the subordinate relationships, which are the foundation for the organization's technical ability, begin to occupy the foreground of consciousness. The characteristic sociology synapse does not occur until a situational change implants that idea in the consciousness as the militia's own purpose" (J. Simmel).

other civil functions. The more remote the possibilities for combat, the greater are the extraordinary activities. The purely bureaucratic function is incompatible with the military man's idiosyncrasy and with his punctiliousness. An inactive army is an army in a surreptitious war, and somehow it is combating against something. When the commanding officers are reduced to drawing high salaries, although this maintains the institution's prestige and the respect for its members, they must—if only for the sake of decorum—deport themselves as if an attack were imminent. No one knows what they will unload against. A border conflict or one of political jurisdiction puts them in action, and eventually war may justify their existence. In general, that is the nature of the professional military all over the world. But the extraordinary function, the honorary civil function so well paid, is the attribute typical to the species originating in South American latitudes. Mutinies and power grabs are ways to justify sumptuous salaries; these violent simulations of war perhaps comply with the right not to remain totally inactive. The military men who incubate revolutions desire to eat their bread without remorse. In the absence of international conflicts and before the sopor and poverty of the bordering countries, those well-fed bodies have to fatidically turn inward and to sublimate their winter maneuvers into the revolt and the usurpation of political power. Contained within the astronomical frontiers by the limits of the desert, the army's natural overflow is inward, in a type of innervation that allows superabundant vital energies to escape.

Fortifications against Defenses

In provinces where there is no need for armies, countless inhabitants walk barefoot, often go hungry, and are deprived of the most elementary instruction. When recruited, it can be seen that they are Sudras and pariahs; they must be discharged because their bodies are only useful for a minimal existence and for being counted in the census. Sixty thousand men under arms and a budget of 180 million pesos are the luxuries of a country that does not have thinkers, scholars, or artists. Poverty

and ignorance are the natural nourishment of armed institutions
that operate inside the hollow thorax. The rifles and the knapsacks
are the protection of those twenty-year-old youngsters who can
scarcely bear their burden; science, engineering, and strategy are
the brain of those illiterates. Poverty brought rancorous isolation;
rancorous isolation brought revolutions and threats of war, and the
frontiers were closed. Those countries only have their armies, and
they have not yet learned to waste their money on luxuries other
than weapons; they are enemies, although there is no reason to
hate—or to love. Those countries are only a danger to themselves,
from their frontiers inward; and yet they live poised for invasions.
They must be feared because they are unhappy with their destinies. It is necessary to flee from any painful reality; thus, the
denial of the sad internal truth can be an evasion-invasion. The
founding of universities is a movement to negate the cultural de-
ficiency; credit exists to negate poverty; the appeal to violent actions is the negation of weakness. Argentina distrusts other countries because she considers them to be the residence of the Indian
who no longer exists in her territory, the repository for her taboos.
The existence of the frontier Indian necessitated the maintenance
of armies of astronomical dimensions; the Indian died, and now
the armed fear localizes the dangers in the unknown. That army
unhinged our finances and those of other countries because the
loans destined for development projects were invested in its maintenance. Thus the Indian's penates wreaked their vengeance. We
view the borders with the same distrustful eye that the farmer used
to peer from behind the fortifications. Somewhere around here
reside the native dangers—the loose dangers that cannot be measured, weighed, or calculated. According to what they are or could
signify on the value scale of culture and of civilization, they do
not exist. But they exist as armies, as explosive forces, as unknowns, as specters of the Indian. We admit that from one day to
the next they could rise in arms, debilitate sovereignty in return for
being supplied with weapons, and attack us with the support of oil,
salt, or metal trusts that would put the latest weapon models into
their irresponsible hands. The forces at their disposal are not

natural forces, but censured weaknesses. We recognize, since we are on guard with excessive defiance, that they have the possibility of becoming strong—even at the price of indignity—and that with their substantial elasticity to become loosened and to degrade themselves they are dangerous.

But, jointly with the pyrotechnical exaltation of a country that rises through the superiority of its army and its navy, there is the decrepitude of another country that descends on the other side of the balance; finally, one country becomes armed fear against danger and the other one danger against fear. The localization of danger in such crude concepts as strips of planet labeled as our neighboring countries and the fear of unprovoked nocturnal aggression divert us from the true internal dangers and debase our values by judging them in contrast to those of our opponents. The degradation of one side emphasizes the exaltation of the other, and everything that symmetrically opposes base conduct appears to be lofty. Our internal enemies are infinite, ranging from endemic illnesses, poverty, solitude, distance, desert, and capitals exploiting noble industry to the other extreme of the superficial and official culture. Our external enemies are those countries which produce the same products that we do and which fulfill an identical destiny in history and in world economy: Canada, Australia, New Zealand, and South Africa. The cannons do not reach that far, and it is easier to fear the dead than the living.

15 THE FLIGHT

The Cunning of Confounded Fear

A life that does not need intellectual satisfactions, or costly emotional outlets, or supernumerary luxuries is satiated with little. It does not nourish the totality of its tissues, and those which are not impregnated with profound, serene joy secrete internally a bitter fluid of pride. Existence is projected to the exterior, as the house is toward the façade; the conscience, restless because of all its tragic flaws, places itself on guard in refined suspiciousness, accumulating professorships and jobs to make respectable the rachitic deformity.

Austere living can maintain a well-equipped house and enhance itself with real cashmere suits when it is bolstered by the robust legs of two jobs and by the perquisites of political influence— valued on equal terms with gold. The conquest of surface has been debased: it does not even refer to hectares of land.

Friendship filters through the living room, and personality disappears in dress; even the eyes of the most sagacious examiner can scarcely perceive what is inside the house or beneath a person's bearing. Twenty years as someone's co-worker does not suffice to decipher the enigma of his budget or of his character. The personality remains a mystery until it is welded to his tegument and skin becomes a cloth. To conceive of a materialistic ideal because any noble human ideal is no more than a baneful fantasy is to play into the hands of the merchants who deal in trivia at a handsome profit. The landlords capitalize on the mania to affect affluence by charging an average of 30 percent of the nominal incomes of the office worker, the public employee, and the ordinary workman—a heavy tax on presumptuous vanity. Socially, such is the practical result of the fear of nakedness, of revealing oneself as ancient man. Tailor's shops, emporiums, and other businesses feeding on the fear of appearing ridiculous collect another substantial portion of revenue— which is how the product of labor has been officially designated— as a tax that people pay without resisting. Rent and dress are the poles of the preoccupations of a people whose Sybaritism consists in not eating meat.

An excessive pride based on credits and debits and the absence of canons of conduct—such as respect for clean and healthy humility and for precise goals in the disciplined march of life—lead to that isolation concentrically imposed by the walls of the house and the cloth of the suit. Ties and gloves are usually the categorical answers to indiscreet questions: once again we witness the palisade that separates the cultivated area from the zone of roaming dangers. The geographical, psychological, and tactical forces of the plain, which enter so strangely transfigured into the urban life, incite one to hide behind appearances and to post sentinels. They are the dramatis personae. The erection of a hasty Babel of values imparts to each builder of his own home a distrustful attitude; even the truthful person exploits his fellow men and invites a pantomimic response to his studied mimicry. All this confusion is engendered by the dread of being caught defenseless, without a knife; it is the fear that after the feast the shadow of hidden pettiness may project on the walls its *mene, mene, tekel, upharsin.*

The feelings of inferiority are transported to the level of rank and of personification; fear of truth, of censured reality, and of not possessing the stable products quoted in the stock market of circulating values leads to the shunning of poverty as being opprobrious and engenders the mimicking of economic stringencies and innate ignorance by fragile, ostensible well-being and counterfeit skill. From such a position, the conscience is converted into a raw nerve for perceiving any allusion to its humiliating secret, and the whole existence reacts by an inferiority complex, as if threatened by the discovery of chambers that cannot be seen from the living room. A people hypocritical about its fate maintains permanent vigilance over its defects, with a morbid sense for the ridiculous that leads to inquiring the mute judgment of each passer-by and each interlocutor. These traits confer such a peculiar, sharp guise to our gestures that the stranger perceives it as soon as he arrives. We are not secure, because the pretense—of which we are aware—is so ubiquitous.

If a conscience issues from a subconscious prone to disguises and it is plagued by its own faults and renunciations, it is like a pool of rancor spawned by the dread of appearing ridiculous. Affectation, *compadre*-like acts, and susceptibility originate from the decrepitude of the forms that martyrize flesh and bones. To overcome intense scruples it does not suffice that a convention be accepted by all or that the key to a fiction be known by all; the concealment is not conducive to anything but scenic illusions—*idola theatri*, as Lord Bacon used to call them. The specter of a physiological taboo: one's own flesh flayed is what is most feared; second, we fear what resembles the indigenous map of the land that nourishes us.

Truth is horrifying in a land where those who have and those who have not feign to be the opposite, because the puppet game corrupts the very essence of the human and tragic plot of life, like bad money that drives out the good. Even nudity becomes a new disguise with which to cover some subcutaneous dress. Sincere feelings rest on deceit, crumbling in a faint breeze. Only in these lands of kinetic fortune is friendship so superlatively exposed to such disconsolate adversity. Friendship and respect are stretched like a sheer film over the ego: one never penetrates through that superficial, false ego to the depths of one's feelings and existence. Everyone unfolds for display only what he desires others to see; the behavior at parties, social circles, and family gatherings hints of an odor of marketplace chitchat. All that we attribute to the lack of moral conscience stems from the mercantile valuation of affections and from the instinctive repugnance for what has no value in barter. When the host and the guest meet at the front door, they measure each other in a manometrical embrace. Then, in a more or less friendly manner, they pass into the living room; from here inward begins the labyrinth shrouding the real nature of the economic position. The contact is not fecund, like love fulfilled only in copulation.

When one adulterates his personality, he achieves the consciousness of an actor who gratifies himself without knowing it in a certain stylistic mastery that he imitates without wanting to. The world becomes a navel whose contemplation explains the varieties of human fate by mesmeric devices. Passion, frankness, rapture, and exaltation toward diaphanous heights become confused in automatically cautious gestures; what functions both on and off stage is a mere puppet of the hidden personality. The man on the defensive, the reptilian being, the cunning gaucho, and the narcissist are inveterate forms of self-indulgence converted into vital habits, something like the child of average singing ability who is sent to a conservatory. The dangers may be of such a nature that only the ego's clothed part, its scenic face, is engaged; the actor, fearing ridicule, solemnly gesticulates his role. Narcissism has an aspect distinct from the conceited joy of seeing oneself live: the fear of seeing oneself discovered. The self-satisfaction demonstrated prima facie is an exaggerated fear of self-examination. Consequently, the care exercised to avoid appearing inferior, weak, and disarranged and the precautions that impel one to live beyond one's means, to deceive friends with the usual frauds, and to present an appearance of affluence without what the old Germans until the days of Goethe called *des Lebens ernstes Führen* [the seriousness of living life] are judgments of material values and not of moral ones. The whole philosophy is one of *Sartor Resartus* [overly tailored tailor].

Agustín Álvarez enjoyed that proud tumefaction of the poor illiterate; he has demonstrated that the itching to pretend to be what one is not, even to the extent of taking pride in perspicacities proper to a swindler, is the comedy's denouement—although not the only one. Such is the end of the pseudonarcissist. It is considered less denigrating to achieve a position by means of a crime than to live in honest poverty: "without honor but wealthy" is the motto of the talented villains.

Supplementary Salaries

It is quite common for the public employee and for the common worker to allege—when it is known how much they earn but not how they live—that they have other occupations, viatica, and extra income, that they receive more or less ignominious subsidies, or that they get along as well as they can with God's help. Fear of ridicule for their poverty is transformed into shamelessness and then into cruelty. The additional alleged income may originate with the man's wife, who works as a teacher, or with his sister, who works as a seamstress; perhaps it is the result of unpaid loans or of a social assistance. The quest for additional income represents the technique of disguise against whose excesses there is no legal sanction or even a repudiation. The weakest being is the most dramatic character in the comedy for concealing oneself. The position of the woman who contributes to the maintenance of a home is false and basically humiliating—regardless of whether she is a teacher, an employee, or a laborer. It is considered shameful to loyally recognize the wife's real contribution, without entirely allowing her to be the assiduous female who takes care of the children, cooks, cleans, and makes love. This is because man fears a slur on his manhood. His equivocal position is derived from a complex in which the woman is also involved: it is an amalgam of scorn, of shame, and of need. The woman is needed, and she is taken advantage of without recognizing her equality of rights; it is expected that on her job in the workshop or behind the desk she convey the image of the typical woman at home.

Confronted by fear, woman was assigned a shameful place. Scorned first and then considered an uncomfortable annex, she now leaves the home to earn her bread; and yet, her latest sacrifice does not inspire respect. Until a few years ago she was expected to exhibit a servile circumspection and to thus clearly differentiate between the wife and the concubine. The married woman always felt threatened, either by a censor or by some wretched soul ready to denounce her for imaginary adultery. Her profession was to be chaste and her rights were limited to the fulfillment of her duties. Later, her life became more harsh when she entered the job contest; she had to work with men, to compete with those who did not even allow her the mercy conceded to a loaded beast of burden. She earned her bread, and she was considered a poor female without a family and with all the stigmas attached to poverty, to spinsterhood, or to an unhappy marriage. With courage she penetrated the machine shops, men's businesses, and offices flooded with man talk. She worked next to them but drew a lower salary for performing the same task. She was courted by the foreman and by the boss who naturally considered themselves entitled to her honor; she was not thought of as an employee or as a worker: she was considered a woman. She was expected to be beautiful and well-built as if she were merchandise in a brothel. The ugly ones were sent to the factories. Gradually, the male gaze was subsiding; the requirement for good looks—which used to be the certificate of competence—was toned down; and after all, since a human being cannot be lower than a dog, it was finally understood that it was a necessity that took women away from their homes and sentenced them—just like the men—to sit in a chair in front of a machine or to pore over accounting books. Men did not conspire against them: it was the fault of society's metallic framework. She had just forsaken her ancient role as a beast of burden, and she did not as yet perform her new function with confidence and determination. She was in doubt, like an old bird that has been freed but perches on top of the cage. There is no sadder parody than that of the flapper, with hands wrinkled by bleach, working in an office as a stenographer. The entire city was not a factory, so she could not sit at the desk in her home. She arrived ashamed, as if she were stealing bread from others, as if the working atmosphere were totally unfamiliar. Unsure of her new role, she arrived at her task as if to an appointment. She was not conscious of her capability as an instrument of action in the big world. Considered for centuries to be an instrument of pleasure, she was bewildered by her phenomenal promotion. She has not as yet terminated all her tremendous duties. She carries man's humiliation in her body and in her character. During the struggle for life, during the trip from her home to the factory, and during days of rest, a return to the old customs is demanded of her; on Sunday she must commemorate her old captivity. During holidays and hours of rest she is forced back into her previous obligations: she has no freedom until she puts everything in order for the following week. From the point of view of morality, the same irreproachable conduct is still demanded of her; she has not been freed to live, as she has been allowed to earn her bread. She is independent from the home to the extent that she may cover the deficit of the male's income, but she is kept censured and submissive, enchained by sexual prejudices. Laws are sanctioned that shelter her, but she has no protection. Tomorrow she will be allowed to divorce and to remarry, and she will be able to vote; but she will not be free. One hundred thousand eyes spy on her when she leaves her home, when she sits in her chair in front of the machine, when she bends over the books, and when she returns. Whether on the street or at home, she is worth no more than she was yesterday although she may now return with a salary in her purse.

Courage and Fear

These forms of hypocrisy and of pride are in accord with other more complicated ones. Evasiveness concerts with mimetic simulations and with challenge consisting of the impudent exhibition of antisocial impulses in an iron-clad defense of the ego. There are three classic reactions to fear: the attack, characteristic of the carnivore; the paralysis or apoplexy, characteristic of the bird and of insects; and the flight, characteristic of the herbivore. The insect's entire body becomes paralyzed, and it is protected by assuming the appearance of its surroundings. The bird remains astonished in a cadaverous fixation, with only its orb and the tremor of its lateral eyelid showing any signs of life. The carnivore does not view the world with the impotence of the defenseless animal, but with the totality of its strength and organic needs; experienced as a successful hunter, the carnivore's movements are endowed with a unity of purpose for stalking prey; when cornered or challenged by another beast, the carnivore attacks, since it knows no retreat and is designed to project forward, to the outside. Fear's only avenue of escape is expressed by attacking the enemy. The ferocity of a powerful, lone carnivore, when it is not triggered by hunger or sexual excitement, is of the same type as the hero's courage in the moment of danger: an instantaneous reversion to fear. On the other hand, the herbivore flees because its strength lies in its legs—so well adapted to flight; escape is its simplest psychological response. Man, both physically and psychologically, possesses all these reactions in some measure. According to the situation and depending on his temperament, man may take varying approaches: he may tackle a problem with determination, face difficulties one by one while symmetrically opposing the logic or methods for contention, or he may remain neutral, foreign to the human significance of the events he witnesses but turning indifference to his advantage; perhaps he may become evasive, hypocritical, mendacious, or cynical, without any of these attitudes necessarily reflecting a concrete posture. These preventive reactions are usually excessive due to the influence of pride, of passion, of interest, and even of timidity—as astute as Nietzsche's description. The military man, the judge, the priest, and the capitalist possess entirely disproportionate power; their demiurgical potential for action is only fully exercised when their self-interests are involved. The first movement, depending on the efficiency of that power, tends to augment the agent's resistance. No one could satisfy his conscience by exercising his disproportionate power over feeble subjects. The tyrant's success commences with his initial grasp of the various degrees of hostility involved in the living forces of the environment. Anyone endowed with a dose of power must conserve around him a certain degree of tension and hostility. The military man conceives of the dangers from potential invaders, and national defense ceases to be a fear of ghosts and becomes something corporeal; without its real existence, the military body's whole reason for being would disappear. Armaments create danger and in principle justify the danger against which they are acquired. By the same reasoning, the judge needs to consider society as an organization secretly sworn against order and justice. Any active movement that does not coincide with the Procrustean codices acquires characteristics of a transgression that conflicts with the judge's most intimate professional sense of justice; finally, he becomes a faithful servant of old prejudices that ultimately constitute society's real juridical framework. Likewise, the priest has the obligation to see sin instead of injustice; by his position as a priest, by the gymnastic development of his faculty to unmask the devil, he converts the world into a hell plagued by traps and evils. Thus, he justifies himself because his reason for being is the expurgation of a diabolical world.

The Euphoric Fears

I

The free man, who was not threatened by major contingencies, desired the quick possession of an easy fortune. In order to triumph and to escape, fear took a hurried slant. The sensation of living without major obstacles generated a false impression of power. Everyone was attacked by the miasmatic fever of enriching himself without working. Gambling was the fastest way to fortune, and a thousand circumstances offered encouragement to adventure. To farm, to buy properties, to invest in mortgages, or to accumulate savings represented alternative means of wagering in a huge gaming house without walls.

Fear did not change although it shifted locations: it was lifted from the homes and introduced into stock-market transactions and speculations. If a person possessed a piece of land, he dreamed about his neighbor's factory; land was like money; money was like a lottery ticket; great fortunes evaporated or multiplied like mirages. Documents, deeds, ballots, contracts, and commercial policies were like playing cards; wealth most resembled diamonds and spades in a fortune teller's deck of cards. Money had no fixed value, and the hideous dance of commercial papers was the delirium tremens of ambition. Gold supplied the same effects as alcohol. After a government obtained a loan, it would fall into a euphoric state, which then drifted over to the people; financial operations have a magical character of buying on credit, and the pound sterling was the rain of manna in the desert. To the people, that alcohol represented confidence, faith, and enthusiasm, and they undertook with intrepidity all the works requiring enthusiasm and courage. The price of goods and of real estate rose with each new loan—as did the salaries. A poison that relieved responsibilities and worries was entering into circulation; it was thought that such a transitory state of euphoria was the reality, the definitive state. The golden manna could be used for electoral frauds in the hands of fortune-telling governments. People imagined they were witnessing the advent of the latent reality; all of Trapalanda acquired the deceitful aspect of inflation, of commercial papers, of railroads, of the telegraph, of books, and of public buildings. Of course, that shameless frenzy for grandeur came from the earth's cretaceous abundance, from seeds, and from the cattle's fecundity in contrast with the sterility of minds, with the human barrenness, and with the leisure. People were content to contemplate general progress, which was not the fruit of their labor but a gift. It was another facet of the adulterous fruit of the sterile man's passion and of fecund nature, a type of mystical rapture under whose enchantment reality became aggrandized. If that is not the reaction of collective fear, then it is the conscience that fears awakening and takes to the road of lies and frauds. There is nothing more cowardly than dreaming with closed eyes before that urgent, superior reality surpassing logic or conjecture. Everyone suspected that he lived at the edge of a crater, and even those who took their savings to the colossus of South America subconsciously contributed their obolus to contain the disaster of awakening. Then, as now, the proclamation of greatness, the progress, the economic potential, and the excellence of our literary and artistic works were transferences from a very complex order; the taboo thoughts, the thoughts strong enough to be vocalized and to destroy the enchantment, were relegated to the subsoil. The parties interested in falsifying the true meaning of that mortgaged reality were those who possessed goods subject to bankruptcy: statesmen, legislators, merchants operating on credit, employees who purchased on an installment basis, and landholders who had mortgaged their lands. Those who had their places assured in the spectacle insisted with all the strength of fear on accentuating the desperate optimism. By virtue of that effort to disfigure reality, the nation acquired those psychological overtones which the foreigner can immediately perceive: "the spirit on the defensive," "the sadness," "the wait for tomorrow." The inevitable maturity of loans created in the people a neurosis in which it was necessary to salvage the present mistake by the extension of a credit taken out on the future.

The eastern and northern provinces, the Republic's geographical sections best endowed with customs, with laboriousness, with culture, and with well-being, were crumbling in everyone's sight because of the distance to the port where the clandestine drug was entering. The population emigrated and concentrated in the good pasture lands of the littoral; illiteracy was as invincible as weeds, and fields that had been cleared for agriculture once again returned to pasture land. The advancements attributable to loans and to capital marched together with the retrogression of reality to which people closed their eyes, thinking they could thus annul it. At the time when the customs house was caving in with the insolvency resulting from a deficit accumulated over a period of eighty years, twenty new banks were being almost instantly created with nominal capital. Public finances were funded by land concessions to railroads and by all types of prerogatives accorded the placement of coined gold. Each railroad, laid out for future grandeur, mortgaged that same future in which everyone so blindly believed. Everyone feared that the use of the horse for traction and the employment of a manual technology, more in accord with reality, would destroy the hypothesis forged by those who came out of tyranny's chaos and wished to recuperate the lost time with one stroke.

II

The fluctuations in property prices have been related to the country's state of security, as if the rules pertaining to real estate were a matter of varying states of mind. The values of real estate and of cattle were judged primarily by the security the owner had in their possession and use. Whatever could not be extirpated, violated, or lost was worth as much as life itself. Things were valued in proportion to the risk and the security involved. Superficially, this is all very simple, as simple as the origins of law and of morality. That is, until a fixed job was held to be more valuable than a farm, a plot of land in the middle of Buenos Aires was considered more valuable than a remote ranch, and a university diploma was worth more than a house.

Faced with persistent and ill-defined dangers and stirred by a basic drive to defend the life-force, the man of the pampa appraised his existence—many times saved as if by a miracle—above its human worth. The undamaged hut and the unscathed body emerged from adventure with a magic factor. Those life defenses later acquired a new meaning, a worth independent of their significance as asylums for man and his soul. Whatever had survived danger had its rights—like the hero—to public merit and to subsidy in addition to the guerdon. Luck was transformed into manna; the sites close to the centers of power increased the poverty of the remote ones. Luck was more than capability; it was dexterity combined with the intangible.

There is, then, an instinctive, animal process in the supravaluation of what has been obtained at a risk; this may give rise to a Mendeleevian periodic chart of economic and cultural values if the concepts of those values should be grouped according to the specific gravities of the worth of goods as assessed by their owners and not by the community. There was an increase of the hostile, the dauntless, and the warriorlike values within an apparently peaceful existence of a barrackslike order. The merit and the cost of those goods depend on the same circumstances that engendered them, mere imitations of states of mind. If moral forces do not develop parallel to daily success, they end by surrendering to the instinctive process of supravaluation of what can be easily seen and touched. And then, the automatic forces of defense and aggression lose any natural control. The calm judgments of the philosopher and of the just man are opposed by the criteria of the trader who measures and weighs and of the sentinel who limits his attention to potential threats. The fall of prices is accomplished by people's depravation, the degree of which is dependent on the extent to which life and material possessions are safeguarded. Typically, what one desires is respected as fellow man's patrimony; one wishes to possess at least as much as can be watched over and protected by one's hand and by the law. The false victory strips the world of its real difficulties, like a revolver that instantly annuls the rival's physical superiority by brutally subduing him with a single shot; what is organized for triumph is not considered—only what is armed.

Prices and values have simultaneously developed common vices. The economic crises endangered lives: with mathematical regularity, the fall of prices produced uprisings and revolutions. There have been seventy revolts between the 1852 defeat of Colonel Hornos and of General Madariaga by the troops of López Jordán and the defeat of Irigoyen by Irigoyenism's right wing. Conversely, the revolts and the riots caused a vertical drop in prices. It could be clearly seen that the orgy of prosperity was a joyful escape from danger and that fear had erected palaces and accompanied the entry of victorious loans. The 1874 revolution sowed such uncertainty that the proprietors of real estate sought to sell their lands at any price; the panic so aggravated the economic situation that it, in turn, provoked the uprisings of chieftains and of generals; the economic chaos was a deeper cause for rebellion than any civilian candidacy for the presidency of the Republic. In that emergency, real estate lost half its value and the commercial and banking failures, which constituted the terrible crisis of fear from 1873 to

1875, swept away with the workers' savings and with the land-lord's storage.[1] The possessors were less secure than their posses-sions; people had not time to situate their construction materials—their lime, their sand, and their brick; a wind from the pampa demolished the sites where fear had taken refuge. Within that seemingly secure economic structure dwelt the palpitating, preying forces tailor-made for hazards and for death; they rebelled under the slightest excuse, eating the fields, the houses, and the paper money. The Provincial Bank, overtaken by the same frightening madness, begat total depreciation; the instability of whatever could retreat from hazard and violence made a colossus of that institu-tion, but it was erected on sand and strengthened by contributions from people who lived in the restlessness and the rush to accumu-late; they deposited in the bank's coffers what they did not want to lose, and when the institution was shattered it spilled the accu-mulated fears over the ruins. It forced the debtors to cancel their obligations on peremptory terms, applying the full rigor of its statutes and resorting to coercive procedures. Those debts had been contracted by mortgaging the rain and the sunshine of future months. And that hope, safeguarded by twenty years of institution-al peace and of guerrilla activity to guarantee that institutional peace, raised the prices and the spirits and played into the hands of speculators, who have always invoked in us the fatherland and the destiny. The debtors had to dump their goods at any price during that time of anguish, as if they were returning a used dress to the Provincial Bank. A measure so opposed with the outlawed prac-tices of primitive revolts served as a call to reality and the native's contact with the land. Fear annihilated the false superfated attach-ment to things, and people rejoiced that they were at least alive; houses performed their essential function, and the fields yielded their legitimate crops—but cut in half.

[1] "A piece of land in Lincoln, in Tapalqué, or in some other deserted spot, when passing in ownership from hand to hand, could produce enormous profits in a few hours; the operation ended with the creation of imaginary towns, ab-sorbing in its fictitious value the savings from one's wage" (Francisco L. Bal-bín).

Although openly violent procedures had disappeared from the area of political interests, they were still in force in the embattled redoubts of finance where they had taken refuge in the tribunals, the Congress, and the Casa Rosada under the attributes of law, of freedom, and of power.

It was thought necessary to calm the frightened spirits, to re-constitute the levigated colossus, to legislate public lands, and to establish the power of the State as an anchor point. Various territorial and monetary approaches for clipping corruption at its roots have been tested since the days of Avellaneda and Pellegrini. The euphoria of convalescence proved the success of the experiments, at least for fifty years. Among those who took time to study the disaster, Don Francisco L. Balbín proposed "political tranquillity" to counter the panic, and Don José A. Terry understood that that crisis and the ensuing crises of progress were products of fear. But that fear is ancient; it composes the tissues of progress and is the natural climate of all South America. It circulates in our blood as a form of solitude. To achieve political tranquillity it was necessary to employ gift-giving and the constitutional use of power in order to tame those militias bred years before in assaults and in despoil-ment; they were lords of the soil who had hypostatized the concepts of fatherland, of property, of heroism, and of patriciate.

Panic was followed by an inverse crisis, an equally intense re-action of hope and of affirmation; property was safe under the pro-tection of a military government that exterminated the Indian, distributed lands, and converted the federal capital into a treasure chest in which the provinces deposited their economies. Progress and peace spread under the protection of the sword, with the reno-vation of uniforms and weapons, and with the law of compulsory military service. Fear could return to its place and collect its plenti-ful harvest.

III

The second crisis of fictitious grandeur was produced in 1880 under a military government. Buenos Aires, still preoccupied with the problems of locating a site for the federal government and counting the income from the customs house, remained indifferent to the unheaval from the pampa. The political problem became an economical one when the emphasis was shifted to the sources of production. The new economic perspectives were still infused with the same political substance; the site for the federal government and the distribution of wealth were the same perennial problems of metropolitan hegemony over the provinces and of the cities against the prairies and the desert. The termination of the Paraguayan war had concluded an economic disaster. An entire loan destined for public works and sanitation was invested in the war, and the national treasury went broke. The preparations for the war with Chile followed the crises of 1873 and of 1880, like the fire that follows bad business.

The wars were a cause of impoverishment, but impoverishment was just as often the cause of wars.[2] The war with Chile was avoided, although at the price of substantially increasing expenditures in weapons. It would have been to our advantage to wage war and to lose it. Terry comments on the subject: "The war of the past was replaced by the longest and bloodiest economic, financial, and monetary crisis registered in the history of civilized humanity, with further complications arising in the years of armed peace." That is the second truth: the peaceful aspect of strained postwar peace.

Forces that were oriented only for attack and a defense system based on aggression led to a Bacchanalia where the abundance of resources was feigned; in truth it was no more than an abundance of vigor and of combativeness. In 1888, the economic unruliness

[2] The civil wars created today's largest fortunes, except for the ones that have diminished from generation to generation because of the heir's irremediable incapacity. During those unfortunate years, subsidiary industries were developed that achieved a sudden flourish and a prolonged existence: tanning industries, blacksmiths' shops, saddleries, and the weaving and manufacturing of clothes. Rosas owned a factory in Santos Lugares and employed over six thousand people in making uniforms and in checking appurtenances and weapons. Men and women formed an industrial city, and even children emulated the adults. Work became a struggle and a game. The ludicrous industry of toy weapons was also exploited, although it had to be prohibited by the imposition of fines and by arrests due to the frightfully increasing number of fights among children.

was the mirror image of yellow fever and cholera. The government and the citizens participated in the orgy within their respective spheres. Any notion of dignity, of responsibility, or of honor was lost; everyone urgently grabbed what he could, robbing his own house and his own city. Banks openly granted credit and opened accounts for anyone; victims of the collective delirium, they contributed to increase the frenzy by reflection. Paper money and mortgage notes were issued without backing. The mortgage note was a true national symbol because everything was mortgaged, even the paper money; and the creditor was an unknown banker. No one ignored that the issues, the notes, and the property values were a lie and a fraud; but they were openly received and traded in a counterfeiter's game. From 1887 to 1888 the funded debt reached 227 million pesos, that is, 87 million more than up to that time. Sarmiento calculated the external debt in 1885 at 300 million pesos, and, parodying a popular quatrain with his tart humor, he wrote, "Silence, the great debtor of the South peeps into the world." Sarmiento, incapable of administering his poor possessions, was part of the financial scandal because of his eagerness to make the country as great as he wished. His successors, who also wished to make the country great, continued to cast it headlong into ruin. In 1900, the funded external and internal debt exceeded 390 million pesos gold. Such a fictitious state of finances and of the economy, typical since 1829, led to disorderly private as well as governmental expenditures.

Basically, in that type of disaster, the worst loss is moral decadence, the unfavorable balance for honesty. The squandering of money by the banks produced from 1889 an equivalent waste in consumption. Private life had molded itself to the immoral forms under which the banks operated. Government and banks became public schools of scandal and dilapidation: they taught how to degrade oneself. No one knew what was the real worth of money, or what were the legal limits for earning it or for protecting it from loss. As with the gambler and the bandit, possession was an excuse for unleashing suffocated instincts. Faced with the difficulty of dealing in gold, people used chips, and the false values slaughtered the authentic gold pieces with impunity. Work began to be scarce, but the unemployment was not so much a true reflection of absent opportunities as of a paralysis resulting from the maladjustment in previous years. Reality was beginning to inspire horror, and it was presumed wiser to distort it through those indecent short cuts. But reality was inexorably imposing itself in spite of the ravings of imagination. Those splendid disguises designed to cover up the ominous reality could justly be called "fantastic creations of imaginations sick with fear."

The appraisal of morality and of intelligence is debased by the disproportionate luxury and by the loss of the realization of the true value of money and of things; these are collective responses to a sudden escape from danger. Europe fell into a similar delirium during the black plague; after the last war there was a renewal of that inflation of signs foreign to culture and to civilization. Who knows to what extent contemporary industrial fever and the thirst for expeditions, for discoveries, and for great mercantile enterprises are a result of those medieval nightmares. Among us, the yellow fever and the cholera produced their moral epidemics without anyone having written a *Decameron*. Here, the horror of death and the certitude of the transitory nature of existence gave birth to the economic immorality parallel to the immorality of customs. The purpose of our efforts is wealth and not life itself.

VI · PSEUDOSTRUCTURES

16 THE FORMS

Cells and Alveolae

A code of laws and a honeycomb are structures corresponding to two types of activities that detail a vivid and methodical history. The honeycomb is a materialized form of group instinct where labor is oriented in a precise direction; a code of laws is also a materialized form of an idea of order and of justice, likewise oriented in a precise direction. Both are a result of a slow process of crystallization and they obey an internal symmetry and method similar to geologic formations or osseous systems. Whatever the value of these forms in the fate of the species—anatomical or mental—they obey an intrinsic need for economy, for meaning, and for experience. They constitute somewhat rigid structures, like the vital and specialized organs of each individual. Within those forms, as inside a body, the action and the evolutionary process of beings find their natural limitations and their strengths. Thus, the infinite possibilities of shapes may be reduced to inextricable, logical, and concrete limits; natural laws impart a fixed direction to the activity. If man would seriously attempt to fulfill his destiny, the infinite causes that force him into other forms of existence would disappear. Within the general structures there are others, concentrically arranged, that delimit a microcosm of infinite forms; these are treated by Simmel in his definition of social circles whose interweaving gives origin to the inexhaustible variety of the themes of life. Each institution, each code of laws, and each honeycomb is a structure, as are morality, religion, language, and all the other families in which signs of civilization or of mere vegetative existence are grouped. It is possible to obtain adult structural forms by crystallization; but, they may also be incorporated by adaptation and be respected as the *sine qua non* of existence. Doubtless, this is the form that constitutes man's totality of life and has overlayed specific norms with others based on convention—mainly education and experience accompanied by their primordial hereditary élan. At birth, man finds his niche within society, and he is imprisoned by the inflexibility of the material and psychic alveolae within which will develop his being and his potential, thus contributing to the increasingly inflexible crystallization of those forms which acquire, as they age, the destiny of a cosmic fatality. Therefore, the degree of civilization may be appraised by the number of forms that have reached the critical point of crystallization while the people simultaneously strive to free themselves and to submit themselves to those norms. Although seemingly foreign to them, they are constituted by a substance that secretes a truly free perspective, rich in possibilities and seeming to envelop them; the outlook unrestrained by those forces seems more graceful and appears to offer a greater number of promises. That possibility of variation and of change, in a capricious metamorphosis, carries the imprint of the perishable, the superficial, and the ludicrous sign within its own fickleness. But, whatever does not crystallize into a concrete shape, whatever does not live beyond its individual life, disappears, leaving at best in the history of the species the sketch of a vain attempt that could well have been beautiful and charged with admirable possibilities. Thus die the extraordinary and teratological beings; the future does not open for them without limits.

Parallel to the crystallographic development of social structures there may occur similar variations, which, at a given moment, may assume the appearance of concrete structures. These are the pseudostructures, firm in the basic outlines of their physiognomies, but hollow in meaning and in substance. They could become orthopedic substitutes for the missing vital organs, but in the long run they cause irremediable damage; the failure and collapse of a segment of that reality may be observed at any time, yet the causes of decrepitude will remain well hidden. Because they are not born from the totality of instincts and attitudes but assume a borrowed crust, they function with a certain anomaly and maintain a precarious equilibrium; the profound observer notes the slopes and deviations, and at times he may be able to detect the weak points along which the fractures are likely to occur. To substitute those technical and natural organizations composed by the anthropological contribution of the infinitesimal sum of individual efforts, we have erected—with the influx of talented men, with the varied and contradictory contribution of the immigrant, and with the adaptation of the native—false forms that are not in accord with environment, life, or national orientation; the resulting asymptotic curve constantly forces the artificially drawn figure to acquire a heretical and schismatic aspect. Lacking ancestral alveolae, we had no other recourse. We ended up with cheap imitations instead of well-formed crystals. We purchased ready-made honeycombs; whatever may be the degree of usefulness and service of those substitutes, they are no more than mere receptacles for inorganic, formless, and fermentable contents. The error—if it can be called that when an overwhelming need forces its acceptance without choice—has been in wanting to adapt with too much haste and excessive rigidity the logical and ineluctable forms of other media to our own, where the natural temper of the inhabitants and the unlimited amplitude of the horizons are oriented in peculiar directions. It would suffice to give one example. Religion, for instance, although it is not the most fundamental or typical theme, has nevertheless reached a point of colloidal density. Among us, religion is a formula and not a bond of faith, an individual belief and not a social force; the lack of faith is one of its outstanding characteristics. Liturgy and the exterior of religion, ecclesiastical doctrine, and the political aspects of social and catechetical action overpowered the embryos of mystical fervor. The environmental elements that could nourish the religious subconscious were absent; the believer found himself in a dilemma with a tradition that did not concert with any of life's external signs and a reality that repelled the chronic forms of Catholicism: the cathedral, the museum, and the weft of cultural, ethical, and sentimental tissues of which it is a fatidical consequence. We fought for religion, but it was a political fight where the shouts of "Long live religion!" and "Down with the heretics!" were used in an attempt to oust Rividavia's system of government and to impose Urien's. More than a system of government, it was one of political ideas; neither that system nor the religion that served as its prop had any kinship with the religion based on faith. The manner in which we lived and fought for freedom to shape our society had nothing to do with Catholicism. From this fact stem the arduous efforts of such patricians as Moreno and Monteagudo to simultaneously reform the historical and the spiritual traditions. Religion became consolidated and was the State's official cult and a secret and omnipotent force in the institutional and administrative arena; but, beneath the conquering framework lies a suffocating, living body that is pressing along the armor's points of least resistance in the hope of making it yield to the unfolding of the cloistered energy—which someday will free itself or it will die.

The Spirit and the Letter of the Law

The man of the pampa felt the full weight of the law before he understood it. To his extended and formless soul, law meant everything that signified obstacles, persecution, prohibition, and unappealable spoliation. He considered the law as a new world of written difficulties that stood in opposition to his will to triumph and to his instinct for preservation. In the open fields, solitude and the knife were his defense. Later, he experimented with ways of eluding punishment by learning about the law: he could evade it if his specific case had not been foreseen. Knowing the law and how to escape through its crevices became the surest safe-conduct to violating the law; usually, those who cheat also write the laws. To be able to live without startling surprises it was necessary to be up to date on the details about ordinances, edicts, and empirical jurisprudence and to know how the law could be evaded with a timely dodge. Without a code of laws, a society would not be viable; neither would one that strictly ruled its everyday acts by such a code. The juridical state should correspond to the essence of the social conscience, be accepted as a moral ideal, and represent a utopian order within a real order. In no case can it appear to be—even though it may be so in reality—a coercive system opposed to or violating the normal flow of life, because the automatic resistance would shake off the law as easily as a bothersome articulation. A people incapable of living in accord with the intimate principles of justice is unworthy of possessing equitable laws; that is to say, it deserves to exist outside the law. A code of laws should be the glorification of common practices, a case of appeal for correcting deviations considered pernicious to the society's integrity and health. Its existence should not even be noticeable, like that of a healthy viscera. If the laws are not inscribed on a people's soul and if the familial and public institutions do not offer a propitious field for their application, the state maintained by the force of law is a false one. The flow of life is subject to variations and sinuosities that may steer it away from the course of law; the most sensible thing from a moral point of view would be to open the floodgates and let it find its own natural level. Justice in life is not a written justice; what matters are the dictates of one's conscience. People, although they mean well, seek respect by pushing into areas forbidden by the laws of nature instead of seeking an intimate accommodation in time and space.

The adoption of a system of government and the ratification of perfect laws can be the most serious ethical, intellectual, and political links in the chain of a people's existence. Each society requires its constitution and its laws; if the citizenry cannot conceive of existence without them, it is because a people that has strayed far from the focus in which life and law form a unit cannot be imagined; the possibility that such a people could suddenly achieve a juridical form is rejected. When young nations adopt laws, disorders may arise from the incompatibility of the written law and the vital law, as revealed by incomprehensible ruptures in the social structure. A discontented reality, forcibly contained, bubbles under the legal appearances. The man who in such circumstances rises against the law, whether or not in some variation of Masaniello or of Karl Moor, is in the right, according to the long, instinctive rhythm; sympathy is on the side of the transgressor. The hero embodies the ideal of rebellion; the employee who embezzles and is caught in the act is awaited at the police station by an admiring and cheering public.

We have struggled for many years to achieve a political and social order to impose on the disordered colonial inheritance. We did not advance by a gradual process, but by violent annexation until Vélez Sársfield established a canon that doubtlessly coincides with the most imperative juridical principles. However, attempts to apply them caused the proliferation of a fauna of stratagems considered as legitimate defenses by the wounded apocryphal interests. Any imposition engenders such a recalcitrant proliferation. Franz Werfel has indicated that within the snob there is potentially an evasive, tangential force opposed to his ancestors, his country, and his person: the suicidal form of three basic feelings in man's life. Jung and Adler have elaborated this point and directly applied it to the study of social phenomena. Snobbery, apparently so obscure and therefore more suggestive, is the destructive force—subjected but not defeated—under the guise of civilization and against which it slowly and constantly struggles, as in the classic example of Burnouf's fig tree. Thus considered, snobbery and barbarous law are components of other more serious and less concrete forces; the depracatory word and the deceitful technique are applied by antonomasia to these less literary and less frivolous forces.

They are states of discomfort in their respective spheres, of the inadaptability of the ego to society's fundamental forms in time, space, and consciousness. They signify social states and not individual ones, with each individual being a receptacle of the collective subconscious. These forms reveal themselves under the most remote and contradictory appearances. Depending on the social class, sex, age, and attitude, those dissident forces may give rise to the criminal, the fraudulent being, and in general the antisocial element, which, nevertheless, is a genuine product of the social forces in tension. Such surreptitious violence may take the form of prostitution, of litigation, of the lack of respect for friendship and for the achievements of others, of excessive ambition, or of the craving for power without accompanying ideals. When the phenomenon covers an extensive area and becomes a dominant characteristic, the defect is usually manifest in the social structure. A social structure that imposes its laws as affronts to individual freedom, that restrains what nature offers abundantly and what the environmental factors inscribe on consciousness as unimpeachable rights, is a fictitious structure. From nature's point of view, social organization is a systematized anomaly. Law and nature, law and man, and law and customs are in perpetual and unmistakable friction. Law is defeated in such a state of discordance; the form of the defeat is not that of an insurrection or of a crime, but of the appearance of parasitical pseudolaws, of ingenious stratagems and tricks that are used to perpetrate a fraud. The parasitical laws may also be observed in the interpretation, in the exegesis, which is also a resource of the vital force deployed against the written force. The good lawyer is not the one who makes justice triumph, but the one who knows how to use the law to evade it. He becomes the sophist of juridical dialectics, like a standard-bearer for life's dark and latent forces. Written law and heterodox law begin to operate as rivals: the logic of sophistry against the logic of reason. The secret affirmation of the conscience seeks to satisfy its anxieties and labors for the triumph of its dark concept of animal justice. It concludes by forming an apocryphal code of laws, infinitely more complicated and captious, which ends by displacing written law and its orthodox interpretation in the name of

"a better law." The appeals that then result from the fracturing of
the law appear as forceful impositions; on the one hand, they pro-
voke the citizen's frank rebelliousness and, on the other hand, the
lawyer's renewed captious dialectic. The attorney defending a disreputable personage has to be aware of the law's complexities; his
art of evading the law is more complex than the law itself. That
insidious system with its complicated procedures designed to deform by equivocation the spirit and the letter of the law emanates
from the original source of discontent: from the mass, the people's
ajuridical and even unjust consciousness. The voice of that mass
is the attorney at the service of the devil; but, the technique of the
courtroom rebounds and infiltrates everyday life like booty that is
sneaked into the cave. Even family life is impregnated by that
skepticism arising from the fragility of the law; family relations
take on overtones that can only be perceived by a foreigner's eye
—accustomed to another panorama. The legal precepts invade the
dictates of the conscience, and they give each life its particular
tone and key, as sometimes can happen when man is conscious of
the meaning of sin. Marriage loses its meaning as a union and becomes a silent partnership; the bonds between father and son become weakened by being limited to rights and obligations, losing
the primitive and intangible factor that makes the relationship
sacred. The ardent desire to be successful leaves no intermediate
alternative between the extremes of poverty and ignorance and of
wealth and wisdom. Knowledge gives rights, possession gives
rights, being a husband gives rights, and being a father gives rights.
A sense of a hierarchical perspective is lacking; justice and injustice, ethos and pathos are not clearly defined. Wife abandonment,
disloyalty, shielding of the protégé at the expense of the outsider's
legitimate rights, usurpation of positions requiring competence, or
penetrating the legislature by the use of fraud become legal acts in
the context of ambiguous life and jurisprudence where morality is
not protected. The examples in our midst are numerous: the vio-
lation or dubious interpretation of the constitution, the imposition
of executive power over the tribunals, the idiosyncrasy of lawsuits,
the appearance of parasitical and fraudulent theories, and the im-

punity of action; it is easy to see why justice and a sense of justice are not in accord.

People instinctively seek out the crafty lawyer and the naturalistic doctor. Even when they are right and the law is on their side, they seek the added protection of deceitful skill against fraud. The client who searches for a shady lawyer and for a quack doctor is a disillusioned man because he believes that occult forces predominate over the forces subjected to order. Our farmer and our public employee shun the true clinical examination and opt for the quack and for politics. The attorney's office, quackery, and politics are the three semidivinities that are best in accord with the popular spirit and with society's structure. The heretical trinity rules according to lateral, *sui generis* laws. The constitution established the trial by jury, but common sense has established that the administration of justice be carried out by the State's ad hoc organs, without taking the risk that juridical heresy might triumph over true rights.

Hollywood

Any artificial structure that is methodically applied, like an orthopedic apparatus, will eventually function with regularity. La Plata is a city, although it lacks a city's organic existence. It was improvised and constituted by one of South America's most powerful banks. The product of a pact, it was born of a political crisis that threatened to destroy the national organization. The bank became bankrupt, but the problem of the federal capital was resolved.

The city would crumble, become uninhabited, and the countryside would once again invade the streets if certain artificial elements supporting the city were to be withdrawn. The city was not made, it was invented. It did not achieve its size through natural growth: it was formed instantly and later had to be filled, be maintained, be lived in. Its own life was an accident. Lacking a social, ethnic, or economic mission, it was a political creation destined to carry on a metaphysical existence. Pellegrini, the juridical engineer of economic bridges, called it a miracle city. It is a miracle city, not because of the speed with which it was edified or because of the imposing buildings that were erected, but because, like miracles, it goes against the natural law and its reality is sustained by faith. Once the public buildings for the provincial administration were created, houses grew around them by mitosis. Twenty thousand cells came from a single cell; from the governmental palace came the dwellings—with the proper number of chromosomes corresponding to their species. A university was erected according to the principles of equilibrium and of didactics. Professors were imported from Buenos Aires and students were recruited from Buenos Aires and the interior. La Plata was the geometrical space, the a priori reasoning of a series of phenomena. It was also endowed with a cathedral, a packing house, and a race track. These are additional attractions designed to maintain a languishing spectacle and to attract the passer-by and the stranger. The workers, the faithful, and the dreamers frequent those places as if on a temporary visit. They go and return without having the impression of having traveled. La Plata is the most remote suburb of Buenos Aires, but the one that most resembles it because it does not have a suburban physiognomy but the integral fidelity of a traced copy. Between Buenos Aires and La Plata stretches a latifundium of over fifty kilometers, a park of Palermo, which is visited on the way. When that latifundium disappears and Buenos Aires extends to La Plata in a continuous plane as it now does to Témperley and Vicente López, the Republic's shape will be that of a continuous and homogeneous public land; we will then think that we know more and are worth more. That latifundium hints to the passenger of La Plata's municipal autonomy because it clearly stands as another city. To augment the distance that the latifundium accentuates with varied landscape and intermediate villages, the train ambles along at thirty-five kilometers per hour; space is expanded in time: eighty minutes seem to be 150 kilometers; 50 kilometers seem like three hours. The train's slowness and the lack of proper heating displaces the city in the distance and avoids the chronological superposition, which would cause the consciousness to juxtapose the two cities. We know that it takes one hour and twenty minutes to travel from one city to the other: one hour of unpopulated countryside—of jungle and of plain—and twenty minutes of country houses and poor men. The train's sluggishness and the desolation make us believe unequivocally that La Plata's life does not depend on Buenos Aires's life and that its government is independent of the Casa Rosada.

Those trains carry La Plata's dynamic population. When the six o'clock train departs, one may think—although falsely—that in La Plata only the watchmen remain and that the city recovers its monotonous rustic platitude until the arrival of the morning trains. Those travelers arrive to drink the city's blood and to eat its bread in return for granting it movement and activity. They eat it as they move from one side to the other. But, simultaneously, the city lives off its parasites—she eats them too. The trains that circulate between the parent city and its affiliate carry the soul of both cities. Its soul is in the circulation. La Plata is the shape of the city, but its spirit is in the trains. A first- or a second-class car is the meeting place of urban and peasant forms. The commuter occupies his seat and takes possession of two seats with his hat or with his books. To go to La Plata is to enjoy certain prerogatives; the splitting of one's personality demands the occupation of two seats, especially if one has two jobs. People sit at ease; they relax because they are going outward, to the suburbs of the metropolis—as when one wears a scarf when going to a ranch. The citizens wearing boots and wrist watches are both masters and guests of the train. By the looks on their faces, it is easy to distinguish those who travel for circumstantial reasons and those who journey from their homes to work. The trains are full of students, public employees, politicians, ranchers, lawyers, and people who speak loudly as they look about them to ascertain whether their importance is recognized by the crowd. The people feel important; some talk and others are immersed in reading; the beggar collects the abundant coins of vanity from all. Whoever habitually travels to La Plata is two, is worth double. If they were more humble or if they considered the train merely a train, La Plata would become indignant of its inhabitants.

The honorary daily citizens are endowed with the importance that La Plata confers on them, and vice versa. There is a tacit pact, for if the spectacle is to maintain its doctoral tone, it is necessary to underline each other's importance.

The Mirrored Plane

Since there are no corpses underfoot and since it is better not to look back at history and at genealogy, the most judicious attitude is to look forward, toward the future. One must speak of a tomorrow and forge a reality out of the future. Our future consists of our flight from the past; it is the fear that looking backward will turn us into salt. Therefore, it is not a future that necessarily issues from our present, but one irrationally constructed over nothingness, with materials transferred from the demolition and shifted about like chunks of masonry. The whole future is the result of lacking a past. But the imprecise shape of the future, the future not conditioned by the present, is the hazard, the reign of chance and the will for "another life." The restless man, the man who is afraid because he is floating between a dark yesterday and a hypothetical tomorrow, only glances at the past as he ponders the future. A nation that projects its existence into the future to eradicate an unpleasant today, not realizing that the people themselves are the roots of a powerful tomorrow, is a nation that does not adhere to life or to the eternal genealogical tree. The certain and the good seem to be not far ahead; the part of the world behind us that we have never seen from our frontal, stereoscopic vision, that mysterious part with its perspective toward a psychic nadir, is the one that pushes us ahead. We live on the eve of great events, on the threshold of a tomorrow; and that tomorrow is an unknown, the tumult of a dream after a desert crossing. The dreamer is anomalous, he is not organized like a man or like a dream; he is the child of centaurs. He lives a meaningless dream; what he does has a phantasmal lack of consistency; the ideas he thinks have that asymmetrical discrepancy of one who just awakens and confuses fragments of his dream with parts of the room. The poet is not a poet, the pedagogue is not a pedagogue, and so on in succession: they are other forms incarnated under those shapes by a violent atavism, submerged to their waists in those circumstantial jobs, as the centaur is in the horse's trunk. No one is the artisan of his destiny, but the destroyer of his nemesis. What one believes himself to be is miles ahead of what one really is.

Self-confidence is lacking, and it is being progressively undermined; missing are the supports of friendship, of love, and of fondness for apparently worthless things. Without the spiritual placenta that allows man to assimilate human substance from the environment, he extracts nutritive substances from multiple beings. The hazards of tomorrow, which are made evident in the obsession for gambling and in the predominant use of intuition over reasoning, make any relationship an accidental one. Any aggregate is made up of digits, not of a global number. Everyone lives true to his destiny or he betrays it by only entering into the most superficial relationships with fellow men. Each work carries the imprint of its author's style and not, as Nietzsche used to say of great works, something of the style of the author's friends. Everyone attempts to exhibit a Sosia, reserving the original for himself; the result is a world of Allan Kardec, where the real beings and their duplicates are all intermingled, equally alive and real.

The friend is an enigma; we know nothing about him, and a great silence obliterates the important characteristics of his person. The wife is a mystery; we encountered her when she was already maturing: we have loved her openly and have agreed by mutual consent not to ask each other about the hereditary mixture of our egos. Any day, a truthful phrase will shatter that friendship, and, in an instant of profound comprehension, hate will be injected into love; and as before, we will once again be alone. The medium in which we live is full of powerful hazards, but it has acquired the consistency of a safe reality; one day, father and son, speaking confidentially, realize that they do not understand each other, that they belong to two different worlds, and that separating their blood is an ocean six thousand miles wide.

17 THE FUNCTIONS

The Advent of Machines

The machine arrived in due time, like a dramatic character making a precise entry in a well-composed theatrical presentation. First was created the mechanical work and then the machine; therefore, the machine is a synthesis and has the same right to life as man. To us it appeared urged on; it was added to the previously existent to substitute complex tools for simple ones and to relieve the tired man. The machine is only superfluous and only establishes a deadly competition in areas where man does not yet have a worthy occupation, where he himself serves as a tool. The loom, the automobile, the linotype, the adding machine, and the airplane arrived when weaving, traveling, printing, and calculating were already jobs of great importance; flesh was replaced by steel. Only the artisan was deprived of a job by the machine that destroyed a system, not a function or a structure. What is harmful is the machine's owner. The machine is only an integral part of humanity when it is logically coordinated with social life, intelligence, and effort. The most technically sophisticated machines have become leviathans that dominate man and impose on him the rude necessity to adapt or to die. The machine is still at the service of the dark forces, but it is surpassing the mortal fate of the metals from which primitive weapons were forged. The organized and mechanized capital found its expression in the machine as the mechanical and not the organic instrument, as a multiplying and not as a creative entity, as matter and not as spirit, representing will and not conscience. The machine was invented by the system of capitalized income, by experimental science, by cities, and by the most profound instincts of *Homo faber*. But its function of multiplying and of producing creates the most perfect system for destruction; the mechanical forms that those mechanisms yield and that advantageously compete with the other forms produced by nature are capital's worse enemies. The machine still defies a very vast sector of human security and well-being, but it is simultaneously resisted by all those forces which it opposes. The machine perishes outside its habitat. Its acclimatization is only feasible with an infinite variety of conditions. The machine cannot create a state of civilization, since the former is a result of the latter; the machine cannot anticipate a need, since it is a symbol and a synthesis. The manufacturing stage precedes the factory stage. The stone ax appears buried where its use signified something vital, where it was the coarse form of man's relationship with the world and a form of psychology, of politics, and of struggle. Today, the machine signifies the same; where it exists, there is something live belonging to humanity.

1. The machine should be correlated with the environment and be an organ of a necessary, precise, and productive function. If it is not, it becomes a destructive device. It can contribute to regression and to misery if it functions outside its medium.

Agriculture provides a livelihood for the farmer, but he must cultivate vast areas to obtain a small profit. Extensive cultivation is a geographical necessity; the farmer's planted area is inversely proportional to the nation's progress. Cultivation of small areas does not suffice; sowing on small tracts would not cover the costs of rent and of transport and would not compensate for work. Wheat is planted, but it means a profit only when produced in great volume. A large crop does not necessarily mean wealth: the costs of renting the field, of harvesting, of transportation, and of the meddling of intermediaries leave a meager profit. Into that primitive rural system was introduced the machine, which doubtlessly can only be justified in areas of extensive cultivation. The maintenance cost was, on the average, ten pesos per hectare; it was more prudent to abandon the tractor and to return to the horse. The machine eliminated the meager profits; the plow and the reaping hook were the most advanced types of machines compatible with our agrarian system. The open range and primitive agriculture were an urgent necessity even though they were less productive methods. We returned—as in Java, according to Spengler—to the forms of manual mechanics.

2. Another dream of the farmer in his prosperous days was the automobile. The distances are immense and the automobile was the machine for great distances. But the automobile requires a road, preferably a paved one, if driving an automobile is to be a different skill than riding on horseback. The plowing machines and the racing machines upped the price of the fields. On roads full of ruts where it is easy to become mired, the horse is the best automobile. Asphalt spreads when the custom of traveling engenders the need for a good road. The appearance of the road is less due to the transportation needs of a particular zone than to the necessity of using fewer tires. The automobile was adapted for ostentation and not for true necessity; therefore, the paved roads are constructed for touring and not for heavy transport. In the middle of the countryside, the peasant without an automobile considers himself to be poor. Those who travel by sulky belong to another category and yet they feel no rancor; they give a helping hand to the automobile stuck in the mud. A touring trip is a trip full of adventures; between Buenos Aires and Córdoba there are many leagues in which to blaspheme.

The use of the automobile is not a solution: it is a problem. Only the North American manufacturer can find a practical use for it;

its wide diffusion adds another reason to contract credit and to discount the future on an installment basis. It did not resolve a transportation problem; it passed over the empty spaces like an escape bridge. Airlines were set up for traveling to the southern coast, to Montevideo, to Chile, and to Brazil with governmental financial backing. The planes transported passengers and correspondence. But the demand was so scarce and the expenditures so disproportionate that most of the flights had to be suspended or subsidized by the national treasury. Aviation, like the automobile, was reduced to the touring phase, and it became the army's by default. The airplane only served for training and for potential raids. Neither commerce nor any type of relations between Argentina and her neighbors or the city and the countryside had a need for that type of locomotion. The ground and the water transportation were not yet resolved, and it was impossible to travel by air. La Rioja and Catamarca had no outlet for their exquisite fruits, so commercial airlines were considered. It was hoped that flying would reduce distances. The flying machine was reduced to its quality as a toy and entered a phase where the inventions that are yet unapplied are known as instruments of recreational physics. Without a doubt, the immensity of the land made people think that the vehicle for great distance would be the most appropriate one. But it so happens that our real territory is very small if we do not include that portion which flatly belongs to geography. Abstract distances cannot be measured; the most adequate use found for airplanes to date in South America is to stage bloodless revolutions.

3. A similar fate befell industrial machines. The only prosperous industries are those of tobacco, shoe manufacturing, saddlery, clothing, and preserved meat: the same ones born of civil wars. Beer and wine are also produced in great quantities, and they are, together with the sugar industry, important sectors of wealth. The machines used in those industries have a life of their own; they function automatically without needing help from the government, unlike the mired car that needs the pull of a horse. Other machines are not of this climate; they begin to function, they move their complicated mechanisms, and finally they come to a stop and must

be dismantled. To protect those machines which never become acclimatized, customs barriers are erected whose basic purpose is to balance the budgetary deficit. But the local consumption of the machine-produced objects is less than the cost of maintaining the factories. Import taxes increase, the national industries fail, and the taxes continue as if the machine, after being taken apart, were continuing to be a spectral wheel spinning in a void. The cows eat the wheelworks, and the alfalfa fields fill the dynamos. Those machines, of a mechanism as complex as that of the needs they are meant to satisfy, would distract capital that is better invested in land, mortgages, cattle raising, or grain cultivation. The pouring of capital into those genuine industries proves that the machine cannot create an economic medium and that in the struggle of forms of universal significance the less adapted succumb. Our machine is the simplest and it functions forever: the brickkiln. For the same reason the peon is our mechanic and our industrial technician. The brickkiln is a machine that transforms raw materials into other raw materials. It closes a most elementary cycle but it serves construction; the land is molded, and man is provided with walls. The peon's relationship to work is that of the brickkiln to the machine. The peon is useful for any occupation that does not require special knowledge; he works with raw material to produce raw material. He is worth the same as the horse and the crowbar on the scale of progress and of meaningful effort. He is a unit of force applied to any task and an undifferentiated state of human energy similar to that of a beast. The product of the brickkiln is a unit of labor similar to that of nature. The peon is necessary where the machine is not; he endures in a climate where the machine could not. The peon triumphs not only because most forms of Argentine ecumenical life are on his side but also because the government, even if it is desired, could not or would not know how to aid the machine and help it to triumph.

For example, in the central post office were installed machines—such as exist in only two countries of the world—for the mechanical conveyance of mail. Once installed, they occupied four of the seven stories of the building; their capacity for work was more than one hundred times what was needed. When this machinery, occupying several stories, was put into operation, the mail would disappear into tubes and conveyor belts and the employees had nothing to do except contemplate the vertiginous voracity with which the letters and newspapers were swallowed. Either five hundred men had to be fired or the machinery—which cost two million pesos—had to be stopped. It was decided to stop the machinery; in twenty years it will still have a disproportionate capacity for work. Such was the struggle between the machine and the peon. The sum of propitious circumstances was on the latter's side; the metallic cadaver of the weaker one remained as an example, undisputably defeated, hanging from four stories of a palace.

4. The weight of machinery, like the weight of civilization, should find solid support in society; no machine settles on earth but rather on the shoulders of a state of civilization. The society that incorporates the machine without having achieved a mechanical structure, succumbs under the inert weight or converts it into scrap iron. The nation that adopts the latest forms of progress and of culture, skipping the transitional stages, regresses to the primordial forms even faster than it left them. There is a hydraulic law that rules those phenomena of culture and of civilization; they cannot be created, acquired, or assimilated phenomena; they must emanate from the depths of a fixed state. If not, they are substitutes of realities, bridges uniting two extremes. The bridge is a jump, the simplest way possible to overcome a difficulty without destroying it. Beneath the bridges the rivers continue to flow and beneath the fictitious constructions reality marches on. Each phenomenon is a problem and has only one exact solution, which should be found if a lasting conclusion is sought. We have always avoided the clear statement of problems because we had at hand a repertory of ready solutions and the problems appeared to be of unpleasant simplicity. Because of these solutions previously acquired, we have not proceeded in accordance with reality. We have made our problems typical, universal problems, and vice versa, and we have tried to make the terms of the equation coincide with the solution found to those universal problems. Therefore, the solutions—which the ma-

chine obviously symbolizes—are simply evasions and bridges of
flight. By those bridges we escape from urgent reality. That process
of transferences may be observed in many other aspects. The problem of elementary education, which is the basis for the purification
of our finances, put into action by Mitre and Sarmiento and later
eluded because of misunderstood shame, led to the founding of universities. In order not to confess that over 50 percent of the population could not read or write, we founded six centers of higher
learning. The university is no more than a building where the
problems of primary education and of professional vocation do not
exist or have not been tackled in concrete terms. It is a bridge. It
was necessary to create the School of Agronomy and Veterinary
Medicine so that the School of Philosophy and Letters could exist.

5. The tenant's son usually studies medicine, and the landlord's
son normally studies law. The School of Philosophy and Letters
admitted students to its classrooms without high school diplomas;
it sufficed to present some literary work: poems published in some
magazine or a book in the current style. That educational body had
to be maintained by fiction; in the same manner, it was necessary
to resort to a stratagem to maintain a normal enrollment in engineering: the graduates were accorded a diploma in masonry. A
new engineer lacked opportunities, but students were incited by a
professional degree, which was something on the order of the
longest side of an isosceles triangle whose other two sides were the
brickkiln and the peon. Without students, the School of Philosophy
and Letters had no life of its own, and a deficit would have quickly
forced its closure; to strengthen it, fifty thousand hectares of land
were adjudicated it as inalienable patrimony. The fifty thousand
hectares formed a bond between the School of Letters and the
School of Agronomy and Veterinary Medicine—a bond symboliz-
ing their disjunction. To Philosophy flocked young men anxious to
learn, for whom the doctorate had great attraction since the days
of coddled liberality; but almost no one attended Agronomy and
Veterinary Medicine. So, experimental schools were created to give
the professors something to do and something to teach. The pro-

fessors in such a state of precarious existence, with the threat that the doors might be definitely closed, discovered another strategem. This time the stratagem was the politics whose critical point of scandal was Santa Catalina. No philosopher or naturalist has come out of those schools; but, hundreds of professors have come out, and beneath them all runs a current of reality. They symmetrically filled the pedagogical holes, according to the plan for public education. A similar statement could be made about the National Library, which since the days of Moreno has been a museum of books. The National Library is a public place where the populace has access to the works that are missing from their homes. The existence of that library seems to have relieved many people of the obligation of having at hand a small shelf with a few books; at times, conscience is discharged in an odd way. The library's pulse is synchronous with that of the Schools of Philosophy and of Veterinary Medicine; it is a place for impoverished students to consult textbooks and for old men to glance at out-of-print novels. From their shelves, which smell of a hypogeum and of greenhouses, books older than our nation watch over young people who absorb ancient emanations in the classroom. The books seem to be in their place: removed from life and from reading, they line the walls and impose silence. The orderlies come and go silently, always tired, always with the same books for the same seats. They are mummies who bring and return pieces of sarcophagi.

Next to culture's bureaucratic organs are the Schools of Engineering, Law, and Medicine. The idealists enroll in the School of Engineering; without a doubt, the soundest youths enroll in the School of Science—the art of the precise and the practical. The classrooms are full, although only engineering diplomas are granted. They know that a harsh destiny awaits a road builder when there will be no roads; it is difficult to be a technician in an environment where performing any task suffices to succeed. A degree in engineering does not bring glory or fortune; and yet, those dreamers of truth embrace that heroic career. They know that their learning will contrast with all of reality; knowledge will often have to humble itself before an experienced improviser who brandishes honors and money; but, a force born from within makes them stronger than anything else.

A career in medicine yields devotion, rank, and wealth; therefore, it is the natural path of the poor man, as a career in law is the natural path of the rich man. A career in law leads to positions in the legislature or in the courts of justice; the career has many incentives, with the preeminent positions crowning the successful life. A doctorate in law is the master key and the most probable title for important people. The school confers the degree, but it is the people who confer the deferential forms of address. The forces that conspire against the doctor and the lawyer are more appreciable; the engineer will be opposed by a structure, by an order, or by a technique; the doctor and the lawyer will be opposed by a normal state of pathological psychology, by people. Material reality rises before the engineer, but before the doctor and the lawyer rise men better structured than that reality. The competition among all will be for money and for power—such is the fruit of the seeds germinated in their spirits during long years of apprenticeship. Descending to a struggle without ideals and without fervor, the doctor and the lawyer will often consent to practicing the knaveries proper to a quack. The trouble is that science is mechanical and precise, but the reality is different; and, everything empties into politics.

6. If one retires to a sufficient distance for observing, he may note the same relationship between the doctor and the quack as between the surgeon and the slaughterman. Both are related to the almost religious figures of the past or those invested with supernatural powers. The quack was the magician, and the sacrificer of cattle was the executioner. Only ninety years ago they were the exponents of a social state that placed them on the demarcation between life and death. At the time when quackery was the only available medicine, killing cattle was the only industry. Both representative beings had their techniques, their arts worthy of respect. In the time of Rosas, incorrect slaughtering was punished. The tyrant, a master of all the ranch tasks, wrote a medical treatise in exile. Beheading became an art; the members of the Mazorca

Society boasted of hacking off a head with one blow; they were familiar with various procedures of killing and of castrating. They respected mastery among themselves, and the most outstanding among them were famous. To flay, to scarify, and to disjoint the cow was a complicated occupation; the hand rapidly became practiced at using the knife like a bistoury along the tissues to separate the fat, the meat, and the bone. Among the professionals, the delicate art of minimal movements was admired—the anatomical dexterity of the blow. Juan B. Justo compared the Chicago slaughterman to the surgeon; they both possess an art of dissection requiring a steady hand, speed, and confidence. It would be interesting to know if Chicago produces great surgeons who are perhaps as good as ours—whose renown is worldwide. But it is indisputable that Chicago may have them fifty years from now, if the butchering of cattle is not only an occupation but also a vocation.

A surgeon has nothing in common with the carver or with the butcher, but the flayer was a man of his epoch as the surgeon is the man of today. I do not believe that Juan B. Justo, who knew about surgery and about history, wished to exaggerate by comparing such extremes. Fortunately, the times when Molière mocked bloodlettings, injections, litigations, and busybodies are remote; however, we should not laugh—the kingdom of magic is not that far. The doctor and the lawyer coincide in their deviations from the strict exercise of their professions by entering politics: the science of evading dangers and of affirming the ego. The doctor finds more favor because he possesses more of the magical qualities, and he subjugates the masses with hidden powers. A doctor is always a person to whom one has to remain grateful after he preserves one's life; the less a people believes in itself, the greater its needs to believe in quacks and in politicians. The rural doctor can be a true doctor and not a quack, he may earn his salary; but the patient cannot cease being idolatrous. Two of the richest and most backward provinces have fallen into the veneration of popular idols who draw their strength from the credulity in political quackery. Not even the federal interventions have managed to weaken them.

One hundred years ago Azara called us litigants and shepherds;

but our grandfathers were more litigious than we are, and the distribution of land obliged each peasant to learn the rural code by heart. Vélez Sársfield, one of our greatest men, was not a lawyer; after a certain point in his studies, he was a self-made man. And yet, he is in a class by himself. Sarmiento, Rawson, and Mitre were expert in law, and they were doubtlessly superior to the specialists when knowledge had to be put at the service of public welfare and when the basic issues were determined by principles and not by virgules. If today the principles are not as respected, the inflation of false values is to be blamed.

Intelligence and Its Program

To have fewer universities than necessary is not an evil; probably, it is less harmful than having too many; but, who would consent to govern an immense country of unlimited prospects and only a few universities? The capacity of our universities to produce professionals is disproportionately greater than the country's demands. The ranks are further swollen by the excessive pedagogical contingent. The overproduction of professionals engenders a type of extraprofessional activity: a type of dumping also practiced by the retired military man. Unless the holder of a degree of questionable worth who finds himself detoured from his dead-end path chooses to resign himself and to succumb, he must plunge into a perfidious competition by making unethical use of his degree. It is not fair that the holder should resign himself to conserving a worn-out degree that is only respected for its potential to generate income. Professional careers are considered to be dignified and capable of providing a level of distinction and comfort; later, the unwary learns otherwise. In a moment of sincere pronouncements at the time of a toast, the minister of justice and education told six thousand jobless teachers and professors that their degrees were worthless. By methods such as these it would be useless to detour student registration into other areas—because they do not exist. The possibilities open to intelligence are limited to university studies. To appeal to politics is to take revenge against the university and against society by demanding that the diploma not be a worthless certification of the number of years and the amount of money spent. The excess of professionals is the edema of the budgets with clauses and provisions that are destined to produce useless posts: afterward, a worthless, subordinate personnel must be added to the service of those posts. Public administration supports the surplus university graduates and thus attempts to remedy mistakes. It is responsible for maintaining the professionals on a level of comfort and of honor and for aiding those who are unable to find an avenue for their professions. Teaching and administrative posts are an indirect form of indemnity paid for damages suffered; consequently, the production of professionals is continued. The State that finances schools that mislead youths in their vocational choices or that shelter students when their vocations find no other way to progress must later finance positions for those youths in order to avoid their protests against the State's irresponsible acts. By the payment of such an indemnity, the government is left alone, the universities continue to overproduce, and the young do not get discouraged as long as they are fed by the prytaneum.

When the natural inclinations are not followed, reality is ignored and false needs are manufactured. The close of each fiscal year leaves a negative balance of morality, of dismay, and of indignation that cannot be restored with a loan. The deficit weighs heavily on the young, victims of an inhuman illusion. There is no complete, continuous social scale of worth between the man with a degree and the man without one. Neither are there possibilities for life between the city and the desert. Outside the dominions of the State and without the university letterhead, intelligence signifies no more than a nuisance. It would become parched in the desert. Whatever the educational curricula may be, life teaches that the conditions for struggle are arduous and inclement; cautioned and prepared, the young people begin their careers. From their first steps they become experienced in the practices that will later prove indispensable; the good advice of older people puts them on guard.

The official program of studies is teaching's outer shell; the young people are also aware of the program of deceit, although they are not the ones to have invented it or to have discovered it. They need to arm themselves against the hidden dangers. The educational deficiencies produce the natural diastases of the student body. The young people's preceptors must have been very weak and ill-prepared to thus deform students, inculcating in them vices typical of senescence. From makeshift classes egress diffident, unenthusiastic, distrustful, and fraudulent young people. For many years, the teacher's ideal was to discourse on a subject as if addressing parliament; classes were taught to merely fill the requirements of a job, taught by those who could not attend to the multiplicities of their tasks. The students secretly scorned their professors and resorted to equivalent slyness—deceit against deceit. They listened to lectures and attended class as they did Sunday mass—without faith. A sector of politics that debased the country was labeled as the old regime; but, an opprobrious chapter was omitted in the condemnation. Perhaps it is the most irredeemable sin of several generations of incompetents who endeavored to shelter their torpidness with the moral corruption of youth. The decrepit sophists perverted the source of life, bastardizing education with politics and pointing to the doctoral profession as the only outlet for intelligence. Ignorance reigned over all but a few nuclei, and spiritual life had no other redoubt in which to take shelter or any other alternative path to follow. The preceptor had an interest in maintaining a certain degree of myopia, which would prohibit the clear perception of his defects; as a turbid committee chieftain, he would complicate the student in his maneuvers and convert him into a sectarian. Defending his professorship with the wiles of a cuttlefish, he contracted irrevocable commitments. The reciprocal connivance suited the professor and the student; both took advantage of it. But the professor consolidated his position, whereas the student was in danger of losing forever his ingenuous belief in knowledge. After a few years, the professor would gain in rank and prestige, and the student would graduate despising him. Spurred to pursue goals unrelated to studies, the student forced the academic councils to view his misunderstood notions as educational problems. He desired statutory reform to enable him to enter into the government of the institutions; finally, he fell into the gears of the political mechanism. He had to rebel against the institution in some way, even if it meant taking the buildings by assault. To pass a subject was judged to be a small victory against the professor, against education, and against the university. Even the severity of the examiners is usually conditioned by a nonexistent pact of implied transactions. Because of the excessive demands of the written curriculum—almost always different from the one taught—and the deficient instruction, the professor is respected at the end of a course as the possessor of a power that until then was not manifested. He had only partially capitulated, and now he demands reparations from the aspirant for his titles and for his social position, impaired in the course of eight months.

The student reaches the conviction that he possesses a certain amount of power, and he puts it into play during the course, as the professor does at the end. As if there really were opposing interests, the retaliation is treacherous and jovial. It is not simply the naturalness, the prank, and the good humor that are peculiar to the students since goliardic times. The force in play is festive, but it is bitter and senile and full of intimate animosities. It is a hostility spilled like vitriol over what surrounds the cult and its culture.

Good humor can madden and kill a world-renowned scientist contracted as a specialist, can cause the resignation of another, can sterilize by disappointment those who dedicate themselves to teaching with some faith. Other more skillful specialists, who do not wish to go mad, or to die, or to depart offended, submit and speculate with praise, divining tomorrow's geniuses from the shell.

In a train car, for example, the common student is startlingly transparent: he is a nebula of bad breeding and of compulsory education. The tone of voice, the gestures, and even the topic of conversation betray a group of young people who have boarded the car allied against the surrounding medium, but who are not in conflict against something they know and do not believe. They are enveloped in an aura of indifference normal for those who ignore the cost of real learning; their reaction is natural, and they enjoy crowded places with their unknown audiences. The stigmas of old regimes reappear in the adolescents; they are withered, with tired blood flowing through their new bodies. In the first place, the student seems forced to carry out a painful task, to drink knowledge although he is not thirsty. Second, he views the university studies as unstimulating, without the respect of those who do not know, and as a compulsory ascetic exercise to gain a privilege. He does not feel respect for studies nor does he believe that education is a trophic need. He sees his destiny in disjointed courses. He knows beforehand that whatever he learns is worthless if it is not strengthened by some prominent relative's influence and that later he will only be alone among equals. His incredulity in education and in culture, which are not values but levers and cranes, leads him to that lamentable skepticism manifested by rudeness, by senile facial expressions. He returns home to another world. Between the environment of the school and that of the home and the street there is a difference of temperature like that which differentiates birds from saurians. The dispersion of studies in train cars and movie houses and the influence of private conduct and of the family life on the classrooms, on the offices, and on the libraries are forces that aspire to somehow establish an equilibrium between the imbalance of the two worlds.

Excesses of Sincerity

The creole, the one who has remained unchanged since the days of the viceroyalty, has only a remote relationship to the immigrant's son. The creole is a being who is born into a constituted home and has already acquired the universal forms of Argentine life. His father is settled and is resigned to the prospects opening before him; the son is born predisposed to accept the reality, and he does not need to deform it or to extol it in order to believe in it and to show concordance.

Differing from the one who came to stay, the immigrant who

came with the idea of returning and then stayed is an unattached, impervious, and refractory being. He carries hidden intentions in his native soul, landscape, climate, and language and he is determined to return to his medium before dying. The son of this artificial being, glued onto society, is born with something untamed, evasive, and recalcitrant. He does not quite manage to enter the mainstream of Argentine life; the more he attempts to tie himself to the whole, the more he accentuates his inborn foreignness. He is not in agreement, and his general attitude, whether for or against, is an affirmation of his dissent. The immigrant's son avenges his parents if they have not fulfilled their destiny, if they have been defeated. The immigrant's son is the avenger, the eternal defender of the absent, the holder of a set of previous postulates that are discrepant with the medium, and one whose interests are not those of the community. Even when he is determined to serve the country and to behave as a proselyte, he is affiliated with a dissident lodge. When he speaks of local things, his voice reverberates with a remote nostalgia, similar to the mountain echo. He assumes his father's position in the criticizing of our accomplishments; when he is in accord, his assent is of a special aspect: he is in accord with his father. But there is another, more interesting facet: the symmetrical inverse. The immigrant's son, who participates in politics, in art, and in science perhaps because of an imperative instinct to use a destructive, corruptive, and dissolving weapon, exaggerates his patriotism, his faith, and his good will to build. As a patriot, he is excessively patriotic; he hides and ignores our defects, appeals to the irritating traps of one who violates the law to benefit a friend, and praises the national institutions until he falls into ridicule and tarnishes their prestige. He affirms as ours what is not ours, and he polishes the surfaces so much that his reflection can be seen in them. He exaggerates in the manner of one who is not entirely convinced, like a converted Jew—Torquemada—more popish than the pope. He forms a part of a society or a club and with the best intentions he corrupts it and brings it to a schism or to closure—perhaps by the desire to achieve a prosperity with excessive speed. Since he is not in agreement with the environment and he is not truly devoted to his actions, his false enthusiasm has the energy of gunpowder. And so, he destroys the native—who by his defects also contributes to the task—without wanting to, pushed by the powerful influence of the hereditary pressure of the subconscious. He characteristically oversteps his authority, and he is acclaimed as the originator of new ideas, as the pioneer of fruitful action, when in reality he is sponsoring worn-out ideas and working with inert forces.

18 THE VALUES

The Mythology of Values

The forging of myths is an intrinsic necessity of the thought process, to such a degree that even the arts only unveil a fragment of the human capacity in that direction. Myths are forged from reality's formless leftovers, conceived during the effort to order reality. Floating in a mass of metaphors and untuned errors, those phantoms perform their demoniacal jests. Even in unemphatic conversation, overlaying the solid foundation of pure and diaphanous ideas there are—as at the end of platonic dialogues—minor myths symbolic of a state of mind, of conscience, and of reasoning that psychoanalysis has investigated as a polypary of extravagant excrescencies. It is the everyday heaven, the natural medium in which the mythical ideas are born, in which they develop and die. But, that mythology forged by the popular imagination and those tangible ghosts conferring upon or denying prestige to people and institutions are the leftovers from the sphere of perfected ideas and feelings. They are the gods and the devils who comprise three-fourths of what we do, feel, think, and speak—the true adjectives and adverbs of the pure language of ideas. In this sense, morality, rooted prejudices, tradition, respect, opinions, proverbs, and all manner of commonplaces in the psychic inflorescence possess a quality of mythological entities, of specters of abolished forms of thinking and of living. If the mechanics of social and psychic life are considered from that angle, the garment is invested with the category of fetish. Such a personage lives within his garment as in a natural medium from which he could not be extracted without detriment to his organization, to his significance, and to his existence. For example, the more a politician attempts to indelibly engrave his image in the electoral mass, the more he accentuates his fetishistic quality until his physiognomy, his height, and his tone of voice become a real complement of his dress. A change of glasses, a shave, or a different suit, shoes, and hat would impair the profiles of the most famous literary, political, and social personalities. It is not in vain that the most ambitious, those who hope to awaken fanaticism rather than admiration, perpetuate themselves with a gesture and with a garment that seem to be eternally the same. They continue being symbols as long as they are wrapped in the garment, which acquires the supplementary significance of ecclesiastical robes. The liturgy is composed of the house in which they live, the comforts they enjoy, their friends, and the stereotyped phrases with which people and events are judged. All this is intended to secure the rigidity of purpose, the ideal. The mythical becomes a supervaluation on a magical level, the somatic aura and the cervical halo that illuminate the restricted body and the strict spiritual preparation. The mythical passes from the individual to the environment and impregnates the cities, the corporations, and the entities—similar to the nimbus of Antigone. The mythical citizens are endowed with a superlative meaning that corresponds not to their importance and significance but to the degree of idolatry of the masses. They engender a multitude of erroneous opinions and of apocryphal emotions, which Lord Bacon classified in four large groups: *idola tribus, idola specus, idola fori,* and *idola theatri.* With that criterion, fundamentally intuitive and hypnotic, one can praise or destroy a business, a cigarette brand, a poetry book, a science prize, or a reputation. In the mythical mental state judgment is made by appearances and impressions created by objects. The mental effort of weighing and calibrating, of disintegrating a concept, or of separating the overtones within a synthetic judgment is a development of advanced civilization because without a doubt, as Nietzsche said, culture consists in affixing an infinite table of values. As we descend along the scale of human sophistication, as we regress from the capacity to discern, as the ingredients of elementary analysis are gradually limited, and as we move toward coarse and disjunctive concepts, we retrace the gradation of the species. Good and bad, black and white, hot and cold are the forms of conceiving a world reduced to two dimensions. The empire, or organized matter, of the great theogonic gods precedes pullulation of the minor, domestic, infinitesimal gods; each one of these figures is the condensation of the intellectual work of centuries. Mythology is a vocation and an essential item for filling the gaps in the structure and in the harmony of the mental cosmos. With the formation of a few idols, composed within our view, religious archeology and ethnology can obtain precise data; but, unquestionably, in that crystallization of the Salzburg branch of values many more beautiful themes are sacrificed for a happy and positive development. When the country's historical heroes are attributed unwithering qualities, they become elevated to the rank of divinities that are neither loved nor feared. To introduce the meaning of history into primary education and to explain the significance of events and the geographical context is to contribute to the romance of myths. After the initial presentation of the myth, certain types of judgments may result that obstruct or facilitate other mental functions applied to the most dissimilar contemplations. History is at times falsified or its real meaning is altered under the pretext of strengthening the national spirit.

Those myths sprout spontaneously, procreated by word and by tradition, although more regularly they are transmitted by the teacher's authority and the catechumen's good faith. The orators, the writers, and the rulers are forgers of infernal myths and of lares and penates. When not countered by honest judgment, their influence is capable of orienting in a particular direction, in accord with the charisma of a leader or with any given purpose. The masses rake up those words and gestures and live in their function, as they think in function of the spoken language.

Naturally, on this conceptual level one is dealing with the formation of transpersonal myths, as the *Quixote* is with respect to Cervantes. Our country's forefathers do not belong to mythology; their actions perhaps do pertain to that sphere; but the works to which they gave life and their example and their teachings fall entirely within the realm of mythology. Rivadavia, Sarmiento, Mitre, Rawson, Avellaneda, Pellegrini, and a few others created myths in that they introduced, as Argentine dogmas, foreign idols that did not address the national faith. They managed to stir admiration and adoration for the simulacra of institutions that existed in other Olympic countries but not in this impetuous nation of urgent needs. Whenever they found that we lacked some organ that functioned well in other latitudes, they squeezed its image into the gap. In such a way the Romans constructed the pantheon on the cell of the aboriginal gods. But, whereas in ancient times they were living gods, participating in the struggles of Trojans and Greeks, here they were sterilized, mummified divinities imported by contraband. With a fixed table of values and under the label of Civilization, the propitious divinities were being forged. Simultaneously, the local, autochthonous idols, considered to be Barbarity, were being dethroned. However, only the barbarian's liturgy was changed, not the substratum of his religious idolatry; faith was not embodied in the divinities, but in the ritual and in the icons. The pantheon of those phantasmal myths had no meaning, no vitality, and no demiurge. Nevertheless, these divinities were believed in and worshipped. The rite of that mythology of the new gods of culture was organized, and the service was taken over by the bacchantes. But, as in some liturgical symbols where it is possible to trace remnants of the phallic cult and of human sacrifices, so in the techniques of promoting, sheltering, and defending the symbols of culture it is possible to track the vestiges of the primitive exploited divinity. Those deities—university, bank, industry, literature, and others—will be deforming themselves soon in a regression to ancestral forms, according to a process that Mendel first studied; in the end, it will be most difficult to separate the hybrid forms from those of a pure genealogy. The gods have assumed the forms of their vaulted niches.

The mythical language is the most adequate for the discussion of myths, and it is necessary for profound mutual understanding.

The Defensive Transferences

The fear of ridicule becomes a defense mechanism through the daily exercise of artificial postures. It is born from the attitude of living as spectators-actors, somewhat withdrawn from intrigue, with coldness and suspicion. The ridicule into which the ingenuous person falls always requires the indulgence necessarily conceded to the stiltlike movements of wading birds. If it is true that the sublime and the ridiculous are but a step apart, grief is very close to the comical; there is an element of the grotesque in the eyes of the contemptuous spectator who witnesses a mother crying for her lost son. But the human element can never be completely lost; the total repression of feelings and the placid observation of suffering betray the temperament of a jobless actor. From the systematization of that imperious attitude is born the fear of ridicule: a state of mistrust that betrays its own ridiculousness. The person who constantly pretends without knowing it, without authenticity, at every moment conjectures the smile of the one who is aware of his true position. That attitude of the actor unsure of himself, of the hypocrite, implies the consciousness of an existing, substantially superior state. The jest is the defensive attitude par excellence. There is no better way to hide a meanness than to turn it into a joke. Homer already described the foul-mouthed mimic who takes advantage of a propitious occasion to insult the majesty of Thersites. Basically, the jest is a stratagem to distract from the fundamental, the recourse to which the hypocrite appeals when he is about to be unmasked, the annoying twitter of a bird. By means of a jest, the serious reality is given a humorous disguise, it is torn away from the human plane and elevated to the plane of fiction.

There is a histrionic quality in every troublesome person; this histrionism and cynicism are part of the struggle of life. To triumph, one must begin by rejecting one's own esteem and the value of one's goods; this rejection may be achieved through heroism and histrionic baseness. The actor is a wonderful defender of his own personality; the tendency to joke is a net of wire entanglements. Another theatrical being is the one who confesses that he is inferior to any position he may occupy; for him, the joke is an evasion, a dodge, a means of detouring the center of interest. The opposite pole is heroism, which for a life without stature is simply the external importance of the position. A public employee, the one manufactured by the grace of a friend's influence, covers himself with a mask of dignity and waits in the expectancy of the ridicule that he thinks will crop out in the slightest insinuation by word or by gesture. His parsimony as a man on guard places him out of reach of the well-aimed shots, and the fear of ridicule leads him to the ridiculousness of leaning on the prestige of his appointment.

In many cases the duties have become technical by that same force of circumstances which creates a diabolical problem of knots from a long thread. The public employee who is faced with discharging the duties of a position is, from the moment of his appointment, the actor in his part; I use this example because Argentine life is the public administration. Napoleon was Napoleon even in Saint Helena, but a general fabricated in an agreement of ministers is but a cheap imitation of a general. A senator may know that he is the product of a fraud or that he lacks senatorial substance; so, he answers recriminations with sarcasm or he hides behind privilege. The general walls himself behind stripes and erects a palisade of hierarchies and of army roles; the senator hides behind his bench and waits out the twenty-four hours that unfailingly signal the prescription by neglect. When a section chief who has been exalted by committee maneuverings is caught in misconduct, he closes his eyes and shouts his approval of the party that protects him and of the president who named him. These three actors of low caliber are the protagonists of our comedy of power; as beings beyond ridicule, they preach by the example of their success that the true ridiculousness lies in living honestly and in resigning oneself to correctly redeeming the role for which one was born.

Historiography

Historical investigation, authentication of documents, and the search for the exact datum in the archives resulted in a methodical arrangement of materials that was called history. The research was not directed to rectify or to distil history, but to make it. The function creates the organ. As the number of parts utilized increased and the various parts were classified, history expanded in volume, in strength, in physiognomy, and in meaning. Events were bent out of shape by the weight of the documents; the importance of events was being slowly diluted, and interest was abating proportionately. The method became the substance. Our history is to be found in ethnography and in paleontology, more so in the latter because of its area, specimens, and importance; the historian limited himself to the spadework of digging for fossils in the libraries' buried treasures. Data are gathered in the same manner as stamps are collected or hectares of land and heads of cattle are accumulated; the materials sought are called history, and the workmen collecting them are historians. There is no history, but, with the existence of historians, sooner or later there will have to be a history, as when there are witches there must be demons by intrinsic necessity. Biography has been the best form of history, from *Facundo* to *Belgrano*, with various autobiographical memoirs; the rest is an inventory of the chattels of the hero's home. The accuracy of a datum is only significant in relation to the importance of the event. And there will be no history, even if its study is carried out according to the most rigorous scientific methods, if there is no basic substance.

After sifting through a pyramid of inexpressive and contradictory materials, the merit lies in the work and not in the mine. Since the events do not have a historical meaning, it is necessary that abundance become important, thus converting the problem of confrontation into one of ontology. Using the same system, a literature has been invented that does not exist; the materials compiled would be rejected as marginal or negative to true literary history wherever it exists. Only where there is no literature or esthetics can those works become histories of literature and of esthetics. Much more important than Argentine history is its historiography; the history of historians does arouse interest. It is incomprehensible that such an inversion of the true values of culture could be reached, such a systematic tergiversation of what signifies civilization, greatness, transcendental event, historical physiognomy, humanity. If Nietzsche could discover obstacles of this type in historical studies—even though he was referring to investigations conducted in the richest deposits—we may speak of obstacles that history presents to the discipline of intelligence and to character formation. Within the cauldron of authentic history, the methods of order, of analysis, and of authentication inevitably led to the rigid forms of embalming specialists. The methodology, unable to base itself on meaningful events and purposes, leads to nontranscendent simulation of history, to its fraudulent practice. The end result of extensive research is a falsification of the meaning of events and the distortion of historical personalities. Logic and didactics replace the nonexistent human truth about affairs and personages.

No one has told the truth about Alvear, Pueyrredón, Rondeau, Güemes, Mitre, Urquiza, Lavalle, Dorrego, and Rosas. Their authentic figures are taboo. Not even Paz withstands an exhaustive analysis without becoming diluted in the tumult of contradictory and disorderly actions. Except for military history, the history of neither commerce, nor culture, nor diplomacy, nor politics has yet achieved the category of historical processes—not even the category of subjects.

Not all countries have produced history; some make history, some live it, and others falsify it; we write it. In general, South

American history pauses at the threshold of history, and its cultural interest does not go beyond the last chapter of prehistory. Our greatest historian was Ameghino. Lafone Quevedo and Outes are closer to history than the professors who elaborate it and then explain it. Those who have prepared a didactic history that is of no interest outside the nation's geographical boundaries, outside classrooms or political circles, mint coins of clandestine circulation; they are true counterfeiters of legal and universal standards because they stamp their own effigies on the coin and leave blank the exergue, as if they were preparing their own pedestals.

Caricatures

When a new age dawned for business, construction, and transportation, sexual mores cloaked themselves with excessive dignity. To bury the past, walls were erected in the present. Sex became confined; it was prohibited to speak of and to allude to such topics; another taboo was added to the many we already possessed. Chastity became the norm for sensuality; the woman embodied, at a somewhat untimely moment, the classical virgin and mother.

Our girl is virtuous and she guards her virginity with heroic integrity. She has not ceased to be old-fashioned and already she is modern; she superimposed her feelings of Castilian honor with the latest finery. She smokes, she wears short hair, she exhibits her leg up to her thigh, she wears a transparent crinoline, and she lines her eyes to hint of a sleepless night. She appears to be a worldly woman, but beyond the superficial shell of the aphrodisiac that she offers lies an incorruptible vestal. The movie houses and the fashion plates show a phase of that courageous postwar life in North America and in Europe; but, she thinks that a change in customs is merely a change in style. She knows all the refinements of concupiscence and the erotic novels; she uses cosmetics and make-up that are cruelly employed in a frivolous exhibition; in the company of respectable relatives, on beaches, in sweet shops, in salons, and in clubs she imitates a risqué style of life. But, whereas the liberal woman from whom she copied those attitudes and temptations surrenders herself to her lover, she resists and retains her honor. The second phase of the movies and of the illustrations is left in charge of other unseen women.

She adopted the outward appearance of the movie vamps and the manners of the variety show artists without in any way abdicating her role as the poor damsel of the Spanish theater. She is pure because she remains enclosed behind a grating; the disguise she wears is not what she is, or what she would like to be, or what she has seen models wear in fashion shows. The brave insinuation in the style of the flapper and of the demimondaine is an ostentation of cowardice that characterizes the bigoted woman devoid of generosity and of beauty. She does everything the women do who lead an easy life but surrender herself. If she has already fallen —to use the language of our comic puritans—she pretends with renewed tenacity the comedy of an unblemished honesty. Once again she dons the disguise of standard honesty. But those censured forces do not submit willingly; they have to break out into anomalous social structures, discharging their duties in the establishments of illicit love.

The faults that she so artfully dodged—as if in a game reminiscent of the bullfight—fell back on society. The revenge of the collective nemesis took many forms: prostitution to which were delegated imperious duties, fomenting its inconceivable propagation; matrimony as a Caudine gallows; monogamy without vocation for fidelity; adultery judged to be deserving of the death penalty; the absorption of the liberal professions into teaching; the invasion of sports stadiums. The average morality achieved was much above normal; the home was consolidated, the woman was respected, and the son had an assured name and education; but, none of these benefits was achieved without the fermentation of perhaps greater evils. Those structures which advanced under a process of magnetization of exotic elements in the social order signified repressions similar to those of the libido; their neuroses were visible in buildings, revolutions, hospitals, work, and culture. Repressed sex took the shape of immense institutional organs and of complicated locksmith's works. Appearance mattered above truth, the shell more than the juicy pulp, until virtue wrapped in an impenetrable network was valued more than the healthy and sincere voluptuousness of joyful youths devoid of mental and utilitarian perversions.

With some careful observation, one may note the same phenomenon in other manifestations of life; when there is no basic substance, when the purity of legal structures can only be ascertained after the closest examination, then we live in an era where we have given values to masks, to phantoms, and to legerdemain. To observe this falseness, it suffices to amble along the streets. The buildings that have a more or less pure style are the ones out of tune. The totality presents a motley language of architectural forms; the pure style represents the same as affected words in disuse. The real style is the promiscuity of many; therefore, the unadulterated style projects artificiality.

We call natural that which is false because we are insensible to esthetic feelings that, for example, provoked an almost physiological repugnance in Ruskin when he viewed stone and marble imitations and the general mystification of elements of construction or of composition. We do not mind a façade constructed of imitation stone or of imitation marble; in advertising, it even serves to enhance properties that are valued according to what they are able to imitate. Since it would have been worse to resign ourselves to the truth, it has been necessary for us to become accustomed to replacing natural and real things with apparent and apocryphal ones. The outside is always of a different style than the inside. Whereas the true artist is offended by all this, the imitative artist must feel a secret loathing for the truth of the original—which affirms his naked existence. In the imitation, in the skillful adulteration, in the ingenious fraud, and in the mirages that console the wounded vanity, we feel the security of a tested road impregnating our conscience, hesitant of its own worth. We are not deceived by the fictitious, but we are disillusioned by the truthful. We could not be any other way; instead of attempting to find our own expression, we shun it and search for mystification; finally, a complicated and even interesting system emerges:

it opens shop, collects proselytes, and functions as the unveiled reality.

Each chieftain minted his coins, whereas the natural, national money was rawhide, bristle, land, and commodities. By the same strange reasoning, technical expressions are learned from a philosophy, teachers are cursed in their own style, studies are limited to the knowledge of outlines and tables of contents, and books are bound to shroud them decently on the shelf. The use of formulas exempts one from understanding the meaning, philosophy acquires bibliographical journals, and science adapts to the style of the time. But, there is a lack of blood, of roots, and of faith, which are necessary to infuse those hollow forms with life and to allow them to propagate. Drawing from cultures foreign to their inherent vocation, some writers have the same style found in poor commercial translations of good authors. The classic style of the publishing house of Maucci and Brothers can be admired in the works of authors who glory in simplicity and rusticity. Translated into Spanish, any work loses its authentic values and becomes a crazy quilt of phrases composed in coarse prose. Verses by Whitman and Claudel become arbitrarily sectioned prose; Lawrence's novels and Freud's studies are transformed into literary dummies of the most unintentional pornography. Since it is difficult to imitate ideas, the forms are imitated; our avant-garde schools lacked creative artists and new values to substitute for the old ones; their success was due, in the main, to the joy of discovering in the foreign poets the style of the cheap translations.

The Science of the Improviser

We are characterized, much more so than other peoples, by the speed with which we perceive and realize in the depths of our soul the subtle allusions, particularly if they refer to another's estimation of our merits. Like the mariners in Athens who immediately perceived the subtle allusions in the Aristophanic dialogues, our peasants pick out the subtle intentions and answer with the most agile dialogues. However, I do not believe that such a mental and verbal feline elasticity is related to intelligence, whose true pace seems to be that of the hyperborean plantigrade. The primitive man's agility does not project beyond the circle of personal defense, and his ingenious and vivacious feints cannot be applied to the greater questions of life. Physical resistance requires agility, but the fine sensibility enabling one to perceive the most delicate cutting edge on the fleshy tip of the thumb pertains to the individual and not to the world.

To live alertly by being our own sentinels is a beautiful predisposition, but, without a doubt, it leads to improvisation rather than to technique, to the formation of a character rather than a temperament, and to intuition rather than reasoning. Quickness of thinking and of reacting gives life a certain rhythm; but, culture is only artificially, superficially enriched because the real truths lie deep in the vital organs. We live in a rush, with a superfluous acceleration that allows us to wait for the completion of the phrase as we sit on the period. Our existence is located slightly ahead of ourselves, and we live, as was customary to say at the time of Rivadavia's innovations, "tugging at the future." Any adolescent discovers a fraud before an adult who is accustomed to a slower pace of life. Everyone introduces his genuine bias into the process of formulating decisions, but the innovation lacks an independent existence and cannot outlive the person. To rush is to improvise; to improvise is to die—with beauty perhaps, but to die nevertheless.

Life should not be rushed, nor should thought be hastened; to live fully is to develop in a unique personal space, exercising a unique function, and moving in a unique time; more than delaying a little, it is "rushing slowly" and not forgetting anything. Unless the soul stops to hesitate, one has not penetrated into the substantive meaning of events; a certain time is necessary to correlate thought with reality. Our way of being is perhaps the spiritual form of a new world where everything remains to be done, where much construction has filled the empty spaces and where the buildings are precariously occupied until the arrival of the real owners. It does not matter that the empty world is an ancient one and that the builder appears much before the definitive inhabitant. We may call it a new world because improvisation within it carries sufficient momentum to erect something that continues standing. The obsession for witnessing the complete construction of a work is manifested in the eagerness to finish the building of a house, to decorate it, and to install oneself in it; but, there is in this an undecipherable disillusionment with life, shown by the inconsiderate use of time and of things. Self-confidence is lacking, the indispensable security needed to wait for the happy conclusion of a long-term project. The peace of perennial contours is not among the comforts offered by the dwelling, although such was not the case in another world.

Haste impedes contemplation, and it hinders the establishment of roots; one is rushing and then waiting instead of moving slowly but constantly. Intelligence must concentrate to grasp the meaning of events; it must interpret them before they, moving at a slower pace than ideas, express their rhythm with timorous precaution. It is necessary to improvise: the variety of forms that constitute the surrounding life and the sparseness of clues in the environmental reality demand that intelligence complete the picture based on superficial and doubtful signs; therefore intelligence is not required to fully employ the qualities of thinking, feeling, and acting. Faced with a world full of simple data, intelligence finds itself endowed with unlimited necessities for action and is capable of more energetic exercises than are required by the state of affairs. The world is simple, and the soul is complicated, as in the good times when the eristic steadied the universe. It is necessary to complete meaningless paragraphs, to conclude other inexpressive ones, and to interpolate an invented appendix in the mutilated text. In that sense, the improviser is a being who overcomes the technical phase of the world about him; he is one who experiments by trial and error. Faced with a set of embryonic forms, he decides to penetrate it instead of approaching cautiously and to imprint upon it his own personal forms, converting it into a tool for the plenitude of his own effort. At the same time, the improviser is the providential tool of that totality of static and empty masses that yearn to be filled. Things, therefore, experiment with man by trial and error. A mechanical equilibrium has not yet been established between our world and ourselves. We are still in the Hesiodic period of improvisation when the poet is faced with the materials of reality but not with its problems; we are in the first steps of a series that ends when man becomes the gnomic poem of things.

There are times when it is scarcely possible to change and modifications are very gradual; there are other times when it is most urgent to build, make, and create quickly and in bold strokes; the world of obligations is not congruent with the world of rights. The former is the world of the engineer and of the statesman who serve it by applying formulas whose preciseness is a basic requirement for success; the latter is the world of the pioneer and of the magician, where reality must first be manufactured and taken to its definite structures in response to an emphatic "Let it be done!" The former are technicians, and they operate taking into account the medium that opposes them with a concerted, mechanical force; the latter react against things by relying on themselves, and they improvise with their heads and their hands. They are the demiurges who end by converting their experience into science; the cities grow and interests become complex and interact freely, absolved from the creator's hand. A reality that has not as yet acquired a physiognomy is a malleable prereality; it is only possible to be vaguely intuitive about the shape it will acquire when it is condensed and organized to such a degree that it will develop in an orderly fashion, when bodies will no longer be static but will function autonomously in accord with cosmic laws. In the presence of a world without concrete forms, man is a perfected being who will stamp his image on that world until reality becomes a hypothesis and his hand a lubricant.

The engineer of this plastic world is the caudillo, in whom are condensed the powers of pioneer and of magician. The caudillo may clothe himself in various disguises, depending on the times and the circumstances; but he is always the antiengineer, the technician of that anodyne reality, stronger than that reality and capable of stamping it with the bias of his talent as an improviser and a creator. In the past, he had a lordly and a corporate role; today, his radius of action is diversified in accord with the empirical divisions of reality into politics, science, economics, and art; the spectral analysis reveals two fundamental lines coinciding with the characteristics typical of the *payador* and of the trail guide. He survives as a technician of a world without metallic structures.

These three protagonists of our history and our culture, who are well described in *Facundo*, are the hypostases of the daring improviser, of the magistrate, of the functionary, and of the leader, who attempt by the exercise of their function to initiate a new era, to inject their personal style into the unfinished reality. Our most secure possession, what has been carved from native dangers and what is best adapted to the environment, proceeds from their enterprise. Compared to them, the improvisers who draw inspiration from consummate techniques are out of tune, like the singer with a bad ear. The road cleared by machete under the guidance of the trail guide's intuitive science leads farther than telegraph lines, as the horse proves superior to the automobile on dirt roads. Everything that differs from the autochthonous is discordant—like an instrument not included in the score. Our best poem is written in verses of *payada*, and it is the work of a *payador*. Our greatest men were those who taught themselves in a self-formed reality and who, in an ethnic, political, and economic chaos, blazed the most secure path possible. The engineer followed his tracks, and those who transported blocks of other cultures also obeyed the eagerness to improvise, although with less skill.

Today, the improvisers study the theories of other realities, the formulas issued from other systems, in order to adapt them to our reality; ignoring Argentine problems, they search for European solutions. In spite of their intentions, they once again fall into the technique of the improviser. The trail guide and the *payador* have become denaturalized. A breath of new air presumptuously wishes to replace divination and inspiration; but, the loss of contact with the land is obvious in the total inefficiency of the new personal style. When machinery is only partially utilized, it becomes rusted and corroded.

The irrefutable vocation of the improviser is most clearly visible in politics and in finances, the areas where the environmental characteristics do not permit the mechanical application of precise calculations. The vastness of our landscape permits approximate calculations; the errors are without immediate consequences. Wilderness, uncultivated land, and manufacturing are the margins in which error is not fraught with grave consequences, and, simultaneously, they are the unknowns that frustrate the efficiency of mathematics. They are the most formless worlds, the most recent, the ones that have not yet been explored or subjected to particular nomes; they are the materials for experimentation, lands still waiting to be mapped and distributed.

Politics provides the clearest example. Our politics of multitudes, applied and incorporated into the science of government, is very recent; the secret and compulsory vote could be most of the State's program. Our people were bestowed with a democratic condition, an unusual right; government was considered a new organism within a new science. The theory was perfect, but there were no able technicians to make it function in the new reality created by the electoral law. To apply theory to reality it was necessary to search for a competent man; the fine instinct of our citizens turned to the representative man: the skilled politician, familiar with the meanders of the country's map and with its inhabitants in whom the theory had to flow and worm itself in. In the new state of affairs, the improvising magician was once again the caudillo— simultaneously acting as the *payador* and as the trail guide. He made the law the school for his career; taking a system with few mistakes, he restored the old political systems that the law precisely intended to abolish. Reduced from its theoretical heights to the level of a most mysterious shortcut through the jungle, an entire program became concretized in a man, as an entire army used to be trusted to the skill of the trail guide. However, that was not the end for which such a system was put in march; the final result was unforeseen continuation of the theory; the trail guide ignored the science of government and paid attention to the imponderables that had created him in the first place; the legislative creation had ignored reality.

The improvisers faced a system that had ceased to function, a residue of outmoded doctrine, ruins of parties that entered into an era of calculation; the attempt had failed forever. The trail guide's science offered efficiency and a simple morality that could not be expected from doctrinaire parties and principles.

The economic world was the back room of politics, an unseen world, like the back face of the moon. No private or collective experience could serve as a base for the study and the practice of finances; theory had nothing to do with practice. Traditionally, the handling of the public treasury was a matter of faith and magic. Although in the financial realm the caudillo outwardly acted as a statesman and a financier, in moments of difficulty he appealed to his old tactics as a *payador*. The founding of banks that grew acromegalic and then failed from one day to the next without visible causes became an almost unvarying procedure. Taxes decreed or sanctioned without the previous knowledge of the economic capacity of the taxpayers or the impact on industries replaced careful estimates. Inefficient and impractical tribute was often raised imperatively without the necessary previous studies and statistical investigation. For example, the recent increase in postal rates reduced the volume of correspondence to less than half. Issues of paper money were authorized, loans were contracted, and budgets were planned without first studying the sources of income, the endurance of industry, commerce, and labor, or the real necessity for investments. Without knowing the possibilities of public and private wealth, obligations were contracted with the future as the only collateral, a future that we continue to abuse inconsiderately. The loans were the margin of error, the means of settling the balance sheet; any mistake in estimates was corrected by special agreements and by the popular formula of importing coined gold in exchange for the future, that is, of importing ready-made solutions to unstated problems.

Some veins of resources became clogged, perhaps forever; others, exhausted, continued to provide money for the famished coffers of the public treasury. For the public treasury to maintain the pomp of the spectacle, it had to resort to tax collections to pay the foreign debts. When Pellegrini founded the Bank of the Nation and created the Reserve Fund, it seemed that we were entering into the period of technology and that the times of empirical administration were ending. Everything apparently indicated that the practical evils had ended, that the funded debt and the fixed value of paper money would impose their standards on the versatile improvisation of governments. It was an illusion. Economic reality had been slowly molded by the influence of perfectly organized interests, foreign to the national economy. The old practice of administering wealth with intuition as the only guide in an economic world of constantly increasing complexity left the financier dangerously unprotected. It was most difficult to manage a reality whose functioning did not depend on the caudillo's will. Crises were unforeseen and suddenly appearing phenomena. The best recourse found to oppose that slow, logical, and internal process was to appeal to magical practices and to instinct for the simplicity that lies dormant in the recondite corners of everyone's spirit. Loans were renewed, gold was removed from the Reserve Fund and thus paper money was left without backing, the Bank of the Nation was forced to provide illegal advances from its treasury, internal loans were contracted, and tariffs and taxes were proportionately increased. By the logic of intuition, the transportation fares were increased; intuition was applied to the solution of three-fourths of the economic, political, and educational problems; emergency therapeutics were borrowed from other countries before a diagnosis of our ills was formulated.

When the world of the past was merely a plain and a jungle, when the lands were flooded and impassable, the trail guide could lead us; when the world afforded only the barest traces of culture, the *payador* could easily interest his audience and overcome any assonant slips. But that world became rigid, mechanical, and categorical, and man strayed behind. He was distracted; he was constructing, assembling, and accumulating materials while those elements free of his influence were becoming organized and distributed in accord with universal specific gravities and architectural laws, obeying internal forces progressively more exact and indefectible.

From the days of discovery, these were the lands of adventure, and this stamp has endured on all institutions as their original sin. The national development follows a genealogical line; the financial, monetary, economic, and mercantile spheres obey international laws and those of political economy. Colonists and entrepreneurs pursued their goals tenaciously and stamped the world with their personalities. The improviser was the demiurge against an untamed nature resistant to the utilization of perfected techniques. But today he lacks the strength to wield that reality in motion. In the struggle for the formation of our country, actions have predominated over thought and learning; what we call crisis, delicate economic problems, lack of industries, low prices and high tariffs, illiteracy, depopulation, instability of property and of life, and the predominance of capitals unrelated to national destiny is the defeat of the improviser.

Civilization and Barbarity

The creators of fictions were the promoters of civilization, in opposition to the agents of barbarity, who were closer to the repudiated reality. During the struggle to displace things European, these very things were being massively introduced against chaos. The procedure used to extirpate the hybrid and the foreign consisted in superficially adopting the European forms. And so, the false was added to the authentic. French and English were spoken, and dress coats were worn; but the gaucho lurked under the pressed shirt. A state of barbarity consubstantial with appearances was being affirmed: the motley superficialities of culture became the building blocks for culture, as can be seen in most facets of our life. The evils were serious, but the proposed changes in the system of government, the reiterated imitation of Vergil, and the hypervaluation of the cultural cosmetic proved to be even more harmful. They were the evils of appearance, of parody that could exist a number of years but that eventually had to be exposed, like the heroic disguise of the actor, which is always shed at the end of the spectacle. The seeds of barbarity were covered with dung, without realizing that nations cannot live off utopias and that civilization is nothing if it cannot be a natural excoriation. It was thought that careful planning could shorten the time needed for development, but the net effect was that of an improperly healed wound. Alberdi realized this danger more clearly than anyone; his physiological enmity for Sarmiento and his diminutive figure before the colossus was upheld by the aim of a David who deals Goliath a frontal blow with a stone.

The most damaging of those dreamers, the creator of images, was Sarmiento. His railroad led to Trapalanda, and his telegraph took a one-hundred-year leap through the void. The word *Barbarous* was affixed at the very top of all works of progress; it seemed to the destroyers of dreams that new elements of backwardness were being incorporated into Argentine life. Sarmiento was the first one to build bridges over reality; Pellegrini was the last one. The former was a genuine son of the colonial period who struggled against the invasion of autochthonous forces; the latter was the genuine immigrant's son who wished to affirm in the financial realm the determination of the European anxious to introduce stability into the environmental disorder. Each man's influence lasted fifty years. When the vigor insufflated by Sarmiento began to falter, it was revived by Pellegrini. In 1910, the utopian dream ended to allow for the revenge of the defeated aboriginal forces. A massive assault gathered force against the spiritual frontiers; the invasion of a suffocated element whose right to life was irrefutable joined with Alem in the demolition of Byzantine domes and initiated the return to normalcy. The generation of 1880 is the typical collective form of the pseudostructure of civilization, forged by an infinite patriotic love; it is a puerile period for assimilation of meaningless forms charged with their own significance; it is an infantile stage. Sarmiento was the first one who spoke of order in the midst of chaos, who defined civilization in the midst of barbarity, who showed the benefits of primary education in the midst of ignorance, who preached in the desert the meaning of society, and who spoke of North America, France, and England in the midst of disorder and anarchy. By reaction, the creator of new values was a product of barbarity. He made war on war; he opposed primitiveness with learning and the native garb with the dress coat; he countered the instincts and the inspirations of the trail guide and the *payador* and opposed the endemic vices of the open country with perseverance, patience, and calculation. He uprooted what there was and planted what there was not. *Facundo* was a school book for adults, and *Conflicto y armonía de las razas en América* ["Conflict and Harmony among the Races in America"] his testament for youth. His uninterrupted sermon provided pedagogical materials for those children with heavy beards. All his foundations, from the Society for the Protection of Libraries and the Society for the Protection of Animals to the National Council of Education and varied scientific institutions, are phalanges in combat against reality, the affirmation of the "other reality." He wished to achieve at any cost that which existed elsewhere; an irreproachable champion of truth and faced with a state of affairs that grieved him, he adopted self-deceit as a system. He dedicated his life and his thought to the solution of Argentine problems; he produced all the great figures of his time, because they either collaborated with him or they opposed him; men, things, and values revolved around him. Thus, General Mansilla, his defender who was also resentful of reality and orthodox to the point of ridiculousness, carried him to the presidency and then went on to combat the heretic dressed like a dandy. He carried Shakespeare's works in his suitcase and inserted his verses in the expeditionary diary.

Men wished to deny the truth, and the tactics employed consisted in ignoring it. A movement of reaction was initiated in all spheres of activity: it began with the construction of public buildings and the laying of rail and telegraph lines, with the proliferation of newspapers, with the imitation of the authors of the analects, with the use of credit, and with the reading of lofty works; it ended with the manufacturing of fiction and with the issuing of unbacked paper to finance works of progress. Twelve banks were inaugurated during the time of Juárez Celman, libraries and universities were opened, the value of real estate increased, and the fermentation of chaos exaggerated the situation; all these conquests were the ideological commotions of twenty men anxious to aggrandize the Nation. It was indeed an imaginative upheaval.

Foreign gold filled the coffers, but it was not diluted in the body of the national economy, or among labor groups, or among private enterprise. Capital flowed, impelled by the winds of immigration; the immigrants followed after the capital—in the movement of the dog chasing its own tail. The credit provided the utopian dream with combustible materials. The dreamers of greatness were rich and demiurgical; but they were not the very wealthy: they lived in average homes and had the same mediocre prospects. The pyrotechnical efforts of imagination were opposed by the hydraulic work of reality that began to conquer bridges, dams, and illusion's artificial mechanisms. The crisis pointed toward a receding of the waters and the formation of a new stratum. All the theories of this dream are embodied in Sarmiento. The fifty-two volumes of his evident, undeniable work correspond to fifty-two years of an also evident and undeniable reality. His illusion had consistency; it was strong enough to assert itself over a categorical and comminatory reality; relief forces of prominent men came to the aid of the utopian dreamer from all sides. If the rider had really been alone he could not have maintained his balance on the colt. They all lived in the heat of the adventure, and, like Rivadavia, Rawson, and Vélez Sársfield, they died infused with the most desolate skepticism. The collaborators in the enterprise of that perfectly logical Jason, judicious and even positivist, worked in behalf of his plans, even when they opposed him.[1] Whoever is still against Sarmiento is so in his function, just as whoever is not with Irigoyen proceeds by reaction, thus furnishing a second proof. Both Sarmiento and Irigoyen unsettled the public treasury, one by

---

[1] That was the danger: if Sarmiento had been a mediocre prose writer and an abstract talent, truth would have been pursued through alternate routes.

building and the other by demolishing. For Sarmiento, reality had acquired the essential characteristics of his own personality; and, if even today his mental and temperamental person seems to us to be so close to reality as to be synonymous with it, it is because the reality that we see is the one he manufactured with his genius. The four fundamental problems of our social life are the four cardinal points of the mind and the life of Sarmiento. We possess a generally uncultivated land where useful plants and untamed weeds can prosper equally well; geography and demography naturally engender illiteracy. The roots of our evils are the lack of institutes for moral and civic character, the lack of teachings in support of tradition and of home, and the freedom used to chain man to his appetites and to his native defects. Sarmiento applied his instinctive vocation to the school that he attempted to mold in the midst of a harsh reality. His self-education and the crudity of contrasts that he encountered in the struggle to develop his ample intelligence made of him what he had lacked: a Teacher. That educational quality, which could be observed even when he tried to encourage wickerworks in the Delta, coincided with that grandiose segment of the empty reality. From that resemblance between what he lacked and what the country lacked came the formulation of the first problem: that of the primary school, which is the nation's basic cultural problem; universities can hardly exist without primary schools.

Sarmiento's traveling spirit, the migratory vitality that he conserved to his last days and that took him outside the country, led him to ponder the problem of communications, which, if they exist at all in South American countries, become routes for separation and distancing. Those towns which Sarmiento observed existing in vegetative isolation, with no contact with the world other than an irregular postal service, surrounded by dangers and difficulties, signified the same on the national map as did his sporadic culture on the map of civilized nations, which he knew with the instinct of a trail guide. The second point of his public program and of his idiosyncrasy is the problem of the communication routes. It suffices to read his itineraries throughout Europe and

America to realize that the distances and the relationships established by the personal knowledge of things and of language would lead him to comical extremes in the defense of the railroad and the telegraph.

Depopulation and ignorance were the a priori conditions of the absent national unity. The towns of the interior still led a stagnated colonial existence. Castro Barros pointed to the magnitude of that danger, infiltrating brains apparently organized for a new understanding of the state of affairs. The visible decadence of the provinces and the dissolution in the chaos of all the forces that should unite people estranged Sarmiento with repugnance from what smelled of original sin in religion and in history. Sarmiento's home was dissolved, and he led an erratic life, without deep affectionate bonds. He was a city man in the provinces, a provincial in Buenos Aires, a foreigner in his own country, an Argentine everywhere else, mad before the inevitable certainty of events, and judicious in the face of the disaster of ignorance invested with power; all this instability impelled him to search for the specific characteristics of Argentine civilization and progress. Therefore, the third problem is one of the formation of the national soul.

Sarmiento maintained himself exempt from the elementary vices of concupiscence, depredation, bribery, and hypocrisy. Humble in his ambition, he was incapable of obtaining glory or fortune except through the road of legality; he never even conceived during his deliria of greatness, as did Lincoln, that he could achieve that greatness at the cost of the most insignificant sacrifice of his honesty. His morbid preoccupation for truth and for honesty contrasted with the secular practices of the national government and the economic life, maintained by exaction, bribery, and fraud. The fourth problem of his psyche and of reality is the probity in the exercise of power. Those four planes enclosed the tetrahedron of our reality and the substance of his soul. But inside those solids, in their mathematical center, there was enclosed an infinitesimal, ultramicroscopic germ, an extensionless geometrical point that fermented disorder in the reality, falsifying it and infecting it. The four fundamental planes, which everyone conceived of as such—

even Alberdi, who is so different from Sarmiento that he looks like him—are Sarmiento's four points of view based on the four cardinal forces of his personality. By luck or by misfortune, his soul coincided with this land; and he became by antonomasia reality's representative being, transfusing into that reality his vigor and his clear-sightedness with the adaptability of two bloods of the same type. Therefore, to declare oneself in favor of the country's reconstruction is to be pro-Sarmiento and to become affiliated with his school, because he and the country are the same truth. It is perfectly logical that after *Facundo*, a history that is an autobiography, civilization and barbarity became antithetical; it was necessary to draw away from the latter and to blindly throw oneself into the former; but to flee from one in order to approach the other or vice versa were the same thing. Barbarity was a past era of the countryside, of the guerrilla armies, and of the ranch administrator in the public treasury. Civilization meant history, the future, the city, the industry, the education, the fundamental basis for the value of things. Civilization was made into a program, and barbarity became taboo. Around Sarmiento and other great Argentines, silence was coagulating over whatever carried stigmas of barbarity, while the voice defining civilization was becoming louder and clearer. Those men, until the times of Pellegrini, possessed the indispensable competence and good faith to call things by their proper names; afterward, what was taboo was not even alluded to, except through the usage of a multitude of synonyms. Ideas, values, themes, and realities were manipulated in accord with that reasoning. Considerable fragments of reality fell into the subconscious with proscribed words, and proscribed words dragged with them into the subconscious fragments of reality. In the end, the world to which everyone aspired came apart, as did that other world which faced everyone and could not be modified. Phantoms displaced men, and utopia devoured reality.

What Sarmiento did not realize was that civilization and barbarity were the same thing, like the centrifugal and centripetal forces of a system in equilibrium. He did not see that the city was like the countryside and that the souls of the dead were being reincarnated in new bodies. The defeated barbarity, with all its vices and its faults of structuring and of contents, had acquired the aspect of truth, of prosperity, and of cultural and mechanical advances. The bastions of civilization had been invaded by specters that were thought to be annihilated. The new aspects of the irremissible truth were cloaked in a world subject to the customs and the norms of civilization. As that immense work and life progressively fall into oblivion, the profound reality returns. We must accept it with courage so that it ceases to perturb us; we must be conscious of it and cause it to dissipate and to allow us to live united in health.

INDEX